Luke Rivington

The Roman Primacy A.D. 430-451

Luke Rivington

The Roman Primacy A.D. 430-451

ISBN/EAN: 9783337021160

Printed in Europe, USA, Canada, Australia, Japan

Cover: Foto ©ninafisch / pixelio.de

More available books at **www.hansebooks.com**

THE ROMAN PRIMACY

A.D. 430–451

Nihil obstat.
SYDNEY F. SMITH, S.J.

Imprimatur.
HERBERTUS CARDINALIS VAUGHAN
Archiepiscopus Westmonasteriensis

7 *Martii 1899*

THE
ROMAN PRIMACY

A.D. 430 – 451

BY THE

REV. LUKE RIVINGTON, M.A., D.D.

Formerly Demy of Magdalen College, Oxford

LONGMANS, GREEN, AND CO.
39 PATERNOSTER ROW, LONDON
NEW YORK AND BOMBAY
1899

All rights reserved

PREFACE

IN preparing a fresh edition of my book on *The Primitive Church and the See of Peter*, which I hope to publish in the course of this year, I became convinced that the best answer to many difficulties raised against the historical proofs of Papal Supremacy and Papal Infallibility would be found in a more detailed account of some one crucial passage in the history of the Church within the first few centuries. Exposition is always, when possible, the best form of controversy; I have therefore selected for the purpose twenty-one years in the first half of the fifth century (A.D. 430-451) and have entered into considerable detail in the exposition of this important episode in the life of the Church. All that appeared on this period in *The Primitive Church &c.* has been rewritten, with the exception of two chapters, which have been merely retouched and illustrated by their historical context. The greater number of the chapters are entirely new.

My reason for selecting this short period is that within those twenty-one years three Councils of peculiar interest were assembled in the East, two of which count among the first four Œcumenical Councils, and the third, which met between these two, was meant to be

Œcumenical. The importance of the two first mentioned is quite unique, as will be seen from the following considerations.

In the Council of Ephesus (A.D. 431) we have actually the first Œcumenical assembly of which the 'Acts'—*i.e.* the transactions of the various sessions—have come down to posterity. This alone would make it a matter of importance to study the history of that Council with peculiar care.

But, further, this Council at Ephesus was concerned with the mystery of the Incarnation in a way peculiar to itself and to the Council of Chalcedon in 451. On these two occasions the Church settled for all time two of the most fundamental points in regard to that mystery of our holy religion, dealing with the 'union' involved in the assumption of our nature by the Eternal Word.

Thus in these two Councils we have our first clear sight of the Church in her combined public action on a large scale, and that action was concerned with the fundamental mystery of our holy faith. History here, at any rate, must have a peculiar interest for us Christians. Principles which are found embedded in the Church at this era must have had their origin in times long anterior; their appearance in full flower and fruit points to a distant past to which their roots must be traced.

Another reason for selecting this episode in the history of the Church is to be found in the circumstances of our English religious life at this present hour. Everything that is going on round about us at this moment in the intellectual and religious world seems to point to the necessity of answering one crucial question: If there is a body of truth revealed by Christ for the permanent welfare of our race, where is its guardian? And to answer this question, it will naturally be asked, Where *was* its guardian in the past? The Councils of Ephesus and Chalcedon give a clear emphatic answer to that question. The guardianship of the faith was entrusted to the Episcopate of the Catholic Church, of which the head was the successor of Peter in the See of Rome—and this by divine institution. The relationship of that See to the universal Church cannot be seen anywhere more clearly than in the records of the Council of Ephesus in 431 and the Council of Chalcedon in 451. Here, when the hour of supreme trial had come, the Primacy of the Bishop of Rome comes before us as a well established provision, of divine institution, for the welfare of the Churches.

It is here, therefore, that the meaning of that Primacy—the principles on which it was obeyed, if it was obeyed—ought to be studied with especial care. If we found ourselves in a system which plainly contradicts those principles, we should have ground for doubting our inheritance in the privileges of the One Body of Christ, and in the sheltering favour of the One Lord. This, as has been recently stated by Professor Sanday, was admitted by those who took part in the religious changes of the sixteenth century. ' It was agreed,' says that distinguished writer, ' that the practice of the Church of the first four Councils—when it could be ascertained—was binding.'[1] 'When it could be ascertained '—but it is impossible in the nature of

[1] *The Conception of the Priesthood*, p. 123.

things to see it in all its effective power, where the records are wanting, as is the case with the Councils of Nicæa and Constantinople. It should, therefore, be studied first in its developed form, when the Church acted as a whole and the records are sufficiently ample to enable us to see the relative action of head and members in the ecclesiastical body. And that is the same as saying, begin with the Council of Ephesus.

The principle here advocated has been laid down with great clearness in a remarkable article in the *English Historical Review* for January 1899. The writer (the Rev. A. C. Headlam) makes this important statement. Speaking of the best method of avoiding the uncertainty caused by the absence of conclusive evidence and of limiting the personal bias in our pursuit of historical truth, he says; 'One method may be suggested as a wise one to pursue, that of advancing from the known to the unknown. The great advance in the study of Roman constitutional history has been made by working back from the known and developed constitutions of the later republican and imperial time to the earlier periods. In a similar way the only true method for the study of Church history is to start from the developed constitution and work back to the earlier period.'

This is a principle which will, it is hoped, commend itself to many for whom this book is written, on this additional ground. Many now believe in common with ourselves that in dealing with the history of the Church we are dealing with that of a supernatural entity placed here by our Divine Redeemer, the laws of whose growth are illustrated by that of the human body, but which is in every stage of its history equally a divine institution.

The Church could never as a whole act in such an episode of her life on a false principle. If the Primacy of the Bishop of Rome was recognised as of divine institution then, it must have been always such. The Church could not go wrong on such a vital matter in the very act of settling the full meaning of the fundamental mystery of the Christian religion—the Holy Incarnation. However at times other powers may have initiated or carried on her work, that institution must have been always there, as the background, just as while prophets and teachers came to the front in early days, the Apostles were there, the final authority, though not everywhere and always conspicuous. So the Primacy was there, and its substantial repudiation would have been an offence against first principles. Neither democratic Christianity nor episcopal aristocracy could have developed into the ecclesiastical monarchy of the years between A.D. 430 and 451.

It will be seen, then, from a close study of this period that the doctrine of the Primacy of the Roman Pontiff was sufficiently developed in the mind of the Christian world before the Council of Ephesus in 431 to enable us to say that the guardianship of the faith lay by divine appointment, not merely with an Episcopate, but with an Episcopate one of whose number was the inheritor of peculiar privileges in regard to jurisdiction and the security of his official teaching, as the successor of the Prince and head of the Apostolic College.

What were these privileges? Not what Mr. Gladstone is pleased to describe them as being, when he tells us that the Vatican Council 'lays it down that the Pope is never to be resisted in any matter, by any persons, or under any circumstance.'[1] It is difficult to see how the Vatican Council could have taken greater precautions to guard against such an idea of absolutism as attaching to its teaching. Neither, again, are the Petrine privileges as declared in the Vatican decrees, what Dr. Bright, Professor of Ecclesiastical History at Oxford, seems to imagine them to be. Speaking of the Vatican definition, he says that 'it makes the Pope practically a universal bishop, holding direct power in and over every single diocese, so that the several diocesans are, in effect, no more than his commissioners and vicars.'[2] This is denied in terms in the *Dogmatic Constitution* of the Vatican Council which says (cap. iii.) :

'So far is this power of the Supreme Pontiff from being opposed to that ordinary and immediate power of episcopal jurisdiction with which the Bishops, who being placed by the Holy Ghost have succeeded to the place of the Apostles, as true pastors feed and govern each their several flocks assigned to them—that the same [power of Episcopal] jurisdiction is asserted, confirmed and vindicated by the supreme and universal Pastor.'

Such is the authoritative teaching of the Vatican Council, which is in direct contradiction to Dr Bright's account of it. And it is equally certain that Dr. Bright's account does not tally with the facts; it is not true in regard to the actual practice of the Church. The actual relation between the Pope and Apostolic Vicars who rule over certain areas before the formation of regular diocesan jurisdiction differs enormously from the relation between the Pope and Diocesan Bishops.

[1] *Soliloquy and Postscript (Later Gleanings,* p. 424).
[2] *Waymarks in Church History,* p. 207.

The fact is that a great deal of recent controversy falls short of its purpose by reason of the assumption which perpetually underlies it, to the effect that the rule of the Pope is, at least in theory, that of an absolute monarch in the full sense of the term 'absolute.'[1] Bellarmine upbraided Calvin for proceeding upon this assumption. He tells him that the Pope himself knows what he is writing, viz. that the Roman Pontiff cannot change the doctrine of Christ nor institute a new worship so as to make it pass for *divine*; and that God alone reigns and legislates without a superior. He alone destroys and saves on His own authority. 'We attribute none of these things to the Pope.'[2]

And so Pius VII. protested that a Pope recognises certain limits which he cannot transgress without betraying his conscience and without abusing the supreme authority entrusted to him by Jesus Christ for edification and not for destruction; and he says that even in matters of discipline the Popes have always observed certain limits and recognised the obligation not to admit innovations in certain matters at all, and in other matters only when most weighty and imperative reasons required it.[3]

So that what we have to look for in the history of the early Councils is the proof, not of an absolutism which pays no respect to contract, usage, rights, and the

---

[1] There is, of course, a sense in which the Papacy may be called an absolute monarchy: viz. as meaning that the form of government in the Church is that of a single ruler. This, however, is not what is meant by those who speak of the 'absolutism' of the Sovereign Pontiff.

[2] *De Rom. Pont.* iii. 19, 21.

[3] *Cf.* Hettinger, *Die kirchliche Vollgewalt des apostolischen Stuhles*, i. 57.

welfare of the community—the Church repudiates such a position for her visible head—but of a full supreme authority, ordinary (*i.e.* attached to the office) and immediate (*i.e.* not necessarily through intermediate authorities), over every member of the universal Church, which is; however, controlled by that respect for laws once established by previous authority, which springs from a sense of duty to God and care for the welfare of the Church.

But while the Sovereign Pontiffs repudiate any such 'autocracy' as Mr. Gladstone attributes to them, or any claim to be 'universal Bishop' in the sense which Dr. Bright attaches to those words,[1] it is certainly held that the Pope is in a very true sense above ecclesiastical, as distinguished from divine laws. Canons have no *coactive* force as against the Popes. While the Sovereign Pontiff is morally bound to rule the Church in accordance with the decrees and laws which have been recognised as part of Church discipline in past centuries, these laws *impose no command* which he has to obey, by divine or human law; as he is the highest authority in the Church, he can accept no rule from any superior except God Himself.[2] 'The Pope,' says a great Canonist, 'is the highest authority in the Church, and as such he has no judge over him externally; for the use he makes of his power he is responsible to God only and his conscience, just as temporal monarchs are for theirs.'[3]

Dr. Bright, in his *Roman See in the Early Church*,

---

[1] *Waymarks*, p. 207; *Roman See in the Early Church*, p. 2.

[2] *Cf.* Hettinger, *loc. cit.* § 25, and Palmieri, *De Rom. Pont.* Pars ii. cap. 1.

[3] Walter, *Kirchenrecht*, § 126.

p. 208, comments on a statement by the present writer that a king is bound to respect the laws, 'not because they are superior to him, but because he is bound by the natural and divine law to set the example,' and that in the same way the Pope is bound to respect the canons, and he asks the question, 'Has submission to ecclesiastical absolutism made Mr. Rivington forget the traditions, the basal ideas, of kingship as understood by Englishmen? He may consult a Roman Catholic historian: it was part of Richard II.'s despotic policy, to "place himself above the control of the law" (Lingard, *H. Engl.* iv. 255).'

I might content myself with replying to this by saying that I have never submitted, nor been asked to submit, to any 'ecclesiastical absolutism'; but it seems only right to protest against the misuse of Dr. Lingard's name in this passage and also against the assumption that the British constitution supplies us with a perfect ideal of kingship. Dr. Lingard (as the next lines would have shown the reader, if only Dr. Bright had quoted them) is speaking of King Richard's attempt to overthrow the constitution by doing away with the action of Parliament after having extorted a subsidy for life. The only parallel (and it is still an imperfect parallel) to this would be the case of a Pope proceeding to govern the whole Church without an Episcopate. But this, according to the Vatican decree, it is not in his power to do. And as for the parallel drawn by Dr. Bright between the British constitution and the government of the Church, it must be borne in mind that that constitution is, indeed, admirably adapted to the genius of the British people, but is not on that account a model form of kingship nor necessarily adapted for the purposes for which the Church exists. Moreover, Dr. Bright's own estimate of the position of the king in the British constitution is not that of most Englishmen. The king is certainly with us, in a sense, above the law; he cannot be indicted for its violation; though he may be induced to resign for the violation of the natural and divine law which bids him care for the welfare of his people and govern them according to the principles of the constitution which he is set to administer. There is a truth in the legal maxim that 'the king can do no wrong.'

But as regards the particular matter at issue, viz. the relation of the Pope to the ecclesiastical, as distinguished from the natural and divine, law, I would ask whether the Oxford Professor of Ecclesiastical History has forgotten the immemorial traditions, the basal ideas, of canon law in the Church of England? These cannot be better represented than by the great Canonist, universally accepted as such by the Church of England, William Lyndwood, Official Principal of the Archbishop of Canterbury's Court, prolocutor of the clergy in the Convocation of Canterbury, who wrote his famous book on the provincial constitutions of the Archbishop of Canterbury in the early part of the fifteenth century. Lyndwood was not an absolutist of the type described by Mr. Gladstone or Dr. Bright; he held that there were cases in which the Pope might be rightly resisted. He mentions just such a case as that about which Bishop Grosseteste wrote his famous letter to Innocent the notary.[1] Nevertheless Lyndwood lays down as the

[1] Not, as Anglican writers suppose, to the Pope, whose name happened to be Innocent: whence the confusion.

unquestioned teaching of the Church Catholic, including the Church of England, that the Pope 'is above the law,' and again, 'is not subject to the laws.' [1]

This, however, does not in the least mean as Dr. Bright understands it to mean, that 'the pope is more than the King, he is the autocrat, of the Church'; [2] neither does the comparison of the position of the Pope with that of the Roman Emperor necessarily imply that his methods must be 'despotic.' [3] The constitution of the Roman Empire did not of itself involve despotism, though, being of the earth, it readily lent itself to abuse in that direction; neither does the position conceded to the Pope in the Vatican decrees involve despotic action. The relation of the Emperor to the laws happens to have been exactly described by the Imperial Count Elpidius at Ephesus in 449, in words which were read at the Council of Chalcedon: 'the Emperor being himself the first to fulfil the order of the laws, of which he is the inventor and the guardian.' [4] He was not 'above the law' in the sense of being under no obligation to observe it, but only in the sense of being responsible to God alone for his observance of it, when it touched his own life.

What, therefore, we might expect to find in history is a certain peculiarly authoritative guardianship of the canons exercised by the Supreme Pontiff, consistent, however, with an appeal to them as the ground of his action, when he felt it impossible under the circumstances to allow their observance to be relaxed. The

---

[1] *Cf.* Professor Maitland's *Canon Law in the Church of England*, pp. 16, 17 (1898).
[2] *Roman See*, p. 209.   [3] *Ibid.*   [4] Mansi, vi. 645.

following pages will show how far this attitude on the part of the Pope is found in the Council of Chalcedon and recognised as part of his office by the Christian world.

And, as regards the whole argument, I have one further remark to make, viz. that it is cumulative. It seems to me that writers like Dr. Bright are perpetually perpetrating the logical 'fallacy of division.' Let any one for instance take the letters (given below: see Index) of Flavian, Anatolius, Theodoret, Eusebius of Dorylæum (all Easterns), and St. Peter Chrysologus of Ravenna, written independently of one another, and all within so short a period, and ask himself whether their cumulative force is not such as to justify the statement that the Vatican decrees were admitted *in substance* in A.D. 451. Would not the fathers of the Church at Chalcedon have said the same as the Anglo-Saxon Church said to the British bishops through the instrumentality of St. Aldhelm, viz. 'In vain he emptily boasts of the Catholic faith who follows not the teaching and rule of Peter'? Would they not have said the same as the Archbishop of Canterbury and his suffragans said in 1318 to the Bishop of Rome, 'We, though unworthy, being included in your pastoral charge, and ourselves derived, as rivers from the fountainhead, from the exalted throne of the Holy Apostolic See'?[1] Would not the Chalcedonian fathers have said exactly what the Archbishop of Canterbury and his suffragans said a hundred years later, in 1412, when having condemned Sir John Oldcastle for denying the Supremacy of the See of Peter,

[1] *Registers of John de Sandale and Rigaud de Asserio*, preface by the editor, Joseph Baigent, 1897.

the Sacrament of Penance, and Transubstantiation, they sent their condemnation to the Sovereign Pontiff, with these words: 'This is that most blessed See, which is proved never to have erred, by the grace of Almighty God, from the path of Apostolical tradition, nor has it ever been depraved and succumbed to heretical novelties. But she it is to whom, as being mistress and teacher of other Churches, the surpassing authority of the fathers ordained that the greater causes of the Church, especially those touching articles of the faith, should be referred for their final settlement and declaration'?[1] In other words, would not the fathers of Chalcedon have endorsed the principle embodied in the canon law of England in these words, 'He is called a heretic who out of contempt of the Roman Church neglects to keep what the Roman Church ordains'?[2]

And all this is exactly what is taught by the *Constitutio Dogmatica* in the Vatican decrees.

I have, in conclusion, to thank the Prior of the Archives at Monte Cassino for kindly sending me a copy of his Dissertation on 'St. Leo and the East,'[3] containing a copy of the important letters from Flavian and Eusebius to St. Leo, which he discovered in the Archives at Novara. These letters have not as yet appeared in any English work on the Council of Chalcedon. The light they throw on the subject of appeals to Rome is considerable.[4] There is one point in the translation of Flavian's letter which is rendered differently by the venerable *doyen* of Catholic apologists

---

[1] Wilkins, *Concilia*, iii. 350. [2] Maitland, *op. cit.* p. 17, note [4].
[3] *S. Leone Magno e l' Oriente.* [4] See *infra*, p. 167.

in Germany, Father Wilmers, S. J. He understands Flavian to ask St. Leo to 'give the type' for the new Œcumenical Synod *by republishing his Tome*.[1] His translation depends on a reading in the Codex which has been emended by Mommsen and Amelli. Father Wilmers is, however, correct so far as the manuscript is concerned; and while I have preferred the emendation, it seems worth while to mention the opinion of so eminent a writer.

Note.

It will be noticed that the name of Dr. Bright occurs very frequently in the following pages, though chiefly in the notes. That writer has thrown down a gauntlet which it has seemed impossible not to take up. In the case of a 'recent proselyte,' he considers that the 'Roman spirit,' when it 'dominates' him, 'absorbs all other considerations into the supreme necessity of making out a case for Rome.'[2] Also his accusations against St. Leo, and against the Papal legates, in spite of the bias which they too manifestly betray, seem to require an answer, owing to Dr. Bright's position as Regius Professor of Ecclesiastical History at Oxford. But I have also felt that in giving an answer to Dr. Bright's numerous criticisms in that work, I am dealing with the line of argument generally adopted by Anglican writers. There can be no danger of misrepresenting their case when given in the words of Dr. Bright, who is its selected champion, and, I am bound to say, its ablest representative. Accordingly, while refraining from any such gross imputations as Dr. Bright has indulged in, I have carefully examined his statements, in the notes, almost one by one.

I am, however, in hopes that such readers as are not conversant with the Greek language will not be deterred by the frequent occurrence of Greek characters in the notes. Such will find, I venture to think, enough of interesting matter in the text to repay their perusal of the following pages. They can leave the notes alone.

[1] *Hist. de la Religion*, Anth. Tr. 1898, § 136.
[2] *Roman See in the Early Church*, p. 211.

I have also thought it well to include an answer to Professor Harnack's treatment of the Councils of Ephesus and Chalcedon, in his *Dogmengeschichte*. The detailed accounts of the *Latrocinium* and of Dioscorus's trial at Chalcedon (pp. 150–250) were written especially with the view of meeting what seems to me a very unjust and unhistorical estimate of these Councils.

LUKE RIVINGTON.

52 MANCHESTER STREET, LONDON, W.
Easter, 1899.

AUTHORITIES

For the sake of those who desire to go further into the history of the important period dealt with in the following pages, I subjoin the names of a few of the authorities whom I have found most useful.

1. MARIUS MERCATOR, *Scripta ad Nestorianam hæresim pertinentia*. Among these, especially *Nestorii blasphemiorum capitula*, and *Synodus Ephesina adversus Nestorium*. According to Garnier, these two works were translated into Latin by Marius Mercator in the very year of the Council (431).

    Also, Father Garnier's (S.J.) two Dissertations, *De hæresi et libris Nestorii*, and *De Synodis habitis in causâ Nestorianâ*, are invaluable.

    All these are to be found in Migne's *Patrologiæ Cursus Completus*, vol. 48.

2. S. CŒLESTINI I. PAPÆ *Epistolæ et Decreta*: *ibid.* vol. 49, or in Coustant's edition in the *Bibl. Vett. Patrum*.

3. MANSI, *Sacrorum Conciliorum Collectio* (Florence, 1761), vols. iv.–vii.

    It is necessary for the student not merely to read, but to study these four volumes. There are Greek words which will only be understood by means of such close study. In regard to the Council of Ephesus, two documents must be particularly noticed, which are not to be found in all the Collections of the Councils, viz. the Roman Council under Celestine in A.D. 430 (iv. 547), and the *Commonitorium* of Celestine to his legates (iv. 556). Harnack's account (*Hist. of Dogma*, iv. 183, Tr.) of Celestine's action is absolutely disposed of by the former; and a great deal of Dr. Bright's contention is pulverised by the latter (cf. *infra*, p. 66).

4. CHRISTIANUS LUPUS, *Synodorum Generalium ac Provincialium Decreta et Canones* (Brussels, 1673), vol. i. It would be difficult to overestimate the value of Lupus's work. His references are, unfortunately, to editions now out of date, but on verifying the quotations in Mansi and elsewhere, I have found them almost uniformly accurate. He is particularly valuable in giving the

AUTHORITIES   xxi

salient points, and the scenery, so to speak, of the drama (for such it was) of the three Councils described in this volume.

5. NATALIS ALEXANDER, *Historia Ecclesiastica*, vol. ix. Natalis never shirks a difficulty, though in his original work he does not always solve them satisfactorily. But his is a work which the student will do well to have always at his side. Only he must be read in the great edition by Roncaglia, with the 'Animadversions' of Mansi, published at Bingen (*i.e.* Bingii ad Rhenum), 1786. These 'Animadversions,' and the accompanying notes, by Mansi, are incomparably the best pieces of writing on many of the difficulties raised by non-Catholics on the history of the Councils of Ephesus and Chalcedon. Hurter in his *Nomenclator Literarius*, iii. 101, calls Mansi ' the most celebrated of all at that whole epoch, and one who deserved superlatively well of the Church and literature.'

6. ALPHONSUS MUZZARELLI (S.J.), *De Auctoritate Romani Pontificis* (Ghent). There is no date to this valuable work. But Padre Muzzarelli accompanied Pius VII. to Paris in 1809, and died there in 1813. Being in the midst of Gallicans, he wrote two or three works on Papal Infallibility, of which the one from which I have quoted in this book was the fullest. His references are very scanty, but I verified the quotations and found them universally correct. The great value of his work consists in its clear and complete refutation of Bossuet.

7. PETRUS DE MARCA, Archbishop of Paris, *De concordia Sacerdotii et Imperii* (Roboreti, 1742). A great work, most useful for its facts, but perversely illogical on the subject of Gallican liberties.

8. BALLERINI FRATRES, *S. Leonis Magni Opera*, 3 vols. (Venice, 1753). A *magnum opus* indeed, quite indispensable for the history of the Council of Chalcedon. Their 'Observations' on Quesnel's Dissertations are masterpieces of erudition and logic.

9. TILLEMONT, *Mémoires pour servir pour l'Histoire*. A monument of diligence, and of immense value even to those who differ from his deductions. Tillemont's work is marred by lack of judgment, owing to his determined Jansenism. Duchesne, speaking of the value of this work, says that it is easy ' *écarter ses préoccupations doctrinales*.' When this is done, it is impossible to speak too highly of his work; but unfortunately it is exactly where his prepossessions have most swayed his judgment that he has been followed by our Anglican friends. For a good estimate of Tillemont see Hurter's *Nomenclator Literarius*, ii. 465. He quotes Schüz, who calls Tillemont ' theologaster semi-Catholicus vel Jansenianus.'

10. HERGENROTHER, *Photius*, and *Kirchengeschichte*, Erster Zeitraum, zweite Periode. Hergenrother's work is sound and thorough. His *History of the Church* may be read in a French translation of exceptional merit, with additional notes by Belet. The portion which embraces the period covered by this book will be found in vol. ii. 312-692.
11. BERNARDUS JUNGMANN, *Dissertationes Selectæ in Historiam Ecclesiasticam*, tom. i. and ii. (Ratisbon, New York and Cincinnati, 1880). A work of pre-eminent value owing to the admirable selection of 'points' and to the soundness of the author's judgment. On the period covered by this book, Jungmann's work is of special value as containing the best refutation of Mgr. Maret's 'Du Concile Général.'
12. PAUL BOTTALLA (S.J.), *The Pope and the Church*, Pt. II. (Burns and Oates, 1870). An admirable summary of the arguments usually adduced in favour of the Catholic doctrine concerning 'the Pope and the Council.'

Other writers, to whom the present writer is indebted—besides the older sources, such as Socrates, Sozomen and Theodoret—are Zaccharia, Palma, and Palmieri. And a careful perusal of Evagrius Scholasticus is to be recommended for the sake of gaining a command of Byzantine Greek such as was spoken at the Councils dealt with below.

The reader is referred to p. 150 *infra* for special authorities on the Latrocinium or Robber-Synod.

CONTENTS

	PAGE
THE COUNCIL OF EPHESUS, A.D. 431	1
THE LATROCINIUM, OR ROBBER-SYNOD, A.D. 449	119
THE COUNCIL OF CHALCEDON, A.D. 451	197

PART I.

THE COUNCIL OF EPHESUS, A.D. 431

Chapter I. ROME DEFINES, AND DELEGATES CYRIL, p. 3
,, II. NESTORIUS WORKS FOR A GENERAL COUNCIL, p. 24
,, III. THE PRESIDENCY AND FUNCTIONS OF THE COUNCIL, p. 34
,, IV. THE DEGRADATION OF NESTORIUS, p. 46
,, V. JOHN OF ANTIOCH, p. 59
,, VI. THE SEE OF PETER 'CONFIRMING THE BRETHREN,' I., p. 65
,, VII. ,, ,, ,, II., p. 75
,, VIII. THE EMPEROR AND THE MONK, p. 90
,, IX. JOHN OF ANTIOCH CONDEMNED, p. 95
,, X. TWO DECREES OF THE COUNCIL:
        1. The Use of the Nicene Creed, p. 104
        2. The Independence of Cyprus, p. 110

NOTES

On the meaning o τύπος, p. 21
On Theodosius s prohibition of καινοτομία, p. 32
On the Council's use of κατεπειχθέντες, p. 57
On Dr. Bright's interpretation of Celestine's Letter, p. 72
Dr. Bright *versus* Mansi, p. 87

PART I

CHAPTER I

ROME DEFINES, AND DELEGATES CYRIL

A PECULIAR importance attaches to the Council of Ephesus from an historical point of view, from the fact that it is the first of the Œcumenical Councils of which we have anything like ample records.[1]

The Council was concerned with the question of the union between the two natures in the One Divine Person of our Redeemer. Was it a substantial or an accidental union? Was He who was crucified on Calvary the Lord of Glory: and is His blood, what St. Paul calls it (Acts xx. 28), the Blood of God? Is the Flesh which gives life to those who partake of It, the very Flesh of God Himself by a Hypostatic Union? Or is the relationship between the Sacred Humanity and the Person of the Eternal Son merely that of a close union between a

---

[1] The records of the Council are in places mutilated, and the whole account of the proceedings in regard to the Pelagians is missing. St. Gregory the Great, who (when at Constantinople) investigated the matter, attributed this to the Eastern love of forgery and tampering with documents (*Epp.* lib. iv. 5, ad Narsen). The account of the sixth session should be read in the old Latin edition published in Mansi's fifth volume. And the account of the Roman Synod in 430 must be supplemented by Baluze's Fragment in Mansi, iv. 548.

created personality and the Uncreated Word? The whole question of the world's salvation hung upon the answer.¹

Both St. Celestine the Pope, and St. Cyril, the champion of the orthodox faith, emphasise this fact.² St. Celestine, in his letter to Nestorius, says that 'we complain that those words have been removed [by Nestorius] which promise us the hope of all life and salvation.' St. Cyril again and again strikes the same note. Dr. Salmon would have done well to have remembered this in his criticisms on this great champion of the faith.³

Up to the time of the Council of Ephesus expressions had been used concerning the union of the two natures in Christ which were meant in an orthodox sense, but which were liable to misinterpretation. St. Ignatius had spoken of Christ as 'bearing flesh;' Tertullian had described Him as 'clothed with flesh;' and the early Fathers had sometimes used the word 'mixture' ($\kappa\rho\tilde{\alpha}\sigma\iota\varsigma$) of the union of the two natures.

But a term had been in use which, if rightly understood, safeguarded the truth as to the union ($\ddot{\epsilon}\nu\omega\sigma\iota\varsigma$) of the two natures. I mean, of course, the term $\Theta\epsilon o\tau\acute{o}\kappa o\varsigma$, or Mother of God, as applied to our Blessed Lady. This term had not been as thoroughly sifted, and authorita-

---

[1] St. Cyril called the union $\ddot{\epsilon}\nu\omega\sigma\iota\varsigma\ \phi\upsilon\sigma\iota\kappa\grave{\eta}$, a substantial union; by which he did not mean, as he clearly explained, a union ending in one nature ($\epsilon\dot{\iota}\varsigma\ \mu\acute{\iota}\alpha\nu\ \phi\acute{\upsilon}\sigma\iota\nu$), but a union that constituted one Being, in opposition to the only union admitted by Nestorians—viz. a purely moral and external one. Cyril distinguished between the two natures in the One Person, but he did not separate them so as to teach that they had any existence after the Incarnation separate from the Personality of the Word.

[2] Mansi, iv. 1049.   [3] *Infallibility of the Church*, p. 312 (2nd ed.).

tively explained by the Church, as, owing to the heresy of Nestorius it was destined to be; but, as the Patriarch of Antioch bade Nestorius reflect, it had been in frequent use.¹

Nestorius had entered upon his career as archbishop with the boast that if the emperor would give him the earth cleared of heretics, he would give him heaven in exchange, and that if His Imperial Majesty would assist him in putting heretics to rout, he would assist him to do the same with his Persian foes. He was inexcusably cruel to his heterodox subjects, but he soon himself plunged into a heresy which cut at the root of the Christian faith—attributing to our Divine Lord a human personality, and thereby denying the substantial union between the two natures. His writings found their way into Egypt, which was in the patriarchate of Alexandria.

The see of Alexandria held a peculiar position in the East at this time. It was the see of Athanasius, and identified with the championship of orthodoxy on the subject of the Incarnation. The Bishop of Alexandria was the greatest person in Egypt;² he had at least a hundred bishops who gave him an enthusiastic allegiance; he had at his disposal an enormous body of monks, 'now in the springtide of popularity and power,' to whom the name of Athanasius was as magic. Alexandria itself was almost synonymous with intellectual primacy; it had been the home of Clement and Origen,

¹ It is much to be regretted that in the English translation of Bishop Hefele's *Concilien-Geshichte*, published by Messrs. Clark, of Edinburgh, the word Θεοτόκος is invariably translated 'God-bearer,' which is an equivocal term, as it might equally be the translation of Θεοφόρος, the very term which Nestorius, through his heresy, would have liked to substitute for Θεοτόκος.

² Cf. Duchesne, *Eglises séparées*, pp. 190, 191.

and was now the source of the correct calculations for the Paschal feast. It had its representative at the Court of Constantinople, and its numerous subjects in that city engaged in the sale of the corn that was regularly shipped thither from the granaries of Egypt. The see of Alexandria had, too, a past of rivalry and contention with the bishops of the Byzantine capital. The Bishop of Alexandria (Cyril) was at this time a man of commanding disposition, great intellectual power, and immense zeal. Whatever may have been his faults in the past (about which there has been much discussion), he was destined to take his place in the Calendar of the Church, and to leave behind him an heirloom of theological exposition on the subject of the Incarnation which she has cherished for more than fourteen centuries.

It is certain that Nestorius's writings had created an interest, not to say excitement, in Egypt itself, in the great monasteries that clustered there. St. Cyril was, in consequence, bound to take notice of the danger; and a correspondence ensued between him and Nestorius. At length he remanded the whole matter to the care of the Bishop of Rome: a step from which he had held off as long as he could, but at last (he says) he felt it to be his plain duty to forward to Celestine the whole correspondence.

St. Celestine, to judge from his letters, was a man full of zeal for the faith, and of great piety and tenderness of heart; Dr. Wordsworth, of Lincoln, appeals to him as the best judge of Cyril's character and conduct, although he underrates his share in the affair of Nestorius. He says: 'Perhaps there could not have been a more impartial judge of the parties in the struggle than the Bishop of Rome. Celestine was a calm spectator of the controversy, and in a review of it it may be well to enumerate his letters as indicative of his bearing with regard to it, and also as a summary of its history.'[1]

We shall presently see that St. Celestine was not exactly a mere 'spectator of the controversy,' and that his letters do not bear out Dr. Wordsworth's general review of the Council. But that writer shows a true instinct in taking the Pope's estimate of St. Cyril, in preference to that of the latter's enemies, whom Dr. Salmon and Dr. Bright follow.[2] 'The Bishop of Rome,' says Dr. Wordsworth, ' did not suppose Cyril to have been actuated by any unworthy motives in this controversy.' In this matter Dr. Pusey is at one with Dr. Wordsworth.[3]

Celestine, on being appealed to by Cyril, summoned a Synod of those bishops who happened to be in Rome at the time, and carefully investigated the matter at several sessions.[4] The result was that Celestine renewed the anathemas of his predecessor Damasus against those who assert that there are two Sons of God, 'One Who was begotten of the Father before the ages, and another who was born of the Virgin . . . and who do not confess that the same Son of God both before and after the Incarnation is Christ our Lord, the Son of God Who was born of the Virgin.' He condemned Nestorius for avoiding the word 'oneness' ($\mathring{\varepsilon}\nu\omega\sigma\iota\varsigma$) and using the

---

[1] Wordsworth's *Church History*, iv. 232-3.
[2] *Infallibility of the Church*, p. 312, and *Waymarks of Church Hist.* by W. Bright, pp. 150-158.
[3] Pref. to St. Cyril's Minor Works, *Lib. of the Fathers*.
[4] Cf. Cyril's letter to John of Antioch, Mansi, iv. 1052.

word 'conjunction' (συνάφεια)—the latter indicating only an external union (*qua nempe connectitur qui exterius adhæret*)—in other words, he defined that the union was Hypostatic, of substance with substance in a single Personality, not of person with Person.

Further, the Pope quoted the Hymn of St. Ambrose, and commenting on the line *Talis decet partus Deum* ('Such a birth befits God'), he set his seal on the word Θεοτόκος (Mother of God), quoting the Greek word itself.[1]

Having thus defined the matter of faith, Celestine wrote to Cyril and gave his decision on Nestorius. He must withdraw his objection to the word Θεοτόκος, or be deposed and excommunicated; and Cyril was to act for the Bishop of Rome in regard to the sentence on Nestorius, if he proved refractory, and also to provide for the government of the Church in Constantinople.[2]

So far St. Cyril's action towards Nestorius had been an office of charity, not an act of jurisdiction. He had not thought that he would do well even to excommunicate him from his own Church without consulting Celestine, although he says he might legitimately have done that much. When he wrote to the Egyptian monks he was writing to people within his own jurisdiction, but he had now laid the matter before one who could deal with cases that concerned the whole Church, and with the question of deposition as well as excommunication.[3] The correspondence that passed between

---

[1] Mansi, iv. 548-552. This invaluable fragment of Celestine's speech at the Synod was first published by Baluze, and is apt to be overlooked through its being separated in Mansi from the collection of documents bearing directly on the Council of Ephesus.

[2] *Ibid.* 1018.   [3] Cf. *Antifebronius vindicatus*, pt. i. 506.

Alexandria and Rome on this occasion is, however, so important that, at the cost of repetition, I will give a summary of the two letters.[1]

St. Cyril begins with giving his reason for breaking the silence which he had kept as long as he dared. The ancient customs of the Churches (he says) persuade us to communicate such matters to your Holiness; I, therefore, write of necessity.[2] Nestorius (he says) from the commencement of his episcopate has been disseminating among his own people, and the strangers who flock to Constantinople from all quarters, absurd ideas, contrary to the faith. He (Cyril) has therefore sent Nestorius's homilies to Celestine. It was in his mind to tell Nestorius at once that he could no longer hold communion with him; but he thought it better to hold out to him a helping hand first and exhort him by letters. Nestorius, however, only tried in every way to circumvent him. At last a bishop, named Dorotheus, exclaimed in Nestorius's presence, 'If anyone shall call Mary the mother of God, let him be anathema.' A crisis was reached by this expression; a great disturbance arose among the people of Constantinople. With few exceptions they refrained from communion—nearly all the monasteries and great part of the senate—for fear of receiving harm to their faith. He had found, moreover, that Nestorius's writings had been introduced

[1] Mansi, iv. 1011, *seq.*

[2] St. Cyril speaks of the Pope as his 'fellow minister,' from which expression Dr. Bright (*Roman See*, p. 145) argues that 'he regards the Bishop of Rome as *primus inter pares*' in the Anglican sense. But what follows decides the sense in which St. Cyril understood him to be *primus*—viz. in jurisdiction. According to Catholic teaching, the Pope is on a *par* with all bishops as regards power of order, but their superior in jurisdiction.

into Egypt, and in consequence had written an encyclical to the Egyptian monasteries to confirm them in the faith. Copies of this finding their way to Constantinople, Nestorius had resented his action. He accused Cyril of having read the Fathers wrongly. Cyril says he wrote direct to Nestorius, with a compendious exposition of the faith, exhorting him to conform to this. All the bishops, adds Cyril, are with me, especially those of Macedonia. Nestorius, however, considered that he alone understood the Scriptures. While all orthodox bishops and saints confess Christ to be God, and the Virgin to be the mother of God (Θεοτόκος,) he alone who denies this is supposed, forsooth, to be in the right. The people of Constantinople now began, says St. Cyril, to look for aid outside their province. St. Cyril felt that a 'dispensation was entrusted to him,' and that he should have to answer on the day of judgment for silence in this matter. He does not, however, feel that he can confidently withdraw himself from communion with Nestorius before communicating these things to His Holiness.

'Deign, therefore, to decree what seems right (τυπῶσαι τὸ δοκοῦν), whether we ought to communicate at all with him, or to tell him plainly that no one communicates with a person who holds and teaches what he does. Further, the purpose of your Holiness ought to be made known by letter to the most religious and God-loving bishops of Macedonia, *and to all the bishops of the East*, for we shall then give them, according to their desire, the opportunity of standing together in unity of soul and mind, and lead them to contend earnestly (ἐπαγωνίσασθαι) for the orthodox Faith which is being attacked. As regards Nestorius, our fathers who have said that the Holy Virgin is the mother of God are, together with us who are here to-day, included in his anathema; for although he did not like to do this with his own lips, still, by sitting and listening to another (viz. Dorotheus), he has helped him to do it, for immediately on coming from the throne he communicated him at the holy mysteries.' He (St. Cyril) has therefore sent his Holiness the materials for forming a judgment.[1]

St. Celestine in a beautiful letter, in answer, expresses his joy at Cyril's purity of faith. He endorses his teaching, and embraces him in the Lord, as present in his letters. For (says the Pope) we are of one mind concerning Christ our Lord! He compares Cyril to a good shepherd, and Nestorius not even to a hireling, but to a wolf, who is destroying his own sheep. Our Lord Jesus Christ, whose own 'generation' is questioned, shows us that we should toil for one sheep; how much more for one shepherd! We ought, therefore, 'to shut

[1] Dr. Bright (*R. See*, p. 145) objects to the interpretation here given of the words τυπῶσαι τὸ δοκοῦν, (1) because the Latin (which he sets aside in Celestine's letter, but prefers in Cyril's!) has *quid hic sentias præscribere*—words which he avoids translating, but which are, to say the least, compatible with the idea of authoritative decision; and (2) because 'Cyril tells Celestine that he ought to make known his mind (σκόπον) to the Macedonian bishops.' Dr. Bright adds: 'We shall presently see that the Oriental bishops did not regard, &c.'

As to (1), the Greek word τυπῶσαι will be commented on directly (p. 21). Meanwhile as to (2), it may be remarked (a) that the question is, not as to what the Oriental bishops thought, but what Cyril here meant. And (β) the word σκόπος, so far from being suggestive of unauthoritative direction, is actually used a few pages further on of the Emperor's commands, which Count Candidian complained had not been obeyed (Mansi, iv. 1233), and it occurs several times in reference to the Emperor later on (cf. 1261, 1264). It will be seen presently that Cyril did consider that Celestine had decided the question.

him out from the sheep, unless there is hope of his conversion. This we earnestly desire. But *if he persists*, an open sentence must be passed on him, for a wound, when it affects the whole body, must be at once cut away. For what has he to do with those who are of one mind among themselves—he who considers that he alone knows what is best, and dissents from our faith? Let, then, all those whom he has removed remain in communion [with the Church], and give him to understand that he cannot be in communion with us if he persists in this path of perversity in opposition to the Apostolic teaching. *Wherefore assuming to you the authority of our See, and acting in our stead and place with delegated authority* (ἐξουσία), *you shall execute a sentence of this kind* (ἐκβιβάσεις ἀπόφασιν), not without strict severity, viz. that unless within ten days after this admonition of ours he anathematises, in written confession, his evil teaching, and promises for the future to confess the faith concerning the birth of Christ our God which both the Church of Rome and that of your Holiness, *and the whole Christian religion* preaches, forthwith your Holiness will provide for that Church. And let him know that he is to be altogether removed from our body. . . . We have written the same to our brothers and fellow-bishops John, Rufus, Juvenal, and Flavian, whereby *our judgment* concerning him, *yea rather, the judgment of Christ our Lord*, may be manifest.'

These two letters contain the following important points.

(i) It was, according to St. Cyril, an 'ancient custom of the Churches,' not simply of Alexandria, for troubles concerning the faith (Mansi, iv. 1011), and such important matters as the deposition of an heretical archbishop, to be referred to Rome.

(ii) St. Cyril asks St. Celestine to prescribe what he judges best in the matter; to give the *decision* on this important case, and to notify his decision to all the bishops of the East. Dr. Bright merely calls this writing in 'very deferential terms'[1] to the Bishop of Rome. Would it not surprise some of his readers to know *how* deferential the terms of St. Cyril's letter were? He uses a word which occurs again and again in the Acts of the Councils in reference to the relation of the Pope to the condemnation of Nestorius, asking him τυπῶσαι τὸ δοκοῦν—words which are a sort of refrain for a year to come; they form the keynote to the proceedings at Ephesus. Bossuet remarks upon this expression, that 'it signifies, in Greek, to declare juridically; τύπος is a rule, a sentence, and τυπῶσαι τὸ δοκοῦν is to declare one's opinion judicially. The Pope alone could do it. Neither Cyril, nor any other patriarch, had the power to depose Nestorius, who was not their subject: the Pope alone did it, and no one was found to exclaim against it, because his authority extended over all.'[2]

(iii) St. Celestine, on being appealed to by St. Cyril to formulate the decision as to Nestorius's excommunication and deposition, at once assumes his infallibility in such a grave matter. The Vatican decree does not go beyond his words, when he says of his own sentence on Nestorius, that it is not so much his, but rather it is 'the divine judgment of Christ our Lord;' and again to the Patriarch of Antioch he says, 'and let your Holiness

[1] *Dictionary of Christian Biography*, art. 'Cyril,' p. 766.
[2] *Remarques sur l'histoire des Conciles*, &c. (*Œuvres*, t. 30, p. 526. Versailles, 1817.)

know this sentence is passed by us, yea, rather by Christ [our] God.' Just as afterwards the Synod, writing to the clergy of Constantinople, calls the executed sentence, being that of Pope and Council together, 'the just sentence of the Holy Trinity and their [*i.e.* the bishops' and legates'] divinely inspired judgment.'

(iv) And again, Celestine is here pronouncing judgment as to what is preached by the whole Christian religion,' and decides to cut off Nestorius *from the common unity.*

Dr. Wordsworth speaks of this all-important letter as being simply a statement of 'the orthodox doctrine of the Western Fathers' upon the controversy![1] Celestine, however, states that he is giving the doctrine of the Church of Rome and Alexandria and 'the whole Christian religion,' or, as he expresses it in his letter to Nestorius (going over the same ground), 'the universal Church.' Dr. Bright has described it thus:

'Celestine gave Cyril a commission of stringent character (Mansi, iv. 1017). He was "to join the authority of the Roman See *to his own*,' and on the part of Celestine, *as well as for himself*, to warn Nestorius that unless a written retractation were executed within ten days, giving assurance of his acceptance of the faith as to "Christ our God," which was held by the Churches of *Rome and Alexandria*, he would be excluded from the communion of *those Churches*, and provision would be made by them for the Church of Constantinople, *i.e.* by the appointment of an orthodox bishop.'[2]

Now, St. Celestine does not say 'join the authority

---

[1] *Church History*, iv. 210.
[2] *Dictionary of Christian Biography*, art. 'Cyril.' p. 766. The italics are mine.

of the Roman See *to his own,*' which Canon Bright gives as a quotation. There is nothing in the Latin or Greek exactly corresponding to ' his own : ' words which would suggest something more than the Papal decision as the source of authority.[1] Neither does Celestine bid St. Cyril warn Nestorius ' on the part of Celestine *as well as for himself.*' He simply constitutes St. Cyril his ' plenipotentiary,' as Dr. Döllinger accurately expressed it.[2] Neither, again, does Celestine speak of the faith held by the Churches of Rome and Alexandria simply, but he adds that it is that of the entire Christian world or religion. And further, he tells Nestorius in the same batch of letters which Cyril was to read and forward, that he will exclude him, not from the communion of ' those Churches ' only, but from the communion also of the entire Christian Church. The latter point is of

[1] In his *Roman See,* p. 146, Dr. Bright urges that to 'assume the authority' would apply to one 'who had no official authority,' and that therefore it could not be said of St. Cyril. He therefore objects to the translation 'assuming the authority of our See' and translates 'the authority of our See having been combined with yours.' But (1) this is a mistranslation of the Greek, which has σοί—*i.e.* 'you,' not 'yours'; and (2) the Latin, which, according to Canon Bright's own principle (*Roman See,* p. 165), is of prime importance in a Papal letter, runs thus: *nostræ sedis auctoritate adscitâ* (Mansi, iv. 1019); (3) Cyril had no official authority over Nestorius: he could not, as Bossuet remarks, excommunicate him from communion with the whole Church, as Celestine at any rate professed to do. Besides, the words 'acting with ἐξουσία' are decisive that the authority was considered to be delegated, even if they had not been accompanied by the words ' using our place,' which Dr. Bright admits to mean delegation. And, lastly, the Greek word συναφθείσης cannot be considered to exclude the combination of two unequal authorities, for it was in constant use at that time to express the combination of the Logos with the sacred Humanity in our Lord: cf. Harnack, *Hist. of Dogma* (Tr.), iv. 171, *note,* and *supra,* p. 8.

[2] 'Bevollmächtiger,' *Lehrbuch* (1843), p. 121; ' *mandataire,*' Duchesne, *Eglises séparées,* p. 35.

importance, but it is strangely misrepresented in the *Dictionary of Christian Biography* (Art. *Cyril*, by W. Bright).[1] In this very letter Celestine speaks of Nestorius being separated from 'our body,' by which, from the contextual use of 'our,' he could not mean simply his own, nor only his own and Cyril's, but the whole body of the Church. Anyhow, in his letter to Nestorius, which St. Cyril was to read and forward, and which covers the same ground, and was read at the Council of Ephesus, the Pope says expressly that by this sentence, unless he retracts, he is cut off from the communion of 'the whole Catholic Church' ('ab universalis te Ecclesiæ Catholicæ communione dejectum').[2] This is a vital point, and it is surely not fair to tell the reader that Celestine bade Cyril warn Nestorius that he was to be cut off from the communion of 'those Churches' (viz. Rome and Alexandria) when, as a matter of fact, he was telling him that he was to be cut off from the communion of the whole Catholic Church. They are words, too, which recur, for in writing to the clergy and people of Constantinople as Celestine did, he repeats the sentence in full which Cyril is to pass on Nestorius. And while he speaks again of the faith held, not only by the Churches of Rome and Alexandria, but by 'the whole Catholic Church,' he says that Nestorius is to be 'excommunicated from the entire Catholic Church.' The same occurs once more in the Pope's letter to John of Antioch. The Pope there again speaks as clothed with supreme authority, calling his sentence 'the sentence passed by Christ our God,' and it cuts Nes-

---

[1] The same misleading expression (Rome and Alexandria) occurs in a later work by the same writer, *Waymarks*, &c. p. 221. The omission is supplied in *The Roman See*, p. 147.

[2] Mansi, iv. 1035.

torius off from 'the roll of bishops' ('episcoporum cœtu').[1]

St. Celestine thus comes before us at the Council of Ephesus as the foundation of the Church in a crisis of her life when the reality of our Redemption was at stake; for this, as we have said, was the real point at issue, as was distinctly stated by himself and St. Cyril. He stands out at once as the 'confirmer of the brethren,' (Luke xxii. 32). He feeds, or governs, the sheep of Christ, supplying them with authoritative direction, with the τύπος, or decree, which was to govern their action. He exercises his Apostolate over the whole Christian Church, directing the Christian flock in Constantinople itself,[2] as well as the Bishops of Antioch and Jerusalem, while he delegates the Bishop of Alexandria, the second throne in Christendom, to execute his sentence.

This sentence, therefore, having been entrusted to Cyril, together with the general management of 'the affair concerning Nestorius,' including the arrangements for providing a new bishop for Constantinople, Cyril wrote at once to John, Bishop of Antioch, and after telling him what had happened, said that it was for him to consider what it was best for him to do. St. Cyril was doubtless well aware that he was treading on delicate ground, for Nestorius had been recommended for the see of Constantinople by John himself; and the event proved how little John was to be depended upon. In describing what had taken place, Cyril says: 'The holy Synod of the Romans has issued a plain decree (φανερὰ τετύπωκε), and moreover has sent it in writing to your Reverence, which [decree] it is necessary for

[1] Mansi, iv. 1050.   [2] *Ibid.* 1036.

those to obey who cling to communion with the whole West.' After saying that the Synod had written to others—the Synodical letters are headed '*Celestine* to our beloved brother'—Cyril proceeds: 'We shall follow the decisions given by him, fearing to lose the communion of so many, who are not angry with us on any other account, and the judgment and impulse given [1] is not about matters of little moment, but on behalf of the faith itself, and of the Churches which are everywhere disturbed, and of the edification of the people.' [2]

The position adopted by Cyril in endeavouring to secure that John of Antioch should do his duty was, therefore, as follows: This is a matter in which we ought to accept the decision of the Roman Synod. The West will themselves obey; they will also make it a condition of communion with others that they, too, should obey the Roman Synod in this matter. Thus, if we disobey, we shall differ from the whole West as to the necessity of obedience, and that, too, in a matter which concerns the faith. 'We shall [therefore] follow the decisions given by him,' *i.e.* by Celestine. If we were to put this into the technical terms of Catholic theology, it would be the same as saying that the decision of Celestine was an *ex-cathedra* judgment; that it would be so regarded by the West, and that the course to be pursued in the East was therefore clear—

---

[1] Gk. κίνησις, which implies that Celestine set the matter in motion, gave its direction and impulse—a direction which the Synod twice say could not be resisted: first in the sentence passed at their first Session, and secondly in their account of their doings to the Papal legates. In this latter case they use the expression ἀναγκαίως κινηθέντες (Mansi, iv. 1296). The same word (κινήσαντος) is used of the Emperor's summons of the Bishops to the Synod, iv. 1276.

[2] Mansi, iv. 1052.

they must obey. That Celestine intended his judgment as what we should now call an *ex-cathedra* dogmatic decision is certain, for he insisted on Nestorius using the term Θεοτόκος (Mother of God) in the sense which he, in his court of judgment at Rome,[1] decided to be the sense of the word in the mind of the whole Church. From that hour this word Θεοτόκος (Mother of God) was destined necessarily to take its place in the terminology of the Church just as much as the term ὁμοούσιος (Consubstantial) in the preceding century. It was not inserted in the Creed, because the very judgment of the Pope was that it was contained in the actual terms of that Creed. It safeguarded, as it was a development of, that Creed.[2]

[1] Mansi, iv. 548-552.
[2] Dr. Bright translates the quotation given above from Cyril's letter as though he said that it was necessary to 'follow' the 'Romans,' changing the order of the words in his translation. But the Greek is not ἀκολουθεῖν (follow), but πείθεσθαι (obey), and the relative pronoun more naturally refers to the decisions (φανερὰ τετύπωκε) than to the Romans. It would mean the Romans in Synod even if Dr. Bright were correct in his rendering of the relative οἷς. He also suggests that lower down we should read παρ' αὐτῶν (by *them*) instead of παρ' αὐτοῦ (by him), *i.e.* Celestine. This is arbitrary; and, moreover, it would not help his case, as he appears to think it would. For why should the West (as Cyril's argument requires) obey the decisions of a Roman Synod as a matter of course, unless it was the court of a superior judge? It must be remembered that that Synod was not composed of bishops delegated by the West. It consisted merely of the bishops, as St. Cyril says, 'found in Rome' at the moment; and that decision is again and again called the decision of Celestine, by Celestine himself, by Cyril, by John of Antioch, and by the Synod of Ephesus. Cyril on this particular occasion naturally spoke of it as the decision of the Roman Synod: *i.e.* he spoke of the Court, the instrument, rather than of the judge, to emphasise the fact that it was a solemn dogmatic settlement of the matter, to which all must adhere who were to continue in communion with the West. He calls it in point of fact, in this very passage, both the judgment of the

John of Antioch wrote to Nestorius on receiving the Papal decision, and urged him to submit on the ground that, although the time given by Celestine (he thus treats it as the judgment of Celestine) was indeed short, still it was a matter in which obedience need not be a matter of days even, but of a single hour; and that the term 'Mother of God,' although capable of abuse, was one which the Fathers had used,[1] and to which, therefore, Nestorius could easily give his consent, attaching to it his own doubtless orthodox meaning. He urges him, in conclusion, to give up his own opinion in favour of the general good.

Cyril wrote also to Juvenal of Jerusalem saying that Nestorius had been 'condemned' by Celestine as 'a heretic' and that Celestine had 'written clear things' (the expression used by him of the Synod in his letter to John), which he has now sent on to Juvenal to excite his zeal to 'save our imperilled flocks'; and he exhorts him to assist in writing both to Nestorius and to the people in accordance with the decree (ὁρισθέντα τύπον), *i.e.* the Papal decision, and suggests that pressure should be brought to bear upon the Emperors.[2]

Meanwhile Cyril had summoned a synod at Alexandria and in conjunction with the bishops he drew up twelve Anathematisms, which he forwarded three months later to Nestorius together with the Papal sentence.

Bossuet describes the situation thus (the italics are his): ' C'est Célestin qui prononce, c'est Cyrille qui exécute, et il exécute *avec puissance,* parce qu'il agit *par*

Synod and the judgment of Celestine, if we accept the only reading supplied us in the Greek (παρ' αὐτοῦ κρίμασι, iv. 1052).

[1] Mansi, iv. 1068. See Harnack, *History of Dogma* (Tr.), iv. 168.
[2] Mansi, iv. 1060.

autorité du siège de Rome. Ce qu'il écrit à Nestorius n'est pas moins fort, puisqu'il donne son approbation à la foi de saint Cyrille, et, en conséquence, il ordonne à Nestorius de se former à " ce qu'il lui verra enseigner " sous peine de déposition.'[1]

Note on the Meaning of τύπος.

Dr. Bright insists upon translating τύπος by 'direction' (*Roman See*, p. 163, and pp. 145, 148) by way of correcting the translation given by Bossuet, which I have adopted in the text, viz. 'judicial decree' or sentence, conveying the idea of authority. And on p. 163 he omits in the text the word ψῆφον in translating the speech of Bishop Firmus, who is giving the Council's view of what Celestine had done. This omission, which originally occurred in his article in the *Church Quarterly Review* for Jan. 1895, p. 289, was pointed out by me in the *Dublin Review*, April 1895—an article which Dr. Bright read, as he refers to it. Yet Dr. Bright repeats the misquotation in the text of his *Roman See &c.*, p. 163, only adding in small print in a note that 'the word ψῆφον, "sentence," precedes.' The reader would hardly gather from this how or what exactly it 'precedes.' And yet a great deal hangs on this. For the contention maintained is that Celestine delivered an authoritative regulation, a decree, a sentence, whereas Dr. Bright persists in translating it merely as 'direction,' which is a more colourless, less 'judicial' word, and is compatible with the idea of no particular authority—something, in fact,

[1] *Remarques sur l'histoire des Conciles*, p. 524, t. 30, Versailles, 1817. For proof of Bossuet's statement as to the Papal 'approbation' of Cyril's teaching cf. Mansi, iv. 1033, where Celestine says of it: ἐσχήκαμεν καὶ ἔχομεν δεδοκιμασμένην = 'we held and hold it as approved,' *i.e.* as sound in doctrine. This was read out in the Council of Ephesus.

that might or might not be followed according as convenience should dictate. Firmus's words are that Celestine ψῆφον ἔπεχε καὶ τύπον, 'gave a sentence and decree.' This fixes the meaning of τύπος. It is simply a 'decree,' and as will be seen hereafter is equivalent to an ὅρος, in spite of what Dr. Bright has said on p. 167. (Cf. *infra*, p. 107.) The words τύπος and τυποῦν constantly occur in the 'Acts' of the Councils for an authoritative decision or decree. As mere examples of literally multitudinous instances : Cyril uses the substantive of the Imperial decree fixing the date of the Council (Mansi, iv. 1229) ; Anatolius uses it of the sentence passed on Dioscorus by the Council of Chalcedon (*Leonis Ep.* 101, § 2) ; the Emperor Marcian uses the verb of the things finally decided by the Synod of Chalcedon (*Leon. Ep.* 105) ; the substantive is used of 'the decision of all the Churches' (Mansi, iv. 1297) ; it is used again and again of decrees of the Nicene Council : once even of the Third Person in the Holy Trinity having made those decrees, ἐτύπωσε τὰ τετυπωμένα (*ibid.* vii. 627) ; it is frequently used of the Imperial decrees, θείους τύπους (*ibid.* vi. 1032). In one instance where, according to Dr. Bright, it does not mean authoritative regulation, he is mistaken in supposing that the idea of 'model' is conveyed by it (*Canons of the First Four General Councils*, 2nd ed. p. 200). The reference is to the public 'typi' or 'tabulæ' of the Roman Empire, settling the division of provinces, territories, camps, and called 'Notitia.' The ecclesiastical divisions were to follow these, according to the 17th Canon of Chalcedon, not because these were 'models' for the ecclesiastical scheme of distribution, but because they were the Imperial regulations or ordinances or decrees on the civil distribution of provinces, &c. That is to say, they were τύποι without reference to ecclesiastical conformity, but because they were authoritative regulations for the Imperial civil administration. In short, τύπος is properly in Byzantine (and especially Conciliar) Greek an authoritative regulation, a decree or ordinance.

In the last three editions of Liddell and Scott's Greek Lexicon (6th, 7th, and 8th), the meaning of τύπος in Byzantine Greek has been added as simply 'decree, or ordinance.' The important point in the description of this word in reference to Celestine's action is that it implies, not any kind of direction, but *authoritative* direction, *i.e.* a decree or sentence.

CHAPTER II

NESTORIUS WORKS FOR A GENERAL COUNCIL

But meanwhile Nestorius had tried to turn the subject. First, he had artfully appealed to the Pope to know what ought to be done about certain supposed disseminators of Apollinarian teaching, with which in Constantinople itself he ceaselessly charged Cyril; and, next, he devised another plan for staying the execution of any sentence against himself. Before a sentence could be served on him in Constantinople—before, that is, it could acquire any canonical force such as the Emperor could recognise—he induced His Imperial Majesty to summon a Council to allay the general disturbance of the Church in the East.

To understand the situation, it will be necessary to glance at the state of things in Constantinople. As Cyril, in his correspondence with Nestorius previous to delating him to the Pope, had charged Nestorius with broaching novelties (καινοτομία), so Nestorius retorted that Cyril was himself the doctrinal innovator in the direction of Apollinarianism. But there were others in the Imperial city just then who were labouring under a sentence passed at Rome for having introduced novel doctrine. The ecclesiastical atmosphere was in fact charged with disturbing influences in the persons of Pelagian adventurers who had found their way to the capital from Antioch, the great centre of strictly Oriental ecclesiasticism.

That city—which first heard the name of Christian applied to the followers of Jesus Christ; honoured by the Church as one of the three sees of Peter; the third throne in Christendom—had long proved a nursery of heretical teaching and religious dissension. Nestorius himself came from Antioch. While there he had come across Theodore of Mopsuestia, the pupil of Diodorus, Bishop of Tarsus, who was the fountain, so far as we can trace things upwards, of all the mischief which occasioned the Council of Ephesus. In opposing Apollinarianism Diodorus had lost the balance of faith, and taught that the union of Godhead and Manhood in the Redeemer was not of substance with substance, but of two persons : a union of name, authority, and honour. Theodore imbibed his error, and so great and lasting was the magic of Theodore's influence that his name had to be condemned in the Sixth Council. Nestorius had come under Theodore's teaching. John of Antioch, in urging Nestorius to obey the Papal decision, alluded to Theodore's withdrawal of certain erroneous expressions as an encouragement. Being both of Antioch, they understood the force of such an appeal.

But there was another of Theodore's pupils, the Bishop Julian, a fellow-countryman of Nestorius, who entered into the lists with St. Augustine in favour of Pelagianism, and, with the usual modesty of heretics, compared himself to David, and Augustine to Goliath. This Julian had been deposed by the Holy See for his Pelagian teaching, and previous to the emergence of Nestorianism had found his way to Constantinople with some others in the hope of moving the Emperor to call a

Council to reverse the sentence of the Pope. Two successive Bishops of Constantinople had refused to present him at Court. But it seems, from a letter of Celestine's, that Nestorius was on too friendly terms with Julian to please the Pope, and that but for his fear of Celestine he would have consented to present Julian to the Emperor. When the see of Constantinople was vacant, Celestine had been anxious about its future occupant for this very reason, lest he should be one that would use his privilege of introduction in favour of such ecclesiastical 'lepers' as Julian, and lead his Imperial Majesty to call a Council for no adequate reason, and so simply disturb the peace of the Church. St. Augustine and the African Church had expressed themselves satisfied with the ruling of the Holy See in regard to Pelagianism. The expression '*Roma locuta est; causa finita est*,' though not the actual words of St. Augustine, are the exact equivalent of what he did say. 'The rescripts have come,' *i.e.* from Rome (which are St. Augustine's words), is the same as 'Rome has spoken'; and the 'case is finished' are his actual words. He was satisfied with the decision of local Councils *sanctioned by Rome*. But the Pelagians wished to appeal to a General Council. St. Augustine had reproved them for their disobedience. Capreolus, Bishop of Carthage, writing in the name of the African Church to the Synod when it was summoned, goes out of his way to press this point, that the bishops of Africa had accepted the decision of the Holy See, and that the Synod of Ephesus had no right to re-open matters already settled by such authority. He speaks of *novel doctrines* which 'the authority of the Apostolic See and the judgment of the bishops agreeing together has defeated,' and submits that to treat these as open questions would be to discover a lack of faith.[1] As a matter of fact, the Synod of Ephesus did allude to their case, not to re-open it, but to signify in express terms their adhesion *en bloc* to the decisions of the Holy See.

Julian, however, hoped much from a Council, and, seeing his opportunity in the appointment of Nestorius to the see of Constantinople, appears to have drawn him into a favourable inclination to himself. Nestorius had gone so far as to sound Celestine as to what could be done in regard to such as Julian.[2] There was, indeed, a natural affinity between their heresies. 'Where Pelagius ends, Nestorius begins,' said St. Prosper ; and 'Nestorius erred concerning the head, Pelagius concerning the body,' said a Council of Western bishops.

Nestorius, then, probably assisted by Julian, turned to the Emperor and tried for a General Council. The Emperor, not unnaturally, welcomed the idea of putting an end to what he regarded as an unprofitable strife.

The long-seated antipathy between Constantinople and Alexandria would also not be without its effect on the situation ; but, in addition, Cyril had quite recently incurred the displeasure of the Emperor by writing privately to the Empresses two magnificent letters on the subject of the Incarnation. Theodosius was just then becoming jealous of the growing influence of his sister, the Empress Pulcheria, which, happily, was always on the orthodox side, while the Emperor himself had come under the subtle influence of Nestorius. It was natural that the best mode of counteracting the supremacy exercised by Cyril over the Catholics of the East, and of Constantinople in particular, and of settling any further troubles from the Pelagians, should seem to his Imperial

[1] Mansi, iv. 1209. [2] *Ibid.* 1021.

Majesty to lie in a General Council. Anyhow the state of confusion was such as to make him feel impatient, and if Nestorius was right, he would have full opportunity for displaying those powers of address which seem to have fascinated Theodosius. Nestorius himself hoped to be President and by bringing Cyril under an accusation of siding with Apollinarian errors, to avert any sentence that might come through him from Rome. The execution of the impending Papal sentence would at least be stayed owing to a technical difficulty; for the Alexandrian Archbishop, if himself in the dock under trial, could not be the executor of a Papal condemnation against the Archbishop of Constantinople. The Council was, as Dr. Pusey expresses it, ' a device of Nestorius.'

But the idea of a Council was also welcomed by the orthodox monks whom Nestorius had so severely persecuted, and who saw their only method of escape from his fangs in the publication of their wrongs at a Council. They accordingly wrote to the Emperor pleading for a Council. Nothing could be more welcome also to the Pope himself, his desire being that Nestorius should have some opportunity of retractation, such as a Council would afford. He expressed himself strongly to this effect in his letter to Cyril, after the Council had been summoned, as also to the Synod itself; and his own words—those of a man whose sincerity and goodness were never questioned by his contemporaries, not even by Nestorius himself (who only thought himself more ' learned ' than the Pope, and, indeed, than anyone else) —are better evidence than the imagination of certain controversialists who cannot conceive of a Pope ever wishing to act otherwise than with a high hand.

The Emperor, then, sent out his summons; and in

his letter he forbade any 'innovations' in the *interim*,[1] *i.e.* any doctrinal novelties such as Nestorius charged against Cyril, and Cyril against Nestorius, and the Catholics in general against Julian and his Pelagian or semi-Pelagian followers. He was, however, careful not to show his leanings in his public authoritative letters, though in Cyril's case he added to the letter of summons a private one complaining of his stirring up strife between himself and the Empresses by his private letters to the latter.

But matters presently took an unexpected turn in Constantinople. The summons for the Council was issued by the Emperor on November 19. By the end of October Cyril had held his Synod at Alexandria, and in the beginning of November (probably November 3) he wrote his letter to Nestorius to be delivered to him by four bishops—one more than the usual number for serving a notice on an archbishop, owing probably to the sentence being that of the Bishop of Rome. Before these bishops arrived in Constantinople the Imperial summons had been issued and was on its way to distant parts. But nevertheless, on November 30, they served the notice of deposition and excommunication on the Archbishop of the Imperial city, together with the Papal letter announcing the terms on which he could be released, and together also with the twelve Anathematisms added by Cyril and his Alexandrian Synod. Thus, in less than a fortnight after the Imperial summons, the whole face of things was changed by the appearance of Cyril's legates in Constantinople, bearing with them the Papal sentence of deposition. Before this had been served, the idea of a Council had

[1] See note at the end of the Chapter.

been devised to settle matters between Cyril and
Nestorius, and with the hope on Nestorius's part that he
would preside. Now all was changed. Nestorius was
condemned by the highest authority known to the
Church, acting, indeed, before the idea of a Council had
been broached, but creating, in spite of that, a new
situation.

We have no means of discovering the feelings with
which this action on the part of Rome and Alexandria
was received by the Emperor. The sentence was
delivered to Nestorius on Sunday as he was about to
solemnise the liturgy. He refused to receive the document at first; but the bearers, taking hold of his garment
from behind, succeeded in lodging the notice with him.
He gave no answer, but each side prepared for the
Council, Nestorius still hoping, it would seem, to be
able to bring on a theological discussion, through the
influence of the Emperor, whose instructions were
entrusted to Count Candidian, and who, according to
Count Irenæus, had settled that Cyril should not sit as
judge at all.[1]

But on arriving at Ephesus some time before
Pentecost, in the hope doubtless of affecting the preliminary arrangements for the Council, Nestorius was
rudely undeceived by the attitude which Memnon, the
bishop of the diocese, at once assumed towards himself
and his sympathisers. The doors of St. Mary's Church
were closed against them. They complained to the
Emperor that they could not celebrate the liturgy of
Pentecost in any of the churches throughout the city.
Bishop after bishop, too, on arriving at Ephesus, must
have strengthened Nestorius's conviction that the Papal

---

[1] οὐδὲ κρίνειν ὡς εἷς ὢν τῶν κρινομένων ἠδύνατο, Mansi, iv. 1393.

sentence was practically accepted, and that the bishops had come, as Count Candidian, the Imperial Commissioner, afterwards complained, not to investigate an open question, but to execute a sentence already passed.[1] Accordingly, as we shall see, Nestorius absented himself from the Synod.

The day of Pentecost had come and the Bishop of Antioch had not arrived. At length bishops came with a message from him that the Synod was not to wait.[2] Some bishops in Ephesus had already fallen ill, many felt the results of heat and bad accommodation, and at last some of them died. As they said the Requiem Mass of one bishop after another, the survivors must have felt keenly the cruelty of the Patriarch of Antioch's procrastination. They knew it to be of set purpose. The Synod in its report to the Emperor assured His Majesty of their conviction that John had delayed from a desire not to be present at Nestorius's condemnation. For no orthodox bishop doubted that the sentence passed by the Pope would be executed. John, they said, allowed friendship [for Nestorius] to gain the day over zeal for the truth. Accordingly the bishops agreed to enter upon the work of the Council, convinced that John of Antioch did not mean, or wish, to be present, for (as Cyril afterwards told the clergy and people of Constantinople) 'he knew that Nestorius [his friend] would be condemned.'[3] He knew that that was not really an open question.

[1] Mansi, iv. 1264. As Dean Milman says, 'The Bishop of Constantinople was already a condemned heretic; the business of the Council was only the confirmation of their [Celestine's and Cyril's] anathema.' *Hist. of Latin Christianity*, i. 206. And Dr. Pusey says, 'The mind of the Church had been expressed in the previous year.' Pref. to Minor Works of Cyril, *Lib. of the Fathers*.

[2] Mansi, iv. 1229, 1332.   [3] *Ibid*. 1232.

On Theodosius's Prohibition of καινοτομία.

Dr. Bright says that Theodosius 'had ruled that "no new steps should in the interim be taken by any individuals"' (*R. See*, p. 153). He refers his readers to Mansi, iv. 1113, and adopts Tillemont's inference that Theodosius had, in effect, 'arrested the decrees of Rome.' Yes, 'in effect'; but it must be remembered that this would constitute no formal opposition to the Papal authority, since the decrees were not yet published. Yet this appears to be the point of Dr. Bright's remark. But, in fact, Dr. Bright, in his translation of καινοτομίας as 'new steps,' has given a complexion to the Emperor's words, which is not warranted by the Greek. The Bishops are told to attend μηδεμιᾶς πρὸ τῆς ἁγιωτάτης συνοδοῦ καὶ τοῦ μέλλοντος παρ' αὐτῆς κοινῇ ψήφῳ ἐφ' ἅπασι δίδοσθαι τύπου καινοτομίας ἰδίᾳ παρὰ τινῶν γενομένης: *i.e.* lit. 'no novelty being broached by any in their individual capacity, &c.' It was not a question of 'new steps' (as Dr. Bright translates), but of what Theodosius, prompted by Nestorius, chose to call 'novelties,' *i.e.* doctrinal innovations, such as Cyril was considered to be instilling on his own account into the minds of the Empresses, and of which the Emperor spoke sharply in his letter to Cyril accompanying the summons. Καινοτομία has a definite signification in the Acts of the Councils. It is the word which Cyril used more than once of Nestorius's teaching (Mansi, iv. 1093, 1307). Nestorius's doctrine had been called καινότητα, a 'novelty,' by Celestine (iv. 1036). The bishops at the Roman Synod said that Nestorius αἵρεσιν καινοτομῆσαι, 'invented a heresy,' (iv. 1052). Nestorius retorted the accusation. He and his sympathisers used the word in regard to the avoidance of doctrinal innovation, or fresh Creeds, by all Councils since the Nicene (iv. 1233). It is the exact opposite of 'rightly handling the word of truth,' ὀρθοτομοῦντες, 2 Tim. ii. 15; cf. Mansi, iv. 1257. It was, in fact, a word that was being bandied about on either side, and consequently it naturally came into the Emperor's letter about their assembling to confirm the ancient faith. Dr. Bright, mistaking the meaning of the word in Byzantine, and especially ecclesiastical Greek, strikes a wrong note as to the situation. The *raison d'être* of a General Council, according to him, was to bring on to the stage a fuller authority than that of Alexandria and Rome. So he renders ἰδίᾳ παρὰ τινῶν 'by any individuals.' But in reality the Emperor's words were meant to 'arrest' any private action of the parties to the quarrel in the East, viz. Cyril and Nestorius, Rome not having yet come on to the scene. It was to stop each of them, but especially Cyril, from pushing what each ascribed to the other, viz. their doctrinal innovations. Even if Theodosius had known of the Papal sentence, he could not have referred to that; for its subsequent promulgation in Constantinople would, in that case, have been a high misdemeanour, whereas it was accepted as regular, and actually spoken of as such by the Synod in its letter to the Emperor himself. Dr. Bright has made a similar mistake in the translation of καινοτομεῖν in a passage in the account of the Latrocinium (cf. *infra*, p. 231).

CHAPTER III

THE PRESIDENCY AND FUNCTIONS OF THE COUNCIL

The Synod began its sessions on the sixteenth day after Pentecost. The orthodox bishops agreed to range themselves under Cyril. Can we doubt why? They themselves in their second letter to the Emperor define their situation thus. They tell His Majesty that the Roman Synod had condemned the teaching of Nestorius and had said that all such should be excluded from the Church, and that 'even before this holy Synod was convened, Celestine commissioned Cyril to occupy his place'—a fact which they seem to emphasise, as suggesting the natural function of Cyril in the Council itself. The Emperor was against Cyril personally; he had complained of his interference; he had not intended him to be President; he ended with imprisoning him. But the Synod suggested the reason why this action was formally valid, viz. that he had been commissioned to represent Celestine '*even before* the Synod'—and therefore, (so they seem to suggest), since the commission had not been revoked, he naturally represented him *at* the Synod. Celestine had also, they add, repeated his decision in a fresh letter; and we know that the view taken by the Synod, in its third session, of its own action was that it had passed a sentence not originally its own, but which it had accepted and made its own. 'You shall execute this sentence,' was the Pope's injunction to Cyril; 'We executed the sentence,' was the plea of the Synod to the Papal legates, when the latter said that they had come to see that the sentence of Celestine was fully carried out.[1]

St. Cyril, then, assumed the Presidency, as having been already commissioned by Celestine to manage 'the affairs of Nestorius,' which were so far from being concluded that they were now to be conducted with the solemnities of a Conciliar decision. The tradition of the Church is quite clear to the effect that Celestine was the real President. Twenty years later the Council of Ephesus was spoken of in the Œcumenical Council of Chalcedon (including some who, as Juvenal of Jerusalem, were present at Ephesus) as having been conducted under the pilotship, or presidency, of Celestine and Cyril—as a Council 'of which the most blessed Celestine, the president of the Apostolic chair, and the most blessed Cyril of great Alexandria, were the leaders,' or (as the Latin translation is) 'presidents.'[2] And in its definition the same Council speaks of the Council of Ephesus again as having been presided over by 'Celestine and Cyril.'[3] And the Emperors, in their letter after the Council of Chalcedon, confirming the sentence against Eutyches and the monks who sympathised with him, speak of the Ephesine Synod as the occasion 'when the error of Nestorius was excluded, under the presidency of Celestine, of the city of Rome, and Cyril, of the city of Alexandria.'[4] The Empress Pulcheria uses the same expression. And the letters from various bishops to the

---

[1] ταύτην ἐκβιβάσεις τὴν ἀπόφασιν, Mansi, iv. 1020; τὸν τύπον ἐξεβιβάσαμεν iv. 1289.

[2] καθηγηταί—Lat. 'præsides' (Mansi, vii. 29). [3] Ibid. 109. [4] Ibid. 501.

Emperor Leo, written after the Council of Chalcedon in reference to the troubles at Alexandria under Bishop Timothy, show by the way in which they attribute the presidency of the Council to Celestine as well as to Cyril that the tradition of the Church was clear on this point.[1] For instance, certain European bishops depose that the Council of Ephesus was gathered together 'under Celestine, of blessed memory, the keeper of the keys of the Kingdom of Heaven, and under Cyril, Pontiff of Alexandria, of holy memory.' And the bishops of Upper Armenia call the Council that 'of which the presidents were Celestine and Cyril, . . . who chiefly shone forth against the wicked blasphemy of Nestorius.' And the tradition was equally strong among the Greeks: witness, besides the instances already quoted, their *Menologium* for June 9, where Cyril is described as 'a most learned man, champion of the Catholic faith, whom the supreme Pontiff Celestine judged a fit person to whom he entrusted his own place in the Council of Ephesus.'

That Celestine considered Cyril, and that Cyril considered himself, to be acting still in virtue of the original commission entrusted to him by Celestine may be gathered from the questions which he asked Celestine before the Council, such as whether Nestorius should be received at the Synod as a bishop, together with Celestine's reply, in which he says 'Yes,' and commits the whole matter to *Cyril and the Synod*. ' It belongs to your Holiness, with the venerable counsel of the brethren, to put down the disturbances that have arisen in the Church, and that we should learn that the matter has been finished by [effecting] the desired correction.'[2] ' It belongs to your Holiness, with the venerable counsel

---

[1] Mansi, vii. 539-623. [2] *Ibid.* iv. 1292.

of the brethren,' is a sufficiently plain indication that Cyril was held by the Pope to be acting under the original commission entrusted to him, only that he would now act with the help of the Council. This letter is dated May 7, and was written the day before the letter to the Synod which was committed to the care of the legates. The messenger who brought Cyril's letter would naturally carry back the answer with all possible despatch, and there was ample time to reach Ephesus before the Council met.

Indeed, it is hardly conceivable that Cyril should have ' occupied ' and ' managed ' the place of Celestine in the Council, as the Acts repeatedly state he did, unless he had some intimation from Rome that he was meant to do so, or unless in the judgment of the Synod he could fairly rest on the original Papal commission. Dr. Bright's suggestion that ' Cyril was not likely to be punctilious in such a matter, and might well assume that Celestine would not disallow him on that head ' [1] ignores the situation. If Cyril was not likely to be punctilious, others were ; we know enough of Juvenal of Jerusalem to feel the weakness of such a suggestion ; and the Imperial displeasure, certain to be manifested, was not likely to be treated as of no account. There must have been some safer ground on which to rest than Cyril's mere assumption.

The letter of May 7, if it reached Cyril in time, satisfactorily explains everything. It shows for certain that Celestine considered Cyril to be already in charge of the whole matter, which would now be concluded in conjunction with the Council. And it is impossible to show that this letter had not reached Cyril before the

[1] *Roman See*, p. 155.

Synod began. It cannot be assumed without some proof, that 'no desire of Celestine's was made known to them until the arrival of the legates.'¹ Cyril's messenger setting off at once would travel much quicker than Papal legates, whose movements were proverbially solemn and measured, and he might well have escaped the storm that overtook the latter and detained them so long.

So that if we take the narrative so far simply as it stands, it results that (1) the Pope had given a decision, (2) the Synod was about to affirm that sentence as a matter of course; and (3) that Cyril acted not merely as Bishop of Alexandria but also as Papal legate. The rule, according to which the Pope now acted, is thus described in a letter by two Alexandrian clerics cited by certain Episcopal legates sent from Pope Anastasius towards the end of this century to the Emperor Anastasius. They say that 'whenever in doubtful matters any Councils of bishops are held, his Holiness who presides over the Church of Rome used to select the most reverend Archbishop of Alexandria to undertake the charge of his own place.'

Cyril, then, acted for Celestine, as having been originally commissioned by him in the previous August to manage the affair of Nestorius, and as having now the office devolved upon him of managing it with the help of a Council: this being clear to the Synod either as a matter of course, or as being acquainted with Celestine's letter saying 'It belongs to your Holiness, with the venerable counsel of the brethren.'

What was the work actually before the bishops? The question has been asked, 'Did they regard themselves as simply Celestine's agents for the carrying out

¹ *Roman See*, p. 158.

of his previous sentence against Nestorius ? This must have been their view if, however erroneously, they had regarded the commission of August as " devolving " upon them.' [1]

To answer this question, we must ask what the writer means by 'simply . . . agents.' But as it is difficult to be sure of the precise meaning which we are intended to attach to these words, and as the matter is one of supreme importance, it will be best to say what the office of bishops in an Œcumenical Council involves on the Catholic theory as expounded by the Vatican Council, and lately again by Leo XIII. in his encyclical *De Unitate*.

According to Catholic teaching, the bishops in Council have, after a definitive sentence by the Roman Pontiff, an office of examination, and a capacity to pass judgment. Their examination, however, is not of that kind which springs from any doubt as to the justice or truth of the Pontifical judgment. It presupposes the binding nature of that. But since every examination is grounded on some doubt, or supposes something that needs clearing up, what is the doubt from which such examination on the part of the bishops proceeds ? The answer is that while the sentence is held to be true, the motives that guide it may be profitably investigated, not to know whether they are just, but simply what they are.[2] As an instance of the first kind of examination which proceeds from doubt as to the truth of an assertion, we might take the case of one who is in doubt as to the immortality of the soul. He begins to search for motives of credibility to satisfy himself as to whether it is a

---

[1] *Roman See*, p. 155.
[2] *Cf.* Palmieri, S.J., *De Romano Pontifice*, 1891, p. 684 *seq.*

truth. But a man may begin with a firm belief that the soul is immortal, and yet examine keenly into the motives which would reasonably lead to such a belief, especially if he had to teach. It would be a case either of *fides quærens intellectum*, of faith seeking to discover its confirmation in the department of the natural reason, or of searching for material for teaching.

Now in the case of bishops in a Synod, there is a very obvious motive for this latter kind of investigation. As bishops they have to teach, and ought to be able to produce the proofs from Scripture and tradition and from the analogy of the faith, in the case of a dogma which they would pronounce to be true, on sufficient authority, even if ignorant of these elucidating considerations. An instance of this kind of investigation is to be seen in the treatment of the dogma of Transubstantiation at Trent. It had always been part of the deposit. When Berenger first started an opposing theory, our own Lanfranc showed him that he was striking against the belief of all ages. It was, he proved, of divine faith. The particular term was made part of the Catholic faith at the Fourth Lateran Council.[1] And yet, three centuries afterwards, the Council of Trent entered upon an investigation of its harmony with Scripture and tradition. Every one of the Tridentine fathers held the judgment of 1215 to be irreversible: that is to say, every one of them believed Transubstantiation to be a matter of faith before it was subjected to this fresh investigation. But in view of surrounding and increasing Protestantism, it was considered necessary

---

[1] Not all that is of divine faith is included in 'the Catholic faith': that is to say, not all that is believed on sufficiently cogent reasons is made an article of external communion with the Church.

to examine it in relation to other truths. As St. Leo says of the examination of his own dogmatic exposition of the faith at the Council of Chalcedon, 'the truth shines brighter, and is held with firmer hold, when what faith had first taught examination has afterwards confirmed.' (*Ep. ad Theodor.*)

The bishops, then, are assembled in Council, not that they may learn the faith, but that they may act as judges and propose their judgment with authority. They are authoritative teachers, not of themselves infallible, nor supreme in authority; but their judgment, nevertheless, has weight and authority, for they are set over their flocks by the Holy Ghost. And they come to a Council, not to see whether the judgment of the Roman Pontiff (if it has preceded theirs) is true, but, whilst using that as their form (τύπος), to make an honest use of their judgment, and add it to that of the Pontiff. The very idea of the Church is, that she contains a successive and permanent series of witnesses owing to the grace of their consecration, though infallible only when in conjunction with the See of Peter. Their judgment in unison with his becomes a conciliar judgment, which has its own special office in rendering conspicuous the unity of the Church, and impressing the faithful with the divine character of the teaching of the Supreme Pontiff. Their judgment in the Synod is not that merely of theologians. These have no authority over the faithful through any grace of consecration; bishops have. If any number of theologians were added on to the Supreme Pontiff, the authority would simply be that of one man. Not so with the bishops; they are not the mere tools of the Supreme Pontiff. They are sheep, but also shepherds; taught, but also teachers; and the authority of their judgment added to that of the Roman Pontiff is the authority of a conciliar judgment. This derives its infallibility from the See of Peter; but although the decision of the Holy See in a matter of faith delivered as obligatory on all would of itself possess the seal of infallibility, it would not have the striking character of a conciliar judgment. The Episcopate is a reality in the Kingdom of God; and its judgments, however dependent for their infallibility on that of the Supreme Pontiff, have, nevertheless, a vitality of their own. Consequently, on the one hand, a General Council is never simply necessary, but it is, on the other hand, in certain cases eminently useful. After the Pontifical sentence, the Catholic Episcopate will, as a matter of moral necessity, conform to it; but while thus not morally free, it is still a gain that the consent of so many should become evident and conspicuous in fact, so that sound doctrine may be the more easily defended, and the subtlety of heretics kept in subjection.[1]

It will be seen from this short exposition of the relation between Pope and Council in Catholic theology, that the devolution of the Papal sentence against Nestorius on the Council would not suppose the bishops of the Council to be simply the agents and instruments and ministers of Celestine in such a way as that they had nothing to do but register his decision.[2] They had to bring their office as judges into play. That decision was the type ($\tau\acute{u}\pi o s$) which they were morally bound to follow. The Pope's injunction to Cyril was, 'assuming the authority of our See and acting with delegated power

---

[1] *Cf.* Palmieri, *loc. cit.*, and Jungmann's *Dissertatio de Concilio Ephesino*.

[2] This is the caricature of Catholic doctrine, presented by Dr. Bright, *Roman See*, p. 155.

[this is the exact meaning of the Greek word] in our stead and place, you will execute a sentence of this sort, &c.' And the bishops, as we shall presently see, distinctly say that they have conformed to this type, or decision. The essence of the decision was that Nestorius should be condemned, unless he repented; a detail of that sentence was, that it should take effect ten days after the notice had been served; but the circumstance of a Council having been summoned to meet, rendered a close adherence to this detail unadvisable. The Council did, as we have said, expressly state that it had adhered to Celestine's decision; but being bishops, with a capacity and duty of judgment, they unfolded the motives which might be supposed to have guided the Pope and showed the grounds on which under the altered circumstances of the case that sentence necessarily stood firm. Their obedience would thus be seen to be materially just, as well as formally good.

Bearing in mind, then, what it is that we have to show when we say that the doctrine of Papal Supremacy is (as the Vatican Council teaches) that of the Primitive Church, let us now see how the bishops acted at the Council of Ephesus.

The first session was held on June 22. The bishops met under difficult circumstances and with this perplexity as compared with subsequent Councils—they had no precedents for an Œcumenical Council. The Acts of the Nicene Fathers, if they had ever been committed to writing, which is improbable, had perished. The Council of Constantinople was not Œcumenical in its sessions, and had not yet taken its place among the General Councils. Neither had they the advantage of the presence of legates from Rome.

One thing, however, was quite plain in the eyes of the Synod. Before Juvenal of Jerusalem had proposed that the Emperor's letter should be read, Peter, the Alexandrian notary, had opened the proceedings by stating the subject before the Synod. Nestorius, he said, had created a disturbance in the Church by certain doctrinal expositions; Cyril had endeavoured to persuade him to come to a better mind; at length the matter had been brought before Celestine, Bishop of Rome, by whom '*what was suitable,* or meet, had been written, comprising a clear decision, or sentence.'[1] This view of Celestine's letter was about to be treated as beyond dispute. All that they did would assume this. For in their third citation of Nestorius, the bishops as a body sent word to him that if he should not come to the Synod and reply to the things objected to him, 'the most holy Synod will be compelled (ἀνάγκην ἕξει) to decide concerning him the things decreed in the canons of the holy Fathers.'[2] It is obvious that, though they do not say so in words, their meaning was that he would be condemned if he did not defend himself by disavowing what he had written, and what he had recently said in Ephesus itself. In fact (to reverse the assertion of Dr Bright) they 'accepted Cyril's and Celestine's estimate of the language used by Nestorius.'[3] When Juvenal of Jerusalem pro-

---

[1] τὰ εἰκότα . . . τύπον φανερὸν περιέχοντα, Mansi, iv. 1129.

[2] Mansi, iv. 1136.

[3] *Roman See*, p. 157. Dr. Bright adds that they did not 'treat it as already proved heretical.' Of course not, if by 'proved' is meant 'proved by a logical process on their own part in Council.' But they did treat it as heretical. Dr. Bright has an extraordinary note on the letter of the Synod referred to above. He says (*Roman See*, p. 155) that 'this' (it is 'these things' in the Greek), 'in the sentence first naming Celestine, expressly refers to the function of all bishops in the

posed, in the first session, that the Nicene Creed should be recited, so that, after the matters under consideration concerning the faith had been compared with that Creed, those that agreed should be confirmed and those that disagreed should be cast out, he prefaced his proposal with saying that Nestorius had 'refused to face the Synod out of a bad conscience': *i.e.* because he knew that he would be condemned. Obviously the bishops had settled in their own mind (and indeed they showed no hesitation about saying plainly) who was in the right and who was in the wrong, and there was no idea of questioning the Pope's *dictum* that what he had definitely settled was the teaching, not only of Rome and Alexandria, but of the whole Church (cf. *supra*, p. 16). To use the words of Dr. Pusey quoted above, 'the mind of the Church had been expressed in the previous year.'

exclusion of false doctrine.' There is not a word about ' the function of all bishops.' The Synod merely adduces the fact that the Western bishops, with Celestine present, had declared that all such (as Nestorius) should be excluded from the roll of bishops. In the same note, Dr. Bright says that Celestine, in his letter of May 7, ' neither says nor implies ' ' that he meant Cyril to be President.' It will be seen directly that nothing can well be clearer than that he did. In the text, however, to which this note is appended, Dr. Bright indulges in an *ignoratio elenchi,* when he says that Celestine had not 'instructed his actual legates to treat Cyril as their chief, but only to take counsel with him.' The question is not as to whether Cyril was to be their chief but his relation to the *Council.* The legates were sent to assist him. The instruction to ' take counsel ' occurs only in the latter part of the letter, and refers only to the possibility of the Council having been concluded and things having gone wrong. In the previous part of the letter, the legates are told to do whatever they shall see to be Cyril's judgment (*Quicquid in ejus videritis arbitrio facietis*), not ' *only* to take counsel,' as Dr. Bright puts it. Cyril ' managed the place of Celestine,' we are told, even when the legates were present—which could only have been possible by reason of himself being a Papal legate. Cf. Mansi, iv. 1301 ; 556.

CHAPTER IV

THE DEGRADATION OF NESTORIUS

No sooner had the Synod opened than a question arose as to the mode of procedure. Peter, the protonotary of Alexandria, assumed that they would commence proceedings by reading what had passed between Cyril and Nestorius, and Pope Celestine. This would have been the strict canonical order. But Juvenal of Jerusalem, who afterwards in the Eutychian disputes gave so much trouble, proposed that the Emperor's letter of summons should be read, and that it should be the 'torch' to guide their steps. He has probably been reported badly: for it seems from what follows as though he alluded to another letter from the Emperor, which Count Candidian, the Imperial Commissioner, had brought with him, giving commands as to the order of their proceedings. This was an irregular, though not an unknown, course to pursue. The Church has sometimes tolerated, but only tolerated, this measure of deference to the Emperor.

Candidian, however, endeavoured to keep the letter to himself until John of Antioch should appear, hoping probably by this means to defer the sessions of the Council indefinitely.[1] But Cyril obliged him to read it, and Candidian soon left the Council, and afterwards

[1] Mansi, iv. 1261.

complained that there was not going to be any real discussion of the matter at issue.[1] He saw, of course, that the bishops had already made up their minds.

The question next arose whether Nestorius should be summoned. Cyril seems to have thought that he had sufficiently shown his contumacy by his doings at Ephesus before the Council met, and by his non-appearance in the Church now. But he was persuaded to act in the most thoroughly canonical way, and to summon him in the usual solemn form.[2] Three bishops, with a lector and notary, waited on him, but in vain. Thrice he was summoned, but at length the messengers returned to tell that they had been treated with contumely by the soldiery that guarded Nestorius's dwelling. The Synod was stupefied. Nothing remained but to proceed at once to examine the facts of the case concerning Nestorius's heretical teaching. They proceeded accordingly to set the case before them. They were not embarking on a theological investigation of the doctrine;[3] that would have occupied them much more than the remainder of the day. What they did consisted of the most summary process consistent with the solemnity of the occasion. They were acting as judges, albeit in obedience to a higher court, and their procedure, however summary, was bound to be marked by judicial order.

Accordingly, at Juvenal's instance, the Nicene Creed was read. For it was against that Creed that Nestorius was accused of having offended. Next came the writings

[1] Mansi, iv. 1263.

[2] Garnier (*Diss. ii. de Synodis*: Pref. to Marius Mercator) thinks that the first formal notification of the day of meeting, having been made to him on a Sunday, would have been invalid.

[3] 'There was no discussion,' Harnack, *Hist. of Dogma* (Tr.), iv. 187.

of Nestorius and Cyril in the earlier part of their quarrel, for this was necessary in order to understand clearly the subject-matter of the Papal judgment. Then Cyril's second letter was read, and he put it to the Council whether this was not in conformity with the Nicene faith. They admitted it as a part of the rule of faith. Their separate short speeches are given in the Acts, and must have occupied considerable time.[1]

Then Nestorius's second letter was read, and on being appealed to by Cyril, the bishops, many of them, one by one, gave their opinion, and at length they all together shouted their condemnation of the letter as impious, heretical, worthy of all anathema. Acacius, Bishop of Mitylene, drew out the points in which it was heretical, and the bishops again shouted their anathemas.[2]

After a silence, Juvenal of Jerusalem proposed that now the letter of Celestine 'concerning the faith'[3] should be read. All that had been read before prepared the way for this: without the letters of Cyril and Nestorius the Papal sentence could not be well understood.

Lastly, Cyril's letter, written in execution of the Pope's commission, which had not been submitted to the Pope, was read as 'consonant with' Celestine's letter, and approved.

It was then clearly established that both Celestine's

---

[1] They occupy thirty columns in Mansi (*cf.* iv. 1138-1168), *i.e.* fifteen columns of Greek.

[2] Dr. Bright calls this a 'laborious examination' (*Roman See*, p. 169); most people would consider it a very summary process, so far as investigation and real examination were concerned. The Roman Synod gave several sessions to the matter.

[3] Mansi, iv. 1177.

letter and also this last, containing the same doctrine and the Papal sentence, had been served on Nestorius, and that he had continued impenitent, not only beyond the ten days originally assigned by Celestine, but even up to the day of the Council. Unless this was established, their action would not have been regular nor in accordance with the mind of Celestine, as expressed in his letter to Cyril.[1]

Next, a number of passages from the Fathers, which had been previously selected—probably by Cyril—were read out, to show that they were acting in unison with the whole past of the Church; and then some passages from the writings of Nestorius.

Before, however, proceeding to the sentence, a letter of Capreolus, Bishop of Carthage, brought by Besulas, a deacon, was also read, in which the Bishop trusted that all novelties would be kept out of the Church, and begged that 'the authority of the Apostolic See and the unanimous decision of the hierarchy' should be considered as final in regard to the Pelagians. More, it is thought, must have taken place on this subject, for St. Gregory the Great, when living in Constantinople, had personally inspected the matter, and tells Narses that the Acts of the Council of Ephesus had been mutilated by some Easterns in respect of Pelagian affairs ($Epp.$ iv. 5).

Then followed the sentence: the terms of which are plain and simple in regard to the relation of the Council to the Pope. They correspond exactly with what we might have expected from the outset. The Synod had been told (what, of course, it knew already) that Celestine had written 'what was suitable, containing a plain sentence ($\tau \acute{u} \pi o \nu$).'[2] The letter containing that sentence

[1] Mansi, iv. 1292.   [2] *Ibid.* 1129.

had been read out to the Synod, after the correspondence between Cyril and Nestorius, which explained the contents of the Papal *ultimatum*. That sentence was not to take effect before an interval of ten days from its reception by Nestorius had elapsed. The ten days, as has been already explained, were naturally (and in accordance with Celestine's mind) prolonged into a considerable interval in consequence of the Council becoming the occasion on which the Papal decision would be executed. It had been established by competent witnesses that Nestorius had not repented of his heresy. The Synod had sent to him to say that if he did not appear ' it would be *compelled* to pass sentence upon him in accordance with the canons of the holy Fathers.' [1]

The Synod accordingly pronounced sentence against him, degrading him from the Episcopal office. And this they did (so the bishops are careful to say), ' being compelled both by the canons and by the letter of our most Holy Father and fellow-bishop Celestine, the bishop of the Church of the Romans.' We are told that during the solemn pronunciation of the sentence many of the bishops' eyes filled with tears, as might well be supposed in the case of a vast gathering of emotional Easterns engaged in placing one of their own number out of the roll of the Episcopate [2]—many of them, as St. Vincent of Lerins remarks, men of great holiness and, we may assume, not without their feelings of tender piety.

[1] Mansi, iv. 1136: ἀνάγκην ἕξει τὰ δοκοῦντα τοῖς τῶν ἁγίων πατέρων κάνοσιν ἐπὶ σοὶ ὁρίσαι.

[2] Dr. Bright pleads that we cannot suppose that they literally shed many tears, as they say they did, and that since this part of the statement is not literally true, we need not take the rest of it as literally true—*e.g.* when they say they were ' compelled ' ! He forgets that the Synod repeated the latter expression.

'Compelled both by the canons and by the letter of our most Holy Father and fellow-minister Celestine'! Such was their position.

First, the canons. The reference is to their having acted in the absence of Nestorius. In several places they speak of their having satisfied the requirements of the canons through their threefold summons of the heretic. They had given him the opportunity of answering the charge brought against him, four bishops having repaired to his house to acquaint him with the position of things; and John of Antioch had expressly commissioned two bishops to tell the Synod not to wait for *him*. 'Do your work,' were his words, 'if I delay.' There had therefore been no violation of canon law. By the canons they were free to act, and indeed compelled, although the guilty party was not present.

But this was not all. The source from which their entire action and their final judgment sprang was the letter of the Pope.[1] They were compelled to act by reason of the letter of him who was at once their 'Holy Father' and their 'fellow-minister:' in other words, their equal in sacerdotal dignity,[2] but their superior in authority. He had been asked by St. Cyril τυπῶσαι τὸ δοκοῦν, to formulate the dogmatic decree. He had given the τύπος in the letters written to Cyril, Nestorius, the clergy of Constantinople, and John of Antioch, but especially in the letter to Nestorius, which was read in

---

[1] The preposition by which they express their obedience to the canons is ἀπό; that by which they express their obedience to the letter of the Holy Father is ἐκ. That the word 'compelled' applies to the letter, as well as to the canons, is clear from the conjunctions used, viz. τε . . . καί.

[2] συλλειτουργοῦ.

Synod. The Council *could* do nothing else than yield obedience to this letter. This the bishops declare they have done. Their action in condemning the Archbishop of Constantinople *in his absence* from the Synod was covered by the canons; their action in condemning him at all was, they averred, a simple necessity after the letter of the Pope. Although exercising a real judgment on the subject, as the record shows they did, they were yet under a moral impossibility of differing from the Papal sentence; they were, they say, 'compelled [$ἀπό$] by the canons and by [$ἐκ$] the letter of the Holy Father'; and in delivering this sentence, which they thus declare to be in its origin and power that of the Pope, they profess to be acting with the authority of our Lord Jesus Christ. It is, they say, His sentence. What Celestine said of the sentence as it passed from his lips, that it was 'the judgment of Christ, who is God,' the Ephesine Council also said of its execution and promulgation by themselves. Pope and Council together claim the prerogative of infallibility: the Pope, in defining the relationship of Nestorius's teaching to the Christian faith; the Council, in judging after the Pope, 'compelled' by his Holiness's decision.

Bossuet says that the Council was not necessary, but it was expedient, on account of the trouble that Nestorius was able to create through his influence at Court. The Council on this account was careful to note that its decision was due to the nature of the Papal decision: that it was, though the act of free men, not, in every sense, a free action; it was a matter of duty to join themselves as members to their head,[1] to use the expression of the Papal legate in the third session; it was their own

[1] Mansi, iv. 1200.

assertion of their membership in the teaching body. The obligation which was thus laid upon them by the canons could only refer to Nestorius's disobedience to the Synod, which compelled it to enter upon the question *without his own defence*. No canon had dealt with his dogmatic error ; but the canons provided for the judicial treatment of a heretic. But the letter of Celestine, which laid them under this obligation to obedience, had respect not only to the deposition of Nestorius, but to his heresy,[1] for it provided that his deposition should follow on his refusal to retract his error in regard to the matter of faith within ten days. And although the Pontiff (as we know from his letter to Cyril) had left the execution of his sentence, including its delay (if deemed advisable), to the Synod, he had (as we know from the same letter) not left it open to them to acquit Nestorius in the event of his obstinate adherence to his error.[2] This obstinacy had now been established by competent witnesses, and the Council, having complied with the provisions of the canons in summoning him three times, was 'compelled,' in obedience to the Papal sentence, to depose and excommunicate the archbishop. But how, as Ballerini asks, could the Ephesine Fathers be ' compelled ' by the letter of Celestine, unless they were ' com-

---

[1] *Cf.* Ballerini, *De Vi et Ratione Primatus Rom. Pontif.* c. xiii. § 11.
[2] Mansi, iv. 1292. If the Fathers had not yet seen this letter, it would only result that they had successfully anticipated Celestine's wish and placed on his injunction to execute his sentence the only rational interpretation—viz. that by consenting to send legates to the Council as they knew he had, he had left his sentence to be executed by the bishops. It is, however, most probable that they had seen Celestine's letter. Father Bottalla, S. J., considers this certain (*Infallibility*, p. 204 [Eng. ed.]).

pelled' to preserve a unity of faith with the Roman Pontiff?

Now, how do those writers who maintain the independence of national Churches deal with this momentous utterance of the Council?

It is not put in evidence at all by Canon Bright in his article in Smith's *Dictionary of Christian Biography* on St. Cyril, nor in that by Mr. Ffoulkes on the Council of Ephesus; neither does it appear in Canon Bright's 'History of the Church,' where the sentence on Nestorius is thus described: ' And the prelates proceeded to depose and excommunicate Nestorius in the name of our Lord Jesus Christ, whom he has "blasphemed"' (p. 333).

There is no allusion to the letter of Celestine here.

It does not appear in Canon Robertson's ' History of the Church '—a work which has figured for so many years on the list of books recommended to candidates for ordination in the Established Church. Dean Milman[1] quotes a part of the sentence, but omits the crucial words ' by the letter of our Most Holy Father and fellow-minister Celestine.' He even gives the Greek in a foot-note, with the same omission, marking that there is an omission. Dr. Wordsworth seems to go a step beyond these writers. He omits the crucial word ' compelled.' His version of the Synod's sentence is:[2] ' They then declared that in accordance with the canons of the Church, and with the letter of their Most Holy Father and brother-minister, Celestine, bishop of the Roman Church,' etc.

' In accordance with ' is certainly not an accurate

---

[1] *Hist. of Lat. Christianity*, i. 211 (4th and revised edition).
[2] *Church History*, iv. 216.

translation of 'necessarily impelled by,' nor is it even a fair paraphrase of the same. A very strong and exhaustive term is here used in the Greek.[1] And not content with a word which contains the idea of tremendous force, they add to it the adverb 'necessarily.'[2] And it must be remembered that the Greek is the original here; that it was drawn up by Easterns, and that it was the Greek which the Eastern Fathers actually signed. Bossuet thus sums up the situation: 'Autre chose est de prononcer une sentence conforme à la lettre du Pape, autre chose d'être contraint par la lettre même aussi que par les Canons à la prononcer. L'expression du Concile reconnaît dans la lettre du Pape la force d'une sentence juridique, qu'on ne pouvait pas ne point confirmer, parce qu'elle était juste dans son fond, et valable dans sa forme comme étant émanée d'une puissance légitime.'[3]

The sentence thus expressed and signed, the Fathers issued forth from their Œcumenical Synod. The citizens of Ephesus were in an ecstasy of joy. They had waited for the sentence in eager expectation, not as doubting the truth, but as looking forward to its confirmation. And upon the Council's leaving St. Mary's at the close of the day, they burst into the wildest applause, and attended the orthodox bishops home with every token of honour, Cyril coming in, as well he might, for the lion's share of their attention. Torchlight processions and incense accompanied the members of the Synod to

---

[1] κατεπειχθέντες, which is a strong form of ἐπειχθέντες.

[2] ἀναγκαίως. *Cf.* St. Irenæus on the necessity of agreeing with Rome, and compare 1 Cor. ix. 16.

[3] *Remarques sur l'histoire des Conciles . . . de M. Dupin*, ed. Versailles, 1817, t. 30, p. 524.

their residences, and the very ladies of Ephesus turned out to manifest their joy at the vindication of the glory of their sex, the 'great Mother of God, Mary most holy.'

Candidian, the Imperial Commissioner, on the contrary, soon had the notices from the city walls torn down. The deposition of Nestorius was then proclaimed by public criers in the streets. Candidian put a stop to this also in the Emperor's name. The Synod had defeated his hopes, and, as the event proved, he was bent on causing trouble. Dr. Littledale thinks that he makes a point against the 'Petrine claims' of Rome when he adduces the fact that 'no practical impression was made on Nestorius or the bishops of his party'[1] by the Papal sentence; and Dr. Salmon holds[2] that the mere fact that the decision of a Council was not received at once on all sides is fatal to the infallibility of Œcumenical Councils—an argument which would summarily dispose of our Lord's Divinity. One of the most recent theories about our Lord's miracles is that since everybody did not at once yield assent to His claims, no miracles could have been worked; and Dr. Salmon's is only the same argument applied to the Church. Certainly Nestorianism did not cease to be; indeed, it seemed for a moment as though after the Council's judgment it might gain the upper hand. But what of that? Men who could repudiate the truth concerning the Incarnation could and did rebel against the Holy See and

[1] *Petrine Claims*, p. 98. This is not quite true: seven bishops came round to the orthodox side, and Cyril preached a magnificent sermon on the occasion, speaking of our Lady as her to whom we owe our baptism and everything Christian, as, in fact, to use a modern term, the Gate of Heaven.

[2] *Infallibility of the Church*, p. 426, c.

against any number of Councils. Nestorius, then, and his followers, instead of submitting to Pope or Councils, had their weapons ready; and John of Antioch was to be led into serious sin before the ultimate triumph of the great Patriarch of Alexandria.

On the Council's Use of κατεπειχθέντες.

It has been objected by Dr. Bright (*Roman See*, p. 159): (1) that the synodical sentence did not presume 'the compulsory nature' of Celestine's decision, but only said that they were 'irresistibly urged' or 'impelled'; (2) that in the missives to Nestorius himself, and to his clergy, the Council mentions the canons and not Celestine; and (3) that the canons and Celestine's letter cannot be treated as co-ordinate, because the Council had not rendered *literal* obedience to that letter.

As to (1): the word used by the bishops for the impulse received from Rome, κατεπειχθέντες, is a strong form of ἐπειχθέντες, 'impelled,' since such is the force of the prefix (see Liddell and Scott on κατά in composition). So that Sophocles translates ἔπειξις 'haste, hurry,' and κατέπειξις 'violent exertion' (Lexicon, *s.v.*); and Liddell and Scott (to whom Dr. Bright refers as his authority) translate τὰ ἐπείγοντα 'necessary matters,' but τὰ κατεπείγοντα '*urgent* necessity.' The word had already been used by the Emperor in his summons to the bishops to attend the Council, which was compulsory: σύνοδον τούτῳ ἡμῶν τῷ θεσπίσματι κατεπείγεσθαι (Mansi, iv. 1113). The Latin version of the sentence, as printed by Mansi, has *coacti*. And the old edition of the Acts (first printed by Baluze), which was used by Gregory the Great (who, when at Constantinople, specially investigated the Acts of the Council of Ephesus) has *necessario coacti* (Mansi, v. 558). Mansi himself in his *Animadversiones in Natalis Alex. H. E.* ix. 475, translates it *coacti*, and remarks on the superiority thus assigned to the Pope. Pope Nicolas I. gives it as *necessario coacti* (*Ep.* 9, *ad Michaelem*). Valesius translates the words when quoted by Evagrius, 'necessitate compulsi' (*H. E.* I. iv.). In the first edition of this book, I translated 'necessarily compelled'; in this I have translated 'compelled,' as sufficient for clearness, and as being beyond dispute. No English word suits the Greek verb so well as 'compelled'; but with ἀναγκαίως added to it, it can mean nothing else. In their letter to the Emperor, the Synod say they 'praised' the letter of Celestine. This does not prevent us from supposing that they did something more than exalt it in word. The chief praise of it that appears in the Acts consisted of their obedience to it (*cf.* Mansi, *Nat. Alex. H. E.* ix. 474). They honoured it as men honour a cheque: ἐκβιβάζειν—the word used in the Synod—contains the idea of a debt paid (Sophocles, Lexicon, *s.v.*).

As to (2): Nestorius already had the Papal sentence; there was no need to state what was obvious, viz. that they were following that. The important thing to state was that they had acted canonically in condemning him *in his absence*. This is what they did state.

As to (3): the canons and Celestine's letter were either co-ordinate or one was inferior to the other. If the latter, either (*a*) the canons were superior—but then the order of the words would be misleading: it would be an anti-climax to speak of the canons and the letter, instead of the letter and the canons—or (*b*) the letter was a superior authority; but no one places the Papal letter here *above* the canons. It remains, then, that they are co-ordinated. Whether the Council had rendered 'literal' or substantial obedience does not affect the question; in their own eyes, they rendered obedience. They said, in the second Session, through Firmus, that they had 'executed the sentence and decree' of Celestine.

CHAPTER V

JOHN OF ANTIOCH

An extraordinary scene now took place in Ephesus. A few days after the deposition of Nestorius by the orthodox Synod, John of Antioch entered the city. He had sent a letter to Cyril when within six days of Ephesus, expressing a hope that he would be there in time.[1] The Synod waited no less than sixteen days, with John of Antioch near and able certainly to reach Ephesus,[2] when two of John's suffragans arrived with a message, saying, 'If I delay, do your work.'[3] During this unreasonable halt, messengers going to and fro became firmly convinced that John was anxious not to be present at the deposition of Nestorius.[4] This, as the Synod told the Emperor, was the real cause of his abstention. Cyril, therefore, and the bishops knew very well that they might delay until they were well-nigh decimated if they waited on for him. Some of their numbers had already died.[5] All this, John of Antioch

---

[1] Mansi, iv. 1121. He must have neared Ephesus just about Pentecost: *cf.* Hefele on the First Session, § 134.

[2] *Ibid.* 1331.   [3] *Ibid.* 1229.

[4] *Ibid.* 1333. All the accounts need to be very carefully compared; the result will confirm Hefele's commentary on this whole incident.

[5] In his *Waymarks in Church History*, Dr. Bright delivers himself of a violent attack upon Cyril. But Cyril's words are seriously misquoted (p. 148); his speech at the opening of the first session is mis-

must have known well; but he was in no disposition to help Cyril to depose his friend Nestorius. 'Plato' was dearer than 'truth.'

Meanwhile he had become the centre of a number of malcontents, whose dubious record in the past necessarily made them a source of mischief to the orthodox party. Some were excommunicated; some had no dioceses; others had been deposed by their metropolitans; some were Pelagians, and some had been ejected from Italy.[1] With these added to his own suffragans, he now entered Ephesus and was met by a deputation from the Synod. He refused to hear what they had to say, and kept them waiting while, after entering his house, he held a Synod composed of the unpromising elements that had gathered round him, assisted by Count Candidian. This Imperial Commissioner, together with Count Irenæus, who had the care of the Imperial provisions for the comfort of the visitors, had set to work to vex the orthodox bishops in the city by every kind of petty persecution, interfering with their accommodation, and making it difficult for them to get the necessaries of life in a strange place. The members of the deputation from the Synod, including bishops, were eventually subjected to physical maltreatment, and presented themselves at a later session with the scars of their wounds still visible.

represented (p 157); and the bishops are merely said to have been 'seriously suffering from the heat.' But some had actually died through want of accommodation and the heat. The blot in Dr. Bright's account consists in his not paying attention to the reports given by the orthodox Synod to the Emperor and to Celestine. And his dates are wrong; *cf.* Hefele, § 134.

[1] Mansi, iv. 1333. The ordinary reading is 'Thessaly': I have adopted Garnier's suggestion.

It is difficult to understand how anyone who has weighed the evidence with care as set forth in the records of the Council of Ephesus, can suppose that John was in earnest about the maintenance of the faith, or that he really wished to be at the Synod. He could have been there easily. Had he wished to uphold the orthodox faith, he would have presented himself at a fresh session of the Council, and would never have connected himself with such characters as went to make up his own *entourage*. As it was, he held what he called a 'Sacred Synod' of his own, with these adventurers and heretics, and excommunicated Cyril and Memnon.

It is much to be noticed, however, that John and his Synod did not defend Nestorius's teaching about which Celestine had written to John in condemnation. Their ground of complaint was that, contrary to the canons, Nestorius had not been heard;[1] and that Cyril's 'chapters' (his twelve Anathematisms) had not been examined, owing to the disturbances fostered by Cyril and by Memnon in Ephesus itself; and that they had not waited for himself and others.[2]

It is to be noted also that he says nothing about the absence of the Westerns. The fact is that the Council of Ephesus was not strictly œcumenical in its first session; for, although Cyril acted as legate of Celestine, his action would naturally have to be confirmed by the Pope in person, or by legates sent for the purpose. It became truly and strictly œcumenical in the second and third sessions,[3] as indeed it seems to plead in its second letter to the Emperor, written immediately after the third session.[4] It there speaks of the agreement of the Papal

[1] Mansi, iv. 1264. [2] *Ibid*. 1267. [3] *Cf.* Chr. Lupus, *Schol. in Can. Ephes.* c. vi. (T. i. p. 427, A.D. 1673). [4] Mansi, iv. 1301.

legates with the synodical execution of the sentence against Nestorius, as carrying with it the agreement of Celestine and the whole West.

So that, although there is no knowing what John of Antioch may have been disposed to do, as a matter of fact his quarrel was not with the sentence of Celestine, but with the mode of its execution by the Synod under Cyril; neither was his contention that Nestorius was free from heresy, but rather that Cyril's twelve chapters or Anathematisms, which he had called upon Nestorius to accept before the Synod, contained matter allied to Arianism, Eunomianism, and Apollinarianism.[1] But he mainly emphasised the uncanonical character of the deposition, owing to the absence of Nestorius and himself. There is one keynote which runs through the utterances of this schismatical Synod: it is 'ecclesiastical lawlessness.' They professed to be the champions of ecclesiastical order. The word for 'order'[2] occurs in every kind of combination. It is necessary to bear this in mind to explain the important utterance of the orthodox Synod in their third session, when they speak of the Legates having spoken 'suitably' (p. 85).[3]

The schismatic Synod, having excommunicated Cyril and Memnon, had their sentence posted on the walls of the theatre, which produced a tumult among the inhabitants. They next induced Candidian to try and prevent these two bishops from offering the Holy Sacrifice on the following Sunday; but in vain—Cyril and

---

[1] Mansi, iv. 1277.

[2] ἀκολουθία; this word occurs again and again in the utterances of Candidian, of John of Antioch, and his Synod. Their boast was that they had acted ἀκολούθως, in canonical order. Cf. Mansi, iv. 1264, 1261, and *passim* in the account of this *Conciliabulum*.

[3] ἀκολούθως.

Memnon refused to submit to such interference, and they had the people of Ephesus with them. These strict adherents to their bishop also precluded all possibility of John and his companions installing another bishop in place of Memnon; and further they prevented the schismatics from using the Church of St. John for a service of thanksgiving which they proposed to hold for having been enabled to excommunicate 'the Egyptian,' as they called Cyril, and his tool, 'the Bishop of Asia Minor,' as they called Memnon.

This being the state of things in the city, we can easily imagine the joy of the people when it became known that the legates from Rome had at last reached Ephesus. Their advent formed the one possible counterpoise to the action of John and of the Imperial Commissioner.

But yet another trouble rendered the presence of the Papal legates a source of thankfulness. Between the first Session of the Council and their arrival from Rome the Synod had sent its letter to the Emperor, who, under evil influence, had quashed the whole proceedings of the orthodox Synod, on the ground that it had met without John of Antioch and had not properly discussed the matter of faith.[1] Candidian's report had, in fact, successfully counteracted the report of the Synod.[2] Cyril at once did his best to answer what he found to be Candidian's falsification of the whole matter. He told the Emperor plainly why John of Antioch had absented himself, and what kind of people the bishops were who

[1] Mansi, iv. 1378.
[2] *Cf.* Hefele, *Conc.-Gesch.* § 135, for proof that the report of the Council had reached the Emperor. Cyril replied to the Emperor's letter on July 1. The second session of the Council with the Papal legates took place on July 10.

had gathered round the 'Oriental' prelate. He claimed that he and those with him had in reality the presence of the Bishop of Rome and of Africa, in fact 'the assent of the whole West to their canonical deposition of Nestorius.'[1] This, of course, was through the fact that Celestine had given the decision which the Council had followed, as we shall presently hear the Council saying *totidem verbis*. The Africans were represented by the letter of Capreolus, Bishop of Carthage, giving in their adhesion beforehand to the destruction of all 'novelties,' as Nestorius's teaching was called.

Palladius, whom the Emperor had sent with an injunction that the bishops should meet together with John of Antioch and discuss the matter of faith, and not leave Ephesus until they had so done, had taken back Cyril's protest. But before anything further could be heard from the Court, the ship that bore the legates from Rome sailed into the port, and soon the gates of the city where St. Paul had preached and St. John had lived with the 'Mother of God' were flung open to receive the representatives of the Prince and head of the Apostles, bearing with them authority to proclaim the divine Maternity of the Virgin of Nazareth—in other words, the literal Godhead of the world's Saviour born of her in time.

With these two Bishops and the accompanying Priest another power, greater than that of earthly kings, had entered upon the scene.

[1] Mansi, iv. 1426.

CHAPTER VI

THE SEE OF PETER 'CONFIRMING THE BRETHREN.' NO. I

ὅρα . . . ποιήσῃς πάντα κατὰ τὸν τύπον τὸν δειχθέντα σοι ἐν τῷ ὄρει.
'See that thou make all things according to the pattern shown thee on the mount.' Heb. viii. 5.

So far, Cyril had been obliged to act under difficulties without the aid of Papal legates. Celestine, however, had in reality sent his legates, but they had been detained on the high seas through stormy weather. They arrived, as we have seen, in July, and on the 10th a solemn reception was held in the Bishop's palace, which counts as the second session of the Council.

To understand the meaning of the legates' action in the next two sessions, we must be careful to bear in mind the instructions they had received. They were to place themselves at once in Cyril's hands—*ad . . . Cyrillum consilium vestrum omne convertite et quidquid iu ejus videritis arbitrio facietis*. They were to take care that the authority of the Apostolic See was maintained. They were to be present at the session of the Council, and if by chance discussion arose, they were to judge concerning the bishops' opinions, or judgments (*sententiis*) but not to enter into the arena themselves —*vos de eorum sententiis judicare debeatis, non subire certamen*. If they should find the Council broken up, they must inquire how matters had been concluded. If

F

they had been accomplished in favour of the Catholic faith and the legates should find that Cyril had decided upon going to Constantinople, they must go there also and present the Papal letters (*epistolas*) to the Emperor (*Principi*). *If things should have gone badly* and matters should be in course of discussion, they must decide what to do, judging by the circumstances, *with the advice of Cyril—cum consilio supradicti nostri fratris agere debeatis*.[1]

The points in this instruction (or *Commonitorium*) which especially concern us here are, that the legates were to act as judges of the bishops' opinions—*vos de eorum sententiis judicare debeatis*—and that if the business of the Synod had been transacted, they were to require to be informed as to how that business had been concluded—*qualiter fuerint res finitæ*.

And if we turn for a moment to the letter of Celestine which they bore with them and read to the Synod, we find that he there describes the office committed to his legates, in these words : ' We have sent, out of our care, our holy brothers and fellow-priests, of one mind with us and tried men, Arcadius and Projectus, bishops, and Philip, presbyter, to be present at the transactions [of the Synod] and to execute what has been already decreed by us, to which we do not doubt you will give your

---

[1] Mansi, iv. 556. This letter has unfortunately been misinterpreted in *Roman See*, p. 154. Dr. Bright there says that Celestine did not instruct the legates to treat Cyril as their chief, 'but only to take counsel with him.' Cyril was to be the Chief of the Council (even in the presence of the legates together with them), which is the only point at issue, and the legates were not 'only to take counsel with him.' This was enjoined in case things went wrong. It is difficult to give one English word for 'sententiæ'; its meaning varies from 'decision' to 'opinion.'

assent, when that which is done is seen to have been decreed for the safety of the Church.'[1]

It is clear, therefore, what the legates were sent to do, viz. to watch the case, so to speak, on behalf of Celestine, and to see that his decree concerning Nestorius was properly executed by the Council, Cyril remaining at the head of the Council, side by side, as it were, with themselves.[2]

At the session, therefore, in the Bishop's palace, Cyril still presided, 'holding the place of the Bishop of Rome,' as the Acts distinctly state.[3] The Western bishops, Arcadius and Projectus,[4] and Philip, a Roman presbyter, were the legates of the Apostolic See, or throne. The West was thus sufficiently represented by these legates from Rome—a significant fact as to the relationship between Rome and the whole West.

Philip now led the way and laid down the order of their proceedings. Celestine (he said) had long ago passed a definite sentence[5] in his letter to Cyril concerning the matter in hand, and he has now sent a letter to your Holiness for the confirmation of the Catholic faith. 'Order that this be read in a fitting manner to the Synod, and entered in the ecclesiastical records.'

Arcadius and Projectus followed in the same strain.

Cyril at once directed that the Papal letter be read 'with befitting respect.' It was read, according to

[1] Mansi, iv. 1287.
[2] So Hefele, *Conc.-Gesch.* § 5 (6).   [3] Mansi, iv. 1279.
[4] These two bishops represented the West, not as having been selected by the Western episcopate, but as having been appointed by the Pope in Synod. They are called, when their office is given in full, 'legates of the Apostolic See,' or of 'the Church of the Romans.' Both Projectus and Arcadius are thus designated, Mansi, iv. 1297, 1299.
[5] ὥρισεν.

custom in the case of a solemn communication from Rome, in the original Latin, by Siricius, a notary of the Church of Rome.¹ The Bishop of Jerusalem at once proposed that it should now be translated into Greek. Philip, the legate, informed the assembly that he had made provision for this, and that the honour due to a letter from the Pope—*i.e.* that of reading the *ipsissima verba* in Latin—having been paid to it, he could furnish them with an authorised translation into Greek, which he had brought with him. The other legates echoed Philip's words.

The burden of the Pope's letter was that, as bishops, they, including himself, had entered into the work and office of the Apostolate, and that their common function was to preserve the faith. 'The custody of what has been delivered is no less an honour than the office of delivering it' [in the first instance]. The Council was as it were the successor of the Council at Jerusalem in the Acts of the Apostles: He who was with the Apostles then will assuredly be with their successors now. They have a common command, a common work, an office in common with the Apostles who sowed the seed which they, as bishops, have now to nurse into fruit. St. Paul's charge to Timothy applies to them his successors—'the same place, the same cause, demands the same office and ministry' (Lat. *officium*, Gk. διακονίαν). 'Let there be prayer made in common to the Lord.' Let them pray that they may be strong to proclaim the faith. Celestine ends with telling the Synod that he has sent his legates to be present at the acts of the Synod and to execute the decision previously given by himself, being assured that

¹ The members of the schismatical Synod all stood up when the *Emperor's* letter was read.

the bishops will acquiesce in this when they see that it was a decision in the interest of the Church (*quæ a nobis antea statuta sunt exequantur* [*i.e.* the legates through the Council]. *Quibus* [*i.e.* the '*antea statuta*'] *præstandum a vestra sanctitate non dubitamus assensum* &c. (Mansi, iv. 1287).

The bishops exclaimed at once: 'This is a just judgment. The Synod gives thanks to the new Paul, Celestine, the new Paul, Cyril'—in allusion to the exhortation of St. Paul to Timothy when Bishop at Ephesus, which Celestine had mentioned in his letter. They continued: '[We give thanks] to Celestine the guardian of the faith,[1] to Celestine of one mind with the Synod, to Celestine the whole Synod gives thanks. One Celestine, one Cyril, one faith of the Synod, one faith of the whole world.'

Projectus, the legate, then took up the practical point of the Papal letter, and requested that the Synod would see that what Celestine had long ago decided, and now recalled to their remembrance, should be accomplished with perfect exactness.[2]

Whereupon Firmus, a successor of St. Basil in the see of Cæsarea, rose and described the nature of the Council's action. He said that the Apostolic See of Celestine 'had previously given a sentence and decree by

[1] These words are omitted in Dr. Bright's list of their exclamations, *Hist. of the Church*, p. 336. His defence (*Roman See*, p. 162) is, that such words are not to be taken literally, because at the Council of Chalcedon the Emperor was called 'a teacher of the faith.' The Emperor, when a Christian, and when he provided for the safe conduct of the bishops and for the execution of their canons, *was* as he is called, a guardian and a teacher of the faith. The Pope was so called because of his corresponding relation to the faith in spirituals.

[2] ἵνα ταῦτα, ἃ καὶ πάλαι ὥρισε [*i.e.* Celestine] καὶ νῦν ὑπομνῆσαι κατηξίωσεν, εἰς πέρας κελεύσητε πληρέστατον ἄγεσθαι, κατὰ τὸν κανόνα τῆς κοινῆς πίστεως (Mansi, iv. 1287).

letters sent to Cyril, Juvenal, and Rufus, and to the Churches of Constantinople and Antioch, which (decree) the Synod had followed.' For the time, he added, fixed by Celestine for Nestorius's amendment had passed, and the day fixed by the Emperor for their assembly had also passed, and Nestorius had not put in an appearance. Consequently 'we executed the sentence [of the Pope] (τὸν τύπον ἐξεβιβάσαμεν), having pronounced a canonical and Apostolical judgment.'[1]

In short, the Synod by the mouth of Bishop Firmus, affirmed that (1) the Pope had issued a decree condemning Nestorius; (2) the Synod had executed that decree; (3) its judgment in execution of the Papal decree was (α) canonical: we know why, i.e. because they had properly cited Nestorius and he had not appeared; therefore they were justified in condemning him in his absence; and (β) it was Apostolical. Why 'Apostolical'? Firmus had spoken in the same breath of Celestine's 'Apostolic See' and Celestine (in the letter just read in which he insists upon the legates executing his sentence on Nestorius, which Firmus says the Synod *has* executed) had urged the bishops to imitate the Apostle St. Paul by boldly proclaiming the faith in common or concert with himself. The meaning, therefore, of Firmus's description of the Synodical judgment as 'Apostolical' is obvious.

The legate Arcadius thereupon asked that the decree of the Synod (τι τετύπωται) should be submitted to their

[1] When, therefore, Dr. Bright says that in the conciliar sentence (*supra*, p. 58) 'the canons and Celestine's letter to Nestorius cannot here be treated as co-ordinate; for the Council had *not* rendered literal obedience to that letter,' he obscures the issue, since the question is not whether *literal* obedience, but whether substantial and formal obedience had been rendered to the Papal letter. The Synod considered that such obedience had been rendered.

inspection. He also spoke of the stress of weather which had detained him and his fellow legates at sea. Philip followed congratulating the Synod on having joined themselves 'as holy members to their holy head by their exclamations' when the letter of Celestine was read. '*For* your blessedness is not ignorant that the head of the whole faith *and of the Apostles* is the blessed Apostle Peter.' In other words, the teaching of the Catholic and Roman Church at this hour was declared by him to be the teaching of all there present. He then expatiated on the stormy weather which had detained them, and requested them to order that what had been done before their arrival should be shown to them, ' so that in accordance with the mind of our blessed Father and of this present assembly, we may confirm them.'[1]

Theodotus, Bishop of Ancyra, after this important speech from Philip, rose and said that Almighty God had shown that the sentence of the Synod was a just one, by the auspicious arrival[2] of the Pope's letter and by the presence of the legates. He added 'for you have

[1] Philip adds ὁμοίως τῇ αὐτῶν καταθέσει, which the Latin translates *conformiter eorum depositioni*. It is difficult, however, to suppose that Philip would speak of the members of the Synod, in their presence, in the third person. And if they (the members of the Synod) were intended, ' deposition ' would more naturally be in the plural. Further, Philip's speech and that of Arcadius is headed ' interpretatio depositionis.' So that the true reading is probably ἑαυτῶν—'our own.' Whichever reading, however, we adopt, the point is that Philip was sent to confirm the judgment of the Synod if it was in accordance with the Pope's, and that the Synod had now declared that it was.

[2] Gk. ἐπιφοιτήσει. It is a strong word, generally used of the arrival of a messenger from God, especially of the Holy Spirit. Cf. Dindorf, *Steph. Thesaur.* iii. 1881. Dr. Bright has made a jumble of Theodotus's speech: he has wrongly connected the limbs of the sentence (*Roman See*, p. 163). He has left out 'the presence of the legates,' which was part of the proof of the Divine approval mentioned by Theodotus,

shown both the zeal and the eagerness concerning the holy faith possessed by the most holy and sacred Bishop Celestine': that is to say, Almighty God has set his seal upon our action by permitting the letter of Celestine to reach us, and Celestine has shown his zeal in his letter (which by anticipation affirms the justice of our sentence) and in sending yourselves with it. Theodotus then said in the name of the Synod that the Acts should be submitted to the legates for their inspection, and that they would in turn see in them the zeal of the Bishops and their 'agreement in the faith which Celestine proclaims with weighty voice.'[1]

The legates accordingly retired for the evening to inspect the transactions of the Synod at its first session.

Note.

It would be wearisome to the reader to be dragged through all the various criticisms which Dr. Bright has passed on the history of the Council of Ephesus as given in the first edition of this book. I have given several and shown what they are worth. I will here select one for greater detail, as a specimen. In reference to Pope St. Celestine's letter to the Synod, Canon Bright asks 'Is not Fleury warranted in saying that Celestine here "places

and which, considering what had just been said, shows that Theodotus looked upon their presence in the same light as Philip did. Theodotus does not say (as Dr. Bright) '*it* shows,' but 'you showed.'

[1] τὴν συμφωνίαν τῆς πίστεως ἣν Κελεστῖνος μεγάλῃ κηρύσσει τῇ φωνῇ. It is impossible to translate the subtle suggestiveness of the Greek here, in the use of the words συμφωνίαν and φωνῇ. The Synod's utterance was one with the weighty utterance of the Pope, is the full meaning.

himself in the rank of bishops"?' Of course he does; he was Bishop of Rome. But Fleury is really quoted to support Dr. Bright's theory that the Popes are on a level with other bishops in point of jurisdiction. Now Fleury mistranslates the words *in commune* in Celestine's letter as though they were the same as the French *également*. Dr. Bright for some years did the same. (Cf. *The Roman Claims, &c.*, p. 11, 1877.)

The origin of this seems to be as follows. Mr. Allies, before he was a Catholic, in his work entitled *The Church of England cleared from Schism* was misled by Fleury in this passage ; and Dr. Pusey in his *Eirenicon* was misled by Mr. Allies and by Fleury, to both of whom he refers. He makes it a difficulty which he calls insuperable, that Celestine should be considered infallible and yet that he should have said to the bishops that the teaching office had descended upon them— himself and them—*equally* (he italicises this word 'equally'). Dr. Bright also refers to Fleury in his *Roman Claims, &c.*, p. 11, and mistranslates Celestine's 'in common' as though it were 'equally.' It is obvious, however, that the two are not the same. A general and a captain may have a common work, yet they are not equal. Their mission may be due to one and the selfsame order from headquarters (an order common to all) to take a fort, or clear a hill. So again 'The Book of *Common* Prayer' does not mean that the clergyman and the people are on an equality in the conduct of the service. Dr. Bright, in reference to this objection, says, 'Where does he' (*i.e.* Celestine in this letter to the Synod) 'say that it' (the teaching office) 'has come to him in a unique sense as the teacher of the Church universal?' But Dr. Bright must know very well that that was not the question. The question I raised was this, Does the expression 'in common,' which Dr. Bright had translated 'equally,' contradict the claim to a superior position in the common work? Dr. Bright used this word 'equally' to establish this contradiction. It would surely have been well not to have introduced Fleury again, considering the way in which Doctor Pusey, and Dr. Bright himself, have been misled by him. Dr. Bright adds (*Roman See*, p. 162), 'It is true that he [Celestine] refers, at the end, to what he had "previously ordained" as to be "carried out" by his three legates.' As so often in Dr. Bright's book, the words 'it is true' introduce something the mention of which saves him from the imputation of not quoting what makes for the other side; but it is something which positively contradicts his conclusion. So here Celestine, having spoken of himself and the bishops as having a common command from Christ, and duties in common, such as proclaiming what they know about the faith, at once places himself at their head in this, their common work, ordering that his previous decree, condemning Nestorius, should be carried out. Dr. Bright is only throwing dust in people's eyes when he says that Celestine 'never claims any sole authority' (p. 161). No Pope ever did, from St. Peter to Leo XIII. They claimed it as head of the body, not as sole in the sense of separate, and excluding the bishops. It is no part of the Papal theory that the Pope should thus be sole in authority, and Dr. Bright ought not to suggest that the writer, whom he criticises, ever made it part of the Papal claim. On the other hand, in calling himself a sharer in a *common* work, Celestine does not place himself on an equality with all other bishops absolutely and in every respect. A common work admits of diversity of share. When Dr. Bright says also of Celestine (*loc. cit.*) that 'he never even alludes to his own see as that of Peter,' he must mean 'in that letter.' But why should he *in that letter*? No one supposes that Philip did not reflect the teaching of Celestine; in fact Dr. Bright sarcastically describes Philip as speaking *more Romano*. Now Philip grounded the Papal action on the fact of the Pope being the successor of Peter.

CHAPTER VII

THE SEE OF PETER 'CONFIRMING THE BRETHREN'— NO. II

On the following day the Council reassembled, the legates having overnight examined the transactions submitted to them. There can be no question as to what the Synod considered itself to have done. It had on the previous day publicly and formally announced that it had executed the Papal sentence in condemning Nestorius. Bishop Firmus had said so in the name of the Synod. But the question still remained, had they done so in canonical fashion? Had they heard, or been willing to hear, Nestorius in his own cause, if he desired it? Had they satisfied themselves that he had not repented in the interval between the sentence of the Pope and the meeting of the Council, as Celestine told Cyril it was incumbent on them to do?[1] The business before them was the formal ratification ($\beta\epsilon\beta a\iota\omega\sigma\iota s$) of the Acts: so it was described by Celestine himself.[2] The legates knew, too, that John of Antioch had accused the Synod of not acting in canonical order ($\dot{a}\kappa o\lambda o\acute{v}\theta\omega s$). Was this true? This was the question to be settled canonically ($\dot{a}\kappa o\lambda o\acute{v}\theta\omega s$).

Juvenal of Jerusalem accordingly rose and asked

---

[1] Mansi, iv. 1292.

[2] 'Requirendum est qualiter fuerint res finitæ.' Celestine's *Commonitorium* to the legates (*ibid.* 556).

the legates if they had read the transactions of the Synod and learnt their purport; to which Philip replied that they had perused the Acts and that all things had been done canonically and in accordance with the discipline of the Church. He asked, however, that these Acts might be publicly read through in their presence, so that in accordance with the order of Pope Celestine (ἀκολουθήσαντες τῷ τύπῳ) they might confirm the decisions of the Synod.¹ Arcadius seconded Philip's request, using the same expression as to the authority on which he acted. The Bishop of Ephesus agreed, and the transactions were now publicly read through word for word. But the Synod added a summary of the reasons for their method of action.² They said that, since Nestorius would not obey their citation, they were compelled to proceed (ἀναγκαίως ἐχωρήσαμεν) to the examination of the things impiously said by him, and that they had detected him both from his letters and his commentaries, and also—and this was a condition on which Celestine had made the execution of his sentence depend, when writing to Cyril, a letter which Cyril had by this time at any rate in his hands³—they had convicted him from the things said by him in the city of Ephesus quite lately, which had been properly substantiated by witnesses.⁴ Having done this, they had proceeded to pass the sad sentence of condemnation

---

¹ Celestine's order (Mansi, iv. 556) was that at the Council they were to act as judges, in regard to the bishops' decisions, or opinions (*de eorum sententiis judicare debeatis*); it is obvious, therefore, that in seeing how things had been transacted they were also to act as judges.

² Mansi, iv. 1293.   ³ Mansi, iv. 1292.

⁴ Of these John of Antioch could have no proper knowledge; for he had examined no witnesses.

upon him, 'being compelled thereto (ἀναγκαίως κινηθέντες) both by the canons and by the letter of Celestine.' This sentence they declared to be the sentence of our Lord Jesus Christ by means of this present Synod.

The stages, then, through which matters had passed were: (i) the reference of the whole matter by Cyril to the Apostolic See; (ii) the condemnation of Nestorius by the Pope in the Roman Synod—an *ex-cathedra* dogmatic definition [1] to the effect that the union between the human and divine Natures in our Lord is hypostatic—a union of nature with nature in one Person, not of two persons, and that this hypostatic union is symbolised by the term 'Mother of God,' which therefore must be accepted by every member of the Catholic Church. On this ground Nestorius was to be excommunicated, unless he repented. This was the ὅρος, or dogmatic decree, of the Holy See.[2] Then (iii) a place of repentance was given to Nestorius, and the execution of the sentence passed into the hands of the Council, which was to make sure as to his persistence in his error, in which case, as the Pope said, he would reap the fruit of his own acts, the Papal 'decrees remaining in force,' *i.e.* by reason of his own obstinacy.[3] At length (iv) the Council assembled, cited Nestorius, proceeded, on his refusal, to read the documents, such as his letters, with a view to giving a conciliar adhesion to the Papal sentence; and (v), having done this in the course of an afternoon and part of an

---

[1] Cf. Bottalla, S. J. (*The Infallibility of the Pope*, [Burns and Oates]) who calls it ' an infallible dogmatic definition,' p. 208.

[2] ἔστι δὲ ὅρος is the heading of the Pope's sentence, Mansi, iv. 1047. For some remarks on Dr. Bright's representation of this matter, see *infra*, p. 110.

[3] Mansi, iv. 1292.

evening, the Synod passed its sentence in avowed obedience to the canons and the Papal letter. Shortly afterwards (vi) the Papal legates appear on the scene with instructions to place themselves in the hands of Cyril, to maintain the authority of the Holy See, and to act as judges of the bishops' judgments.[1] They proceed to inquire, in accordance with express orders, as to the precise way in which the business of the Synod had been conducted. The Synod distinctly and emphatically claims to have 'executed the sentence' of Pope Celestine.[2] But the legates require that the report of the Acts should be submitted to their inspection, that in accordance with the order given by the Holy Father they may confirm them. The Synod willingly acquiesces. And the legates proceed to approve of all that had been done, and to give their assent in writing. The whole scene is one of emphatic deference to the representatives of the Apostolic See. And (vii) this deference was paid to it, not as the see of the older Imperial capital, nor of the Apostolic See of the West, but as simply 'the Apostolic See.' This was the term perpetually applied to it—not, as has been suggested[3] (with scant deference to the historical situation), because they 'would not care to magnify Antioch by emphasising its Apostolic character, and Jerusalem was still subordinate to Cæsarea,' for this would not account for Alexandria's title to 'Apostolic' being also subordinated, nor could it in any way account for the application of the word 'Apostolic' in a unique sense ('*the* Apostolic See') by *Eastern bishops* to the See of Rome, even under the circumstances of Antioch's opposition to the Synod. No; Philip gave the reason of its Apostolicity, not as his own opinion, but as *their*

[1] Mansi, iv. 556.   [2] *Ibid.* 1287.   [3] Bright's *Roman See*, p. 160.

belief (*supra*, p. 71). In the way of deference the Papal letter was read in the original language as well as in a translation; the Acts of the Synod were submitted to the Papal legates; they were solemnly read out from end to end in their presence *after they had themselves read them through*, and the moving cause of the decision arrived at was then declared by the Synod to be 'the canons and the Papal letter' (ἀναγκαίως κινηθέντες, Lat. *coacti*).

Let us pause for a moment to consider the situation outside of Ephesus. The Emperor was against Cyril and in favour of Nestorius; the Bishop thus deposed was the Bishop of the Imperial city. The great central see of the East, that of Antioch, had professed to excommunicate Cyril and Memnon, the Bishop of Ephesus, for the irregular way in which they had acted. What was Rome, that, in the face of all this, its Bishop should occupy the transcendent position that it did in the person of the Papal Legates?

Rome had not been for the past century and more the habitual residence of her Emperor. At this moment Theodosius in the East, by whose order the Council had been summoned to Ephesus, was the overlord of Rome, and the child whom eight years before he had placed on the throne in the West was with his mother at Ravenna, for safety's sake. Byzantium was as politically powerful as Rome was politically weak.[1] There was nothing in the city of Rome but the prestige of the past; while Constantinople was ablaze with the glamour of an Imperial Court. The bishops of the East were mostly Courtbishops, perpetually truckling to the Imperial favour. Fifty years ago they had endeavoured to give the Byzan-

[1] Gregorovius, *Hist. of Rome*, pp. 168, 179 (Tr.) Dill, *Roman Society*, p. 128 (1898).

tine capital a lift above Alexandria and Antioch. That Council had not indeed taken its place among those called Œcumenical; the bishops at Ephesus considered themselves to be sitting only in the second Œcumenical Synod. Still, the Imperial city had advanced step by step. What was it that under such adverse circumstances secured the deference now paid by Eastern bishops to the Bishop of desolate Rome, sinking as she was civilly to comparative insignificance in the life of the Empire? Philip, the Papal legate, had already explained the secret; he had struck a note which awakened no single dissonant utterance in that second session of the Synod. He spoke, *not* of 'older Rome,' but of 'the Apostolic See.' He had congratulated them on their having 'joined themselves as holy members to their holy head' by their exclamations uttered immediately upon the Papal letter being solemnly read; and he had explained this expression of his by appealing to their universal acceptance[2] of the truth that Peter was 'the head of the whole faith, and of the Apostles'; hence Celestine, the present Bishop of Rome, was their 'holy head'—an exposition which was followed by a sympathetic speech from Theodotus of Ancyra.

But now in this third session, after the form of procedure had been dictated by the legates, and a considerable time had been spent in publicly reading, for form's sake, the whole Acts of the first session; now that the Synod had avowed its indebtedness to the Papal judgment, 'compelled by the canons and by the letter' containing that sentence, the legate Philip rose and delivered a speech in which he at least professed to voice again the belief of every member of that Synod as

[1] Mansi, iv. 1289. [2] οὐ γὰρ ἀγνοεῖ ὑμῶν ἡ μακαριότης.

to the reason why they had thus deferred to the judgment of the Holy See. The reason was to be found in the teaching of Holy Scripture and the constant tradition of Holy Church as to the See of Peter. He said:

'It is doubtful to none, yea and has been known to all ages, that the holy and most blessed Peter, the prince and head of the Apostles, and the pillar of the faith and the foundation of the Catholic Church, received the keys of the Kingdom from our Lord Jesus Christ, the Saviour and Redeemer of the human race, and that the power of loosing and binding was given to him: who up to this time, and always, lives and exercises judgment in his successors. Therefore our holy and most blessed father Bishop Celestine, being his successor and holding his place, has sent us to this holy Synod to supply his presence.' He then speaks of the Emperor having summoned the Synod for the preservation of the faith, and continues: 'Therefore Nestorius, the author of this perverse novelty [Gk. *lit.* new perversity] and the head of the evils, having been summoned, as we have learned from the Acts of the Synod, and having been warned, according to the decrees ($\tau\acute{u}\pi o v s$) of the fathers, and the disciplinary provisions [*lit.* discipline, or science] of the canons, contemptuously refused to come to judgment, when he ought of his own accord to have offered himself, that he might have been healed by the spiritual remedy [thus provided]; but having a seared conscience, although he was legitimately and, as I have said, in accordance with the canons, admonished, he refused to come to this holy Synod, and allowed, not only the interval allowed by the Apostolic see, but a much longer time to pass by. Therefore,'—notice how exactly the legate has repeated the reasons given by the Synod itself for their condemnation of Nestorius, viz. the requirements of the canons and of the letter of Pope Celestine—'that which has been pronounced [1] against him who with hostile spirit and impious mouth has uttered blasphemy against our Lord Jesus Christ, stands firm, according to the decree ($\tau \acute{v} \pi o v$) of all the Churches, since in this Council of the hierarchy are gathered together the priests both from the Eastern and the Western Churches, either in person or by legates. Therefore following the decrees ($\tau \acute{v} \pi o \iota s$) of the Fathers, this present holy Synod has passed a definite sentence ($\mathring{\omega} \rho \iota \sigma \epsilon \ldots \pi \eta o \sigma \epsilon \nu \acute{\epsilon} \gamma \kappa a \sigma a\ \mathring{a} \pi \acute{o} \phi a \sigma \iota \nu$) against the rash blasphemer. Wherefore let Nestorius know that he is excluded from the communion of the Catholic Church.' He thus ratified the sentence of the Synod in the name of the successor of the Apostle Peter.

The two other legates made similar formal utterances as to the validity of the Synodical condemnation of Nestorius. Arcadius is called 'the legate of the Apostolic See,' and Projectus 'the legate of the Church of the Romans.' As such they were, as has been already remarked, taken to represent the West sufficiently— although they were not deputies selected by the West, but representatives deputed by the Holy See.

Such, then—to return to the speech of the legate Philip—was the plain teaching concerning Papal Supremacy, as grounded on the words of our Lord to Peter, who is called 'the foundation of the Catholic Church.' And this belief was given as that of every bishop there, and indeed of the whole Catholic Church —'it is doubtful to none'—and as that of all past ages —'it has been known to all ages.' This statement of Papal Supremacy did not occur as an *obiter dictum*;

[1] τὸ ἐξενεχθέν.

it was made the pivot upon which the whole action of the legates hinged. It was a case in which, if ever there was one, silence on the part of the bishops would involve acquiescence. At a time when the city of Rome was politically in the dust, when no one would have called her, from a natural point of view, the Eternal City—for no one, except those who believed in her as the See of Peter, could have dreamt of the vitality she was to exhibit, owing simply to the prerogatives of the Prince of the Apostles, whose seat and centre was in that city—at that era of apparent decadence, the legate of the Bishop of Rome stood in the midst of this great Eastern assembly and spoke of the position of 'the Apostolic See' in the Kingdom of God, as inheriting the prerogatives of 'the foundation of the Catholic Church,' the Prince and head of the Apostles.

There was no protest made. None said that this was not his faith, not even the ambitious Juvenal of Jerusalem, equal, at any time, to the task, if he had really held a different faith. Had the teaching of Philip on the Papal Supremacy been open to question, had any-one, contrary to what Philip said, doubted it, we could hardly have failed to catch some murmur of dissent.

But Philip's simple statement of the belief of all the bishops there present was met with something even more significant than silence. He had made his deposition, as the saying was, and it had hinged on the Divine institution of the supreme position of Peter's See in the Catholic Church. What of such a deposition?

Cyril spoke for the Synod. He said: 'The depositions made by the most holy and God-fearing bishops Arcadius and Projectus, *and moreover by the presbyter Philip*, have been made plain to the Synod; for they have deposed, filling the place of *the Apostolic See* and of the bishops of the whole Western Synod. So that they have executed the things already decided by the most holy and God-beloved Bishop Celestine and they have given their assent'—obviously that of a superior—' to the decree pronounced against the heretic Nestorius by the holy Synod assembled here in Ephesus. Wherefore let the transactions of yesterday and to-day be joined on to the previous " Acts "; so let the records be brought, that they may manifest in the usual way by their own signature their canonical agreement with all of us.'

Now no honest man could have used the expression which Cyril here used of the Holy See, if he did not believe the doctrine just delivered by Philip concerning that see and asserted to be the accepted teaching of all who sat there. Cyril spoke of the legates as filling the place of ' the Apostolic See,' as well as, of course, of the bishops of the West. Philip had explained in what sense the See of Rome was '*the* Apostolic See'; and Cyril immediately used the expression without any counter-explanation. We know, too, what Cyril thought of it. It seems almost incredible that anyone should endeavour to establish a difference of opinion between Philip and Cyril by drawing attention to the fact that Cyril ' takes care to describe the legates as representing, not only " the Apostolical See " but " all the holy Synod of the West."'[1] Why, *Philip had done the same.* Nor is it less surprising that the same writer should consider that he makes a point in saying that Cyril also distinguishes ' *their* (*i.e.* the legates') action, as Celestine's real " agents," from the sentence already pronounced by

[1] Bright's *Roman See*, p. 164.

the Synod to which he requests their "assent" in writing.' No one, surely, ever dreamt of supposing that the Synod was the 'agent' of Celestine in the sense that the legates were. The action of the legates was that of men, strictly representing the Holy See, sent to pass judgment on the action of the Synod. The action of the Synod was that of bishops, who had their own duty of judgment, though that right would be used amiss if it ended in differing from the Papal sentence.

One of the legates who represented the Synod of the West, but who is immediately spoken of as 'the legate of the Church of the Romans,' replied that, 'in view of what had been done in this holy Synod, they cannot but confirm their teaching with their own signatures.' And the Synod at once said—and the words are conclusive as to their view of all that had happened—' Since the most pious and God-fearing bishops and legates, Arcadius and Projectus, *and Philip*, presbyter and legate *of the Apostolic See*, have spoken suitably,[1] it follows that they

[1] Gk. ἀκολούθως. Dr. Bright thinks that this means 'in accordance with the Synod.' If so, it must be remembered that the Synod professed to have executed the sentence of Celestine (cf. Firmus's speech, *supra*, p. 69); and that the legates were *consequently* in accord with it. But, as a matter of fact, the word ἀκολούθως is generally used in the Acts of the Council of Ephesus and Chalcedon as a synonym for 'canonically or in ecclesiastical order.' The schismatic Synod under John of Antioch had laid the greatest stress on the breach of canonical order of which the Synod under Cyril was supposed to have been guilty, using this same word again and again in its substantive form (ἀκολουθία). Nestorius had done the same (Mansi, iv. 1233). So that here the Synod says that the legates had spoken in agreement with the canons, especially Philip. The Synod used the same word in the fifth Act (Mansi, iv. 1321) : 'Ακολούθως ἡ ὑπόμνησις γεγένηται, where the Latin is ' *Qualem oportebat*.' ἀκολούθως καὶ κανονικῶς is a regular expression for a thing done in canonical order, in Byzantine Greek. The burden of Cyril's accusation against John of Antioch and his schismatic

should make good their promise and by their signature confirm what has been done.' In other words, the whole Synod accepted the situation as described by the legate Philip. Thus the assent required by the law of the Church was secured. The Greek historian had said that it was not lawful to make regulations or canons contrary to the judgment of the Bishop of Rome;[1] nor would the proceedings, therefore, of an Œcumenical Synod be valid without the assent of the Apostolic See. That assent had now been given, so far as it could be given by legates, and it had been given in agreement with the canons, as they themselves had stated.

Each of the legates signed, Philip first, as 'presbyter and legate of the Apostolic See': Arcadius and Projectus as 'Bishop and legate of the Apostolic See.' Neither of them signed as representing, in a direct way, the Synod of the West; but as Philip said —and Cyril echoed his statement—the West was present in them, that is to say, by implication. They acted in obedience to the Papal injunction; by that authority, which they placed in the front in their depositions, they were justified in agreeing with the Synod, in following suit in their signatures, in confirming what the Synod had done.

---

action was ἐχρῆν τοῖς κανόσιν ἐξακολουθῆσαι, and that he insulted πᾶσαν ἀκολουθίαν ἐκκλησιαστικήν, all ecclesiastical order (M. iv. 1308); whereas John of Antioch claims that his Synod will see that things are decided ἀκολούθως (iv. 1264). ἀκόλουθος came to mean 'canonical,' because the canons were arranged in a consecutive series. *Cf.* Lupus, *Synod. Decret.* i. 903.

[1] Socrates (a lawyer of Constantinople in the middle of the 5th century), *H. E.* ii. 8.

NOTE ON DR. BRIGHT v. MANSI.

Dr. Bright, in the *Church Quarterly Review* (Jan. 1895, p. 290), and in his book on *The Roman See, &c*, p. 165, has committed himself on this incident, first to a patent mistranslation and then to an equivocal withdrawal or a reassertion of his mistake. I do not know which is intended. In the *Church Quarterly Review* he translated the Synod's words calling upon the legates to confirm its Acts, thus: 'Since they have spoken ἀκολούθως, it follows that they should make good their own promise and *affirm what has been done* by their signatures.' Now the legate Arcadius had said in the preceding sentence that 'in view of what had been done'—considering, that is, that all had been done in canonical order—they felt obliged to 'confirm their teaching with their signatures.' There can be no question what Arcadius meant by 'confirming.' Dr. Bright, however, anxious to get out of the awkward witness which would be rendered to Papal Supremacy if the Synod consented to have its transactions reviewed and confirmed by Papal legates, actually translated (*Church Quarterly Review*) βεβαιῶσαι 'affirm,' and made the Synod ask the legates to 'affirm what has been done' by it. What could be meant by *affirming* what had been done, when all that had been done had been written down and read out, unless in the sense of 'confirming'? But, if in that sense, why not use the word 'confirm'? This was pointed out by me in an article in the *Dublin Review* to which Dr. Bright alludes elsewhere, showing that he had read it, and in his book on the *Roman See* (p. 165), he alters his translation thus far, 'it follows that they should make good their own promise, and affirm [or "confirm"] what has been done.' It is surprising that one who deals with such accusations about scholarship and logic as Dr. Bright does, should have had recourse to such a singular procedure as this. When he says on the next page that 'the sense of βεβαιόω is somewhat elastic; its sense in any particular passage must be settled by the context; and we learn by Cyril's phrase " canonical assent " in what sense the legates were expected to "confirm" the Council's proceedings,' Dr. Bright needs to be reminded that a single expression does not make a context, and this one word 'canonical' itself receives ample explanation from the whole context. And certainly of all men, Cyril is the last whose use of 'canonical' could be supposed to exclude what the whole context establishes, viz. the right to judge of the action of bishops, which resides in the Apostolic See. The legates had refused to give their assent to the Acts of the Synod until they were certified that all had been done in strict accordance with the canons. Their assent would not be itself canonical, unless this condition were fulfilled.

But since the name of Mansi occurs so often in these pages, it may be well to give the estimate which that most learned and illustrious writer formed of the first three sessions of the Council. It occurs in his ' Animadversions ' on Natalis Alexander's History ($H. E.$ ix. 473 [1787]). Mansi quotes a remark of Baluze, who, as he says, though a disciple of De Marca, yet admitted that the discovery of Celestine's *Commonitorium* to the legates (cf. *supra*, p. 65) was fatal to his master's theory, so far as that theory was founded on the Acts of the Council of Ephesus. Baluze says that if Baronius had seen this *Commonitorium* he would have been able to say still more confidently that the legates were sent, not that the case of Nestorius should be subjected to a fresh examination, but to see that the sentence already passed was executed. Mansi quotes the words from the sentence of the Council ' compelled by the canons and letter of Celestine ' as showing the obedience paid by the bishops to Celestine; and he deduces the same from the words of the Synod to the Emperor, viz. 'praising Celestine &c.' He quotes the words of Firmus as proving the same. He then deals with the fact that the Council examined the teaching of Nestorius, and remarks that 'not merely the definitions of the Pontiffs, but those also of Œcumenical Councils were discussed in particular Synods, not from any doubt as to their truth, but because they believed that they could pass a fresh judgment on them. The Pontiffs themselves, who believed that it was not lawful to refuse assent to their own definitions, willed that Councils should be called to prove what they had defined.' He then lays stress on the words of the sentence at Ephesus, 'compelled by the canons and by the letter of Celestine,' adding: 'No one but a superior can compel.' He thinks that Bossuet has given away his case by appealing to the Council of Ephesus. We might say the same with tenfold force of Dr. Bright and our other Anglican friends. As for the Council's issuing a sentence in its own name, Mansi says that a lower court can always do this when ordered by a higher court. He then quotes Pope Nicolas I., who adduces the same words from the sentence passed by the Council: 'necessarily compelled' (*necessario coacti* is the Pope's translation). He then shows that the explanation of a 'canonical' sentence, adopted by Dr. Bright, will not hold. And Bossuet's notion (also adopted by that writer), viz. that the legates only manifested their assent to the Synod's transactions, is, says Mansi, quite untenable when we consider 'that the legates said that the Acts were then to be confirmed by them after they had been submitted to their investigation for the especial purpose that they might see if they agreed with the judgment passed by Celestine.' Mansi then shows that Philip, in saying that Peter, the pillar of the faith and foundation of the Catholic Church, lives still in his successors and exercises judgment, predicates 'the infallibility of the Pontiffs when they define *ex cathedra*; for if they can err in defining, who would dare to say that Peter the pillar of the faith and foundation of the Church lives in them and exercises judgment?' Mansi then shows that the legates came to see that Pope Celestine's judgment was executed, and that Cyril said that the legates had done that for which they were sent.

CHAPTER VIII

THE EMPEROR AND THE MONK

We must now return to Constantinople and its young Emperor. After the Council's first session at Ephesus, the bishops sent the Emperor a report of the proceedings, in which they explained why they met together without the Bishop of Antioch, and then, taking up the two points of their sentence in which they had alleged the canons and the letter of Pope Celestine as the moving cause of their decision, they showed how both in proceeding to their work without Nestorius and in the conduct of their task they had acted in accordance with the canons, and how they had 'praised'—that is (as their sentence explained), deferred to and acted in unison with—'Celestine the most holy and God-beloved Bishop of Rome, who condemned the heretical dogmatic teaching of Nestorius *before we did, for the safety of the Churches, and of the holy and saving faith* delivered to us by the holy Apostles and Evangelists and by the holy Fathers; which he [Nestorius] endeavoured to overthrow by his depraved teaching, which he disseminated far and wide after his condemnation.'[1] They therefore begged the Emperor to take

---

[1] Mansi, iv. 1240. The Greek text here presents a difficulty in the last sentence. It runs, πολὺ τὸ πλῆθος ὃ καταγνωσθεὶς ἐξέχεε. Judging from the Latin edition in use before the sixth century (Mansi, v. 562), the meaning is that a great quantity of heretical talk was poured forth

measures for removing this teaching from their midst, and to have Nestorius's writings committed to the flames.

It is to be noticed that the bishops in this letter speak of the part played by Pope Celestine as being that of safeguarding the 'Churches' and the Apostolic faith, and of Nestorius's condemnation as having dated from the decision of Celestine. As a matter of fact, they had especially established the fact of his *continued* false teaching, as indeed they were in natural justice bound to do. But the gist of this paragraph in their synodical letter is this: Celestine condemned Nestorius; we followed suit, Nestorius having persisted in his depraved doctrine, even after his condemnation by Celestine, (καταγνωσθεὶς ἐξέχεε).

But after the third session, when the Papal legates had confirmed the synodical condemnation of Nestorius, the bishops wrote a second report, in which they began with speaking of his condemnation by the Roman Synod, which they considered necessarily carried with it the entire West. They thus, as a matter of fact, brought out the special feature of a conciliar judgment as given above in our *résumé* of Catholic teaching on the subject of Œcumenical Councils (p. 41). Where a Papal decision has gone before, a conciliar judgment exhibits in the most striking way possible the unanimity of the entire Church in that decision. This was the burden of the bishops' letter to the Emperor now. They mention the letter of Celestine to themselves as having supervened on the decision given by the Roman Synod

by Nestorius. But the important point is that, whatever this means exactly, the statement is clear that in the eyes of the orthodox bishops Nestorius had aggravated his crime by teaching as he did after his condemnation by Pope Celestine.

presided over by him, and the presence of the legates from Rome and their confirmation of the Acts of their first session, as involving the acquiescence of the entire West in what they had done. They also emphasise the fact that Cyril had been originally entrusted by Celestine with the conduct of the matter, an important point, as it suggested that in the government of the Council he was not taking upon himself to act simply as the bishop of the rival see of Alexandria. They end with a petition which assumes that they now at length have a right to consider their action as final, and ask to be released from further attendance at Ephesus, and to be allowed to arrange for the consecration of another bishop for Constantinople. The letter was signed by Cyril and the rest of the bishops, but apparently not by the legates, perhaps because it concerned their own assent to the transactions of the Council, of which Cyril was president—they themselves having been sent to 'judge of the bishops' sentences or opinions' as Celestine had said in his *Commonitorium*.

But every effort had been made at Constantinople in the end of June to prevent the Emperor from receiving a true report of the doings of the orthodox Synod.[1] Candidian had succeeded in poisoning his Majesty's mind against Cyril, and leading him to believe that Nestorius had been uncanonically condemned. No one disputed the justice of the original sentence of the Pope on Nestorius; it was against the conciliar execution of that sentence that all their efforts were directed. Still the Emperor was destined to receive some further information as to the transactions of the orthodox Council. A simple mendicant succeeded in reaching the great monas-

[1] Mansi, iv. 1428.

tery in Constantinople, and having hidden a copy of a letter from Cyril in a reed—probably his pilgrim's staff—he was able to throw fresh light on the distressing state of things in Ephesus. And now a scene occurred which left an indelible impression on the people of Constantinople and assisted the Emperor in forming a true judgment of the case.

There lived in Constantinople an aged man, an Archimandrite, and a patriarch among monks (who swarmed in the Imperial city), to whom, as the Synod said in its letter of thanks,[1] God had from the first revealed the real temper and tone of Nestorius's episcopate. He used to say to his monks: ' Beware, brethen; an evil beast has settled in this city: and he has to injure many by his teaching.' For forty-eight years this venerable ascetic had never left his monastery; but within and without its precincts his name was one with which to conjure, by reason of the sanctity with which he was universally credited. The Emperor had ere now visited him in person, to induce him to join in litanies and processions when Constantinople was trembling with the shocks of earthquake; but Dalmatius (for that was his name) turned a deaf ear to the advances of his highest earthly superior; nothing could prevail on him to leave his monastic home. But now a voice from heaven seemed to say to him that he must break through his cherished seclusion and go in person to visit the Emperor.

The scene in Constantinople as the recluse quitted his cell to make his way to the presence-chamber of the young Emperor Theodosius is described in a letter written to the Synod of Ephesus by the bishops in

[1] Mansi, iv. 1260.

Constantinople[1] who clustered there and became the resident Council round the Archbishop. A great crowd of the orthodox accompanied the holy monk through the streets, and as he passed into the palace with some attendant Archimandrites the crowd remained outside chanting their psalms antiphonally. And when the Saint emerged from the palace, a long procession accompanied him through a principal thoroughfare to the other end of the city, still singing their psalms, until he entered the basilica of St. Mocius, where he was to communicate the Imperial answer. It had been favourable, Cyril's proposal that a deputation from the Council should wait on his Imperial Majesty and explain their transactions had been accepted. The crowd of orthodox shouted ' Anathema to Nestorius ! '

[1] Mansi, iv. 1428.

CHAPTER IX

JOHN OF ANTIOCH CONDEMNED.

In the next (fourth) session of the Synod at Ephesus Cyril still presiding ('managing the place of Celestine,' say the Acts) with the assistance of the other legates, brought forward his own case and that of Memnon, the bishop of the diocese. John of Antioch, had, as we have seen allowed himself to be so far led away by the bad company in which he found himself, that he had synodically condemned, excommunicated and deposed both Cyril and Memnon. Cyril could have afforded to treat such madness with contempt, if he had not had to deal with an Emperor who was opposed to him, and with all the enemies of the faith. He might have fallen back simply and solely on his union with the successor of St. Peter and the whole West; but the matter was one which had arisen since his actual communication with Celestine. Accounts were already being sent to the Emperor by Candidian; and Nestorius and the Bishop of Antioch both leant on the Imperial arm. At any moment he might find himself in prison, as indeed eventually happened. Every moment, therefore, was of importance.

Accordingly the Synod was again convened and Cyril asked the bishops for their vote on John of Antioch's conduct towards himself and Memnon. After explaining how the proceedings of the Council had been conducted in an orderly and judicial manner, and how John of Antioch had delayed when he might have come, and had been joined by certain disorderly persons, some without sees, some under accusations, he pointed out that the so-called deposition which John and some thirty bishops had pretended to pass on himself and Memnon was absurd, considering the number and character of the real Synod. 'And indeed,' he added, 'he has no power from ecclesiastical laws or from an Imperial decree, either to judge any one of us or to attempt anything of the kind, *especially against a greater throne.*' And anyhow he ought to have called upon us, together with the whole Synod, to answer his charges.[1] Cyril seems here to speak of Alexandria alone as a ' greater throne,' although at this time Ephesus may perhaps have considered itself also to be in the same category, being more than a metropolitical see.[2] But Alexandria was a ' See of Peter.'

Accordingly, on Cyril's proposal, three bishops were now sent to the Bishop of Antioch to summon him to appear before the Synod. But they found him surrounded with soldiers, and were insulted with the blasphemous talk of his retinue. On the return of the episcopal messengers, Cyril proposed that the Synod should at once proceed to declare the sentence of the Antiochene party null and void. But Juvenal of Jerusalem interposed suggesting that John should be cited again. In the course of his speech Juvenal roundly condemned the Patriarch of Antioch for not hastening

[1] Mansi, iv. 1308.
[2] Cf. Duchesne, *Origines du culte chrétien*, p. 25 (2nd ed.), for the position of Ephesus at this period. Bossuet considers that the expression refers to Alexandria alone.

to appear before the Synod, considering its character, 'and to obey and respect the Apostolic throne of Rome sitting with us.' He also in some way brought in the Apostolic throne of Jerusalem. But he spoke of the see of Rome as that 'before which especially it has been the custom for the see of Antioch to be directed and judged, according to Apostolical order and tradition.'[1] In fact, he took up the line of thought suggested by Cyril, when he spoke of Alexandria as a 'greater see,' and while echoing Cyril's contention that a 'greater throne especially' could not be judged by Antioch, he probably added some glorification of his own see, which was, in fact, the characteristic of his rule at Jerusalem. All this was in accordance with the principle that the sees that were under no metropolitan, but were afterwards called Patriarchal sees, could only be judged by 'the Apostolic See,' or by a General Council, which, of course, in order to be general, must include, or be confirmed by, that see. For Rome was in conciliar language '*the* Apostolic See,' not *merely* the Apostolic See *of Rome*, or of the West; it *was* this latter, but it was also the former—'*the* Apostolic See' simply—a designation never bestowed on any other. The Councils speak of the Apostolic See of

---

[1] Mansi, iv. 1312. The grammatical order of this long sentence is confused in the original Greek. Juvenal seems to speak of the Apostolical see of Jerusalem as 'sitting with *us*,' and as though that were also to be obeyed by Antioch. But it cannot be supposed that he spoke quite such nonsense as that. He had a quarrel with Antioch, and in this very Synod tried to wrest from its jurisdiction some of its fairest provinces; but he was baulked by Cyril (cf. *Leon. Ep.* 119). But he never claimed any jurisdiction over Antioch itself. In speaking of the traditional subjection of Antioch to Rome, he is doubtless alluding to the case of Paulinus of Antioch, in the last century, and Paul of Samosata at a more distant period.

Alexandria, and the Apostolic See of Jerusalem and the Apostolic See of Rome; but when 'the Apostolic See' simply is spoken of, all the world knew that Rome was meant.

Bossuet puts the whole matter with his accustomed terseness and lucidity. He says:

'Lorsque Jean d'Antioche, avec son concile, osa déposer Cyrille et avec lui Memnon, évêque d'Ephèse, on lui reprocha non seulement d'avoir prononcé contre un évêque " d'un des plus grands sièges," ce qui regardait Cyrille, patriarche d'Alexandrie, mais encore d'avoir déposé deux évêques sur lesquels il n'avait aucun pouvoir, ce qui convenait également à Cyrille et à Memnon. C'étaient là, dit le concile d'Ephèse, deux attentats qui renversaient tout l'ordre de l'Eglise. Mais quand le Pape prononce, surtout en matière d'hérésie, contre quelque évêque que ce soit et quelque siège qu'il remplisse, loin d'y trouver à redire, chacun se soumet: ce qui prouve qu'il est reconnu pour le supérieur universel.'[1]

John was twice more cited, but with similar and even worse results, the bishops being personally treated with ignominy, and John saying that 'since the causes of the Court are transferred to the Church, he was transferring the cause of the Church to the Court.' The Synod thereupon proceeded on the following day to pronounce all that John of Antioch had done null and void,[2] and passed sentence of excommunication upon him and his associates, depriving them of episcopal faculties, until they should acknowledge their fault,

---

[1] *Remarques sur l'histoire des conciles*, Œuvres, xxx. 526 (Versailles, 1817).

[2] They called the petition of Cyril and Memnon ἀκόλουθος = in order. Cf. *supra*, pp. 62, 85.

adding that 'unless they do that quickly, they will undergo the complete sentence of the canons.'[1]

They then wrote their third letter to the Emperor. In this they described the real character of John of Antioch's crew, and the uncanonical nature of his procedure against Cyril, their 'head.' The burden of their complaint against John was that his action was out of order [2]—ecclesiastical or canonical.

But a more important letter, so far as our subject is concerned, was now written to Pope Celestine. It was their first report to him. And it opens in a way in which a Synod of Eastern bishops would never address any but the occupant of '*the* Apostolic throne.' They say: 'Your Holiness's zeal concerning religion and care concerning the orthodox faith, a care so dear and well-pleasing to God, the Saviour of us all, have come to be worthy of all admiration. For it is your wont, who are so great, to be distinguished in all things and to make the stability of *the Churches* the object of your zeal. But since it was necessary that all things that have followed should be brought to the knowledge of your Holiness, we write perforce.'[3] They enter into some detail as to John of Antioch's delay, proving that it was quite possible for him to have been with them, if he had wished it.[4] And after describing the action of the

---

[1] Mansi, iv. 1823.
[2] ἔξω πάσης ἀκολουθίας ἐκκλησιαστικῆς, iv. 1328. Cf. *supra*, pp. 62, 85.
[3] Mansi, iv. 1329.
[4] Dr. Bright's elaborate condemnation of Cyril on this point in his *Waymarks*, &c., pp. 150-158, amounts to a condemnation of the very position of the Synod as a canonical gathering. Garnier notices that if, as John of Antioch insisted, they were violating the canons in not waiting for him, then they were not merely not an Œcumenical Council,

Synod in regard to Nestorius, they reach a climax when they say that Celestine's letter was read, ' by which [1] he was with good reason condemned as having written blasphemy and inserted unholy sayings in his own interpretations, more especially as he was so far from repenting' (the allusion is obviously to Celestine's letter to Cyril about a time for repentance being given through the Council being summoned) ' that he dared to say in discussion with certain holy and learned bishops at Ephesus, "I do not confess a God two or three months old;" and other things he said more disastrous still.'

They then proceed to give a detailed account of John of Antioch's doings on his arrival in Ephesus, and report that they have excommunicated him, but not degraded him from his office. ' *This* ' (they say) ' by way of conquering his precipitancy by long-suffering '—that is to say, overcoming evil by good—' though he would justly and lawfully have suffered it, we have reserved for the judgment of your Holiness.' There were, in fact, two superiors of Antioch, which was one of the ' greater sees '—viz. the See of Peter itself, and a General Council, which included the See of Rome, or must be confirmed by it. The Council was now Œcumenical in any matter that came properly within its cognisance,[2] by reason of the presence of the legates from Rome, and

---

but their acts had no validity at all. But the Synod itself answers every objection brought by Dr. Bright against Cyril for beginning without John. Dr. Pusey's account, which Dr. Bright is engaged in contradicting, keeps much closer to the documents and is supported by Hefele's account. See also Garnier's Preface to Marius Mercator.

[1] δι' ἧς, 1332.

[2] It could not overstep the programme laid down at Rome; but Celestine had expressly included the treatment of erring bishops in its work.

might lawfully have degraded John of Antioch; but by way of forbearance they left it to Antioch's natural superior. The Synod goes on to contrast the ludicrous sight of a Synod acting as John of Antioch's did, consisting of men of such character, and being a mere handful. 'What authority could they have against a Synod gathered from all quarters under heaven? For there sat with us also the bishops sent by your Holiness, Arcadius and Projectus, and with them the presbyter Philip; these secured your presence to us and filled the place of the Apostolic See.' They are sure that the Pope will be indignant, considering what harm must come to the Church 'if freedom is given to those who choose to insult even the greater sees and to pass sentences illegally and uncanonically on those over whom they have no jurisdiction.'[1] Clearly it was the presence of the legates that put the Council within its rights in passing sentence on a Bishop of Antioch, and as clearly the Bishop of Rome could do the same himself. The bishops left it to him, not as their deputy, but as occupant of 'the Apostolic See.'

They conclude with praising Cyril as the mainstay of the faith, and with speaking of their action with regard to the Pelagians. They say that 'the things decreed by your Holiness' concerning that set of heretics were in the judgment of the Synod to remain firm. Notice that what Capreolus spoke of as due to the Apostolic See and the agreement of the bishops, the Synod here speaks of

---

[1] Mansi, iv. 1336, 'the greater sees'—the plural being used possibly because a general law is laid down, not because Ephesus was included. The definite article would probably have been omitted in that case. At the same time, just then Ephesus, as has been remarked above, may have regarded herself as a 'greater see.'

as decreed by Celestine simply ; and it must be remembered that to judge that decrees should remain firm was the formula used of their adhesion to the decrees of Nicæa.

Note.

Dr. Bright has a characteristic criticism on the passage concerning the 'greater sees,' as it appeared in the first edition of this work. He says :
'And here is an illustration of Mr. Rivington's "ways." (1) He makes the Council give as its reason for this reservation that " the matter concerned one of the ' greater thrones ' " . . . (2) He glosses the assertion of a right to depose John as if it depended on the presence of Roman legates ; and (3) he omits the reason actually assigned for not doing so—"that by forbearance we might overcome his temerity"' (*Roman See*, p. 168). The numeration is my own.

As to (1) : it is untrue that I ' made the Council *give as its reason*, &c.' The words were ' They left the severer sentence,' not ' They said that they left.' When their words were quoted it was made plain in that same paragraph. I have enlarged the passage in this edition, so that, at any rate, there may be no mistake about its meaning.

As to (2) : the 'gloss,' in the passage alluded to, is the actual explanation given by the Synod itself, only Dr. Bright, as so often in his book, just gives a turn by omitting the definite article, which makes a difference. It was the presence of the legates as a matter of fact which gave the Synod the right to deal with John of Antioch. They would have had that right, if assembled for the purpose of dealing with it, without the presence of Papal legates. But in this case they put forward the presence of the legates in contrasting their authority with that of John. Cf. *supra*, p. 101.

As to (3) : they imply that they would not have exercised this forbearance had it not been that Antioch had a natural superior at Rome. It was because Antioch was one of the greater sees, and therefore naturally under Rome directly, that they decided to overcome evil by good—*i.e.* exercise forbearance where he had been so precipitate—by letting the severer sentence rest with Rome.

CHAPTER X

TWO DECREES OF THE COUNCIL

1. *The Nicene Creed.*   2. *The Independence of Cyprus.*

THE Council concluded its sessions with two decisions of unequal importance; both of them, however, have figured in recent controversy.

I. In the sixth session, the fathers decided that no Symbol or Creed was to be composed or promulged or proffered to any who sought admission to the Church, save only the Creed of Nicæa.[1] Ever since the Council of Constantinople, and indeed before it, various 'Symbols' or Creeds had been drawn up and used, some in agreement with the Nicene, others not. An instance of the latter was now produced before the Synod by a certain Charisius, who had been cajoled into signing a Symbol which is generally referred to Theodore of Mopsuestia and was much in vogue among the sympathisers with Nestorius. The Council accordingly did what the Nicene Council itself could not well do, nor the Constantinopolitan; it strictly forbade any other *Creed* but that of Nicæa from being used. That was the ὅρος in the sense of a Symbol which was to suffice, at any rate for the

---

[1] Mansi, iv. 1361. The old Latin edition of the Acts published by Mansi in his fifth volume (p. 559) should be consulted. The Acts of his session have been mutilated.

present. In this way the Third Council of the Church strengthened the material rule of faith; the Apostolic deposit was embodied and expanded in the Nicene Creed, and the fathers had met, as Cyril said in his statement to the Synod, for the purpose of strengthening the definition of the Apostolic faith and investigating the heresy of Nestorius.[1] They effected this by insisting on the Nicene Creed as the one Symbol to be offered to heretics before their reconciliation with the Church, or to Pagans on seeking admission into the Fold. The term Θεοτόκος (Mother of God) was not inserted in that Symbol; although several words were added which indicated the agreement of the fathers at Ephesus with those at Constantinople in 381.

Two difficulties arise. How could they consistently endorse the use of the Constantinopolitan form of the Nicene Symbol, since this contained additions to the original Creed? and how had they safeguarded the Nicene Creed against the misinterpretations of Nestorius?

The answer to the first question was debated centuries afterwards—not, indeed, for the first time, but most fully—at the Council of Florence in 1438. The Bishop of Ephesus at that Council inveighed against any even verbal alteration in the Nicene Creed, on the ground that the Œcumenical Council of 431 had strictly prohibited such change. The Archbishop of Rhodes in his answer pointed out that an addition was one thing—implying, as it did, something added from without—and development or explication from within was another. An explanation was not, he argued, an addition. And so the Constantinopolitan Symbol, being but an explication of

[1] Mansi, iv. 1305.

what was already in the Nicene Creed, made the two—that of 325 and that of 381—but one. The Bishop of Ephesus had himself already excused the elongation of the Nicene into the Constantinopolitan on the ground that they were but one. So that the principle underlying the injunction of the Ephesine fathers in 431 is contained in the original meaning of the word they used, ἑτέρα πίστις, lit. a *different* Creed. The Constantinopolitan form of the Symbol was not that. But in order to preserve the Creed intact, they forbade in reality, as the context shows, any *other* Creed, which is frequently the meaning of ἑτέρα in Byzantine Greek. This particular form of prohibition was, in its nature, temporary. They could not bind a future Council. They could not prohibit the use of the Athanasian Symbol, when it should come on to the scene, nor—to leap some centuries forward—the Creed of Pope Pius IV., which contains the Nicene Creed. But they did strengthen the Apostolic faith by corroborating, for the first time in full Œcumenical Synod, the Creed of Nicæa in its Constantinopolitan form, making it the only Creed for use in the reconciliation of heretics.

But if this canon, or decision, of the Council of Ephesus consisted in simply prohibiting the use of any other Creed but that of Nicæa, how could they be said to have safeguarded that Creed? For if merely signing the Nicene Creed were sufficient, was not Nestorius prepared to do that? If the mere reaffirmation of that Creed were sufficient, what heretic would have been condemned in the fifth century?

St. Cyril himself touched upon this difficulty in his letter to Nestorius. 'It will not suffice for your Holiness merely to confess with us' [*i.e.* merely to reaffirm] 'the

Symbol of the faith once put forth by the Holy Spirit by the holy and great Synod once assembled at Nicæa. For even if you acknowledge the words with your lips, you have not understood it rightly.'[1] Cyril then went on to say that Nestorius must further withdraw his own writings and sayings and teach what the rest of the Church teaches—as contained in his (Cyril's) writings, which, he says, had been sanctioned by the Roman Synod and by all the bishops at Alexandria. 'For this' (*i.e.* the interpretation of the Nicene Creed given in those writings) 'is the faith of the Catholic and Apostolic Church, with which all the orthodox bishops, West and East, agree.' It is clear that Cyril understood by 'the right definition of the Apostolic faith' the Nicene Creed as interpreted by Celestine's decree and by the already consentient witness of East and West. This, in the fullest sense, was the definition (ὅρος) which from Cyril's point of view, the Council assembled to strengthen. This decree of Celestine's, involving a particular interpretation of the Nicene Creed, which he sent to Nestorius and to the people and clergy of Constantinople, is called in the Acts of the Council the ὅρος [2]; it was a decree concerning the faith, as Cyril had impressed on John of Antioch. It was 'not about matters of little moment, but on behalf of the faith itself and of the Churches which are everywhere disturbed;' such are his words.[3] Nestorius, said Celestine, was to teach what the Roman and Alexandrian Churches and the whole Catholic Church and the Church of Constantinople in past times taught as to the faith of Nicæa. This, therefore, was the ὅρος or decree of the Apostolic See, which related to an individual archbishop on a matter of faith. And if we

[1] Mansi, iv. 1071.   [2] *Ibid.* 1048.   [3] *Ibid.* 1052.

ask further what exactly the definition of the faith was, the answer is that it was that interpretation of the Nicene Creed which was given in the Roman Synod of 430, when Pope Celestine insisted on the Hypostatic union as enshrined in the term Θεοτόκος (Mother of God).[1]

And so the Bishop of Ephesus at the Council of Florence, in its fifth session, points out how careful the Ephesine fathers of 431 were not to violate their own rule of not adding to the Nicene Creed; seeing that while they 'then sanctioned the word Θεοτόκος (Mother of God) in opposition to the delirious dreams of Nestorius,' they did not insert it in the Creed, 'although the term was most necessary in the dogmas'—*i.e.* to be included in the dogmas—'of our salvation.'[2]

Thus there was a definition of the faith on a particular point given by Celestine at the Roman Synod; it was involved in the decree concerning Nestorius; it was accepted by the Synod; it explained the Nicene Creed; that Creed was now understood to contain it, and the Synod decreed that no other Creed should be proposed to heretics or Pagans. But always in the case of heretics, the abjuration of their particular heresy was required, and this, in the case of those tainted with Nestorianism, included an acknowledgment of the single Personality in the two Natures of our Incarnate Lord.

Every Synod had its ὅρος, its definition of some kind; so that the Sixth Council renewed expressly (to use its own words) the 'definitions' (ὅροι) of the five preceding Synods.

There was another reason why Celestine's definition of the faith would not naturally lead to the insertion of

[1] Cf. *supra*, p. 7.   [2] Mansi, xxxi. 538.

its crucial term in the Nicene Creed. It was there already in a peculiar sense, in the very terms of the Creed. The Creed said that the 'Son' was 'born of the Virgin Mary.' Now the Consubstantiality of the Son to, or with, the Father had already been defined: it followed that Mary was the Mother of God.

But that this truth was defined at Ephesus was the constant tradition of the Church. Photius thus describes the Council. He says that the fathers 'dogmatised,' *i.e.* taught dogmatically, that 'our Lord Jesus Christ is worshipped and proclaimed, in accordance with the tradition of the Fathers, in one and the selfsame Person,' and that they 'delivered or handed down that accordingly His immaculate and ever-virgin Mother is rightly and truly called also the Mother of God.'[2] This is the short description of the Council's work by one who has been called 'the most learned man that ever sat on that throne'[3] (Constantinople). And elsewhere Photius has preserved a fragment by one of the most orthodox successors of Cyril in the See of Alexandria, St. Eulogius, the friend of our Gregory the Great. Eulogius says that certain heretics had arraigned the Council of Chalcedon for 'having put forth a definition of the faith' (ὅρον ἐκθεμένην) contrary, as they asserted, to the injunction of the Council of Ephesus. They apparently misunderstood the difference between a definition and a Creed.[4] Eulogius accordingly answers that the Council of Ephesus could not have meant what these heretics supposed, for it had done the same thing itself. 'Decreeing this very thing, it defines what no other Synod defined before'; and

---

[1] Lupus Christianus, *Synod. Decr.* Pars I. p. 815 (Bruxellis, 1673).
[2] Mansi, iv. 457.   [3] Puller's *Primitive Saints*, &c., p. 153.
[4] Lupus, p. 963.

'the Hypostatic union is its definition, which had not been defined by the older Synods.'[1]

Where is this definition? The Council itself drew up no definition; but it accepted Celestine's definition enshrined in his decree concerning Nestorius. (Mansi, iv. 548-552.) This decree the bishops had professedly executed, and in doing so had given a Conciliar, as distinguished from a Papal, definition: in other words, Celestine defined, *i.e.* definitively settled, the truth as to the Hypostatic union contained in the term 'Mother of God,' and the Council made the definition its own.[2]

II. Three Cyprian bishops also brought before the Synod their grievance about the assumption of jurisdiction over them on the part of the Bishops of Antioch.

---

[1] ὁρίζει αὐτὸ τοῦτο τυποῦσα & μηδετέρα τῶν πρὸ αὐτῆς διωρίσατο .... ἀλλὰ καὶ ἡ καθ' ὑπόστασιν ἕνωσις αὐτῆς ἐστιν ὅρος, ὃ ταῖς πρεσβυτέραις τῶν συνόδων οὐ διώρισται. *Photii Biblioth.*, cod. ccxxx.

[2] It will be seen from this how very wide of the mark Dr. Bright is when he writes that 'Celestine's "direction" was not a definition of the faith; and a little more acquaintance with ancient dogmatic phraseology would have saved Mr. Rivington from this blunder' (*Roman See*, p. 167). There is here, first, a wrong translation of τύπος, which is 'decree,' not 'direction'; and secondly, the idea which he goes on to express that the office of the Council was merely that of 'synodically reaffirming' the Nicene Creed, shows how little he has based his interpretation on the history of the Council as a whole: and, thirdly, we see such a writer as Photius and such a person as Eulogius (not to speak of others innumerable) differ from Dr. Bright as to the meaning of 'ancient dogmatic phraseology.' And to come to more modern times, is anyone more entitled to speak on 'ancient dogmatic phraseology' than Mansi? Yet Mansi again and again speaks of Celestine's 'definition of the faith.' See his *Animadversiones in Natalis Alex. H. E.* ix. 473, 477, and 558. But in truth the matter is settled by Philip's words to the Council, when he says 'Celestine ὥρισεν.' The 'blunder' of which Dr. Bright speaks and the 'ignorance of ancient dogmatic phraseology' which Dr. Bright imputes to me must be assigned to another quarter.

It had been held on the one hand that Cyprus, which belonged to the civil province of which Antioch was the centre, was included by the sixth canon of Nicæa in the ecclesiastical province of the Bishops of Antioch, but that during the Eustathian schism at Antioch this order had been disturbed by the Arians. On the termination of the schism, Pope Innocent I. wrote to Alexander of Antioch, and on the strength of his assertion decided that the Cyprians ought to return to their obedience in accordance with the Nicene canons. The Cyprians, however, maintained that they had not originally been under Antioch, and that therefore their subjection to that see was not contemplated by the Nicene canon. Great violence, moreover, had been used by the Antiochene party to induce the Cyprian bishops to surrender their independence.

The Synod accordingly decreed that if the facts were as the Cyprian bishops stated, and the facts appeared to be established as such, the Cyprians were right to resist the pressure of Antioch; and they decreed, what indeed, except as bearing on the particular case, hardly needed decreeing, that if anyone seized a province and subjected it by force to itself, he should be bound to restore it to its independence, and the provinces were to remain with their territories undisturbed, in accordance with ancient custom.[1] The decree doubtless had reference to the attempt which Juvenal made in this Synod to encroach on the province of Antioch, as well as to the violent occupation of the Cyprian province by the Bishop of Antioch. There was at that moment in the East, and had been for many years, a lust of power and attempts to extend their jurisdiction on the part of the more im-

[1] Mansi, iv. 1469.

portant sees, and the Council, accordingly, very properly spoke of the danger of worldly pride in these ambitious projects.

But Dr. Bright and other Anglican writers see in this provision and this expression an allusion to Rome—on the ground that the actual expression used by the Ephesine fathers—' the arrogance of authority '—closely resembles an expression used some years before by the Africans in deprecating the presence of legates, viz. ' the smoke of worldly pride '; and that this close resemblance, not identity, of expression, ' seems to demand some explanation.'[1] The explanation of the use of the words ' arrogance of authority ' is not far to seek when we consider the history of Juvenal of Jerusalem on the one hand, and of the Antiochene party on the other. And since no one, with the actual historical situation before him could suppose that the Council were thinking of anything going on in the West at that moment, Dr. Bright has recourse to the fact that ' Eastern bishops ninety years before had shown some jealousy of Roman self-assertion ' and therefore it is not ' incredible ' that they ' should have thought the words opportune in case of its recurrence '! Such an interpretation of historical documents only needs to be stated: its statement is its refutation.

As regards the encroachment on provinces not belonging to an exarch, it would be difficult to bring in the claim to universal jurisdiction made by ' the Apostolic See.' The two things are not on the same plane. And as regards universal jurisdiction, we have seen that the Ephesine fathers admitted this in the Apostolic See; and consequently their canon must be interpreted in

[1] *Roman See*, pp. 169, 170.

accordance with their belief. And in view of various precarious applications of this decree, it must be remembered that these bishops at Ephesus could not fix the territorial limits of provinces for ever and aye. They were providing for the East and for things as they were.

Once more, Dr. Bright asks ' How, on Vatican principles, could a General Council, even provisionally, reverse the alleged "decision" of a Pope?'[1] The answer is that a decision which avowedly rested on the assertion of one party to a suit,[2] as this did, and which said (as the Pope's decree did) 'we persuade them,' could be ' provisionally reversed,' on fresh evidence being produced, without any violence done to ' Vatican principles.' Infallibility does not come into the question; for that has to do with *ex cathedra* pronouncements, and there was no pronouncement of that kind in Innocent's decision. No dogmatic fact was concerned; no matter of faith. It was a matter of discipline. Neither was there disobedience in regard to the supreme jurisdiction of the Apostolic See: for the whole question was one of facts. If it was proved that the claim of Antioch was not involved in the Nicene canon, because Cyprus had not been in her jurisdiction before the Nicene Council met, the very ground on which Innocent avowedly went would sanction Cyprus being recognised as independent of Antioch.

[1] *Roman See*, p. 169.
[2] 'Cyprios sane *asseris*' are Innocent's words (*Ep.* xviii. c. 2).

CONCLUSION

THE story, interesting as it is, of the Imperial assent to the condemnation of Nestorius, and of the eventual reconciliation of Cyril and John of Antioch, does not belong to my subject. This only may be noticed, viz. that no amount of Imperial displeasure constitutes an argument against the binding nature of the laws of the Church on those who believe in her divine constitution; and that the Bishop of Antioch too clearly showed the original cause of his quarrel with Cyril for any serious weight to be attached to his objections to the Anathematisms drawn up at Alexandria.[1] Further, the Church owes to St. Cyril an inexpressible debt of gratitude for his firmness and zeal in the defence of what he clearly saw, and all now see, to have really involved the whole question of the world's redemption. If the child ' of two or three months old ' that lay in Mary's lap was not literally Almighty God, the world was not saved by Jesus Christ.[2]

---

[1] It is true that he fixed on one expression of Cyril's ($\mathring{\epsilon}\nu\omega\sigma\iota\varsigma\ \phi\upsilon\sigma\iota\kappa\acute{\eta}$) and on Cyril's use of $\phi\acute{\upsilon}\sigma\iota\varsigma$, which could be misunderstood, but it is clear that but for a certain perversity, which led him into his schismatic action at Ephesus, he would not have misinterpreted Cyril.

[2] Dr. Bright (*Waymarks*, p. 172) carries his depreciation of Cyril to such a pitch that he even allows the idea that Cyril had to do with the subsequent hardships of Nestorius, not merely to cross his mind, but to inspire the following sentence. Speaking of the severities dealt out to

The Church also had in Celestine, the Bishop of Rome, one of whom she is justly proud, who saw, equally with Cyril, what was involved in the contest, and omitted no pains to support the great Bishop of Alexandria. Before his death Celestine wrote one of his most touching letters to the bishops of the Synod,[1] after their dispersion to their homes, full, as all his letters are, of beautiful applications of Holy Scripture, and displaying the firmness of a ruler and tenderness of a father. He strikes the note of joy in the opening sentence; he then congratulates them on having faithfully carried this affair into execution 'with us'; he applies to himself the words of the Psalmist (Psal. xxiv.), 'The innocent and the upright have adhered to me,' showing that he conceived of the Synod as the Synod conceived of itself, as the executor of his own sentence. He praises their choice of a successor to Nestorius, and congratulates them on the emperor's assent. He then tells them that they must not stop here: they must induce the Emperor to rescind his decree about Nestorius being allowed to go to Antioch. He must be removed further. 'Solitude alone becomes such men.'

'We,' says the Pope, 'are further off than you are, but by solicitude we see the whole matter closer. The care of the blessed Apostle Peter has the effect of making all present; we cannot excuse ourselves before God concerning what we know. . . . We ought to have

Nestorius by the governor of the Thebaid, Dr. Bright says: 'We may hope that he was not seeking to gratify the primate of Egypt.' Then why suggest such an idea, for which there is not an iota of evidence? Dr. Bright also in quoting Garnier on Cyril's character (*ibid.* p. 145) omits the words 'animus erat excelsus erectusque,' giving no intimation that Garnier had said this in praise of Cyril.

[1] *Ep. Cel. ad Syn.* March 15, A.D. 432.

care for all in general, but it behoves us specially to assist the Antiochenes, who are besieged by pestiferous disease.'

Such is the care which he evinces for them, in accordance with the title accorded to him by the Synod, viz. ' our most holy Father,' and with his own conception of his relationship to the Prince of the Apostles. He then decides what shall be done with respect to those who seemed to think with Nestorius. Although the Synod had passed sentence on them, ' still we also decide what seems best. Many things have to be looked into in such cases, which the Apostolic See has always regarded.' He accordingly orders that they shall be dealt with in the same way as the ' Cœlestians,' and desires that the same method of treatment shall be observed in regard to those who have imagined that ecclesiastical cases could be removed to Christian princes. He then instructs them how John of Antioch should be dealt with in case of his correcting himself.

The letter, considering all the circumstances, is a very remarkable one. It is that of a God-fearing man providing as father for the wants of his children. There is not a trace of any consciousness that he is doing anything but fulfilling the duties of an office recognised by all; and that office is clearly in his judgment the government of the universal Church entrusted to him as the successor of Peter. On the same day he wrote to the Emperor congratulating him on his better mind, and giving him some exquisite exhortations as to the performance of his high functions. He also wrote to the clergy and people of Constantinople, praising Cyril and drawing attention to Nestorius's sleepless energy. But Rome (he adds) is not behindhand in watchfulness.

'The blessed Apostle Peter did not desert them when they were toiling so heavily, for, when the separation of such an ulcer [as Nestorius] from the ecclesiastical body seemed advisable by reason of the putrid decay which became sensible to all, we offered soothing fomentation together with the steel. It was not by the swiftness of our sentence that he became to us as a publican and heathen man. We could not delay longer lest we should seem to run with the thief, and to take our portion with the adulterer against faith.' Celestine here treats his own sentence and its execution by the Council as one.

It is difficult, after all we have seen, to understand how Dr. Salmon could say that 'the only one of the great controversies in which the Pope really did his part in teaching Christians what to believe was the Eutychian controversy.'[1]

Sixtus succeeded Celestine, and took up the work in the same spirit. In the following year he wrote to Cyril, praising him for his magnificent conduct and directing what was to be done about the followers of John of Antioch, and eventually wrote a most beautiful letter to John himself after the reconciliation between him and Cyril, in which he did not spare the bishop for his past conduct, although he acquitted him of any heretical teaching. He summed up the whole matter, saying, 'You have learned by experience what it is to *think with us.*'[2]

From all that has gone before, we may deduce the following conclusions as to Church principles in A.D. 431.

1. The Bishop of Rome held the Primacy in the Church as the successor of Peter, *i.e.* by Divine institution.

---

[1] *Infallibility of the Church*, p. 426, 2nd edition. [2] Mansi, v. 379.

2. This Primacy of the Bishop of Rome involved:
   - (*a*) the right to depose a Bishop of Constantinople;
   - (β) the right to determine with authority whether or no the said bishop had contradicted the common faith of the Church.

3. The bishops of an Œcumenical Council exercised a real right of judgment, but in subordination to the defining power of the Bishop of Rome.

4. There were certain 'greater sees' in the Church over which only an Œcumenical Council (which included the Bishop of Rome), or the Bishop of Rome himself, had jurisdiction.

5. The denial that Mary was the Mother of God constitutes an offence against the faith of the Church.

6. The meaning of this term Θεοτόκος (Mother of God) is that there is but one Person, although two distinct Natures, in our Lord Jesus Christ.

7. It is not enough for Christians to agree to a formula which they interpret in a different way. It is not enough to recite the Nicene Creed; but it is necessary for a teacher in the Church to abjure the heresies which wrongly interpret that Creed. In her guardianship of the faith the Church eschewed the principle of comprehension in regard to matters on which she had spoken.

8. The Church is a living body that can speak, and propose with authority fresh definitions to guard the old truths.

9. The Church is one in the sense that she is under one form of government, and her several parts are visibly united. Visible union is not for her a matter of hope and aim, but a necessity of her life.

PART II
THE LATROCINIUM or 'ROBBER-SYNOD'

Chapter I. The heretical Archimandrite, p. 121
  ,,   II. Papal Intervention, p. 133
  ,,   III. The Acquittal of Eutyches, p. 150
  ,,   IV. The Deposition of Flavian, p. 161
  ,,   V. Flavian's Appeal to Rome, p. 167
  ,,   VI. Leo proposes, Theodosius refuses, a Council, p. 181

PART II

CHAPTER I

THE HERETICAL ARCHIMANDRITE

THE throne of Peter was now occupied by one of those majestic figures which occasionally dominate a whole period. His name was Leo: and well did he merit his name, and rightly has posterity called him 'Great.' The Council of Chalcedon called him the 'wonderful' Leo, and again spoke of his zeal as equal to that of the Apostle Peter. The Oriental bishops in their letter to Pope Symmachus speak of Leo as 'among the Saints'; Facundus, of his 'weight' and 'constancy'; Saint Maximus, the Greek theologian, of his strong-heartedness and great sanctity; Nicolas I., of his having saved the Christian faith; Photius, of his sanctity, great renown, and zeal in piety and religion; and the Greek Menology, of his virtue, wisdom, and sanctity, and of his having left conspicuous monuments of his virtue, but especially of his witness to the true faith.

The sum and substance of Christianity was again at stake; the true Glory of its Founder was again in question under another form, and Leo the Great was the instrument chosen by the Divine Founder of the

Christian Church to vindicate the truth of His Incarnation.

But it was as occupying the throne of Peter that St. Leo achieved the triumph of Chalcedon. More than once had he quoted the words of Christ, 'I have prayed for thee, that thy faith fail not,' as the source of his confidence, and the words 'confirm thy brethren' as the rule of his conduct.[1] And in that confidence he acted throughout his troubled reign, as he guided Patriarchs, Bishops, Emperor and Empress, through the maze of heretical subtleties. He said nothing different from what others had said before him as to the prerogatives of his see; but the circumstances under which he had to act developed a fuller apprehension of the truth that St. Peter was the appointed 'confirmer of the brethren' in the matter of faith. It was in the counsels of Divine Providence that the whole force of the 'Petrine Privilege' should be felt on a large scale and under the pressure of unparalleled needs, so that the Church might realise more fully where her strength lay and never

---

[1] St. Leo taught that Peter was placed over all the Apostles: 'De toto mundo unus Petrus eligitur, qui et universarum gentium vocationi et omnibus Apostolis cunctisque Ecclesiæ patribus præponatur, ut . . . omnes proprie regat Petrus, quos principaliter regit et Christus.' And quoting the words in St. Luke, he says 'pro fide Petri proprie supplicatur, tanquam aliorum status certior sit futurus, si mens Principis victa non fuerit. In Petro ergo omnium fortitudo munitur, et divinæ gratiæ ita ordinatur auxilium, ut firmitas, quæ per Christum Petro tribuitur, per Petrum apostolis conferatur.' St. Leo also taught that the prerogative of Peter descended to his See: 'si quid etiam nostris temporibus recte per nos agitur, recteque disponitur, illius operibus, illius sit gubernaculis deputandum cui dictum est: *et tu conversus confirma fratres tuos*' (*Sermo* iv.). The references to the writings of St. Leo are to his Sermons and Letters in the Ballerinis' edition, *Leonis Magni Opp.* vol. i. Venice, 1753.

suffer her locks to be shorn. But throughout his emphatic exercise of his prerogative as the guardian of the Nicene Faith and of the Nicene canons, not a note of surprise, as at any novel claim, was heard. Heretics or politicians might endeavour to evade the force of that prerogative or to use it in their own behalf, but as to the prerogative itself no challenge was ever made. For, as had been said at the Council of Ephesus without challenge, ' It is doubtful to none and has been known to all ages, that the blessed Apostle Peter, the head and prince of the Apostles, received from the Saviour of the human race the keys of the kingdom, and that he lives and exercises rule in his successors.'

But to proceed to the actual history. The utterances of a ' foolish old man,' as St. Leo called him, erring more from stupidity than the subtlety that misled Nestorius, were the occasion of the storm that now burst with terrific suddenness over the Church—a foolish old man, who boasted that he had kept his vow of continency in the monastic life, and who had all that peculiar influence which is invariably exercised for good or evil by men of recognised austerity. Such was the Constantinopolitan Archimandrite, Eutyches.

To understand the situation it will be necessary to revert briefly to the events immediately following the victory of Cyril over Nestorius. John of Antioch, who had played such a bad part in the Council of Ephesus, after two years of resistance accepted the decrees of that Council through the joint persuasion, or pressure, of the Emperor and the Pope. And having once done so, he became an influence for good throughout the East. About five years after his submission and reconciliation, he wrote to Proclus, the Archbishop of Constantinople, saying that the whole East was quiet and that they were enjoying a breathing-time from the unforeseen evils which the world had experienced through 'the accursed Nestorius.'[1]

But many elements of mischief were at work. The partisans of Nestorius, of Diodorus, and of Theodore of Mopsuestia, were numerous and excited. Monks and clerics might be heard in the streets of Alexandria and Constantinople wrangling over the rightness or wrongness of Nestorius's condemnation and Cyril's Anathematisms. But so long as John of Antioch, Cyril, and Proclus lived, these elements of disturbance were kept in check. Each, however, of these sees changed hands within the decade. First, Cyril was succeeded at Alexandria, in A.D. 444, by his nephew and archdeacon, Dioscorus, a man of ungovernable ambition and violent temper, and accused by some of his clergy of an altogether immoral life. He has been called 'the Attila of the Eastern Church.'[2] Next, John of Antioch had been succeeded two years before by his nephew Domnus, a man of weak character, whose career proved to be nothing less than a tragedy. He had experienced a call to the solitary life. Fired, however, with the idea of recalling his uncle from his Nestorian sympathies, he had left his cell, contrary to the advice of the Abbot Euthymius, who predicted the misfortunes that actually befel him. At Antioch he now won his way to the episcopal throne as successor of Saint Peter in the

---

[1] Mansi, v. 974.

[2] For Dioscorus's character *cf.* Theophanes, *Chronogr. ad annum* 439, and Nicephorus, *H. E.* xiv. 47; Liberatus, *Brev.* c. 10. Theodoret (*Ep.* 60) gives him a good character before his elevation. He appears to have fearfully deteriorated.

third See of Christendom. A deadly animosity sprang up between him and Dioscorus. He had allowed Proclus of Constantinople to take precedence of him at a Synod, and had thus seemed to countenance the provision of the third canon of 381, a mortal offence in the eyes of Dioscorus.[1] The latter had also interfered in the diocese of Antioch, and had requested Domnus to publish a letter of his, which Domnus refused to do, grounding his action on the second canon of 381.

But thirdly, in A.D. 447 the see of Constantinople itself became vacant. To the disappointment of the Archimandrite, Eutyches, who was connected by birth and friendship with the Emperor's favourite chamberlain, Chrysaphius, and who is said by Theophanes and Nicephorus to have looked forward to the post of archbishop, Flavian was appointed to the see. And, moreover, according to Evagrius, Flavian on his appointment sent Chrysaphius some sacred vessels instead of the gold coin for which the covetous chamberlain looked on such occasions.[2] And again, Flavian was a friend of Domnus. Dioscorus omitted to send the usual letters to Flavian on his appointment.[3]

It will be seen from all this that it would require but a spark to produce any amount of dissension between the three sees of Alexandria, Antioch, and Constantinople,

---

[1] Cf. Theodoret, *Ep.* 86. This letter is now recognised as written by Domnus, not by Theodoret. The Syriac version differs slightly; probably it was a Synodal letter, and consequently varied slightly according to the bishop to whom in each case it was sent. Cf. *Actes du Brigandage d'Ephèse*, par M. l'Abbé Martin, Amiens, 1874, pp. 139–143.

[2] Evagrius, *H. E.* ii. β.

[3] We learn this from the recently discovered letter of Flavian to Leo. *Cf.* p. 173.

and that there is no need, as there is no justification in the record, for bringing in the West to explain the troubles that now arose.[1]

Further, we are told by the historian Facundus that Domnus of Antioch was the first to denounce Eutyches to Theodosius.[2]

To complete the picture, we must remember that Dioscorus about the same time picked a quarrel with Theodoret, the historian, and Bishop of Cyrrhos, and the *quondam* critic of Cyril's Anathematisms. Dioscorus looked upon himself as the hereditary champion of the great Bishop of Alexandria, his uncle and predecessor, Cyril, and he wrote to Domnus complaining of Theodoret, whose see was in the 'Diocese' (Patriarchate) of Antioch, on account of certain reports as to Nestorian tendencies having appeared in Theodoret's teaching while on a visit to Antioch. Theodoret defended himself, but in vain so far as Dioscorus was concerned. About the same time[3] Domnus took a step calculated still further to inflame the minds of those who were making anti-Nestorianism their one cry. There was one prominent figure among the lay attendants at the Council of Ephesus, the Count Irenæus, who had been commissioned by the Emperor to look after the bishops assembled at the Council in temporal matters. Being strongly attached to Nestorius, he had proved a terrible scourge to the orthodox bishops. He had made their

[1] It will be seen from the whole narrative that Harnack's endeavour to account for the turn that the events took by attributing political motives to Leo, is simply without foundation in the record—indeed, is contradicted by it.

[2] *Pro Trium Defensione Capitulorum*, Lib. viii. cap. 5.

[3] The chronology is difficult to settle. I have followed the Abbé Martin, *Le Pseudo-Synode*, Paris, 1875.

stay in Ephesus almost intolerable, and had afterwards induced the Court party to pronounce against Cyril. This Imperial officer had now professed to be converted to the orthodox side and sought the priesthood; and Domnus had consecrated him Bishop of Tyre.[1] The Monophysites, not believing in Irenæus's conversion, resented the appointment, and the Emperor Theodosius, whose ear they had gained, when he renewed his edicts against the Nestorians, deposed Irenæus, on the ground that he was a bigamist.

I have used the word Monophysite [2] by way of anticipation. The champions of Cyril as against Nestorius had unfortunately taken as their watchword Cyril's declaration that there is but 'one incarnate $\phi\acute{v}\sigma\iota\varsigma$' in our Divine Lord, by which he meant 'one Person.' But the word $\phi\acute{v}\sigma\iota\varsigma$ meant literally 'nature,' and the opponents of Nestorianism (which denied the single Personality in our Incarnate Lord), now losing their balance, spoke of there being not merely one Person, but 'one Nature' in His Incarnate Being, due to a certain mixture or confusion of the Divine and human natures.

The Emperor, having deposed Irenæus, proceeded a step further and confined Theodoret to his diocese. Thus the situation was critical. Domnus was left without his chief adviser, except so far as Theodoret could support him by his letters. He was moreover induced to cancel the appointment of Irenæus to the bishopric of Tyre and to consecrate Photius in his stead. The Monophysites were thus carrying all before them.

At this juncture (A.D. 448) a Synod was assembled at Constantinople under its archbishop, Flavian, to decide a

[1] Mansi, v. 939.
[2] *I.e.* maintaining 'one nature,' after the Incarnation.

difference between the metropolitan of Sardis and two of his suffragans. At this Synod, to the astonishment of many, Flavian himself included, Eusebius of Dorylæum stepped forward and accused his *quondam* friend, the great Archimandrite Eutyches, of heresy.[1] Cicero's burst in the opening of his oration against Catiline in the Roman Senate, 'How long, I pray thee, O Catiline, will you abuse our patience?' did not more take the assembly by surprise than this sudden accusation on the part of Eusebius, who had been the great opponent of Nestorius.[2] He accused Eutyches of teaching and disseminating a heresy opposed to that of Nestorius, but a heresy none the less. He accused him of teaching contrary to Cyril's second letter to Nestorius, which, as was afterwards explained, taught the co-existence of two Natures in our Incarnate Lord's single divine Personality. He accused him of renewing the heresy of Apollinarius, who made the human nature of our Lord an unreality. After being summoned and refusing to attend the Synod, Eutyches made his appearance, and after much fencing threw off all disguise (as Flavian explained in his letter to Leo), and said that 'we ought not to confess that our Lord subsisted in two Natures after becoming man,' and that 'the Body of our Lord, although born of the Virgin, who is consubstantial with us, is not itself consubstantial with us.' In this, says St. Flavian, 'Eutyches ran counter to all the expositions of the holy Fathers.'[3] Eutyches eventually withdrew the latter statement, but clung to the former. He was degraded from his ecclesiastical rank and deprived of the superintendence[4]

[1] Mansi, vi. 652.   [2] *Ibid.* 653.   [3] *Leon. Ep.* 22.
[4] τοῦ προιστάναι, Mansi, vi. 748 and 820. In the restoration of

of his monastery. But the Synod did not go on to expressly anathematise his teaching.

Eutyches afterwards maintained that he had made a formal appeal at this Synod; but he was not consistent in his statements as to the authority to which he professed to have appealed. It is agreed on all hands that he told a falsehood in saying that he made any formal appeal *at the Synod itself*. The patrician Florentius deposed at a subsequent Synod, in 449, that Eutyches said to him in a soft low voice [1] just as the Synod of 448 broke up, that he appealed to the separate Synods of Rome, Egypt, and Jerusalem. The monk Constantine said (falsely) that Eutyches had appealed to the holy Synods of the Bishop of Rome and Alexandria, and Jerusalem and Thessalonica, while the sentence was being read.

His reasons for mentioning these particular bishops are obvious. The Bishop of Rome could not be passed over, and Eutyches had lately written to Leo about what he considered a recrudescence of Nestorianism, and had received a gracious answer. He hoped to deceive Leo now, and Anastasius of Thessalonica as Papal Vicar in Eastern Illyricum might be expected to follow suit. The Bishop of Jerusalem, as the event only too fully proved, was not likely to side with the opponents of Eutyches, viz. the Bishops of Antioch and Constantinople. Eutyches carefully omitted the name of the Bishop of Antioch. His pretended appeal, therefore, was to the synodical decisions of these selected prelates. At the Latrocinium he spoke of having appealed to the Synod

---

Eutyches, his position is called ἡγεμονία and ἀρχή indifferently, the two words being used as synonyms; cp. 836 and 861.

[1] πράως, Mansi, vi. 817.

itself, but he presently explained this by saying that it was to certain archbishops. Flavian, he said, 'ought to have written before all things to the archbishops to whom he [Eutyches] appealed.' It has been erroneously imagined that Eutyches professed to have appealed in terms to a General Council.[1] But he never once uses the expression, and it is certain that he did not mean to have Domnus, of Antioch, for one of his judges, without whom (if intentionally omitted) a Council could not be General in the full sense of the term.

He probably wrote letters to every quarter whence help might come. His letters, however, with one exception, are not extant, and we can surmise nothing as to their contents, except, of course, that he asked them to look into his case and to condemn Flavian's decision.[2] But what is certain is that Eutyches wrote to Rome sending the Pope, together with Eusebius's accusation and some testimonies (mostly supposititious) to himself, two documents: one a profession of faith, and the other a notice of appeal to Rome which he pretended to have handed in at the Synod of Constantinople, a notice

[1] Dr. Bright imagines this. But he has probably been misled by the wrong reading in the Latin version of the Council under Dioscorus, included in the Acts of Chalcedon. It runs thus: 'Cum magis oportuerit ante omnibus pontificibus scribere, quos et appellaveram,' 'when he [Flavian] ought first to have written to all the Pontiffs to whom also I had appealed.' But the true reading is 'when he [Flavian] ought rather, before all things, to have written to the archbishops to whom also I appealed :' ὀφείλων πρὸ πάντων τοῖς ἀρχιερεῦσιν ἐπιστεῖλαι κ. τ. λ. Mansi, vi. 641.

[2] Liberatus (*Brev.* cap. 12) says that Eutyches wrote to Dioscorus in this sense, which might be taken as a matter of course. Dr. Bright (*Roman See*, p. 262) refers to Mansi, vi. 820. But there is not a word in that passage about his having written to Dioscorus. He only professes there to defer to the Bishops of Rome and Alexandria as fathers.

which contained a promise, alleged to have been made to the Synod, *to follow the Papal decision in every way.* He asked St. Leo that he might suffer no prejudice pending the appeal, and begged for a decision on the matter of faith. It is absurd to suppose that he wrote to anyone else in the same way.[1]

But his statement in his letter to Leo, that he had appealed to him in the Synod at Constantinople, implies that the bishops in the East held that such an appeal if formally made during a Synod must have the effect of suspending their sentence. This was the point of the statement, viz. to stay the proceedings at Constantinople. He knew that the Pope had only to suppose that an appeal had been lodged at the Synod and he would be able to enforce a suspension of the sentence.[2]

---

[1] 'Omnibus modis me secuturum quæ probassetis' (*Leon. Ep.* 21, c. i.). Dr. Bright (*Roman See*, p. 173) thus pretends to summarise what I said in the first edition of *The Primitive Church and the See of Peter*: 'We know nothing, he [Dr. Rivington] argues, of any letter from Eutyches, except the one to Leo; therefore, we may practically treat the application to Leo as standing alone.' Instead of this, I had said that Eutyches 'probably wrote letters to every quarter whence help might come' (1st ed. p 366). And I mentioned some in particular. Consequently there is no suggestion that the 'application' to Leo 'stood alone,' in the sense that no other applications were made to anyone. But I suggested that the character of Eutyches's letter to Leo was unique; and that much is certain. A person in his senses could not write to more than one archbishop as he did to Leo, promising to obey his judgment. Dr. Bright proceeds: 'This is a short and easy method, indeed; but it happens that Eutyches, in 449, charged Flavian with ignoring his appeal to a General Council.' Now Dr. Bright himself says 'We may take it as certain that he [Eutyches] made no formal appeal whatever during the Council.' How, then, can what Eutyches said, and *falsely* said, a year afterwards affect what he *did* in 448? How could his falsehood in 449 affect the question of his 'application to Leo' standing alone, in the sense of being unique, in 448?

[2] Cf. Ballerini, *Leon. Opp.* T. ii. 'De Causa Eutychis.'

I have said that Eutyches made application in other quarters, though necessarily of a different character, since he could not have promised to obey others as he did promise Leo. His object was clearly to enlist anyone that he could in his favour, and accordingly he wrote to a bishop known to have special influence with the Emperor Valentinian, viz. St. Peter Chrysologus, Bishop of Ravenna. This saintly archbishop, however, replied that he could not intervene in such a matter[1] without the leave of the Bishop of Rome. He appears not to have learnt from Eutyches anything about the Synod of Constantinople, and he knew nothing about the dogmatic epistle of Leo.[2] He accordingly advises Eutyches what to do. Eutyches had obviously said nothing about a General Council, but simply asked St. Peter Chrysologus for his judgment on the matter of faith. We are indebted to an important discovery of an old copy (dating between A.D. 453 and 455, and therefore strictly contemporary) of St. Peter's letter in Greek, for the whole text of the saint's words. He advises Eutyches to 'attend obediently to whatever is written from the most blessed Pope of the city of Rome, because blessed Peter, who both lives and presides in his own see, gives to those who seek it the truth of the faith.'[3]

---

[1] πίστεως αἰτίας, cases concerning faith (*Leonis Ep.* 25).

[2] *S. Leonis Magni Opp.* Tom. I. ed. Ballerini. *Admonitio in Ep.* 25, § 6.

[3] *Ibid. Ep.* 25.

CHAPTER II

PAPAL INTERVENTION

ARCHBISHOP FLAVIAN also had written to St. Leo immediately after Eutyches's condemnation at Constantinople, sending him the Acts of the Synod. He notified, indeed, the condemnation of Eutyches to other bishops, but he sent the *Acts of the Synod* to Leo, a measure which implied a formal appeal to a superior court. His letter, however, did not arrive in due time, whether owing, as is supposed, to the management of Eutyches and his friends, it is impossible to say. Accordingly St. Leo, on receiving Eutyches's letter, wrote at once to the Emperor and Flavian. The letters are both of them of the highest importance as showing what the Pope could assume as admitted by the Emperor of the East and the Archbishop of Constantinople, as to the right of a Bishop of Rome to pass judgment on a matter of faith.

The origin of his writing to the Emperor was this. Eutyches had set to work through his friend and relative Chrysaphius, the Emperor's favourite chamberlain, to gain the help of the Imperial power for the reversal of of his condemnation. Pulcheria had, according to Nicephorus, been removed from the Court and had retired temporarily to a convent. By this means the one influence over Theodosius in behalf of orthodoxy was out of the way, and the weak Emperor fell under the complete sway of Chrysaphius, or, which was the same thing, of Eutyches himself. His Majesty accordingly wrote to Rome on behalf of Eutyches.[1]

Leo, however, tells the Emperor that he needs to hear from Archbishop Flavian before he gives judgment.[2] He blames Flavian to the Emperor for not having sent the Acts of the Synod to Rome as he ought to have been the first to do.[3] The Pope was not aware that Flavian had, as a matter of fact, at once despatched the Acts, but that from some mishap they had been delayed. If the Emperor and Eutyches and Chrysaphius were acting in concert to get judgment from Rome before the cause was properly heard, they were much deceived in their estimate of Leo. For the latter simply told the Emperor that he was displeased that Flavian had not written, and that he had written to him to say so and felt sure that after this 'admonition' Flavian would send a report of all the proceedings, ' so that judgment may be passed in accordance with evangelical and Apostolical teaching.'[4] To Flavian the Pope wrote in terms of censure for not having done his duty, since he had already heard from the Emperor, and also from Eutyches, and the latter had said that he 'had given in a notice of appeal at the time of the judgment itself.' The failure, therefore, with which Leo reproached Flavian was not merely that he had not written quickly on an important matter, but that he had not respected Eutyches's appeal to Rome. He therefore desires Flavian to send an account of the

---

[1] *Leonis Ep.* 24 (Ball.).
[2] 'Ut possit congrue de bene cognitis judicari.'
[3] 'Cum studere debuerit primitus nobis cuncta reserare.'
[4] *Ep.* 24.

proceedings and to hold everything over until he [Leo] has cognisance of the matter.¹

It is impossible not to see in these letters plain evidence of the recognised position of the See of Rome as the court of appeal from distant sees in the East. It was not Valentinian, but Theodosius, to whom St. Leo thus wrote, and it was of no less a personage than the Archbishop of Constantinople that he thus complained. He refuses to listen to the application of the Emperor, but requires the formalities of a judicial procedure to be complied with, so that 'judgment may be passed in accordance with the evangelical and Apostolical teaching.'² No mere patriarch would thus write to an Emperor concerning a matter beyond the limits of his own patriarchate.

This was in February A.D. 449. The next step on the part of Eutyches was in imitation of Nestorius. He made for a General Council, without waiting for a reply from Leo, whose judgment he had solemnly promised to obey. His friend and relative, Chrysaphius, turned at once to Alexandria, and enlisted the ambition of Dioscorus in the strife, promising him all his own influence at Court (which was immense) in furtherance of Dioscorus's well-known aims at supremacy in the East, if only he would espouse the cause of Eutyches as against Flavian. Dioscorus seized his opportunity, and at once wrote to the Emperor suggesting a General

---

¹ *Ep.* 23: 'usque ad nostram notitiam cuncta deferri.' Dr. Bright's account of this letter is inadequate. He says that Leo 'naturally thought that Flavian "ought to have written" to him as soon as Eutyches did' (*Roman See*, p. 173). But why 'naturally'? Leo says, because of the supposed appeal—the point which Dr. Bright ignores.

² *Ep.* 24: 'ut in lucem ductis his quæ adhuc videntur occulta, id quod evangelicæ et apostolicæ doctrinæ convenit, judicetur.'

Council. In this suggestion there was not as yet formal opposition to the idea of a Papal judgment, since it is not likely that Chrysaphius or Eutyches told Dioscorus of the appeal to Rome. Neither could the Emperor have received the Pope's reply, or have divined its contents. Not that, as events proved, Theodosius, Eutyches, or Dioscorus, to say nothing of Chrysaphius, would be in the least troubled with scruples about the Church's order or the common rules of justice. They appear to have now tried the experiment of a second Council at Constantinople itself, in which the trustworthiness of the documents containing the official account of Eutyches's condemnation was impugned; and when this failed they addressed themselves to the actual working of the Œcumenical Council.[1]

But before entering upon this subject, we must consider the correspondence which now ensued between Rome and Constantinople. Archbishop Flavian, when he wrote his second letter to Leo in answer to the censure passed on him for not sending the report of the Council of 448, had not heard of the Emperor's *definite* decision to summon a General Council, but rumours of it were in the air.[2] His letter is of great interest in more ways than one. The whole tone is that of deference to a superior authority. He in no way resented St. Leo's censure of his silence. As a matter of fact, he had written and sent the Acts of his Synod, but they had miscarried, or been delayed on the way. The archbishop recognised the duty which lay upon him to report proceedings to Rome. He describes the whole situation, narrates the deposition of Eutyches, and says that the latter has appealed to the Emperor, thereby

[1] Liberatus, cap. 12. [2] ἡ θρυλουμένη γίνεσθαι σύνοδος, *Leon. Ep.* 26.

trampling under foot the canons of the Church. Further, Flavian tells Leo that what Eutyches had asserted, unknown to him, in his letter to the Pope, viz. that at 'the time of judgment,' *i.e.* at the Synod, he gave notice of appeal to Rome, is untrue. He implies that, had it been true, he would have suspended proceedings. Flavian does not afford in this important letter the slightest indication that in his judgment St. Leo was stretching his prerogative in writing to him as he had done. On the contrary, he ends by invoking that prerogative as the only means of securing the peace of the Church. He asks the Pope to be bold with the boldness that becomes the priesthood, to 'make the common cause his own,' and to 'deign to give his decision by means of a brief in accordance with the canonical deposition of Eutyches at the Constantinopolitan Synod.'[1]

[1] συμψηφίσασθαι καταξίωσον. Dr. Bright thinks this means 'be so good as to give assent,' and implies no deference. He notices that συμψηφίσασθαι is literally 'vote with' (*R. See*, p. 174). But elsewhere he translates ψῆφος 'sentence' (pp. 163, 166) when it is used of the bishops in the Council of Ephesus. This is its general meaning in Conciliar language, the character of the sentence depending on the position of the person who pronounces it. Here the context settles that it is a superior sentence. In an old Latin copy of the letter the word is translated 'simul decernere' (*Leon. Opp.* Ball. i. 791). καταξίωσον is simply 'deign,' not (as Dr. B.) 'be so good as.' It is often an expression of deference. Out of seventeen letters written by Leo to the Emperor Marcian, its Latin equivalent (*dignare*) occurs in thirteen, always by way of deference to his Imperial Majesty. It is used three times of the Emperor Theodosius and twice to the Empresses. In Leo's letter to the Emperor Theodosius (*Ep.* 43), of which we have the Greek and Latin, Leo says ἀποσοβῆσαι καταξίωσον, *avertere dignare*. Once the Latin word is used of Almighty God (*juvare dignetur*, *Ep.* 37), and once of Divine Providence (*Ep.* 29). For the Greek word see Liddell and Scott's Lexicon (ed. 8). Flavian writes throughout in the most deferential mood. Eusebius uses καταξιῶσαι of Archbishop Flavian, clearly as speaking to a superior (Mansi, vi. 656). But what must be considered to settle the question against Dr.

He asks the Pope also to 'confirm' the faith of the emperor (using, not the usual word, but that which occurs in our Lord's command to St. Peter in St. Luke xxii.[1]); and he says that 'the matter only needs your impulse and help, which is bound by virtue of your own consent, to bring everything into peace and calm; and so the heresy which has arisen, and the trouble that has ensued, will be brought to a happy conclusion, with the help of God, through your holy letter; and moreover the Synod, about which there are rumours, will be prevented from taking place, and so the Churches in every quarter will not be troubled.'[2]

Flavian, therefore, profoundly distrusted the value of the rumoured Synod, as anybody would who grasped the situation; he looked to the timely exercise of the Papal prerogative as alone sufficient to secure the peace of the Church.

And in expressing this conviction he bears witness to the fact that an equal reverence was attributed to the authority of the Apostolic See by the rest of the orthodox bishops in the East.[3] Otherwise there would be no point in his remark, and no ground for his hope.

The principle, therefore, of Church government which the Archbishop of Constantinople assumed as

Bright is that the Count Elpidius said in the Latrocinium to the bishops: καταξιώσατε, συμψηφιζομένου ὑμῖν τοῦ Θεοῦ, περὶ τῆς πίστεως ἀποφήνασθαι. Elpidius was speaking to the bishops as superiors in matters of faith; and Almighty God is spoken of as σύμψηφος. This disposes of a number of objections raised by Dr. Bright on account of the word σύμψηφος being applied to Leo (Mansi, vi. 621).

[1] στηρίξαι. Dr. Bright explains this as meaning 'to tell on the mind of Theodosius'!

[2] *Leon. Ep.* 26.

[3] Cf. 'Obs. Baller. de Diss. Quaesn. de Eutych. Appell.' *Leonis Opera*, ii. 1128.

Catholic was this—he did not consider that matters should necessarily be concluded where they began. There was, as yet, no thought of the independence of national Churches, nor of each province finally settling its own matters. His connection with Rome was intimate and obligatory; and it is clear that it did not depend on the civil position of that city. He wrote to Leo as to him to whom it belonged to 'vindicate the common affairs of the Churches;' he prayed him to issue a brief which might settle the disturbances of the Eastern Churches, and he alluded to the passage in St. Luke xxii., 'Confirm the brethren.' St. Leo had requested him, not merely to notify the deposition of Eutyches, as he would do to other Churches, but to send him the Acts—precisely what is done for the revision of a sentence by a superior court. And Flavian fully recognised his obligation to enable St. Leo to do his duty, which St. Leo had said was impossible without a full report of the proceedings.[1] He states distinctly that not only was there no need of the judgment of any other Eastern patriarch, but that not even a General Council was needed; and Flavian knew well what the other Eastern bishops thought.[2] This was in March A.D. 449.

[1] *Ep.* 23.
[2] Mansi, v. 1356. *Adnot. Baller.* Dr. Bright thinks that as regards a Council, 'if Theodosius had recognised Leo's See as the supreme court of appeal, he would not have entertained and acted on this scheme in spite of Leo's objections.' He ought to have added 'and in spite of the Archbishop of Constantinople's objections.' These two were better judges of the matter than an Emperor under the sway of a eunuch (Chrysaphius), *plus* a heretic (Eutyches), *plus* the 'Attila of the Eastern Church' (Dioscorus). But, in fact, Dr. Bright's misconception of 'Roman' teaching on the relation of a Council to the Pope underlies his objection. Theodosius did not contemplate a Council apart from the See of Peter; but he hoped that a conciliar expression of opinion would

But in May Leo had received Flavian's report, and he at once took in the whole position. The 'lion' was roused, and from that day onwards his activity, his decision, his wisdom, his piety, his tender charity and his indomitable courage were such as to mark him out as one of the most extraordinary characters that have filled the pages of history, even were we to forget the effect of his noble presence on Attila leader of the Huns, outside the walls of Rome, or his influence over Genseric within the city. He had already given the death-blow to the remnants of Priscillianism; he had baffled the clandestine movements of the Manicheans, and he had sent Pelagianism to its grave. But here was an enemy that threatened to shake the foundations of the Christian religion by a direct assault on the person of its Founder. All that activity, and ingenuity, and worldly prestige, all that the favour of princes and the friendship of the great could do, was enlisted in its favour. But St. Leo was more than a match for these. He was so in virtue of the divine promises to Peter, for we shall see that it was as the successor of St. Peter, *and through the Church's recognition* of the authority of the Apostolic See, that Leo eventually triumphed. Had he been compelled to vindicate the authority of St. Peter's See—that is to say, if men had been able to resist him on the ground that our Lord did not include the successors of St. Peter in His commission to that Apostle—the posi-

---

influence the Papal judgment. Leo would hardly have ventured to speak of the Emperor's wish to have the faith defined by St. Peter, and to say this in a public letter to the Synod, if he had had no foundation for the statement. Theodosius, though under bad influence, had his better moments.

tion would have been an impossible one. But the faith of the Church had been declared in the most explicit terms at the Council of Ephesus. East and West had there agreed in the position that ' it had been known *to all ages, and was doubted by none*, that the blessed Apostle Peter, Prince and Head of the Apostles, received the keys of the Kingdom from the Saviour of the world,' and that Peter ' lives and exercises judgment in his successors.' Such were the undisputed terms in which the Papal legates at Ephesus had expressed the general teaching of the Church, which by common consent had been placed in the archives of that Œcumenical Council, as containing nothing strange to the ears of the assembled bishops of the East, nay, as spoken ' suitably ' *i.e.* in accordance with the canons ($ἀκολούθως$).

It was, then, as the successor of the Prince of the Apostles that St. Leo now acted, and that he claimed to act ; and no voice in the East was raised to deny this truth, save, indirectly, one, and that was the voice of the man who became the patron of Eutyches, and who was extruded from the Church at her Œcumenical Council at Chalcedon.

The ides of June had come, and Leo, having been already engaged on his longer epistle to Flavian, saw the necessity of taking more stringent measures to meet the difficulties in which Flavian was placed. He decided upon sending representatives to Constantinople to inquire into the whole matter, and instead of sending his letter by Flavian's messenger, he sent it by these messengers, together with letters addressed to Theodosius, to Pulcheria, to the Archimandrites of Constantinople, to the Synod, of which he had now received notice, and in which he acquiesced,[1] and to Julian, Bishop of Cos, of whom more hereafter.

The 'Tome of St. Leo,'[2] as the epistle now sent to Flavian is called, stands almost alone, after Holy Scripture, in the reverence with which it was regarded for ages by the entire Church. Its reception was equalled only by the position assigned in the primitive Church to the letter of St. Clement, the third successor of St. Peter, written to the Corinthians in the first century. It was frequently read in the East after a General Council in professions of faith. St. Gregory the Great says: 'If anyone ever presumes to say anything against the faith of these four Synods, and against the Tome and definition of Pope Leo, of holy memory, let him be anathema.'[3] The Sixth Œcumenical Council calls it 'divinely written,' and says that 'by it they [the fathers] made void the understanding between Eutyches and Dioscorus.'

It opens at once with judging Eutyches, and then proceeds to that magnificent exposition of the 'sacrament of our faith,' which on its first perusal in youth has impressed so many much as the first sight of the sea.

It is, however, with the ending of St. Leo's Tome that the purpose of this book is concerned. The Archbishop Flavian (be it remembered), to whom the Tome is addressed, had come before Leo as the judge of first instance, having synodically condemned an Archimandrite of his own archdiocese. He brought him before Leo in

---

[1] This was clearly the case, in spite of the apparent contradiction given at the Robber-Synod, which will be explained hereafter.

[2] *Leon. Opp.* Baller., *Ep.* 28. A 'Tome' was a doctrinal formulary. The word itself means a part of a book done up (rolled up) by itself—a volume.

[3] Lib. vi. *Ep.* 2.

his letter as already condemned in the Constantinopolitan Synod, to be condemned more solemnly and by a final peremptory judgment passed by the Apostolic See.[1] For he did not merely notify the deposition of Eutyches, but asked for help, and asserted that peace could only be obtained by Leo's approval of the Synod of Constantinople (whose Acts he sent) and by his issuing a brief to that effect. Accordingly at the end of his Tome St. Leo gave his judgment.

Without referring the matter to a Council of the whole West, he reviews the synodical Acts, and in part confirms, in part disapproves, of the judgment of the Constantinopolitan Synod. He confirms the condemnation of Eutyches; but he reprehends the acts of the Synod as inadequately conducted. He blames the bishops for not having proscribed under anathema the heretical saying of Eutyches, 'I confess that our Lord consisted *of two natures* before the union, but I confess only one nature *after* the union.' And then he directs that Eutyches should be received back again if he repents, and gives the exact method of such reception. The matter, therefore, needed to be done more exactly and canonically than in the Synod of Constantinople. Eutyches, he says, might have thought that he had spoken some of these words 'rightly,' or that they were such as could be tolerated ('tolerabiliter'), so far as any expression of the Synod to the contrary was concerned. 'In order, however,' the Pope concludes, 'to bring this whole matter to the desired end, we have sent, in our stead, our brethren the Bishop Julius and the priest Renatus, with my son, the deacon Hilarus, with whom we have associated the notary Dulcitius, whose faith has been approved by us,

[1] συμψηφίσασθαι καταξίωσον.

trusting that the help of God will be with us, that he who had erred may abjure his false opinion and be saved. God keep thee safe, dearest brother.'

Such was the exercise of Papal jurisdiction contained in this letter, one of the most celebrated documents of Christian antiquity. It contains an exercise of authority such as only belongs to the judge of a supreme court. None of the other Patriarchs are taken into account; St. Leo speaks in full authority, and that he was not usurping an authority which was disallowed by others is certain from the fact that the Council of Chalcedon and the whole Catholic Church accepted the Tome as a solemn judgment and sentence within the competency of the Pope's authority.

Thus, not only did Eutyches pretend that he had appealed to the Pope, when it suited his purpose, on the understanding that his appeal would be sure to suspend the sentence of the Eastern bishops against him; not only did the Archbishop of Constantinople send the synodical Acts to be reviewed by the Pope as judge in the matter; not only did Leo act as judge and decide the case so far as could be done at a distance, and send legates to do the rest in his stead—but, as we shall presently see, an Œcumenical Synod, and the universal Church for ever after, accepted as an authoritative exposition of the Nicene faith the Tome which contained this exercise of authority, against which not a protest, not a murmur, not a whisper was ever raised.[1] But how could this be unless the position of judge which he assumed therein was in accordance with Apostolic doctrine?

Together with his 'Tome' or Epistle to Flavian, Leo

[1] Cf. 'Observ. Baller. de Eutych. Appell.' *Leonis Opp.* ii. 1130.

sent a letter to the Emperor Theodosius, which is of importance as showing the grounds on which he acquiesced in the convocation of a General Council. He says that Eutyches has been proved to have erred—there is no question, according to St. Leo, about that; but since the Emperor has settled upon a Council at Ephesus 'that the truth may be made known to the unskilful old man,' he, the Pope, sends legates to supply his place. 'The legates,' says St. Leo, 'are commissioned to carry with them a disposition to justice and benignity, so that, since *there can be no question as to what is the integrity of the Christian confession,* the depravity of error may be condemned.' If Eutyches repents—which the kind heart of the Pope always contemplates—the benevolence of the priesthood ('bishops' in the Greek version) is to come to his aid. Eutyches, says St. Leo, had promised him, in his original petition, that he would correct whatever the Pope condemned.[1]

The idea of the Council, then, was that it was a fitting machinery to impress on Eutyches the importance of obeying the Papal decision, and to deal with him properly if he asked pardon. It was in this that the Constantinopolitan Synod had come short of perfect justice and charity.

But St. Leo continues with the following descriptions of the position occupied by the decisions contained in his Tome or letter to Flavian. He says to the Emperor: 'But what things the Catholic Church universally believes and teaches concerning the sacrament of the Lord's Incarnation are more fully contained in the writings which I have sent to my brother and fellow-bishop Flavian.

[1] *Ep.* 29.

At the same time the Pope wrote to the Emperor's saintly sister, who had brought him up in his tender years under all the best influences of the Christian faith. It was not her fault if her Imperial brother now sided with heretics; and it was to be her lot to assist the saintly Pope in the Church's struggle with the new heresy. To her—the Empress Pulcheria—St. Leo described the error of Eutyches as 'contrary to our only hope and that of our fathers,' and told her that, if he persists in his error, he cannot be absolved. 'For,' he adds, the 'Apostolic'[1] See both acts with severity in the case of the obdurate, and wishes to pardon those who suffer themselves to be corrected.' It is obvious to remark that he considers the absolution of Eutyches to rest with the Apostolic See. He hopes that Pulcheria will do her best to help on the Catholic faith, and says that he has delegated his authority to those whom he has sent, that pardon may be bestowed if the error is done away.

It is here, as elsewhere, the Apostolic See that is assumed to be the agent in the matter, and the Council is to be concerned, not with settling what is the true faith, but with moving Eutyches to repentance by the display of unanimity among the bishops.

Still more important, if possible, are the terms of the letter which he sent to the Archimandrites of Constantinople.[2] They are his 'beloved children.' He is sending to them persons 'a latere' to assist them in 'the defence of the truth,' not for the investigation of the faith. He sets his seal to their condemnation of Eutyches. If he

---

[1] Literally, 'The moderation of the Apostolic See observes this discipline that it both' &c. *Ep.* 30.
[2] *Ep.* 32.

repents and makes full satisfaction—which is the constantly recurring thought in Leo's mind—then 'we wish him to obtain mercy.' But 'as to the sacrament of the great love of God (*pietatis magnæ*) in which we have justification and redemption by the Incarnation of the Word of God, our teaching from the tradition of the Fathers [1] is sufficiently explained in letters to Flavian, so that you may know from your chief (*per insinuationem Præsulis vestri*) what in accordance with the Gospel of our Lord Jesus Christ *we wish to be established in the hearts of all the faithful.*'

Still more definite are the words of the Pope to the Synod itself, which was to meet in August. He gives as the ground of its being convoked the Emperor's wish to add the authority of the Apostolic See to his edict,[2] as though his Majesty desired 'that the meaning of the answer given by the *Prince of the Apostles* to our Lord's question should *be declared by the most blessed Peter himself*,' *i.e.* through his own see. The object of the Council is further defined to be that 'all error may be done away with by a fuller judgment' ('pleniori judicio') —exactly the idea of a Council which has been given above.[3] The Council was as it were the fuller and more

[1] 'Nostra ex Patrum traditione sententia.'
[2] *Ep.* 33. 'Ad sanctæ dispositionis effectum'—'dispositio' being a term in use for Imperial edicts.
[3] P. 39. So Mansi says: 'Non ergo concilii judicium plenius appellavit, quia a superiore potestate dimanare indicaret, sed quia in majori numero ibi judices assident.' Mansi, *Animadv. in Natal Alex. H. E.* vol. ix. Diss. xii. Harnack says: 'The Council is merely an *opus superadditum* "ut pleniori judicio omnis possit error aboleri."' Thus the condemnation of Eutyches is already decided upon, and the Council merely repeats it. The Pope enjoins this.' *Hist. of Dogma* (Tr.), iv. 203. The 'mere repetition,' however, is of immense value to anyone who believes in the supernatural character of the Church, and is exactly what is calculated

emphatic utterance of the Papal judgment. Its action was to consist in adhering to the judgment of the Apostolic See—in as it were prolonging its utterance, and applying it materially and visibly to the person in hand. It was not a higher judgment, not the confirmation of a superior authority, but the sentence of the Pope swelling out and completed by its synodical proclamation, as the sufferings of Christ were completed by those of His followers. His legates were to preside over its actual utterance; they were to determine with the holy assembly of the episcopal brotherhood by a common sentence 'what things will be pleasing to the Lord.'[1] The Pope then goes on to give a sketch of what Eutyches should do, and repeats what he had already said to Flavian, viz. that Eutyches in the document ('libellus') which he had originally transmitted had promised to obey the Holy See. He also speaks of his Tome as having been written to abolish error and unite the world in one and the same confession of faith.[2]

One other letter he wrote on the same day to Julian, Bishop of Cos, in the course of which he says he has sent letters to Flavian 'from which both your beloved self *and the whole Church* may know about the ancient and only faith, what we hold and preach as of divine tradition.'

No sooner had the messengers set out with this batch of letters than Flavian's original letter (written immediately after the Constantinopolitan Synod) arrived, containing another copy of the Acts of the Synod which

to impress those who do not. Bishops do not always repeat what they do not believe. *Cf.* p. 42.

[1] *Ep.* 33. *Communi vobiscum sententia*: not, as Dr. Bright is fond of translating *communis*, 'by a sentence in which all the agreeing parties are *equal*,' for St. Leo taught that the common sentence of the Apostolic See and the bishops was that of the head and members.

he had spontaneously sent to Rome, and which had been mysteriously delayed. Leo at once wrote to him briefly, saying that the Synod was not really needed. And he took the opportunity of writing once more to the Emperor, excusing himself from attendance at the Synod on three grounds: first, because there was no precedent for a Pope attending such a Council in person; secondly, if there were, temporal necessities at home were in the way (the barbarians were wellnigh at the door); and thirdly, because the case was so clear that there was no real need ('rationabilius abstinendum'). Still, he says, he sends legates.

CHAPTER III

THE 'ROBBER-SYNOD' OR *LATROCINIUM* [1]

1. *The Acquittal of Eutyches*

ON August 8, A.D. 449, the ill-fated Council met at Ephesus. Its salient feature may be described in the

---

[1] Besides the ordinary sources of information on the 'Robber-Synod,' such as Prosper, Liberatus, Facundus, &c., the following should be consulted: (1) Martin, '*Actes du Brigandage d'Ephèse*, Tr. faite sur le texte Syriaque contenu dans le MS. 14530 du Musée Britannique par M. l'Abbé Martin,' Amiens, 1874. This Syriac text was published by Perry, and is to be seen in the Oriental room at the British Museum. (2) *Le Pseudo-Synode*, Paris, 1875, by the same author. (3) *Récits de Dioscore*, originally in Greek and translated into Coptic—one of the treasures of the Jacobite Church of Alexandria, read liturgically every year in our Lady's Sanctuary. It will be found in the *Revue Egyptologique*, 1880, p. 188. Not much in the way of fact is to be gleaned from this, but it helps to realise the tone of Dioscorus. (4) The appeal of Flavian and of Eusebius in the *Spicilegium Casinense*, vol. i. (5) Evagrius's account of the whole Eutychian controversy, which is graphic and gives the Oriental (Antiochene) point of view, and is useful for comparison of the Greek terms with the Acts in Mansi. (6) Christianus Lupus, *Synodorum Decreta et Canones*, vol. i.: Appendix ad Ephesinum Latrocinium (Brussels, 1673). The value of Lupus's account, to which I am indebted in the following pages, consists in the way he seizes salient points. His references are scanty, but, after verifying his quotations, I have found them uniformly correct. (7) Nothing will make up for a careful study, if somewhat toilsome, of the narrative in Mansi, vi. 587-927. The account of the Latrocinium is included in the account of the first session of Chalcedon, and in that again is included the account of the Councils of 448 and 449

words used by Tillemont of the immediate result, 'Dioscore règne partout.' It had been the dream of this unhappy man to lower Constantinople and to undo the mischievous canon of 381, which placed Alexandria below the 'upstart' Imperial See. So far Dioscorus was within his rights. But his political ambition connected itself with a question of the faith, in which, although not originally heterodox, he took the wrong side. As the hereditary champion of the memory of Cyril, his great predecessor at Alexandria, he saw Nestorianism everywhere, and his theology lost its balance. But the support of what he took for orthodoxy was clearly secondary to the attainment of a certain ecclesiastico-political supremacy, which was thwarted by the third canon of Constantinople in 381. Against this Synod his bitterness knew no bounds. These two features of the situation must be borne in mind throughout, if we would not miss the meaning of much which now took place at Ephesus. Whatever should be proclaimed orthodox must be shown to be in accord with Cyril's teaching, and the action of the fathers at Constantinople in 381 must be in every possible way depreciated.[1]

The Council presented every possible feature of irregularity. Its composition was open to the charge

at Constantinople, under Flavian and Thalassius. I have thought it well to quote these authorities here, because Harnack, without any scholarly treatment of the subject, has minimised the atrocities of the *Latrocinium*, even likening it to the Œcumenical Councils (*Hist. of Dogma*, Eutychian Controversy, vol. iv. Eng. Tr.).

[1] A layman of his diocese, Sophronius, deposed at the Council of Chalcedon that Dioscorus 'considered himself above everyone else and would not allow the Imperial decrees ($\tau \acute{\upsilon} \pi o \upsilon s$) nor the highest judicial sentences ($\mathring{\alpha} \pi o \phi \acute{\alpha} \sigma \epsilon \iota s$) to be carried out, saying that the country [Egypt] belonged to himself rather than to the rulers.' Mansi, vi. 1032.

of 'packing.' Its first session was due to a sudden summons to meet at dawn without consulting the bishops in common.[1] Dioscorus took precedence of the Papal legates, who, under protest, retired from the circle of bishops and remained standing aloof. He seems to have justified his position on the ground that the Emperor had ordered it, and that legates were not the same as the person whom they represented. This at least is a fair deduction from the words of the legate Hilary.[2] The Papal letter to the Synod was handed to Dioscorus to read, and he took it together with the letter to Flavian, (the Tome) as Tillemont suggests,[3] and the notary, in collusion with him, immediately spoke of another Imperial letter. Juvenal of Jerusalem, who played the grand Patriarch throughout and sat above Domnus of Antioch, proposed that the Emperor's letter be read at once. The Papal letter was simply suppressed. The Emperor, in his letter, lauded Barsumas to the skies, and this miserable monk, the accuser of Domnus, and the inciter of violence later on, was allowed, contrary to the rules of the Church, to take his seat as a constituent member of the Synod.

The Emperor had ordered that all those who had taken part in the condemnation of Eutyches should now be under trial. The Imperial letter was summarised by the prejudiced notary in his digest of the Acts thus: 'Concerning Flavian of holy memory as introducing certain disturbances[4] in regard to the faith against

---

[1] This is a detail we owe to the recently discovered letter of Flavian to Leo.   [2] Mansi, vi. 613.
[3] Dioscorus was condemned at Chalcedon for not reading the Tome. See *infra*, and Evagrius, *H. E.* ii. 4.
[4] ἀνακινοῦντός τινα. This was the word used in his final condemnation. Mansi, vi, 621.

Eutyches.' This was the keynote of the Acts, viz. unsettlement or innovation, and it was really aimed at the Council of Constantinople of 381, which in its third canon placed Constantinople above Alexandria, and which, as we have seen, enacted certain additions in regard to the Apollinarian heresy—a heresy akin to the error of Eutyches.[1]

After Juvenal, Thalassius was the next to speak. He had been appointed President, together with Dioscorus and Juvenal, by desire of Eutyches and Chrysaphius. He was a neophyte, a secular official who had been irregularly foisted into the see of Cæsarea Cappadocia, and, it is interesting to note, had a special grudge against Domnus and Flavian by reason of their compact as to the third canon of 381, Domnus having allowed precedence to Flavian's predecessor. He had a natural prejudice against the see of Constantinople, as its occupants, one after the other, were endeavouring to include his own 'Diocese' of Pontus in their jurisdiction. He was consequently a ready instrument in the hands of Eutyches. He carried his antagonism to Constantinople to the extent (as we shall see hereafter) of at least delaying his adhesion to the twenty-eighth canon of Chalcedon. This prelate now proposed, and justly, that the question of faith should take precedence of everything else, and Julian, the Papal legate, who, with his co-legate 'stayed to see the end,' seconded the proposal. But Dioscorus at once objected. His aim was not in the least to discuss the matter of faith, but to get rid of Flavian on the ground of his deference to the Synod of

---

[1] Apollinarius spoke of the body of our Lord as not strictly human, but as fashioned straight from the Substance of Deity. The heresy of Eutyches equally made the body of our Lord unhuman.

381. Throughout the Latrocinium this was the object, however suppressed in terms, which Dioscorus kept in view. He urged that they had met to consider the question as to whether the matters which had arisen (that is, as he meant, Flavian's condemnation of Eutyches) were in accordance with the 'statutes of the Fathers,' or whether they were innovations. 'Do you wish,' he imperiously asked, 'to innovate [1] on the faith of the holy fathers?' [2] Again, 'For the confirmation of the faith I search the statutes of the fathers who met at *Nicæa and at Ephesus*' [3]—deliberately omitting the Council of Constantinople in 381. The whole Synod exclaimed that Dioscorus was 'the guardian of the canons,' 'the guardian of the faith,' most of them quite unintentionally condemning the Creed of Nicæa as expanded by the 150 fathers of Constantinople in 381.

Eutyches was now introduced to the Synod. He opened with a little personal vanity as to his labours for the faith against Nestorius, and handed in a document containing a confession of his faith, which consisted of the Nicene Creed shorn of the Constantinopolitan additions.[4] This was afterwards pointed out in the Council of Chalcedon.[5] He omitted, that is, the words 'of the Holy Ghost and the Virgin Mary,' which had been inserted in view of Apollinarian teaching. In a word, he handed in the original form of the Creed, which was not that in common use in Constantinople, where his monastery was situated. It was the Creed in the form in which Apollinarius himself was willing to accept it. Not that Eutyches was averse to condemning

---

[1] ἀνασκευάσαι, another of the words used in Flavian's final condemnation.
[2] Mansi, vi. 624.   [3] *Ibid.* 625.   [4] *Ibid.* 629.   [5] *Ibid.* 632.

Apollinarius by name, and those who say that the flesh of our Lord Jesus Christ came down from Heaven,'[1] but he had evaded using the Creed as formulated by a Council (viz. that of 381) which had condemned Apollinarius. In this last declaration, however, as to the Body of our Lord not having come from Heaven, he receded from the position he had taken up at the Council of 448 under Flavian.

He added that he accepted the Nicene Faith as confirmed at the Council of Ephesus under Cyril. He had learnt to misinterpret Cyril, and therefore had no difficulty in professing agreement with him and retaining his own heresy. As a matter of fact, the Nicene Creed as contained in his profession of faith was not exactly that which the Council of Ephesus accepted from Charisius at the session at which the decree prohibiting any alteration was enacted. This latter was longer in the portion relating to the Third Person in the Holy Trinity.

His indictment against Flavian was, that he (Eutyches) had been accused before him at a Synod of bishops who happened to be staying in the Imperial city, which was not a Synod for the purpose of dealing with heresy[2]; that the accusation was too vague and ill conceived; that Flavian had been on familiar terms with his accuser, Eusebius, while the case was going on, a fact suggestive of collusion; that Flavian had been prepared to condemn him unheard, trusting to his keeping at home in the silence of his monastery; that whereas (and this was the real point that commended itself to

[1] Mansi, vi. 633.
[2] This was the 'Resident Synod,' as it was called, and in this matter Eutyches had the appearance of Canon Law in his favour.

Dioscorus) he had offered to confess by word of mouth and in writing the Nicene faith as interpreted at Ephesus in 431, Flavian required certain additions to that faith, so that he was really condemned for adhesion to the Council of Ephesus; and that Flavian had not respected his appeal to the Council before which he now appeared, 'whereas he ought before all things to have written to the archbishops to whom he [Eutyches] had appealed.'[1] He wound up with an appeal to the Council to stop the mischief at its root by confirming the Creed as the holy fathers at Nicæa handed it down, which the holy fathers at the second Council (that held at Ephesus) confirmed —thus indirectly setting aside the Constantinopolitan additions.[2] 'These,' said Bishop Diogenes at Chalcedon, 'he passed by as being Apollinarian.'

Flavian now asked that Eusebius of Dorylæum, Eutyches's accuser, might be heard in answer.[3] But the Count Elpidius demurred on the ground that all who had acted as judges in the Council that condemned Eutyches (A.D. 448) were there to be judged and that they could not admit the accuser to have his say over again in this Council—a decision contrary to the most ordinary rules of justice.

It was now proposed that the Acts of the Council of 448, in which Eutyches was condemned, should be read through; but the legate Julius interposed and claimed that the letter of Pope Leo should first be read. This was a difficulty for Dioscorus. It was a serious matter

---

[1] Viz. Leo, Dioscorus, Juvenal, and Anastasius, but not the Archbishop of Antioch.

[2] Mansi, vi. 640-644.

[3] Eusebius, in his letter of appeal to Leo, speaks of Leo's having ordered his attendance at the Council.

to suppress a Papal letter, and also he could hardly recede openly from his express promise that the letter should be read ; and yet to read it would be to overthrow his whole plan. Bishops might be expected to rally round it who could otherwise be cajoled into the belief that in acquitting Eutyches they were only supporting the Ephesine fathers of 431. But Eutyches, probably by arrangement, came to his rescue. He deposed that Flavian had entertained the legates at his archiepiscopal residence, who were thus in collusion with the archbishop, and that therefore no harm ought to accrue to him from what they might say. Ignoring the point at issue, Discorus decided thereupon that the Acts of the Council under Flavian in 448 should first be read and then (though this was never done) the letter of the Bishop of Rome.[1]

When the reader came to Eusebius's accusation of Eutyches in 448, in which he had thought it wise, by way of barring any charge of Nestorian proclivities, to speak of the Nicene Creed as confirmed at Ephesus, the Synod at once burst into exclamations of assent. The bishops were really emphasising the decree of 431 which forbade any additions to the Creed and (though many of them without knowing it) were ignoring the Council of 381 which made the additions. The legate even joined in under a delusion. And when the Acts of the Latrocinium were read at Chalcedon and these Acts of the Council under Flavian were in consequence repeated there, the Synod of Chalcedon burst into the same expressions of assent.[2] We see from this how adroitly Dioscorus laid his plans. He was now contriving to get the Synod of 381 slighted under cover of loyalty to the Council of 431.

[1] Mansi, vi. 649. [2] *Ibid.* 653.

Another difficulty now confronted the patrons of Eutyches. In the Constantinopolitan Council of 448 Cyril's letter on behalf of peace written to John of Antioch and his Synod had been read by order of Flavian. As they were now reading at Ephesus the Acts of the Council of 448, Cyril's letter had to be read also. But nothing could be plainer than Cyril's declaration (in this letter) of two natures in Christ after the Incarnation, which Eutyches denied. Consequently Bishop Eustathius rose and said that Cyril had afterwards expressed himself more exactly and explained more carefully what he meant in letters to certain bishops, in which he had said that there was 'one nature of the Word which was incarnate' and that Cyril had supported this expression from Athanasius.[1] In defending himself afterwards at Chalcedon for saying this of Cyril, Eustathius advanced to the middle and held out the book with the passage from Cyril. 'One nature' meaning 'one Person consubstantial with the Father' was not an unorthodox expression, and Eustathius was right in asserting this, but wrong in denying that our Lord, as Cyril taught, had also two natures, *i.e.* after the Incarnation.

At length in their reading of the Acts of the Council of 448 they came to the words in which Eusebius had summed up his accusation against Eutyches in the question: 'Do you, my lord Archimandrite, acknowledge two natures after the Incarnation, and do you say that Christ is consubstantial with us, or do you not?' Whereupon the bishops at Ephesus cried out: 'Take and burn Eusebius; let him be burnt alive; let him be cut in

---

[1] Mansi, vi. 676. Cyril used the word φύσις (nature) here with the meaning of person. This is quite certain. His reference to St. Athanasius was a mistake.

two; as he divided [into two] so let him be himself divided.'
Dioscorus now put to the Council the question 'Will
you tolerate that expression, that there are two natures
after the Incarnation?' And a cry arose 'Anathema to
him who says so.' But Dioscorus evidently saw that
the cry did not arise from the entire body of bishops,
and accordingly he said that he must have their hands
raised. And again a cry arose: 'If anyone says "two"
[*i.e.* two natures in Christ] let him be anathema.' And
every hand was raised. At Chalcedon the bishops
deposed that only the Egyptians had *said* that there
was but one nature after the Incarnation. The rest
merely held up their hands in terror.[1]

When at last they read the Acts of the second
Council held at Constantinople in this same year by the
Emperor's order for the purpose of examining the Acts of
of the Synod under Flavian, and when Eutyches now
repeated his already refuted accusation that those Acts
had been falsified, Flavian could no longer restrain
himself. He rose and said: 'It is false.' Dioscorus bade
him write down whatever he might have to say.
Flavian protested that he had not been allowed to speak
in his own justification. On this Dioscorus appealed to
two or three individual bishops and then to the whole
Synod to say if he had prohibited Flavian from speaking. Flavian contented himself with saying that his
acts as contained in the second, slightly revised, copy of
the documents, gave him no fear as before God. He
had not, and should not, be of another mind about it.
Dioscorus went on to ask the bishops what each thought
of Eutyches and what each decided concerning him.[2]
They decided, one after another, that Eutyches should

[1] Mansi, vi. 737, 739.   [2] τὶ περὶ αὐτοῦ τυποῖ.

be restored to the priesthood and to the government of his monastery, and one after the other spoke of adhering to the faith of Nicæa as confirmed by the Council of Ephesus. We have only to compare these signatures with those at Chalcedon respecting the Tome of Leo, to see the significance of the signatures at the Latrocinium. The omission of all allusion to the 150 (*i.e.* the fathers at the Constantinopolitan Council of 381) was the measure of Dioscorus's victory. The '150 fathers' disappeared at the Robber-Synod, but reappeared in the signatures at Chalcedon. Dioscorus signed last and said that he 'confirmed the decisions of this holy and Œcumenical Synod.'[1] Thus Eutyches was acquitted.

[1] οἰκουμενικῆς συνόδου ψήφους, Mansi, vi. 861.

CHAPTER IV

THE *LATROCINIUM* OR 'ROBBER-SYNOD' (*continued*)

§ 2. *The Deposition of Flavian*

THEY might have stopped at the acquittal of Eutyches, if the object had been simply to vindicate what they considered the truth. But nothing would satisfy Dioscorus short of seeing the Archbishop of Constantinople at his feet. Accordingly, after receiving a deputation from the great monastery in which Eutyches was Archimandrite, and assuring the memorialists that they were perfectly orthodox since they held the same faith as Eutyches (of whose removal from their headship they had complained), and after reinstating them as a body, Dioscorus had portions from the Œcumenical Council of Ephesus read out to the assembly. While the notary was reading the rule laid down at that Council that no one was to transgress its orders as to new Creeds, by adding to the Nicene, and that if a bishop or cleric did so, he should be deprived of his charge, Onesiphorus, one of the bishops, whispered to his neighbour that this was aimed at Flavian. His neighbour replied that such madness was inconceivable, and that it

[1] Mansi, vi. 829.

could only concern Eusebius of Dorylæum. But it was only too true that Dioscorus was making for the ruin of Flavian.

The long day was now drawing to its close, and the wax candles were lighted for Vespers, when Dioscorus said that he presumed that all were satisfied with the Nicene exposition of the faith as confirmed, and alone recognised as valid, by the sacred Council held in this city in which they now sat, and that anyone who should say anything besides (παρὰ) this or think, or innovate, or seek for anything beyond, became subject to condemnation. Bishop after bishop expressed his assent to this principle. Hilarus, the Papal legate, took the opportunity of proposing that the Papal letter be read, and they would see that 'the Apostolic See' taught the same. But Dioscorus paid no heed to the suggestion. He had now reached the climax of his programme. He first repeated in full the Ephesine condemnation of anyone who put forth any exposition besides that of Nicæa, 'which the Council assembled here confirmed, and decided authoritatively[1] that it alone should be held and delivered in the Church,' 'so that it is not lawful to put forth another Creed besides this or to seek for or introduce anything fresh, or to disturb (or initiate) anything concerning our holy religion,' but those who do so ' have subjected themselves and do subject themselves manifestly to penalties, so that if they are bishops they should be deposed from the episcopate.' He then asserted in the name of the Synod that Flavian, Bishop of Constantinople, and Eusebius, Bishop of Dorylæum, had clearly done this by unsettling and changing almost everything, and so becoming the occasion of scandal and

[1] τυπώσασα, Mansi, vi. 908.

CHAPTER IV

THE *LATROCINIUM* OR 'ROBBER-SYNOD' (*continued*)

§ 2. *The Deposition of Flavian*

THEY might have stopped at the acquittal of Eutyches, if the object had been simply to vindicate what they considered the truth. But nothing would satisfy Dioscorus short of seeing the Archbishop of Constantinople at his feet. Accordingly, after receiving a deputation from the great monastery in which Eutyches was Archimandrite, and assuring the memorialists that they were perfectly orthodox since they held the same faith as Eutyches (of whose removal from their headship they had complained), and after reinstating them as a body, Dioscorus had portions from the Œcumenical Council of Ephesus read out to the assembly. While the notary was reading the rule laid down at that Council that no one was to transgress its orders as to new Creeds, by adding to the Nicene, and that if a bishop or cleric did so, he should be deprived of his charge, Onesiphorus, one of the bishops, whispered to his neighbour that this was aimed at Flavian. His neighbour replied that such madness was inconceivable, and that it

[1] Mansi, vi. 829.

could only concern Eusebius of Dorylæum. But it was only too true that Dioscorus was making for the ruin of Flavian.

The long day was now drawing to its close, and the wax candles were lighted for Vespers, when Dioscorus said that he presumed that all were satisfied with the Nicene exposition of the faith as confirmed, and alone recognised as valid, by the sacred Council held in this city in which they now sat, and that anyone who should say anything besides ($παρὰ$) this or think, or innovate, or seek for anything beyond, became subject to condemnation. Bishop after bishop expressed his assent to this principle. Hilarus, the Papal legate, took the opportunity of proposing that the Papal letter be read, and they would see that 'the Apostolic See' taught the same. But Dioscorus paid no heed to the suggestion. He had now reached the climax of his programme. He first repeated in full the Ephesine condemnation of anyone who put forth any exposition besides that of Nicæa, 'which the Council assembled here confirmed, and decided authoritatively [1] that it alone should be held and delivered in the Church,' 'so that it is not lawful to put forth another Creed besides this or to seek for or introduce anything fresh, or to disturb (or initiate) anything concerning our holy religion,' but those who do so 'have subjected themselves and do subject themselves manifestly to penalties, so that if they are bishops they should be deposed from the episcopate.' He then asserted in the name of the Synod that Flavian, Bishop of Constantinople, and Eusebius, Bishop of Dorylæum, had clearly done this by unsettling and changing almost everything, and so becoming the occasion of scandal and

[1] $τυπώσασα$, Mansi, vi. 908.

confusion to the holy Churches and the orthodox people everywhere, and had subjected themselves to the penalties decreed by the holy fathers. Then he added:

'Accordingly we, confirming what they decreed, have decided that Flavian and Eusebius are deprived of all sacerdotal and episcopal rank.'

Each bishop was then called upon to deliver his judgment in turn.

Flavian now protested to Dioscorus, 'I refuse your jurisdiction.'[1] And Hilarus, the Papal legate, said in Latin, 'It is contradicted'—thus supporting the protest.

Then follow the signatures in the Acts, the Bishops of Jerusalem, Antioch, Ephesus, and a number of others, emphasising the reason of their judgment, viz. that Flavian and Eusebius had offended against the rule which forbade any addition to, or diminution of, the Creed of Nicæa, confirmed by the Council of Ephesus in 431.[2]

So the Acts of the Synod ran. But at the Council of Chalcedon it was deposed that this sentence and the signatures had not been managed in the quiet way in which the Acts of the 'Robber-Synod' would lead one to suppose.

When Dioscorus proposed the sentence against Flavian, Onesiphorus, Bishop of Iconium, who, as we have seen, guessed what was coming, rose and knelt before the throne on which Dioscorus sat, and holding his knees, in Eastern fashion, passionately entreated him

---

[1] παραιτοῦμαί σε. Tillemont, quoted by Dr. Bright (*Roman See*, p. 272), says that one does not see why Flavian did not say this earlier. But at that period it was a common way of appealing, to decline the jurisdiction, even after the definitive sentence. The contrary way was introduced by Justinian. *Cf.* De Marca, *De Concordia Sacerd.* &c. Lib. VII. cap. vii. § 1.

[2] Mansi, vi. 909.

not to proceed to such an extreme measure as the condemnation of Flavian. Dioscorus rose from his throne and standing on the footstool said, 'Are you stirring up sedition? Fetch the Counts.' A scene of utter confusion followed.[1] The military entered the church with clubs and swords, the proconsul himself appeared with chains, and presently Barsumas,[2] with his monks, joined in the scene of violence; the writing tables of the notaries were upset and their papers blotted, and Dioscorus with violent gestures bade the bishops sign, or they would have to reckon with him; blows were freely distributed as the soldiers and monks stood over the reluctant bishops, to whom a blank paper was presented for signature, to be filled in afterwards with the sentence on Flavian and Eusebius.[3] Flavian himself was beaten and kicked, but in the midst of the indignities he suffered he remained firm, and, driven into a corner with Eusebius, handed to the legates his appeal to the throne of Peter.[4] He was not destined to prosecute his appeal in person, for, owing to the injuries he received, not many days elapsed before he passed to his martyr's crown.

Dioscorus, secure of the vote of his Egyptians, made sure of the signatures of the Orientals first (the bishops of the Antiochene 'diocese') and the Egyptians signed afterwards.

To this unparalleled scene of confusion and violence we have, not merely the witness of the bishops who deposed at the Council of Chalcedon, but also, though only recently known to historians, two separate accounts by Flavian and Eusebius in their letters of appeal to Leo.[5]

---

[1] Mansi, vi. 832.   [2] *Ibid.* vii. 68.   [3] *Ibid.* vi. 601, 625.
[4] *Libellus Appellationis*, Spicilegium Casinense, i. 132.
[5] See next chapter.

It is therefore not possible to doubt the truth of the main features of this scandalous exhibition of unscrupulous violence. 'Where swords are, where is the Synod?' said one of the bishops at Chalcedon. Well might many of the bishops there, on the recital of the treatment of Flavian, call Dioscorus a second Cain, who had murdered his brother Flavian.

Domnus, the Bishop of Antioch, was deposed, as also Theodoret, of whom we shall hear more hereafter. Maximus was irregularly chosen in the place of Domnus, but Theodoret's see was left unfilled. Ibas was also deposed and his see filled by Nonnus. Dorylæum, the see of Eusebius, was left vacant. This prelate, whose name is so conspicuous in the history of Eutychianism, had, in spite of his impetuous zeal, shrunk from pursuing his accusation of Eutyches at the Council of Constantinople in 448, on the ground that he had everything to lose, since Eutyches had money at his command and Court influence, and he himself had neither.[1] He had now, to all appearance lost everything, except his soul: Dioscorus, he afterwards informed the Emperors Valentinian and Marcian, had 'by money and by the brute force of his troops, overwhelmed the orthodox faith and confirmed the heresy of Eutyches.'

No one knows what became of Bishop Julius, the Papal legate, in this scene of disorder, but Hilarus, the deacon, his co-legate, fled for his life and escaped to tell the tale to his master at Rome. St. Leo gave the Synod a name by which it has been known ever since, viz. the Latrocinium or 'Robber-Synod.'

But Dioscorus, who was now omnipotent with the Emperor, took one further step, which was eventually

[1] Mansi, vi. 736.

the chief ground of his condemnation. On one of his visits to the Court, inflated with pride, on the very spot where the 318 fathers promulgated the Creed of Christendom—at Nicæa—he gave expression to the inordinate notion which he had conceived of his ecclesiastical position. One bishop in his signature to the acquittal of Eutyches had called Dioscorus the 'universal bishop.'[1] He now acted on the notion of at least supremacy over the whole Church, and in presence of some ten bishops, excommunicated St. Leo himself, probably on the ground that he was supporting bishops excommunicated by the authority of a universal Council. The Council of Chalcedon gave to this act its proper name, viz. simply 'madness.'[2]

---

[1] Mansi, vi. 855.

[2] In my first edition I had supposed, in accordance with the marginal note in Mansi, vi. 1010, that this took place just before the Synod of Chalcedon. But I think it more probable that Dioscorus acted thus in the lifetime of Theodosius. It is, however, difficult to say for certain. Cf. Ballerini, *Leon. Opp.* ii. 1535. Quesnel thinks it took place at Alexandria (*ibid.*). Cf. also Tillemont, xv. 609.

CHAPTER V

FLAVIAN'S APPEAL TO ROME

Now let us suppose that the Church at this moment possessed nothing more for the purposes of her government than a 'first patriarch,' *primus inter pares* in every respect, jurisdiction included, with a precedency, a pre-eminence,' and (in a sense not formal or technical) ' a leadership,' but without ' definite powers '—which is the highest Anglican description of the official position of the Holy See. Suppose, too, that this precedency was owing, not to a divine institution, but to the secular position of the city of Rome, to its having been 'organised by Apostolic hands,' and having been connected with ' the majesty of the names of Peter and Paul,' and become 'famous for its bountiful generosity ' and for ' its traditional immunity from heretical speculations.' This is the account given by a representative Anglican writer, of the ' place both lofty and distinctive ' 'undoubtedly assigned by ancient Christianity ' to the see of Rome.[1]

Would such a leadership have proved equal to the crisis that had arisen in the East under the Emperor

---

[1] Cf. *The Roman Claims tested by Antiquity*, p. 8, by W. Bright, D.D., Canon of Christ Church, Regius Professor of Ecclesiastical History. 1877.

Theodosius? Could such a leadership (which does not include the *right* of being appealed to as a higher court) have been able to reverse the catastrophe of the Robber-Synod without a miracle? Could such a position, with no 'definite powers,' no inheritance of rule and judgment from the 'Prince of Apostles' (for this is excluded by that theory), have sufficed to enable even a Leo the Great to counteract the tremendous success over the orthodox faith which had now been achieved at Ephesus? Peckham, Archbishop of Canterbury, complaining to Edward I. of the conflicts that had arisen in England between the Church and State, says that nothing would avail to set things right except that state of things in which Catholic emperors bent before (1) the decrees of the Sovereign Pontiffs, (2) the statutes of Councils, (3) and the sanctions of the orthodox Fathers. And in regard to the first he says, 'the sovereign Lord of all gave authority to the decrees of the Sovereign Pontiffs, when He said to Peter in the Gospel of St. Matthew, "Whatsoever thou shalt bind on earth shall be bound in heaven."'[1] Could anything short of this inherited privilege of Peter, which was the teaching of St. Anselm and every other Archbishop of Canterbury, and which is the distinctive feature of Catholic and Roman teaching at this hour, have been adequate to deal with the state of things that had now arisen in the East?

But, putting aside *a priori* considerations, let us ask, On what did St. Leo actually rely? He had already expounded the faith which he 'desired to be implanted in the hearts of all the faithful,' as he told the clergy of Constantinople. He had already given an 'interpretatio benigna' to the Emperor's desire for a Council as neces-

[1] *Ep.* 199: *Registrum Epistolarum*, ed. C. T. Martin (1882), i. 240.

sarily involving the wish to have Peter's answer at Cæsarea Philippi explained by Peter himself (*i.e.* through his see), as he told the Synod itself; he had reviewed and revised the Acts of a previous Synod of Constantinople, and laid down the conditions of Eutyches's restoration, and, in his letter to the Empress, he had assumed, on the ground of his occupying 'the Apostolic See,' the office of absolver of the heretic in case he repented. But he had now to lift up the fallen East. He had the Emperor against him; the Patriarch of Alexandria was his unscrupulous foe, a new patriarch had been elected to Antioch, the Bishop of Jerusalem had sided with the enemies of the faith, and but one bishop, besides his own legate, had dared to lift up his voice in favour of the murdered archbishop.

On what, then, did Leo rely in dealing with bishops, patriarchs, and an Eastern Emperor? His position as Bishop of Old Rome could avail him nothing, for Theodosius was Emperor of New Rome. His position as occupant of *an* Apostolic See would not suffice: the Bishop of Jerusalem was his equal there, to say nothing of the Bishop of Antioch. The traditional orthodoxy of Rome would be of no use to him here; the East had gone in for its own opinion. He had with him the hearts of many, but the voices of few, while the Emperor professed to believe in an Eastern Council of bishops under his own royal supremacy. What right had Leo to intervene at all?

The ground that he did assume was his position of Sovereign Pontiff. He knew well that though they might rebel against it, they could not deny it. He knew that the East to a man believed St. Peter to be 'the Prince and head of the Apostles,' and that Peter 'lives and exercises judgment in his successors.'¹ And on this belief he acted throughout. And in the whole course of the Council of Chalcedon not a single protest was raised against the assumption made to Emperor, Empress, to the Synod, and to individual bishops—made publicly and given as the ground of Leo's action : there was, I say, not a solitary protest against the perpetual assumption on the part of the Pontiff that he was the successor of St. Peter, and that as such he had the power of the keys, not exclusively, but pre-eminently ; with a precedence, not of honour merely, but of spiritual jurisdiction over the entire Church of God. 'It is idle' (so we are told) ' to bid us acknowledge her bishop' (*i.e.* the Bishop of Rome) 'as first patriarch, when he will not be acknowledged as anything short of a Supreme Pontiff.'² But the history of Eutychianism and the Council of Chalcedon are distinct in their evidence to the truth that the Pope was held to be the successor of the Prince of the Apostles, and as such was, as St. Cyril called Celestine, ' the archbishop of the universal Church.' Leo, in leaning on his inherited prerogative, had the conscience of the Church with him, as will now be seen.

Flavian upon his condemnation at Ephesus had handed to the legates an appeal to Rome. He appealed to ' the Apostolic See : ' so Liberatus, in his *Breviarium*, states after inspecting the documents. And the Western Emperor, Valentinian, distinctly states the same in his letter to Theodosius : ' the Bishop of Constantinople appealed to *him* (viz. the Bishop of Rome) by formal notice.' De Marca, whose theories would not incline him to emphasise this, says : 'It is clearly proved by

¹ Cf. p. 81.   ² *Roman Claims*, &c., by Dr. Bright.

Valentinian's letter that Flavian appealed to Pope Leo;' and again, 'so as that he appealed to the Roman Pontiff alone.'

But in such matters it was the invariable custom of the Roman Pontiff to act in concert with the Roman Synod. A synodical declaration was a more formal utterance; it was like the emphasis to speech, as when a man gathers up his whole self for a special effort. It was a kind of proclamation that the utterance was formal. It was not indeed a necessary means of signifying that the sentence thus delivered was, so to speak, *ex cathedra*, for the Tome itself was not a synodical utterance, but it was the usual way in which at that time the Pontiff dealt with serious cases such as the deposition or reinstatement of bishops. It was a means of bringing into play that consultative function of the Episcopate which the Vatican Council spoke of as included in the normal action of the Papacy. The authority of the Roman Synod emanated from its President as successor of Peter; but its unanimity was a factor in the impressiveness of the Papal judgment. St. Leo himself speaks of certain writings of his as sent to Constantinople, 'not only with the authority of the Apostolic See, but also with the unanimity of the holy Synod which had assented in great numbers.' The *authority* was that of the Holy See; the unanimity of the Synod was an additional advantage.[1]

And so the Empress Placidia, writing from Rome, says that Flavian had sent a formal notice to the

---

[1] Dr. Bright (*Roman See*, p. 177) quotes these words in Latin, italicising the words 'not only' (*non solum*) and 'but also' (*sed etiam*), ignoring the vital distinction between 'authority' and 'unanimity.' St. Leo does *not* say that his writings went forth '*not only* by the authority of the Apostolic See, *but also* by that of the Synod.' The authority was his.

Apostolic See 'and to all the bishops of these parts,' which was perfectly true. But 'these parts' did not mean that all the bishops of the West were to be consulted, but the bishops round about Rome and others happening to be in Rome, where the Empress was. These bishops did indeed represent the West, but only as the head represents the body; they did so, not because of any delegation, but because they were as it were the Cabinet Council of the Supreme Pontiff. How else could they exercise authority over the East? How indeed could a comparatively few—for the numbers of which Leo speaks (*frequens convenerat*) are to be compared with the ordinary meetings, not with the numbers of the entire West—how could this comparative handful of itself, and without any express delegation, represent the West as it did, except from the fact that the head was there? We have, however, irrefragable evidence in this case that 'these parts' are not the entire West, *except so far as the West was involved in the acts of the Roman Synod*, for Hilarus, in writing to the Empress Pulcheria, speaks of the Roman Synod which responded to Flavian's appeal, as 'the whole West'; and again, St. Leo, writing to Theodosius, speaks of the tears of 'all the Churches in our parts,' by which he certainly did not mean the entire West, for his letter is headed 'Leo, Bishop, and the holy Synod which met in the city of Rome.'[2] When, therefore, Galla Placidia spoke of Flavian's having written 'to all the bishops of these parts' she did not mean that the entire West was to be gathered together by represen-

---

[1] *Leon. Ep.* 46.
[2] *Ep.* 43. The 'Resident Synod' of Constantinople was the counterpart of the Roman Synod. Only the Roman Synod was constitutional, because of the position of its President, the successor of Peter.

tation, but that the appeal was to the Pope in his Roman Synod which was the normal representative of the West. The appeal was to the successor of Peter *as such*, acting as he did in such cases with the solemnity of a court composed of such bishops as could be got together at the time. Nothing else will suit the expressions used and the acts that followed.

Such was the state of the argument before a valuable discovery was made which has set the seal to the position maintained by the Ballerini and Mansi, as against Quesnel and others, whom Dr. Bright has followed. The Prior of the Archives at Monte Cassino (Dom Ambrogio Amelli) had the good fortune to discover in the Archives at Novara a Latin copy of the letters written to Rome by Flavian and Eusebius. Both letters are of great interest as containing two separate accounts of the Robber-Synod from those most nearly concerned in it, written immediately after its close, if not, indeed, in part during its proceedings.[1]

We gather from Flavian's letter that Dioscorus had

[1] These letters have been inserted by Mommsen in his *Neues Archiv*, xi. 362. They are referred to by Duchesne in his *Eglises séparées*, p. 202, and by Harnack, in his *Dogmengeschichte*, on the 'Eutychian Controversy.' Amelli gives good reasons for supposing that they belonged to Dionysius Exiguus, who is known to have been compiling materials for a History of the Council of Chalcedon. Cf. *S. Leone Magno e l' Oriente*, p. 24 (Monte Cassino, Tipo-Litografia Casinense, 1894). The letters in question have also been inserted in the *Spicilegium Casinense*, tom. i. (1893), with Mommsen's emendations. This may be seen in the British Museum. I had not had the advantage of seeing it when I published the first edition of this book. Christianus Lupus deplored the loss of this letter of Flavian's, which he says would have stopped *os loquentium iniqua*, by which he meant Quesnel and his followers. It is satisfactory to find that the arguments of the Ballerini and Mansi (*Nat. Alex. H. E.* vol. ix.) are supported by the discovery.

conceived an implacable animosity against him from the day of his consecration to the see of Constantinople, and had not sent him the customary letters on his appointment to that see. But Flavian says that notwithstanding this he had 'obeyed' Dioscorus 'in everything.' The third canon of Constantinople does not seem to have influenced their respective dealings. But the interest of Flavian's letter centres in the expressions he uses in appealing to Rome. Did he appeal to Rome as to the see of the 'first Patriarch' or as the see of the Apostle Peter?

His letter is addressed to Leo himself in person. He tells him how Dioscorus acquitted Eutyches, and did not allow 'the letter of your Holiness to be read, though it suffices for the confirmation of the faith of the Fathers.' He then speaks of 'the unjust sentence which he issued against me according to his own good pleasure, *while I appealed to the throne of the Apostolic See of Peter the Prince of the Apostles and the universal blessed Synod which is under your Holiness.*' These last words clearly do not refer to an 'Œcumenical' Synod, both by reason of the expression 'which is under your Holiness,' evidently referring to something in regular action, and because of the sequel. They can only refer to the Roman Synod as constitutionally representing the West,[1] as, in fact, its normal exponent.

Flavian then proceeds to describe the scene of

---

[1] The contention of the Ballerini that Flavian did not appeal to a General Council even of the West cannot be maintained since the discovery of this letter. But their main contention is supported by the letter. A really representative Council of the West was never summoned. Any fair number of bishops sufficed, as long as the Holy See was satisfied.

ruffianly violence which took place. His account confirms what has been already described. 'A crowd of the military surrounded me and, when I was desirous of taking refuge at the altar, would not allow me, but did its best to turn me out of the church. In the midst of a fearful tumult, I managed with difficulty to get to a corner of the church and to remain there with those who were with me. But even this I could not do without being carefully watched, lest I should manage to report to you all the ills I suffered.'

The archbishop then proceeds to formulate his prayer to his Holiness. It was, first, to busy himself in the cause of the faith, 'which has perished through licence.' Next, to see after the overthrow of ecclesiastical constitutions and simply to narrate the whole matter both to the people who are in a majority, 'and also to teach the Emperor by a suitable letter; moreover to write to the clergy of the holy Church of Constantinople and to the monks; also to Juvenal, the Bishop of Jerusalem' (who had taken a prominent part in the last scene) 'and to Thalassius of Cæsarea' (who had been appointed by the Emperor a coadjutor to Dioscorus), 'to Stephen, the Bishop of Ephesus' (where the disaster occurred), 'and to Eusebius of Ancyra and Cyrus of Aphrodisia' (prominent members in the iniquitous scene), 'and to the rest of the holy bishops who consented to the unrighteous sentence against me, and to Dioscorus, who held the principal authority in the holy Synod at Ephesus.'

This was certainly not a programme to be set before a 'first Patriarch' with no 'definite powers' but a mere precedency of honour without effective jurisdiction. But Flavian entreats for more in addition to this. He asks Leo ' to issue a decree ¹ which God will inspire your mind to frame, so that a Synod both of the West and of the East being held, a like faith may be everywhere preached, so that the statutes of the Fathers may prevail, that all that has been done may be rendered void— things done somehow, as they have been, unrighteously and in the shade, and not without levity; and [so] to apply healing to this horrible wound which has spread serpent-like almost through the whole world.'

Flavian concludes with saying that the bishops who were forced into signing against him were but few—a statement which conflicts with the records of the Council. But, as Dom Amelli points out, Flavian would not be aware of what was done outside his own immediate purview and after he had escaped from the church.²

At the same time, Eusebius, Bishop of Dorylæum, appealed to Leo to reverse his deposition by Dioscorus and his Synod. Until the discovery of his letter by Amelli, this was a fact unknown to historians of the Councils. He forms another witness to the ruffianly treatment of the bishops at the Latrocinium by Dioscorus and his associates, and he adds a few touches to the picture, just as an independent witness naturally would. It seems that being forbidden to enter the Synod, although St. Leo had ordered him to be admitted, he was nevertheless incarcerated in some dark place in the church, guarded by soldiers. Dioscorus, he says, threatened to have some of the bishops thrown into the sea if they ventured to dispute his ruling. No one was allowed to approach Eusebius,

---

¹ *Dare formam*: the word used almost always (when *decretum* is not used) to translate τύπος, a decree. Cf. *supra*, p. 21.

² *S. Leone Magno e l' Oriente*, p. 45.

though several bishops had signified their willingness to solace him in his 'passion.' The bishops' signatures were obtained by violence, ' as they know who were sent by your Holiness in the place of your Blessedness, to whom I presented the formal notice (*libellos*) of my appeal, in which I have demanded the cognisance of your See.' There can be no question, therefore, to whom Eusebius appealed.

We must, however, notice the reason of his appeal to the Holy See. In the beginning of his letter, addressed to 'the holy and most blessed Father and Archbishop Leo,' he says: 'The Apostolic throne has been wont *from the beginning* to defend those who are suffering injustice, to assist those who have been the prey of unavoidable factions, and to raise up those who lie on the ground, according to the possibility [power of so doing] which you possess, and the compassion which you have towards all men. The reason is that you have a right understanding, and *preserve the faith* towards our Lord Jesus Christ *unshaken*, and exercise charity without dissembling towards all the brethren and all who call on the name of Christ. Wherefore I, being entangled in unavoidable [embarrassments], fly to the only refuge, after the help of God, in my affliction and extremity, desiring to find a release from the ills that have befallen me.'

His only refuge was 'the Apostolic throne' with its inerrancy in the faith and traditional charity towards the whole Christian brotherhood. After describing, as we have already seen, the catastrophe of the Latrocinium, and stating the formal nature of his appeal 'to your See,' he says: 'I entreat your Blessedness, touching your knees at least in word if not with my hand,[1] pronounce the reversal (*evacuatio*), and nullity of any unjust condemnation by the most religious Dioscorus, and of their decree, who were forced into consenting to his will, and give me back the dignity of my episcopate, and communion with yourself, by letters from you to my lowliness, bestowing on me my rank and communion'—*i.e.* the rank of bishop, and communion with the Apostolic See.

The whole of the letter is in the plural number, but the title and the expressions 'your See' and 'the Apostolic throne' prove that it is the 'majestic plural,' not a plurality of persons addressed.[2]

It is impossible not to see in these two letters a unique position of authority assigned to Rome as 'the Apostolic throne,' or, as Flavian expresses himself, 'the throne of the Apostolic See of Peter, the Prince of the Apostles,' written, too, from Ephesus, where it had been said in the Œcumenical Council of 431 that 'Peter . . . the Prince of the Apostles . . . lives and exercises judgment in his successors.' The position of Leo clearly in Flavian's mind resulted, not from the city, but from the position of Peter in the Apostolic College. He says that the Tome of Leo (his letter to Flavian himself) 'suffices for the confirmation of the faith.' It was already authoritative. He treats the Apostolic See as the proper court of appeal for an unjustly deposed Archbishop of Constantinople exercising its authority in a Synod 'under' Leo, as in the case of injured bishops the

---

[1] Just as, in Eastern fashion, Onesiphorus and others knelt at Dioscorus's knees in the Synod, entreating him not to depose Flavian.

[2] The letter is said, in a footnote in another hand, to have been sent by Chrysippus and Constantine, names which occur in the Acts (Mansi, vi. 574, 719, 744, 1062 ; cf. Amelli, *Leone Magno*, p. 49).

Pontiffs invariably did. Then in regard to the breaches of the ecclesiastical order that had taken place, he looks to Leo to communicate with his own (Flavian's) flock, with the Emperor, and with those Eastern bishops whose conduct had been so unseemly and so cowardly, and with Dioscorus himself. Further, he hopes that Leo, besides respecting this appeal to his see and the Synod under him, will issue an authoritative decree, which, by means of a Council, not merely of the West, but West and East together, a truly Œcumenical Council, will secure unanimity of teaching throughout the world, and the rest of the bishops deposed will have their cases investigated, and all the injustice done will be rectified. He does not ask Leo to act despotically, but he does ask for an exercise of authority; while Eusebius asks Leo simply to restore him to his position of Bishop. It must be remembered that the Catholic thesis, while it maintains that the successor of St. Peter is more than a 'first Patriarch,' does not maintain that he is by virtue of his office an absolute ruler. He is Supreme Pontiff, and no cause like that of Flavian's has run its course to its end until Rome has spoken her word—whether with or without the aid of an Œcumenical Synod depends on the judgment of the Sovereign Pontiff himself. As a matter of fact, Leo's action in this case followed exactly on the lines proposed by Flavian, *i.e.* first his Synodical judgment and then a General Council.[1]

Theodoret also appealed, a short time afterwards, to

[1] On the mistake of supposing that the rule of the Sovereign Pontiff is absolute, in the sense of being uncontrolled by contract, by usage and by rights, see Hettinger on *The Supremacy of the Apostolic See in the Church*, i. 27. Pius IX. protested against the idea; and Bellarmine had already said distinctly that the one absolutely free ruler in the Church is Christ (*De Rom. Pont.* iii. 19).

Leo and his Council, giving as his authority the precedent of St. Paul. 'If Paul, the herald of the truth, the trumpet of the Spirit, ran to the great Peter ... much more do we in our littleness run to your Apostolic throne, that from you we may receive healing for the wounds of the Church.'[1] But his case will be dealt with in connection with the Council of Chalcedon itself.

[1] *Ep.* 113.

CHAPTER VI

LEO PROPOSES, THEODOSIUS REFUSES, A COUNCIL

ON September 29, A.D. 449, St. Leo was holding one of his customary annual Synods of the suburbicarian sees and of the bishops who happened to be in Rome, assembled to celebrate the anniversary of his own birthday and to conduct the affairs of the Church, when Hilarus, the deacon and legate, arrived from Ephesus with the sad tidings of the Robber-Council. The Roman Synod was accordingly prolonged to consider what steps should be taken to retrieve the disaster which had befallen the true faith. They had now before them the appeals of Flavian and Eusebius. They knew nothing as yet, it would seem, of the death of Flavian or the election of a successor to the see. Hilarus had escaped at the close of the first session, having refused to attend a second. They only knew of the triumph of heresy in a Council of bishops which had received St. Leo's acquiescence on the understanding that it met to promulgate the condemnation of Eutyches, if he did not withdraw his heretical propositions, and to absolve him by the authority of the Holy See, if he did.[1]

St. Leo in concert with his bishops at once repudiated the Council at Ephesus, so that Hilarus, who was

---
[1] Cf. *supra*, p. 143.

present, could write to the Empress Pulcheria saying 'that everything done in Ephesus by Dioscorus uncanonically and tumultuously and through worldly hate, is condemned by the aforesaid Pope with the whole Western Council.' This was the first step in the programme proposed by St. Flavian, who had appealed to 'the throne of Peter and the universal Council which is under your Holiness.' He had originally declared that the exercise of Leo's authority would supersede the necessity of a General Council in the East; he had now appealed to that authority, and it had nullified his deposition.

A few weeks [1] after Hilarus brought the tidings of the catastrophe at Ephesus, and after the whole matter had been well weighed in Synod, the Pope wrote to the Emperor Theodosius precisely on the lines suggested by St. Flavian in his appeal to the Holy See. Leo expressed his intense disappointment at the result of the Synod at Ephesus and his confidence that all would have been well with the bishops there, and there would have been no doctrinal innovation,[2] if only his legates had been allowed to read his letter [3] to the Synod or that to Flavian, 'for the tumult would have been so quieted by the manifestation which, inspired divinely (*divinitus inspiratam*), we have received and hold, that neither unskilfulness would have pursued its folly' (in allusion to Eutyches), 'nor rivalry' (in allusion to Dioscorus

---

[1] For the date see *Leonis Opp.* Ep. liv. and *Diss. de Ep. deperd.* n. 38.

[2] μηδὲν δύνασθαι καινοτομεῖσθαι.

[3] These particular letters were not those of the Roman Synod. They were *Ep.* 33 and *Ep.* 28 (Ball.); see also *Ep.* 45, in which the same letters are spoken of as the teaching of 'the See of the blessed Apostle Peter.'

against Constantinople) 'have had the opportunity of doing further harm.' After speaking of the protest of his legates against what was dogmatically proclaimed,[1] saying, as they did, ' that the Apostolic See could never accept it,' the Pope in the most touching terms urges the Emperor to look to God and think of the judgment-seat of Christ. 'Behold I, O most Christian and worshipful Emperor, with my fellow bishops . . . entreat you in presence of the inseparable Trinity of the one God, Which is the Guardian and author of your empire, and in presence of Christ's holy Angels, that you would order that all things should remain in the same state in which they were before any judgment' [had been given].[2]

He now tells the Emperor that ' all the Churches of our regions, all the bishops, entreat your Clemency that you would order a General Synod to be assembled in Italy.' Two reasons are given for this: first, the protest of the legates at the Latrocinium itself, and secondly, the appeal of Flavian. Each of these pre-

[1] δογματισθέν. The Greek, as we have it, is older than the Latin. It dates from two or three years only later than the sending of the letter.

[2] It seems necessary to protest against the absurd cavil of Bishop Andrewes, as it is reproduced by Dr. Bright (*Roman See*, p. 178), that there is 'no mandate here' from the Pope; as if Leo could not be Supreme Pontiff because he *entreated* the Emperor to do his duty. No one who has read it will easily forget the Conference of the Pastor Adolphe Monod on 'the tears of St. Paul.' St. Leo occupied the Apostolic throne, and nothing better befitted the successor of an Apostle than tears and supplications at a crisis like this. Leo could be true to his name when occasion called for it, as in the presence of Attila; but when the truth of the Incarnation was at stake, and a Christian Emperor was in danger of losing his soul, he could be the embodiment of tenderness. When the bishops at Chalcedon use the same word of entreaty (παρακαλοῦμεν) to Leo, Dr. Bright translates it ' request ' (*Roman See*, p. 205). Cf. *infra*, p. 373.

vented the Synod at Ephesus from being final. The object of the new Council was to be the overthrow of heresy and the healing of schism. St. Leo then adopts a slightly altered tone and says that in point of fact to ask this has become 'necessary'; 'the decrees of the canons of Nicæa, which have been established by the bishops throughout the whole world, bear witness' to the necessity; and from this passage he continues in the mood of exhortation, more tersely and decidedly. The letter obviously comes from one and the same pen, and is in parts a personal appeal to the Emperor in person.

In this letter, however, Leo strikes the note which resounds to the end of the matter. He assumes the championship of Nicene rules, as of the Nicene faith. Theodosius had been misled into imagining that in supporting Eutyches he was supporting the Nicene settlement: St. Leo, in effect, tells him plainly that it is he who is guarding both the faith and the rules of Nicæa. This was an essential element of the Papal prerogative. The primary idea of Papal supremacy is that it exists for the preservation of the Apostolic deposit; this aim took the shape, after 325, of a guardianship of the Nicene settlement. The faith of Nicæa could never, according to the teaching of Rome, be allowed to suffer innovation; the Nicene canons could only be changed or dispensed from for good reason and by competent authority, to be found in the Apostolic See. Nothing but the most profound misunderstanding of the teaching of the Church as formulated in the Vatican decree could have led some writers to see in Leo's championship of the Nicene settlement an abatement of his claim to supreme authority. It was, on the contrary, the most prominent and proper feature of that supremacy.

As regards the particular provision to which St. Leo referred in this letter as Nicene, it will be observed that he uses a curious phrase, 'the decisions of the canons of Nicæa.'[1] The provision was that of the fourth and seventh canons of Sardica. The periphrasis perhaps expresses most accurately the real state of the case. It might simply mean the 'canonical decisions' of the Nicene Council. But, on the other hand, it may point to matters on which the Nicene fathers agreed, but which were not embodied in definite canons until the Council of Sardica met and the necessity for such promulgation of Nicene principles had been shown by the Athanasian conflicts. But the emphatic assertion that 'the decisions of the canons at Nicæa,' of which the canons of Sardica, to which he referred, formed part, had been 'established throughout the world,' shows that the African troubles about these Sardican canons had ended well, and the Church had set her seal on the term Nicene being applied to those canons. Leo wrote this letter some thirty years after the African investigation; and as he was the most accurate of men, his witness is fair evidence that all were now agreed that 'Nicene' was a proper term to apply to the Sardican canons. In the same way the Church has settled that the Niceno-Constantinopolitan Creed, which was certainly not drawn up by the Nicene fathers but which is recited throughout the world as the 'Nicene' Creed, is rightly so called.

But, as we shall see, we have not simply an assertion by Leo, made at a time when it is inconceivable that he should lay himself open to the retort that no such Nicene provision existed, to say nothing of his profoundly Christian character; we have also the acceptance

[1] τῶν κατὰ Νίκαιαν κανόνων αἱ ψῆφοι.

of this provision in the East. The essence of these canons was that the fact of a bishop having appealed to Rome from a Synod of bishops enforced the suspension of his sentence of deposition, until the Bishop of Rome had settled upon another court, whether his own or another in the same region, to try the case.

At the same time St. Leo wrote to the Empress Pulcheria as to one who had never failed the religion and faith of Christ, telling her of his letter to Theodosius, and repeating that his legates had protested at the Ephesine Council that they would never suffer themselves 'to be separated from that faith which, fully expounded and authoritatively defined by the See of the blessed Apostle Peter, they had brought with them to the holy Synod.'[1] He says that Flavian remains in the communion of Rome, and that he has moved for a Council to be held in Italy, that all things that had caused the trouble might be rehandled with greater care and so they might return to the peace of God. He then says, 'Let your Piety deign to explain our supplication to the Emperor, considering that you hold a special commission as from the blessed Apostle Peter.'[2]

Leo also wrote a very beautiful and touching letter to the people of Constantinople, the flock of Flavian, whom he imagined to be still alive. In the course of this letter he tells them plainly that if any bishop should

---

[1] Greek: πίστεως ἣν πλήρη ἐκτεθεῖσαν καὶ διατυπωθεῖσαν ἐκ τοῦ θρόνου τοῦ μακ. ἀποστόλου Πέτρου. *Ep.* 45. The Latin is a translation, not the original. Notice the use of ἐκτέθεις and διατυπώθεις, and cf. *divinitus inspiratam* of *Ep.* 44. διατύπωσις is used at the end of this letter for the authoritative action of the Emperor.

[2] *Pietas vestra dignetur*: Gk. ἡ εὐσέβεια . . . καταξιωσάτω. Would Dr. Bright refuse (cf. *supra*, p. 137) to translate this 'deign'? Leo is writing in a strain of deference to the Empress.

be elected to Constantinople during Flavian's lifetime, 'he will never be considered in communion with us, nor can he be numbered in the roll of bishops. For as we have anathematised Nestorius in his perversity, so we anathematise with equal execration those who deny the truth of the flesh in our Lord Jesus Christ.' He bids them see in the person of their bishop (Flavian) Him for Whom he has not shrunk from suffering, and desires that they may imitate him, and obtain a common reward of faith with him.[1] There was no question with Leo as to the illegitimacy and nullity of Flavian's deposition, nor of the heretical nature of Eutyches's teaching. It was the letter of an Apostle both in its tender care for the flock in Constantinople and its unconscious courage in defying all the forces that were at work in favour of Eutyches. There is also one sentence in this letter which was prompted by a certain tact which Leo combined with the lion-like courage that marked his dealings in this tremendous crisis. In exhorting the Constantinopolitan Catholics to stand firm, he speaks of the faith on which they were built, 'and in which we know the most Christian Emperor remains firm.' This was really the case: for Theodosius was being simply misled by those around him.

At the same time Leo wrote to certain Archimandrites of Constantinople, urging them to adhere to Flavian, and to be ready to suffer for the Catholic faith.

Theodosius kept perfect silence. But after the lapse

---

[1] *Ep.* 50. The letter is entitled 'Leo and the holy Synod, which met in the city of Rome, to the Clergy, nobility, and laity, most beloved sons.' It is not likely that the Synod would call itself the Fathers of the clergy of Constantinople. The fact is, that these letters are really Leo's, written after consultation with the Synod.

of three months the Emperor Valentinian came to Rome with the Empresses Eudoxia and Galla Placidia, his wife and his mother, on the Vigil of the Feast of the Chair of St. Peter (February 450). They came into St. Peter's for their devotions, and there met the Sovereign Pontiff. They were at the tomb of the Apostle in the basilica. After service, when his Holiness approached their Imperial Majesties, hardly able to speak for the tears and sobs that choked his utterance, surrounded by a number of bishops, whom, says the Empress Placidia, 'he had assembled by virtue of his commanding position,'[1] he described the state of things, and told them of his petition for a General Council, and besought them to use their influence with their Imperial relative to induce him to return a favourable answer to the petition. The sorrow of the great Pontiff moved them; the Empresses describe it in their letters. That of the Empress Galla Placidia is of special interest. She speaks of Flavian's appeal ' to the Apostolic See and all the bishops of these parts, through the legates of the Bishop of Rome, who according to the definitions [or canons] of the Nicene Council are wont to be present' (the canon being that of Sardica). She urged that the Emperor should arrange that ' according to the decree and decision [2] of the Apostolic throne, which we in like manner venerate as at the head of matters,[3] Flavian should remain in his Episcopal status and the judgment should be transferred to the Synod of the Apostolic

[1] ὑπὸ τῆς ἀρχῆς τοῦ ἰδίου τόπου καὶ τῆς ἀξίας.
[2] τὸν τύπον καὶ τὸν ὅρον.
[3] ὡς προηγούμενον προσκυνοῦμεν. The Empress uses the word προσκύνησις in the opening of her letter for 'the veneration of the Apostle Peter' which they had come to render at his tomb on the Feast of his Chair.

throne, in which he who was counted worthy to receive the keys of heaven first adorned the Episcopal rule ;[1] when it becomes us to guard the reverence due to this greatest of cities which is the mistress of the whole world.'

The special interest of this letter lies in the kind of argument which the Empress felt it suitable in the present distress to use to her Imperial relative. That she should press home the dignity of the Apostolic throne on the ground that it is the See of Peter and fixed in the Eternal City witnesses to a general belief to which she felt she could safely appeal. Also the expression ' Synod of the Apostolic throne ' is significant.

But the letter which Valentinian wrote to Theodosius is of greater importance still. It is impossible to suppose that he would enter upon any disputed ground as to jurisdiction. His letter was doubtless inspired by Leo. And who can read the letters of Leo at this period without feeling that his supreme motive was the honour due to our Divine Lord and his devouring zeal for the truth of the Incarnation? It is true that Harnack, from his rationalistic point of view, sees only a political motive in Leo's conduct. At this period he was dominated by fear of Alexandria's pre-eminence; presently, his motive would be fear of that of Constantinople. The theory is certainly read into the record, for there is nothing in that record which explicitly states it, and it involves a complete repudiation of the religious side of Leo's character. It is a theory which would be impossible to one who accepted the teaching of the Church on the mystery of the Incarnation; and in dealing with motives, it is necessary

---

[1] Gk. ἐπισκοπὴν τῆς ἀρχιερωσύνης.

to have some sympathy with the deeper currents of a man's mind.

A very different, but also unjust, estimate of Leo's action is suggested by Dr. Bright. Leo, according to this writer, was at the same time engaged in 'magnifying his own bishopric and consolidating and formulating the "Petrine" ideas which had long grown up among its clergy.' In this he 'went too far.'[1]

Now let us see what ground Leo had to stand upon. It will be admitted that for twelve hundred years the 'Petrine ideas' as formulated by St. Gregory the Great have held their own in the West. 'I know not what Bishop is not subject to this See,' are his words. But was there sufficient in the past to exonerate Leo from the charge of having formulated a *new* Petrine tradition —that is, from 'consolidating and formulating the Petrine ideas which had long grown up among its clergy'—in the sense of innovating on the immemorial teaching of the Church concerning the see of Peter? The previous pages of this book supply an answer. In no single passage of his writings does St. Leo say more than had already been said in the beginning of the century by his predecessor Innocent I.[2] And St. Augustine detected no sign of 'innovation' in this teaching of St. Innocent. But, further, St. Leo does not in the whole conduct of the Eutychian controversy go one whit beyond St. Julius, the first champion of the Nicene settlement. St. Julius claimed that a Bishop of Alexandria must be judged from Rome, and he grounded his claim on the possession of a Petrine tradition. In that case the bishop was St. Athanasius and Julius acquitted him, and Athanasius preserved

---

[1] *Roman See*, p. 176. [2] Aug. *Epp.* 181, 182.

the letter in which Julius asserts his claim, and is responsible for handing it down to posterity among the proofs of his innocence. Now in the case before us, Leo had to do with an unworthy successor of Athanasius in the same see, and he claimed the right to judge him. He preferred to exercise his judgment through the instrumentality and with the assistance of a General Synod, but his duty of judgment was in his own mind derived from his relationship to the Apostle Peter. It was simply and absolutely his duty to stand in the breach as the responsible person in the last resort, and in doing so, if the Apostolic throne appeared with a fresh jewel in its crown, it was not he, but circumstances that put the jewel there. He certainly did not 'formulate' the Petrine ideas in any sense of innovation. But the Petrine prerogative was of that nature that, while always clearly before the minds of the Popes, its *rights* were capable of consolidation, as circumstances called for their appropriate exercise. As a matter of fact, however, what we owe to St. Leo in this respect is mostly the clear statements of a great theologian, and the providential preservation of a considerable literature in which Emperors, Empresses and Archbishops figure, and all this in connection with the mystery of the holy Incarnation. It has been well said: 'That Leo, alike in his high official position, and in his force of character and religious earnestness, was *the* man to stand forward amid the Eutychian peril, will be admitted by all who believe in the One Christ as perfect God and perfect Man, with gratitude due to him for that firm theological equipoise whereby, while the error for the time is being exposed, no advantage is given to its Nestorian opposite.'[1]

[1] *Roman See*, p. 176.

It was under the influence, as we may rightly suppose, of this great Pontiff, that the Emperor Valentinian now wrote his own letter to Theodosius. His letter was shorter than that of his mother, but to the same effect. After mentioning his visit to Rome for the Feast of St. Peter's Chair—he had not yet lost the effects of his training and fallen into the excesses which disfigured his after life—he speaks of the duty incumbent on them as Emperors to defend the faith received from their ancestors and to preserve the veneration due to the blessed Apostle Peter. He then says that 'the most blessed bishop of the city of the Romans, to whom antiquity yielded the episcopal rule over all, ought to have opportunity and facility for judging concerning the faith and concerning bishops. For this reason, in accordance with the custom of the Councils' (in allusion probably to the cases of Athanasius and Chrysostom, and to the canon of Sardica), 'the Bishop of Constantinople [Flavian] formally appealed to him.' At Leo's request, therefore, Valentinian says he prefers his petition to Theodosius ' that the aforesaid bishop, the rest of the bishops from the whole world having been assembled within Italy, and the whole previous judgment [of Dioscorus] having been set aside, may carefully investigate the case in hand afresh, and promulgate the sentence which the faith and the idea (or doctrine) of true Godhead (*ratio veræ Divinitatis*) demands, &c.' (*Leon. Ep.* 55).

It required no development of Petrine ideas to suggest this procedure. It was in strict accordance with the wish of the Archbishop of Constantinople. Flavian had both appealed to the Roman Synod, and expressed a desire that another General Council should be assembled to counteract the effects of the Pseudo-Synod at Ephesus. The plan commended itself to Leo, and thus, after repudiating Flavian's deposition, he wished for a General Council to assemble in Italy. The case of other bishops had to be considered, and Leo had to draw the Episcopate round himself. It was a bold request, for it meant the removal of the investigation from the influences of the Court of Constantinople. Now it would have been the merest folly to write thus if there had been no common agreement as to the prerogative of the See of Peter in a matter of this kind. The answer could and must have been given straight and at once, that the Church knew of no such prerogatives as were assumed by Leo, and recognised by the Emperor Valentinian, by the Empresses Galla Placidia and Eudoxia, by the martyred Archbishop of Constantinople, by the champion of orthodoxy, the Bishop of Dorylæum, and by the ablest bishop of the day, Theodoret of Cyrus (or Cyrrhos), and by the saintly and orthodox Empress Pulcheria in the East. This answer was not given, and the whole course of the proceedings for the next two years shows that it was the one answer that could not be given by orthodox Christians.

Galla Placidia wrote also to the Empress Pulcheria in the same strain as to Theodosius, entreating her to take care that all that was done in that 'tumultuous and miserable' Synod at Ephesus should be repudiated, and that the whole cause should be remitted to the 'Apostolic throne in which the most blessed of the Apostles, Peter, who received the keys of Heaven, first adorned the high priesthood,' adding that 'we ought to give the precedency in all things to the eternal city.' Apparently, her thought was that the eternal city had a right to precedency in the civil order, because, as she says, it has filled the

o

world and the like, and in the ecclesiastical order, because it is the See of Peter; and so in 'all things' it deserves the pre-eminence.

Now we must either suppose that St. Leo had suddenly converted the Emperor and these two Empresses to a new view of the Papacy, and that untoward circumstances had likewise converted the Archbishop of Constantinople and the orthodox Bishop of Dorylæum to the same view, or, if this seem unlikely, we can only see in their writings a witness to a common consciousness that the See of Peter was, in the last resort, the proper judge in matters of faith and in regard to the deposition of bishops, and that St. Leo was not starting a new 'school of thought' in the Church, but simply working on an accepted belief, in his defence of the faith. That he did assume such a belief as the common inheritance of Christendom is certain, as has been already shown, and as is, if possible, still more conspicuous in the letters which he wrote to Constantinople, under the very eye of the Emperor Theodosius. His letter to the clergy and laity there contains a magnificent exposition of the dogma of the Incarnation, shorter far than the letter to Flavian, but a perfect summary of the Church's teaching against Nestorius on the one hand and Eutyches on the other. He bids them work on the Emperor 'that he may deign (*dignetur*) to grant our petition, by which we have demanded that a plenary Synod be called.' But later on he wrote to the Archimandrites Martin and Faustus, and spoke of his letters having been sent to Constantinople, 'not only with the authority of the Holy See, but also with the unanimous consent of the holy Synod, which had met in great numbers,'[1] letters which

[1] 'Quæ ad nos frequens convenerat.' St. Leo calls the letters *scripta*

being thus sent showed ' what care we have for the whole Church.' ' Meanwhile let your love take care that what we preach contrary to the impious sense [of Eutyches] and in accordance with evangelic doctrine, may be known to all the children of the Church. For although we wrote fully what had always been and was the opinion of Catholics, still we have now added no little exhortation to confirm the minds of all. For I am mindful that I preside over the Church in his name whose confession was praised by the Lord Jesus Christ and whose faith destroys all heresies, but specially the impiety of the present error: and I understand that nothing else is permitted to me than that I should spend all my efforts on that cause in which the safety of the universal Church is attacked.'

' I preside over the Church in the name of him whose confession was praised by the Lord Jesus Christ '—such were the plain terms in which the Saint described his responsibilities in writing to orthodox Eastern Archimandrites.

But what of the Emperor Theodosius? It is most unfortunate that the correspondence which ensued between Leo and Theodosius has been lost. The Emperor speaks of several letters which had passed between them, none of which are extant. The question of Flavian's deposition necessarily fell through in consequence of his death, owing to the fearful scenes at the Synod in Ephesus; and the correspondence appears to have turned on the question as to whether there was any

nostra, sent by the authority of the Holy See, and with the unanimous consent of the Synod: the authority was his, the consent was the Synod's. The letters were Leo's own letters. This is shown by the next paragraph in this letter.

ground for a revision of the Synod's utterances as to the faith. Leo wrote in December to the Emperor pointing out that they in the West held to the Nicene faith, evidently endeavouring to open his eyes as to the delusion into which he had been led. But the Emperor in his reply to Valentinian assumes that the facts of the case were not well known when he and the Empresses wrote at the instance of Leo, to his correspondence with whom he refers them. He in no way denies the jurisdiction of the See of Peter, but he managed to elude its exercise in this instance. We cannot, indeed, argue much from his silence, since we do not possess the correspondence to which he alludes; but certainly it would have been natural to have given some hint to Valentinian, in his answer to him, that his views as to the authority of the throne of Peter were exaggerated if Theodosius really thought they were. But there is not the most distant approach to such a hint, not a word about the honour due to the Byzantine capital, but mere assertions that if Valentinian had known the whole facts of the case, he would recognise that their adhesion to the Nicene faith remained intact. The position was certainly one of extreme difficulty for Leo. The Emperor appeared to be completely in the hands of the Eutychian party. And it was impossible in those days for the Pope to exercise his right of calling a General Council without the concurrence of the Emperor, who could forbid his subjects passing from city to city, and whose financial aid was absolutely necessary. But, as before in the history of the Church, so now, man's necessity proved to be God's opportunity. Theodosius was removed from the scene. He died from a stumble of his horse.

Part III

THE COUNCIL OF CHALCEDON

Chapter I. The Council of Chalcedon Convoked, p. 199
,, II. The Deposition of Dioscorus:
      1. Placed on Trial, p. 221
      2. The Trial, p. 229
      3. His Contumacy, p. 240
      4. The Sentence, p. 244
,, III. The Need of a Definition, p. 257
,, IV. The Adhesion to Leo's Tome, p. 270
,, V. The Definition itself, p. 280
,, VI. The Restoration of Theodoret, p. 297
,, VII. Antioch's Dependence on Rome, p. 312
,, VIII. Previous Encroachments of 'New Rome,' p. 318
,, IX. The Byzantine Plot; or the 28th Canon, p. 336
,, X. Eastern Recognition of Papal Supremacy, p. 350

NOTES

On Theodoret's Use of ἡγεμονία, p. 219
On Dioscorus being put on Trial, p. 252
On the Meaning of ἔκθεσις, p. 292
On the Restoration of Theodoret, p. 308
On Maximus of Antioch, p. 316
On Dr. Bright's Accusation against the Legates, p. 347

Appendix I. Dr. Bright and the Letter of the Synod to Leo, p. 367
,, II. The Tome irreformable from the first, p. 378
,, III. The Papal Legates' version of the 6th Nicene Canon, p. 394

CHAPTER I

THE COUNCIL OF CHALCEDON CONVOKED

IT has been said that before the accident by which he met his death, Theodosius had seen his errors.[1] He had banished his intriguing chamberlain Chrysaphius, and recalled Pulcheria. What is certain is that he selected her for his heiress.

This extraordinary woman, whose life was one of prayer and fasting in the midst of Imperial cares; who rose night by night to sing the Psalms with some of her equally devout family; who had made a vow of perpetual virginity; and who had been the recipient of one of Cyril's most magnificent letters on the subject of the Incarnation, now became a Deborah in the crisis that had arisen. The Council of Chalcedon saluted her as a new Helena. St. Cyril says that in her 'every kind of virtue and every adornment pleasing in the eyes of the Divine Majesty shone with wonderful splendour.'[2] No woman, however, had as yet held the reins of empire; and accordingly she offered her hand and throne to the most distinguished general of the day, on condition that he should respect her vow. Marcian, for that was his name, was a worthy husband to St. Pulcheria, renowned as well for his piety as for his military skill and sense of

---

[1] See last chapter.
[2] Cyr. Alex. *de Fide, ad Pulch. et Sorores Reginas.*

justice.¹ His accession to the throne was welcomed alike by the senate, the army, and the people at large.

Everything was now changed. The governing motive was no longer primarily political but religious. It is not too much to say that Harnack's appreciation of the situation ignores the main facts. Pulcheria's accession was the new factor, and the determining feature of the conflict as it entered upon its second phase was the passionate attachment of the new Empress to the orthodox faith. Her entreaties to Theodosius that he would accede to the Pope's request for a fresh General Council to be called in Italy had failed. But in her new position her first care, as also that of her husband, was to carry out the earnest wishes, as they understood them, of the Sovereign Pontiff.²

Their very advent to the throne had made a Council unnecessary. This, however, they did not see; and Marcian accordingly wrote to Leo, as ' bishop and ruler of the divine faith,'³ acquainting him with the fact of his accession, asking for his prayers and saying that he hoped that by the Synod assembled with Leo's authorisation⁴ peace would be effected among all the bishops.

¹ τὰ πρὸς Θεὸν εὐσεβὴς, τὰ πρὸς πολιτευομένους δίκαιος (Evagrius, *H. E.* II. i.).

² Of course, political quiet was the aim of the new Emperor; but his religious instincts grasped the fact that the peace of the State was best attained through unity in the faith, and he believed Leo's to be the true faith.

³ τὴν σὴν ἁγιωσύνην ἐπισκοπεύουσαν καὶ ἄρχουσαν τῆς θείας πίστεως— words which Dr. Bright understands to mean that ' as chief Christian bishop, he was that faith's foremost guardian ' (*Roman See*, p. 179). The Latin, which is probably from Marcian's own pen, is ' principatum in episcopatu divinæ fidei possidentem.' *Principatus* on Marcian's lips would imply sovereignty, not, of course, over the faith, but over others in regard to the faith.

⁴ διὰ τῆς συγκροτηθείσης ταύτης συνόδου σοῦ αὐθεντοῦντος (*Leon. Ep.*

Some correspondence ensued, which is not extant, and Leo sent legates to deal with the Emperor's proposal. Marcian wrote again to Leo in November, and asked him to signify his wish as to attendance at the Council, at which all the bishops were to meet, and at which 'whatever conduces to the peace of the Christian religion and to the Catholic faith shall be settled as your Holiness in accordance with the ecclesiastical canons has defined.'[1] The allusion is to Leo's letter to Flavian.

Pulcheria also wrote, and spoke of the Council in which the bishops 'would decide with your authority,'[2] as the faith and Christian piety demand, about the Catholic confession and the bishops who were separated.' In neither of these letters do their Imperial Majesties imply that the doctrine contained in Leo's Tome was an open question. They imply the contrary. Marcian speaks of Leo having the 'rule' in regard to the faith,[3] and of the bishops settling things in accordance with Leo's decision; and Pulcheria in the letter just quoted speaks of 'the Apostolic confession of your letter' and rejoices that Anatolius, the new Bishop of Constantinople, has signed it—treating it as a standard of faith. But

---

73). The last two words obviously refer to the gathering of the Council, which was due, as Marcian considered, to Leo's origination. If it is referred to the establishment of peace, the inference as to the scope of Papal authority would be stronger still. But the best scholars understand it as referring to the Council. Dr. Bright understands it as relating to the settlement of peace, by Leo's authority (*Roman See*, p. 179).

[1] διετύπωσε.   [2] σοῦ αὐθεντοῦντος ὁρίσωσιν.

[3] ἄρχουσαν τῆς πίστεως. Mansi remarks on the words 'as your Holiness ordained' &c.: 'Thus the Emperor acknowledged the definitions of St. Leo, which obviously consisted of the Tome, and were to be looked into by the Synod in such wise as that they were bound to assent to them' (Nat. Alex. ix. 521).

there were bishops who had been led away at the Latrocinium and (it was thought) needed to have the faith set before them, and the lapsed but penitent bishops needed some public restoration which would be made at the Council with Leo's authority.[1] The Empress told St. Leo that the body of the martyred Flavian had been brought back in great honour to Constantinople, and that the bishops who had been sent into exile for siding with him had returned to their sees.

Leo, however, now felt that there was no need to hurry on the Council. It might well wait. The deposition of Flavian was no longer in question, and the dishonour done had been repaired by the solemn transference of his body to Constantinople; the bishops driven out by Dioscorus had returned by Imperial order; and the Tome had been practically accepted. Matters, therefore, could be now readjusted without the excitement of a General Council; and, indeed, a Council could not be materially œcumenical by reason of the alarming state of things at this moment in Italy. Attila was on the warpath, and bishops could not move about. The West was, indeed, always sufficiently represented at a Council by the Papal legates, but the actual presence of Western bishops was impossible. On the whole, therefore, he discouraged the immediate convention of a General Synod. But Marcian had gone too far to recall the step, unless, of course, Leo actually refused to send legates, in which case it would have been merely an Eastern Council. Leo, however, knowing that Marcian had originated the

---

[1] σοῦ αὐθεντοῦντος ὁρίσωσιν. Pulcheria, *pace* Dr. Bright (*Roman See*, p. 179), is speaking here of what was to take place 'in the Council.' The sentence begins κἀκεῖσε γενομένης συνόδου and ends with the words just quoted, to which the subject is 'all the bishops.'

idea of a Council purely from a desire to carry out his strongly expressed and reiterated wish, and knowing that matters were safe in the hands of Marcian and Pulcheria so far as the external ordering of affairs was concerned, decided to send his legates. It was of no importance now, that it should be held in Italy, as Leo had originally desired, for the Court influence was no longer opposed to the true faith, and Pulcheria had expressly promised that nothing should be decided without the authority of Leo.[1] Marcian, therefore, had his way: a fact which has no bearing on the question of Papal rights; for any such question would only have emerged if Leo had refused to have anything to do with the convocation of a General Synod. But their Imperial Majesties and the Sovereign Pontiff were now working in concert, and the one desire of their Majesties was that the authority of the Pontiff should have full sway both in the matter of faith and in the discipline to be observed in regard to the bishops who had failed in their duty at the Latrocinium.

Everything, therefore, now promised well, mainly owing to the influence of the saintly woman who, in God's providence, was now at the helm. Political issues were subordinated to religion; and the influence of the great Pontiff was destined to hold its proper place in the fourth Œcumenical Council of the Church.

But before entering the church at Chalcedon in which the Council was held, to listen to the discussions, it will be well for us to consider the circumstances under which two of the bishops proceeded to take their seats, viz. (1) the new Archbishop of Constantinople and (2) the celebrated historian, Theodoret, Bishop of Cyrus.

[1] σοῦ αὐθεντοῦντος ὁρίσωσιν.

1. Upon the death of the martyr St. Flavian, the clergy and people of Constantinople had elected to the vacant see an Alexandrian priest who had acted as secretary to Dioscorus and was in high favour with the Emperor Theodosius. The latter had relied on him in his ecclesiastical administration, and had probably procured his election as archbishop of his capital. Anatolius, for such was his name, wrote to Leo announcing his consecration. What else he said we do not know. It is not correct to say that he 'simply announced his consecration, without asking for any consent to it on Leo's part,'[1] if by the latter words anything unusual is implied. The purpose of announcing his consecration would naturally be that of receiving Leo's consent. Anatolius's letter, as we have it, is confessedly a fragment: but St. Leo's letter to the Emperor clearly implies that Anatolius sent his notice for the sake of confirmation. We do know, however, that he omitted a statement as to his teaching; he gave no account of his faith.[2] Leo accordingly waited some months before answering, and then he wrote, not to Anatolius himself, but to the Emperor Theodosius. Now it would hardly be possible to give clearer indications of the relation of sovereignty on the part of the See of St. Peter towards the See of Constantinople than are afforded by this and some succeeding letters. It must be remembered that Leo was then writing to an Eastern Emperor who was opposed to his condemnation of Eutyches; he was writing, too, about the bishop of that city which was the very apple of the Imperial eye. We know from the 'Constitution' of Valentinian in 445, which bore the name of Theodosius, that the latter accepted in theory the

[1] *Dict. of Chr. Biogr.* art. 'Leo,' by C. Gore. [2] *Ep.* 69–71.

sovereignty of the See of Peter over all the sees of Christendom; for although such 'Constitutions' ordinarily ran in the joint names of the Emperors as a matter of form, yet they would not on such a vital point contain a doctrine, bearing on politics, which was not accepted by both. It was a matter of course that they agreed in what as a matter of course ran in their joint names. But this sovereignty of the Apostolic See was now expressed in a form most calculated to excite the Emperor's indignation, and to jeopardise the whole position, unless that sovereignty were beyond dispute. A mere diplomatist would not have ventured on such a course. But in truth the Huns, tumultuously crowding into Italy and advancing towards Rome, were not more dreadful in the eyes of Leo than the incursion of heretics into that vineyard of the Lord with which the Eastern bishops declared him to have been entrusted by the Saviour of the world.[1] The time had come when that energetic nature, which had hardly its peer in that half-century, must exercise the authority of his position to the full. The Divine Majesty of his Lord was at stake. It was enough for Leo. He 'made full proof of his ministry.'

Now there was good ground for suspicion as to Anatolius's teaching. Indeed, his conduct after the Synod showed that there was a taint of heresy about him, such as Leo feared. Accordingly Leo wrote to the Emperor, in July 450, and praised him for deciding to adhere to the Nicene Creed. It was on this point that Theodosius had been misled by the Eutychian party. They were, as we have seen, for ever proclaiming their adherence to the Nicene Creed, and made believe that they were con-

[1] Letter of the Eastern bishops to Leo after Chalcedon.

tending for that Creed and for the Ephesine decree. So the Pope gives the Emperor credit for sincerely believing that he was acting in defence of the Nicene settlement; and on this ground he expresses his surprise that Anatolius has not sent him an account of his faith. Consequently he has deferred acknowledging him—'not that he refused his affection, but because he awaited some manifestation of Catholic truth.' He says that he is not exacting from him anything but what every Catholic would do. He then refers to their predecessors' writings as sufficient tests for those who preceded them, but as insufficient for themselves under present circumstances. Anatolius is to 'read carefully' 'what the holy Fathers have given as guard to the faith in the Incarnation,' 'and he must understand that what Cyril wrote against Nestorius is consonant with this.' Cyril's letter, says the Pope, is a clear exposition of the Nicene definition, and has been placed in the archives of the Apostolic See.[1] Anatolius is to read carefully the Acts of the Ephesine Synod against Nestorius; and he is 'not to disdain to read also my letter, which he will find agrees in all things with the Fathers.' St. Leo thus places his Tome side by side with other standards of faith, using it as, with them, a test of the bishop's orthodoxy.[2]

[1] 'Apostolicæ Sedis scrinia susceperunt.' In other words, it was a standard of faith.

[2] 'Let him not disdain' is an expression of courtesy. It is strange that Dr. Bright does not see this, and that he should ask the extraordinary question: 'Can words be plainer as against the assertion that the Tome, *qua* Leo's, was deemed infallible?' (*Roman See*, p. 181). This is exactly what the words do show—viz. that the Tome was already used as an infallible test of orthodoxy in regard to the Eutychian controversy. Notice that Leo gives Anatolius no alternative here—he must read Cyril's letter and St. Leo's own letter. Dr. Bright misses the reason why Cyril's letter was to be read—viz. because it *had been accepted* as a

But this is not all. St. Leo tells the Emperor that Anatolius, having recognised that all this is demanded and expected of him,[1] is to sign the confession of the Common Faith, and make a declaration before all the clergy and the whole people—a profession of faith which is to be 'publicly notified (1) to the Apostolic See, and (2) to all the Lord's priests [*i.e.* bishops] and Churches.' Further, he is to send a written statement as soon as possible, plainly (*dilucide*) declaring that if anyone believes or asserts anything else concerning the Incarnation of the Word of God than what 'the profession of all Catholics and my own' declares, he will separate such a one from his communion. And to expedite this important matter, he says he is sending four legates, whose business it will be 'to declare the exact faith which we hold, *the form of our faith* [*i.e.* the Tome], so that if the Bishop of Constantinople consents to the same confession of faith, with his whole heart, we may feel secure and rejoice in the peace of the Church. If, however, there is any dissent from the purity of our faith and the authority of the Fathers,' a Council must be held in Italy, so that it may not be open to anyone to talk about the Nicene Creed and yet be in opposition to it.[2]

Now, had there been an idea that there was the slightest dogmatic ground for denying the prerogative thus claimed by Leo of dealing with the Archbishop of Constantinople as a subject, and of imposing on him the Roman 'form of faith,' it is not possible to suppose that standard of faith. Leo's letter was *such* previous to any conciliar acceptance: it was such *qua* Leo's.

[1] 'Expeti desiderarique'—'desiderari' expressing Leo's feeling that something of the kind ought to have been done sooner.

[2] *Ep.* 69.

either Theodosius or Anatolius would not have resented this exercise of jurisdiction. It would be impossible to imagine a more extreme case. There is every circumstance that could emphasise the impossibility of such a tremendous assumption (if it were a gratuitous assumption) passing muster without a challenge. The archbishop in question was not naturally disposed to submit quietly to anything that could be called a usurpation for the sake of uniting against a common foe, for he had a tender spot in his heart for the party of Eutyches; neither was he the occupant of a see which had no ambition or no political friends, for it was the Imperial see, and was soon about to attempt a rise in the scale of patriarchal honour over Alexandria and Antioch. Here, too, was an Emperor not favourable to Leo and the orthodox party, but under the influence of Dioscorus and his friends. Such were the circumstances, and they simply preclude the idea that there was not ample recognition of the headship of the See of St Peter on which St. Leo could work; for Leo was neither a dullard nor void of care for the faith. He lived for the faith, and he knew something of men.

To Pulcheria Leo wrote to exactly the same effect. Anatolius must consent to the letter of Cyril and to the Tome, and must without delay acknowledge the 'unskilful folly' displayed by the definition of the Robber-Synod. And the reason he gives is the same as Leo XIII. would give under similar circumstances, viz. ' because both my confession of faith and that of the holy Fathers concerning the Incarnation of the Lord is in all respects concordant and one.' [1]

[1] *Ep.* 70. Some of the best MSS. make Leo say that Anatolius is to acquiesce in Cyril's letter '*vel* epistolæ meæ, &c.' There can, however,

At the same time he wrote to the Archimandrites of Constantinople (a still stronger step in some respects), and complained of Anatolius having given no sign, as if there had been no scandals connected with Constantinople.

Leo seems to have had no fear that he was placing the cause nearest to his heart, the maintenance of the 'peerless sacrament of the faith,' in any jeopardy. If ever there was a case in which the authority of the Apostolic See needed to come forward, it was here, and if ever there was one case more than another in which that authority was used with holy boldness and singleness of aim, it was this. The result was everything that could be wished, owing (we know not how far) to the accident of Theodosius's death, which occurred a week or two after Leo had thus written. The legates appear to have acted promptly, and in November the Empress Pulcheria was able to announce to Leo that 'Anatolius embraces the apostolical confession of your letter,' and has without delay signed the dogmatic epistle to Flavian, which she calls 'the letter of the Catholic faith.'

be no doubt that if 'vel' is the true reading, it = 'and.' The previous letter, just quoted, shows this. And it is quite certain that 'vel' = 'and' in *Ep*. 67, where Leo tells the Bishop of Arles that the Tome and ('vel') Cyril's letter are to be made known to all. And again in *Ep*. 131 'vel' is used for 'and.' Dr. Bright here again thinks this would dispose of the idea that the Tome was infallible *qua* Leo's. He says (*Roman See*, p. 180): 'Cyril's letter and the Tome are put side by side.' Exactly: the one was a standard of faith because of its conciliar acceptance; the other, apart from such acceptance. That is to say, Cyril's letter had already been erected into a standard of faith; the Tome, in taking rank with it, was proclaiming itself also a test of orthodoxy for the Archbishop of Constantinople. This would hold good even if Ballerini's remark about 'vel' were not true. But, I repeat, the previous letter just quoted (*Ep*. 67) is decisive.

Anatolius's letters to Leo are unfortunately lost.[1] Leo answered him and congratulated him, and, after giving directions about the reception of such bishops as had given way at the Latrocinium, he says, ' the favour of communion with us is to be neither harshly denied nor rashly bestowed.[2] He says that he had received Eusebius into communion, and therefore requests Anatolius to have Eusebius's Church taken care of, and desires that all should know that Anatolius has been received into communion with Rome, ' that those who serve our God may rejoice that your peace has been concluded *with the Apostolic See.*' He further tells the Emperor that he has directed the legates to co-operate with Anatolius,[3] and in another letter he tells Anatolius that he joins him with them in the execution of his decree,[4] and gives his directions about the lapsed bishops in general and the leaders in particular. As regards the latter, if they repent he 'reserves' their case 'for the maturer counsels of the Apostolic See,'[5] and bids Anatolius ' to strive to execute such things as befit the Church of God ' in union with his own legates.

At the same time, as if, in God's providence, history was to settle for those who search it the lines of Papal jurisdiction, St. Leo exercised the same authority over

---

[1] There is, however, a valuable fragment of the minutes of the Council held at Constantinople, in which Anatolius publicly pronounced his adhesion to Leo's Tome, which was read through. This fragment is contained in a Life of Abundius, the legate sent to Constantinople for the purpose. He speaks of Leo 'who sent us from Rome to teach (*ad insinuandum*) the Catholic faith to all' *Cf.* Ball. *Leon. Ep.* i. 1487, or Mansi, vii. 775-778.

[2] *Ep.* 80. [3] *Ep.* 83.

[4] 'Executionem nostræ dispositionis. *Ep.* 85. (*Cf.* the use of *dispositio* for an imperial edict in the same series of letters, viz. *Ep.* 91.)

[5] *Ep.* 85. 2.

the members of the archdiocese of Constantinople that Zozimus did over Africa. Two Constantinopolitan priests had repaired to Rome to clear themselves of suspicion as to heresy, and Leo sent them back, saying that 'at great cost they had opened their hearts to [literally *in*] the Apostolic See, and shown that they receive nothing save what we, *by the teaching of the Holy Spirit*, have both learned and teach;' and he exhorts Anatolius to assist them, as 'being adorned with the favour of Apostolical communion,' *i.e.* communion with the Apostolic See.[1]

It is difficult to imagine a more perfect anticipation of Catholic ecclesiastical life in the nineteenth century. And so far there is not a solitary protest recorded, not a distant idea that St. Leo was doing more than exercising his proper prerogative in a natural way, and fulfilling the responsibilities of his sacred and divinely instituted office.

A very important step was now taken by the new archbishop. For the second time he called together his 'home-synod,'[2] and the bishops not merely themselves signed the Tome or letter to Flavian, but sent it to the absent metropolitans.

Abundius, the Papal legate, thereupon returned from Constantinople, and obtained, in accordance with the request of Leo, the subscription of the metropolitan of Milan and his Synod to the Pope's dogmatic epistle. The same had already been obtained from the provinces of Gaul.

So that this letter to Flavian, which had been sup-

[1] *Ep.* 87.
[2] Consisting of the bishops sojourning at and living around Constantinople.

pressed at the Robber-Council had now received the signatures of well-nigh the whole Christian world. It was issued as an *ex cathedra* pronouncement on the part of the Pope; it had now been received as the dogmatic expression of Christian belief at Constantinople, at Antioch,[1] and in the entire West. No bishop who had signed it could henceforth treat its teaching as an open question;[2] it only remained to issue a definition in accordance with it, and to induce the Egyptians to withdraw their complicity with Dioscorus and his teaching, and to arrange the return of the lapsed but penitent bishops. St. Leo had already laid down the conditions of their return, but had made an exception in the case of the ringleaders at Ephesus. This, however, he also eventually left to the discretion of the Council on application from Pulcheria.[3]

2. Such were the circumstances under which Anatolius took his seat. But how did matters stand with Theodoret? He had been condemned by Dioscorus at the Robber-Synod. Thereupon he appealed to Rome. He wrote to Leo,[4] and said 'If Paul, the herald of the truth, the trumpet of the Holy Spirit, betook himself (lit. *ran*) to the great Peter, *so that from him he might convey* to those in Antioch who doubted about the proper observance of the law the solution of their difficulty, much more do we in our littleness fly to your Apostolic throne, that from you we may get healing for the wounds of the Church. For on all accounts the primacy fitly belongs to you. For your throne is adorned with many advantages.' He then enumerates the glories of the Apostolic throne. Its seat, the city of Rome, has a

[1] *Leon. Ep.* 88. [2] *Cf.* Appendix on the Tome, p. 378.
[3] *Ep.* 85. [4] *Theodor. Ep.* 113. *Leon. Ep.* 52.

harvest of blessings as compared with others. They indeed may have size and beauty and a multitude of inhabitants, or none of these, but the splendour of certain spiritual graces. But Rome has both. 'The giver of good things has bestowed on yours a vast crop of blessings. For it is the greatest of all cities and the most splendid, presiding over the world,[1] and is swollen with inhabitants, and in addition to all this it has produced a still prevailing sovereignty [2] and has given its own name to its subjects. But [unlike other cities which have only one or the other of the advantages mentioned] the faith adorns it above all others,[3] and of this the divine Apostle is an unimpeachable witness when he cried aloud ' Your faith is announced in the whole world ; ' but if immediately after receiving the seeds of the saving doctrine it was laden with such wonderful fruits, what terms suffice to do justice to the religion which prevails within it now? It has, moreover, the tombs of the common fathers and teachers of the truth, Peter and Paul, illuminating the souls of the faithful. Now, this thrice blessed and divine pair arose indeed in the East and shed their rays on every side, but gladly came to the end of their days in the West, and thence they illuminate the whole world. *These [Apostles] have rendered your throne most illustrious. This is the culminating point of your privileges.* Further their God has even now shed light on their throne, by placing in it your Holiness [who is] shedding forth the rays of orthodoxy.'

---

[1] τῆς οἰκουμένης προκαθημένη : for the use of the genitive, *cf.* προκαθημένη τῆς ἀγαπῆς (Ign.).

[2] 'Sovereignty': thus translated by Dr. Bright (*Roman See*, p. 191, *note*). The Greek is ἡγεμονίαν.

[3] διαφερόντως, in a distinct and special way. *Cf.* Liddell and Scott, *s.v.*

It will be seen from the above quotations that Theodoret taught that St. Peter was treated as a court of appeal by St. Paul himself in certain matters; that the whole world was illumined with the doctrine of St. Peter and St. Paul; that the see of Rome was the see of the blessed Apostles Peter and Paul, but (as the opening sentence shows) of St. Peter in a peculiar sense. Moreover, Theodoret hands on a truth which had found expression in St. Cyprian and other Fathers, viz. that the praise accorded by St. Paul to the Church at Rome in the opening of his Epistle to the Romans described a unique and abiding fact,[1] and, further, that it was not the Imperial position of the city of Rome that gave to the See its predominant character, but its being the see of the two Apostles, one of whom, however, was so subordinate to the other that he conveyed the necessary teaching to the Christians at Antioch *from the other*, i.e. *from Peter*.

Theodoret then proceeds to express his agreement with the Tome of Leo, showing clearly in a single sentence that he repudiated both Nestorian and Eutychian heresy, and says that he joyfully recognises 'the grace of the Holy Spirit speaking through' Leo. He then describes his own condemnation by Dioscorus, adding, 'But I await the sentence of your Apostolic throne.' He desires to know from Leo whether he is to acquiesce in this unjust deposition or not. 'For I await' (he repeats) 'your sentence, and if you should command me to abide by the adverse decision, I abide by it, and will henceforth trouble no man, but wait for the just judgment of our God and Saviour.' He had said also, 'I beseech and entreat your Holiness that your upright and just

---

[1] *Cf.* Cyprian, *Epp.* 30, 59, 60 (Hartel).

tribunal would assist me, who am appealing to it,[1] and would bid me come to you and show that my teaching treads in the footsteps of the Apostles' (c. 5).[2]

Theodoret wrote also to Renatus, the priest of the Roman Church who had been sent as legate to Ephesus, but was now dead. To him he said: 'Concerning this case, I beseech your Holiness that you would persuade the most holy and blessed archbishop to use his Apostolic authority, and bid me fly to your Council,' *i.e.* the Council which the Pope used in the determination of greater causes, to which Flavian also appealed.

Its authority was derived from the authority of the Holy See, and that it was the authority of the Holy See which Theodoret was invoking is certain, both from the expression ' *his* Apostolic authority,' and from the words that follow. He says that he flies to that Council, ' for that most holy See has the sovereignty over the Churches which are in the whole world on many accounts; and before all these, in that it has remained free from the stain of heresy and none has ever sat in it with thoughts contrary [to the faith]; it has kept the Apostolic grace whole and uncorrupt.' He then expresses his readiness to acquiesce in its judgment, whatever it may be.[3] It is clear from this that it was not the judgment of the Synod

[1] ἐπικαλουμένῳ, the technical term for an appeal.
[2] *Ep.* 113.
[3] ἔχει γὰρ ὁ πανάγιος θρόνος ἐκεῖνος τῶν κατὰ τὴν οἰκουμένην ἐκκλησιῶν τὴν ἡγεμονίαν διὰ πολλὰ κ. τ. λ. (*Ep.* 116). Ἡγεμονία is the word used in *Ep.* 92 for the sovereignty of the Imperial city over the world in the civil order. It may be noticed that the paramount reason for exalting the See of Rome is, with Theodoret, that it has never erred from the faith, but has kept ' *the Apostolic grace* whole and uncorrupt.' The peculiar maintenance of the faith was due to a special grace. *Apostolic grace* is not the grace of the Episcopate simply, but of the See of the Apostles Peter and Paul, as his previous letter shows, and particularly

at Rome in itself that he sought, but the judgment of the Sovereign Pontiff, expressed, as it was wont to be, in Synod. The Synod was the apparatus, the machinery, the setting of the Papal judgment. The bishops of this Synod could not be considered infallible as compared with other Synods, except by reason of their relationship to the Holy See. It was the infallibility of that see on which he distinctly placed reliance. It never had gone wrong; its faith had been something special as compared with that of all other sees from the days when St. Paul spoke of it until now. *The inference is that it will not go wrong now.* Theodoret salutes its decision on the matter of faith as the teaching of the Holy Ghost— 'the Holy Spirit speaking through you' are his words.

At the same time he wrote to the 'Patrician' Anatolius to induce him to persuade the Emperor to allow him (since a bishop could not move without Imperial leave and sometimes the assistance of the Imperial purse) 'to go to the West and be judged by those bishops most beloved of God,' *i.e.* the bishops of the Roman Synod. Now Theodoret was not simpleton enough to ask the Emperor's leave for anything that contravened the laws of the Church as understood in the East; and yet he did ask Anatolius to get him leave to have his case tried at Rome. From this we may justly conclude that the transference of the case of a Greek bishop to Rome was not considered to be in contravention of the Church's laws. It was not here the case of anything claimed by the Pope, but a glimpse of how Greek bishops understood the matter. These Western

of the See of Peter, as the opening of the same letter proves. As Paul repaired to Peter, so Theodoret repairs to the Apostolic throne, *i.e.* the See of Peter.

bishops 'most beloved of God' could possess no rights over an Eastern bishop, except as being the Council of the sovereign ruler of the Church, as Theodoret called the Roman Pontiff.[1] But as the custom was ever to exercise the Pontifical authority by means of a Council it was all one to appeal to the Episcopal Synod at Rome or to the Bishop of Rome himself. Theodoret was in distress, and disposed to lean on any arm that was likely to support him. This may be freely granted and may be thought to discount somewhat his expressions of loyalty to Rome. In fact no one ever does appeal to any authority except when in some distress. But it must be remembered that he had to save his position with others, and that he was both an historian and (in spite of the bad part he took for a time against Cyril) a theologian of no mean order. Men in his circumstances do not appeal to a court that nobody recognises, nor could there be any reason for emphasising the doctrine concerning the relation of Peter to the See of Rome in making his appeal, if it was not a dogma generally accepted. He was a Greek bishop and belonged to the Antiochene jurisdiction. His evidence, therefore, must be allowed to take a conspicuous place in the great body of proof which we have seen to be accumulating, as our narrative proceeds, to the effect that Rome as the See of Peter held the sovereignty of the whole Church in its hands, however imperfectly at particular times and by particular persons the measure of its jurisdiction might be understood. The Vatican teaching was there *in substance*; indeed it would be difficult to express in clearer terms, using the language of that age, the teaching of the Vatican Council concerning the relationship of the Holy See to the rest

[1] *Ep.* 116. *Cf.* Ballerini, *Obs. in Diss. x. Quesnelli*, § 3.

of the Church than has been done by Theodoret. According to him (as we have now seen) that see was 'the all-holy throne'; it was 'the Apostolic Throne'; it was the See of St. Peter and St. Paul; it 'held the sovereignty over the Churches throughout the world'; and it was the one pure, true channel of the Church's faith.

It seems that the writings which Theodoret promised to send to Leo for inspection and judgment did not reach Rome until after the legates had left for the East; but on receiving them Leo at once passed sentence in Theodoret's favour. He was worthy to be restored to his see, which, as a matter of course, it would rest with the Council to effect.[1] Both St. Leo and the Commissioners speak of the Papal 'judgment.'[2] So that there can be no doubt that the Sovereign Pontiff passed actual sentence on Theodoret's case as that of a formal appeal on his part. We may assume that there was a careful examination of the case at Rome, considering the caution invariably exercised by this great Pontiff in admitting anyone to communion who had been suspected of heresy. And Theodoret had exhibited sympathy with Nestorius and opposed Cyril, though he had detached himself from all connivance with heresy when the reconciliation took place between St. Cyril and John of Antioch. It is therefore in the highest degree improbable that St. Leo would pass judgment without careful and, presumably, conciliar examination of his present teaching. At the same time there was a certain incompleteness about the affair, seeing that Theodoret had not appeared at Rome in person, owing to his having been cited to Nicæa (afterwards to Chalcedon); and he had not definitely anathematised Nestorius,

[1] *Leon. Ep.* 77.   [2] *Ep.* 120, § 5. Mansi, vii. 189.

although St. Leo might well presume that he was prepared to do so when opportunity offered, as Anatolius had been compelled by Leo to anathematise Eutyches. When, therefore, Theodoret came to Chalcedon, he was in the position of a man whose right to the position of bishop had been juridically declared by the Papal judgment, but whose *actual restoration* would be completed at the Synod.[1] He was entitled to act as bishop if he complied with the usual forms, and as such to be the accuser of Dioscorus.

NOTE ON THEODORET'S USE OF ἡγεμονία.

In a note on Theodoret's letter to the priest Renatus, quoted above, Dr. Bright says: ' In this letter the Roman see is said to have " on many accounts the presidency, τὴν ἡγεμονίαν, over all Churches." Mr. Rivington mistranslates this by his favourite "sovereignty"' (*Roman See*, p. 193, n. 1). Now Liddell and Scott's translation of this word is ' the hegemony or *sovereignty* of one state over a number of subordinates' (*s.v.* II.) ; and, again, it is (they say) 'used to translate the Roman *imperium*' (II. *b*). And certainly in Byzantine Greek ἡγεμονία and ἀρχή are used interchangeably : *e.g.* Μαρκιανὸς ... τὴν 'Ρωμαίων ἀρχὴν περιβάλλεται. "Α δ' οὖν καὶ ὑπ' αὐτῷ πέπρακται τῶν ἐῴων ἡγεμονεύοντι (Evagr. *H. E.* i. 22). τῶν στρατιωτικῶν ταγμάτων ἡγούμενος (*ibid.* ii. 8). ὁ Ζήνων διέμεινε κρατῶν τῆς ἡγεμονίας, *i.e.* the Empire (*ibid.* ii. 17). And when Theodoret in a previous letter had used ἡγεμονία of the superiority of the city of Rome over other cities Dr. Bright himself renders the word in that letter by 'sovereignty' (*Roman See*, p. 192). In the passage in Thucydides to which Dr. Bright refers, in another work '(*Waymarks*, p. 213), a distinction is drawn between ἡγεμονία and ἀρχή, which was very much lost in the 800 years that intervened between

[1] *Cf.* Ballerini, *Obs. in Diss. x. Quesnelli*, § 10.

Thucydides and the Byzantine Greek of the Councils of Ephesus and Chalcedon. So in Homer, from whom the distance downwards in time was not as great as between Thucydides and later Byzantine Greek, the verbal form ἡγεμονεύω almost always has its original sense of merely leading, whereas in Thucydides it is already attaching to itself the meaning of rule, command, authority (iii. 61). In Greek Testament use it has generally the meaning of government (Matth. xxvii. 2, Luke ii. 2, Acts xxiii. 24), and the participial form is translated by the A. V. ' those that have the rule over you ' in Heb. xiii. 7. In Byzantine Greek, with which we have to do, it generally implies effective jurisdiction. It is used as a synonym of ἀρχή in describing the relation of Eutyches to his monastery. Compare the votes of Domnus and Eusebius in Mansi, vi. 836, with that of Barsumas, vi. 861. The two former use ἡγεμονία, the latter, ἄρχειν, of the same relation.

CHAPTER II

THE DEPOSITION OF DIOSCORUS

§ 1. *Placed on Trial*

THE great Council met, not, as was originally intended, at Nicæa, but at Chalcedon, in order that the Emperor might attend to his Imperial affairs and yet be near at hand in case of need. The Papal legates had stipulated that the Emperor should attend. Their experience of the Latrocinium led to this request. The Council was in reality summoned, as Evagrius puts the matter in brief, because the legates of Leo, who were in Constantinople at the time of Marcian's accession to the throne, 'said that Dioscorus at the second Council in Ephesus had not accepted the Tome of Leo, *which was a definition of the orthodox faith*,[1] and because those who had been insulted by Dioscorus entreated that their affairs might be synodically adjudged.'[2]

Leo wrote to Anatolius of Constantinople telling him that in the case of any bishops who repented of their part in the Ephesine gathering, which was not worthy of the name of a Synod, the communion of the Church was to be restored to them, on condition that they

[1] *H. E.* ii. § 2: τὸν Λέοντος τόμον ὀρθοδοξίας ὅρον τυγχάνοντα.

[2] Harnack says that ' Dioscorus had to submit to a judicial process of an extremely disgraceful and unjust kind ' (*Hist. of Dogma*, iv. 217, Tr.). He gives no proof. I have therefore here given a full account of the proceedings—the best answer to Harnack.

distinctly anathematised Eutyches and his teaching. But an exception was to be made in the case of Dioscorus, as the ringleader. If he showed signs of repentance, his case was to be 'reserved for the maturer counsels of the Apostolic See.'[1]

It must be remembered, moreover, that the whole case turned on the assertion by Dioscorus and the denial by Leo, that the teaching of Eutyches was merely a reflection of Cyril's. Cyril's teaching was the teaching of the Church, not because it was Cyril's but because, as expounded in his two letters to Nestorius read at Ephesus in 431, it had been sanctioned by the Church. It was the teaching of Rome. The bishops in the Council now gathered together, referred to this when they exclaimed: 'Celestine confirmed what Cyril said; Xystus confirmed what Cyril said,' *i.e.* two successive Popes confirmed his teaching. But on Cyril's teaching Eutyches had professedly built his heresy and claimed that his version of that teaching represented the teaching of Nicæa. Leo had written his Tome to show that the Nicene faith was mispresented by Eutyches. The acceptance of this Tome had now been made the touchstone of orthodoxy, and the Council met to enforce this view of the matter. In the words of the Archbishop of Constantinople himself, in his letter of December, the Council had 'to drive away all novelty by confirming with a common decision the faith of the blessed fathers [the Nicene] and the

[1] *Leon. Ep.* 85. The Pontiff writes of 'those who claimed the highest place in the same unhappy Synod'—but it is evidently Dioscorus that he has in view. Anyhow, Juvenal and Thalassius, who might be also alluded to, showed that they did not come under the same category. Leo thus consented beforehand to the Synodical deposition of Dioscorus, but did not give the Synod power to finally absolve him if he repented.

Epistle of your Holiness consonant with this.'[1] This, and the restoration of those bishops who had been illegitimately excluded from their sees and the condemnation or absolution as the case might be, of those bishops who had subscribed to the condemnation of Flavian by putting their signatures to a blank paper, was the proper and the only regular business of the Council.

The bishops met in the church of St. Euphemia, on whose intercession they avowed their reliance, and on whose altar they placed their definition that (as they afterwards told the Emperor, and St. Leo) it might be presented through her to Almighty God before all saints and angels. In other words, the whole Church in solemn assembly avowed their reliance on the intercessory mediation of a great local saint.[2]

There were at least six hundred bishops present, the largest number that had ever met in Council. They were, almost to a man, Eastern prelates, the West being sufficiently represented by legates from Rome. The scene of their meeting is described in glowing terms by Evagrius and is to this day one of the most exquisite spots in that beautiful but ill-fated region. The bishops sat in a circle stretching from the sanctuary into the nave and a copy of the Holy Gospels was placed in the midst.

Dioscorus at once took his seat, as Archbishop of Alexandria, on the right hand of the Commissioners and Senate, with Juvenal of Jerusalem; while the Papal legates (Paschasinus, whom the Pope had sent from

---

[1] *Leon. Ep.* 101, § 1.
[2] For the miracles she was considered to have performed see Evagrius, *H. E.* ii. 3.

Sicily, and Lucentius, both bishops, with the presbyter Boniface) sat on the left, the side of honour, with Anatolius, Maximus of Antioch, Thalassius of Cæsarea Cappadocia and Stephen of Ephesus. Dioscorus had—some little while before, though it is difficult to be sure of the exact time—executed the farce of excommunicating St. Leo—an act of madness which eventually afforded the bishops their chief ground for deciding upon his own excommunication. Whether by this means he thought to make it technically impossible for the legates to sit and condemn him, or whether he acted out of mere *bravado* to show what a Bishop of Alexandria could do, and by way of insulting the Apostolic See, it is impossible to say. He now sat down in the place of honour as the occupant of the second see of Christendom.

His action naturally produced a scene: and it gave an occasion for showing the general acquiescence of the Council in the position of the Bishop of Rome as their head. The Papal legates at once stepped into the centre and said that they held instructions from 'the most blessed and Apostolic Bishop of the city of Rome, *who is the head of all the Churches*,' to the effect that Dioscorus was not to 'sit with the Council.' They threatened to withdraw unless Dioscorus was ordered out.[1] The Commissioners endeavoured to induce the legates to specify the charges brought against Dioscorus, which, however, they refused to do. They refused to act as accusers, Lucentius said. 'Let him give an account of his own judgment, for he usurped the character of judge which did

---

[1] μὴ συγκαθεσθῇ τῷ συνεδρίῳ (Mansi, vi. 581). The legates added to this that he should be sent out of the church altogether, a detail which was not regarded.

not belong to him and he dared to arrange¹ a Synod without permission from the Apostolic See, which has never been done, and *is not competent, i.e. lawful to be done.*' Paschasinus chimed in, saying that the directions of the bishop ' who occupies the Apostolic throne,' as well as the canons of the Church and the traditions of the Fathers, must be obeyed. The Commissioners still urged that ' it is fitting that you should show in particular what is his fault.' On their refusal to act as accusers, the Commissioners turned to Dioscorus and said that he could not hold the position of judge and accused at the same time, and ordered him in effect to take the place of one under accusation.² He had to move out of his seat and remain in the middle, whereupon the legates resumed their seats in the place of honour. The decision of the Bishop of Rome given as ' the head of all the Churches ' was thus obeyed, and Eusebius of Dorylæum now advanced to the middle and entered upon the office of accuser, which the legates had refused to fill.

Dioscorus maintained that Flavian had been rightly condemned by the Council which the Emperor had convened at Ephesus. Accordingly the Acts of the ' Robber-Synod ' were read. In these the name of Theodoret occurred and he was at once sent for, on the ground that he had been restored to his episcopate by Leo and commanded to be present by the Emperor. A scene of wild confusion ensued. The Egyptian bishops, a disorderly set of untrained minds, attached to their ' national Church ' under Dioscorus, and the Illyrian and Palestinian Bishops, saw in Theodoret only the enemy of St.

---

¹ ποιῆσαι. It was the arrangement of the Synod, by assuming the office of president, which was objected to Dioscorus. So Hefele.

² Mansi, vi. 645. See note at the end of this chapter.

Cyril. They shouted and protested and maintained that to admit Theodoret into the assembly was to cast out Cyril, whom Theodoret had once opposed.[1] The statement which the Commissioners and Senate made as to Theodoret's reinstatement and as to the Imperial command, availed nothing for awhile with these Egyptian partisans. They were furious at the idea of one who had anathematised their former patriarch appearing in the Council as bishop. But the Orientals (*i.e.* the bishops of the Antiochene diocese to which Theodoret belonged) and the bishops of Asia, Pontus and Thrace cried out that, on the contrary, Dioscorus should be turned out of the edifice as a murderer. They also affirmed that they had signed Theodoret's condemnation at the Robber-Council under pressure of violence. The Imperial Commissioners hereupon insisted that Theodoret had entered—and was qualified to enter—the assembly as an accuser, and the bishops must simply allow the business which they had begun to proceed. They guaranteed that 'no prejudice should arise to anyone' through the presence of Theodoret, but that the opportunity of arguing their case against him was reserved, if they wished to enter upon any mutual discussion, and they insisted that the Egyptians should bear in mind that Theodoret's exarch, Maximus, had, though informally, certified to his orthodoxy.

Accordingly Theodoret took his seat in the Council,

[1] It must be remembered that the Egyptian, Illyrian and Palestinian bishops—a trouble in the Council afterwards—were a small minority. The Egyptians were not more than twelve or thirteen, the Illyrians were only thirty-two, and the Palestinians sixteen. The great mass of the Council was against them. Juvenal, after his acceptance of the definition at Chalcedon, had grievous trouble with his subjects in Palestine.

but in the middle, as being an accuser. But this was not likely to put the Egyptian bishops at their ease, for Theodoret was there to exercise an office which could only, according to the Sixth Canon (as it is often called) of the Council of Constantinople in 382, be fulfilled by one who was not excommunicated nor deposed, who, in fact, had one of the distinctive rights of a bishop. When, therefore, he took his seat, the Orientals exclaimed, 'Worthy, worthy'—a term applied in ancient times to a newly consecrated bishop, by acclamation. They thus acknowledged his partial restoration.[1] But the Egyptians objected: 'Do not call him a bishop; he is not a bishop.' To which the Orientals returned fire with their clamorous assertion of satisfaction at the decision: 'The orthodox in the Synod,' *i.e.* it is right to admit such as Theodoret to the Synod. 'Cast out the seditious,' *i.e.* the Egyptian bishops themselves. The Egyptians, in no way behindhand in clamour, shouted out: 'Cast out him who has insulted Christ. Long live the Empress!' *i.e.* Pulcheria, Cyril's friend. 'Long live the orthodox Emperor! This fellow anathematised Cyril'— which was only too true. And again: 'We cast out Cyril if we accept Theodoret.' The Commissioners, however, simply stopped the tumult with the remark that all this excited shouting befitted a mob more than bishops, and, leaving Theodoret where he was, ordered the reading of the minutes of the Ephesine meeting (the Latrocinium) to continue.

In promising the Egyptians that they should be allowed to have their say with Theodoret afterwards if they wished to enter upon a struggle,[2] the Commissioners

---

[1] *Cf.* Chr. Lupus, *Synod. Decret.* i. 896 (Brussels, 1673).

[2] φυλαττομένου . . . . παντὸς λόγου καὶ ὑμῖν καὶ ἐκείνῳ εἴ τινα ἀμοι-

were only doing what Leo himself would have been the first to allow. For the case of the bishops was, according to Pulcheria, to be decided (1) at the Council (2) by his authority,[1] and Leo himself in his letter to the Synod had expressly said that with regard to bishops driven from their sees by the Latrocinium, they were to apply the medicine of justice to their wounds so that no one of them should be so deprived of what belonged to him as that one should have what belonged to another.[2] As a matter of fact the Synod did not allow the subject to be mooted at all, until the whole question of the faith had been transacted and the definition drawn up, and the Emperor had left the scene. And Theodoret was included in the list of bishops who sat in Council during the second Act;[3] was allowed to sign himself 'Bishop of Cyrus' at the end of the fourth Act; and in the sixth also he signed, saying 'I, Theodoret, Bishop of Cyrus, defining have subscribed,' which is conclusive as to the *interim* acceptance of his episcopal position by the Council, since he thus exercised the highest prerogative of a bishop, giving his judgment as to the doctrine of the Catholic Church. And all this was done on the ground that he had been restored to his episcopate by Leo. The attestation of Maximus to his orthodoxy was not a judicial act, as was that of Leo. He acquiesced in Leo's decision from personal knowledge of Theodoret. He said he had heard him preach. And Leo's decision must be taken together with his request that the cases of bishops should be, all of them, subject to conciliar investigation.

βαίως ἐγγυμνάζειν βουληθείητε. Dr. Bright *seems* to follow a corrupt reading of the Latin. *Cf.* Baluze's note in Mansi, vi. 591.

[1] σοῦ αὐθεντοῦντος ὁρίσωσιν (*Leon. Ep.* 77).

[2] *Ep.* 93, c. iii.   [3] Mansi, vi. 943.

Thus far, then, Dioscorus had been obliged to pass from the position of judge to that of accused, by order of Leo as 'the head of all the Churches,' and Theodoret had been, at least temporarily, admitted to the rank of bishop in deference to Leo's decision.[1] He took the same place in the middle as did the orthodox champion, Eusebius of Dorylæum (Mansi, vi. 645).

§ 2. *The Trial. The 'Acts' of the Robber-Synod*

Point by point was now proved against Dioscorus, as the 'Acts' of the 'Robber-Synod' at Ephesus (449) were read in the church of Chalcedon.

1. In the account of those who sat in that Synod the name of Dioscorus came first, before that of the Papal legate. This was the signal for cries of indignation from the bishops: '*The name of Leo was cast out*;' and as the Secretary proceeded to read out the names of Juvenal of Jerusalem, Maximus of Antioch, and Flavian of Constantinople, the 'Orientals' (*i.e.* the Antiochenes) and other bishops exclaimed at Flavian being put in the fifth place.[2] It might seem at first sight remarkable

[1] What happened in the Eighth Session will be dealt with in its proper place (*cf. infra*, p. 297). Dr. Bright speaks of Theodoret as being 'kept waiting through several sessions as one who was still open to accusation' (*Waymarks*, p. 231), and 'as an accuser who might himself be accused' (*ibid.* 227), and again as 'capable also of being accused' (*Roman See*, p. 194). There is a false rendering of the Greek in Mansi's Latin text, which uses the word 'accusation.' But Mansi gives Baluze's note, which says that none of the old copies have this reading. At the same time, even if this expression were accurate, the action of the Council so far would afford an emphatic testimony to the supremacy of the Apostolic See, since on no other supposition but that of supremacy could the Papal judgment of a Greek bishop, in the Patriarchate of Antioch, be accepted as conclusive even so far as it was in this case.

[2] Mansi, vi. 608.

that the Antiochenes should exclaim against an arrangement by which their own mother see was placed above that of Constantinople. And it is still more curious that the Papal legate should have come forward and called attention to the fact that they—*i.e.* himself and the present Council—had put the present Bishop of Constantinople first after Rome. And Diogenes of Cyzicus alluded to the canons, meaning of course the third Canon of Constantinople, which Rome had not received. But it was not really on the ground of that canon that Paschasinus, the legate, had proceeded, but out of respect to the *compact* whereby Proclus of Constantinople and Domnus of Antioch had agreed that the status of Constantinople as decreed by that canon should be accepted by them. Paschasinus's weakness in this matter was afterwards repudiated by Leo, and Maximus was blamed for not taking his proper place.

That, however, was a minor matter compared with ousting the representatives of Rome from their proper place in favour of Alexandria. This was the first criminal offence committed by Dioscorus.

2. Next in order, as the recitation of the Acts of the Ephesine catastrophe continued, came the question of Leo's letter to Flavian—his Tome.[1] '*It was not read*,' was the accusation. Dioscorus endeavoured to shift the blame on to the shoulders of Juvenal and Thalassius, but in vain. This was the second serious offence.

3. They now in the natural course of the reading entered upon the question of Eutyches's teaching which had been sanctioned by Dioscorus. The violent behaviour of Dioscorus soon came to the front, for the accuracy of the account as entered in the minutes of the Robber-

[1] Mansi, vi. 616.

Synod was questioned by some of the bishops, and this elicited the declaration from several bishops that they had been unable to use their notaries at the Latrocinium, owing to the party of Dioscorus having overturned their desks and destroyed their tablets and almost broken their fingers. But when they came to the place where Dioscorus was said to have given out that he was acting in harmony with the decrees of the fathers at Nicæa and Ephesus, which he said he had carefully searched, Eusebius of Dorylæum interrupted with the exclamation, 'I search, said he [*i.e.* Dioscorus]; and I too [Eusebius] have done that.' To which Dioscorus now replied, 'I said, " I search," not " innovate," ' *i.e.* ' I do not introduce doctrinal novelties ' (as he had charged Eusebius with doing). ' For our Saviour commanded us saying, " Search the Scriptures." But he who searches does not innovate,' *i.e.* he is kept from doctrinal novelties. To which Eusebius replied in effect, 'That depends on the spirit in which you search.' He suggested that Dioscorus would have found the truth if he had searched in a spirit of prayer.[1] 'The Saviour said " Seek and you shall find." ' The reading was then resumed, and when they came to the place where Dioscorus was reported as saying that the decisions of the fathers of Nicæa and Ephesus could not be rehandled, for this would be to

---

[1] Mansi, vi. 625. It is worth noticing that all these Greeks understood the word ' Search ' in John v. 39, as the imperative. Dr. Bright (*Roman See*, p. 283) has curiously missed the point of this little incident. He translates Dioscorus's words thus : ' Our Saviour bade us examine the Scriptures ; that is not innovating.' The words are ὁ δὲ ἐρευνῶν τὴν γραφὴν, οὐ καινοτομεῖ. Nobody suggested that reading the Scriptures was an innovation. Dioscorus was maintaining that there must be no introduction of doctrinal novelties, and that he was preserved from this because he searched the canons and the Scriptures.

rehandle what the Holy Ghost had decreed, and the Synod (the Robber-Synod) was reported as having thereupon exclaimed that Dioscorus was 'the guardian of the faith,' Bishop Theodore burst in with an indignant denial that they ever said that, to which Dioscorus now rejoined (at Chalcedon) that Theodore might as well say he was not present.[1] So far as presenting a bold front was concerned, Dioscorus was equal to the situation.

But when they came to the account of Eutyches's profession of faith handed in at the Latrocinium, and to his quotation of the decree of the Œcumenical Council of Ephesus (431) against drawing up or presenting any other Creed than that of Nicæa to persons suspected of heresy or to converts of Christianity, Eusebius of Dorylæum bluntly declared that Eutyches lied, for that there was no definition or canon that said exactly what Eutyches did.[2] Dioscorus thereupon interposed, saying that four codices contained this 'definition.' He drew a distinction between a 'definition' and a 'canon.' But the Bishop of Cyzicus explained on behalf of Eusebius that the decree of Ephesus did not forbid what Eutyches had quoted it as forbidding: for Eutyches, following in the footsteps of the Apollinarians, had omitted the addition made at Constantinople in 381, viz. the words 'of the Holy Ghost' and 'the Virgin Mary.' Eutyches therefore (said this bishop) acted 'deceitfully' in quoting the Ephesine decree for his own purpose. But the Egyptians at once shouted out that 'no one accepts an addition'—in a word, they did not accept the Niceno-Constantinopolitan form of the Creed—and they added: 'Let the things decreed at Nicæa prevail; the

[1] Mansi, vi. 628.   [2] *Ibid.* 632. οὐκ ἔστι κανὼν τοῦτο διαγορεύων.

Emperor ordered this.'¹ And it was true that the Emperor Theodosius had ordered that the Nicene Creed (and he seems to have understood it in its shortened form) should be the norm and test of the bishops' faith. But the Emperor was under the heretical influences of Eutyches and Chrysaphius. And Eutyches (as has been already remarked) had purposely adopted the programme of accepting as Nicene only that which was actually expressed at Nicæa. The orthodox bishops accordingly now exclaimed, in answer to the Egyptians' plea that no addition was to be allowed but that they were to adhere to the decrees of the fathers at Nicæa, ' Eutyches said that ' —which was true. The Egyptians, however, clung to their ground, and the reading was resumed.

Eutyches's profession of faith being continued, Eusebius interrupted again at the assertion that 'the flesh of our Lord and God, Jesus Christ, descended from heaven.' This was a point in Eutyches's teaching which, as it had been defended by Dioscorus, showed that the latter was really unorthodox. The indictment against him was growing more and more unanswerable. This was a third serious count against him.

4. After a passage of arms in which Dioscorus elicited that the Bishop of Isauria had shown the white feather, the Antiochenes and their party owned their cowardice in not having withstood Dioscorus when he induced them to sign the deposition of Flavian by putting their names to a blank paper. Even Thalassius, who had so supported Dioscorus, joined in with his *peccavi*.²

The reading being resumed, Flavian's request at the Latrocinium that Eusebius of Dorylæum might be admitted as having been the accuser of Eutyches at the

¹ Mansi, vi. 633. *Cf.* Rusticus's annotation.   ² *Ibid.* 640.

Constantinopolitan Synod of 448, the Chalcedonian magistrates, recognising the monstrous injustice of Eusebius's exclusion, asked Dioscorus why Eusebius had not been allowed to enter. Dioscorus again threw the blame on others : this time on the Emperor, whose representative, the Count Elpidius, had ordered Eusebius to remain outside. Juvenal and Thalassius disavowed any overt action in the matter. The magistrates naturally refused to accept such excuses, saying: 'In case of a matter of faith being tried, this is no defence.' It was an offence against natural justice. Dioscorus, however, endeavoured to blunt the edge of their condemnation by turning to another subject and suggesting that it was as bad for them to have allowed Theodoret to enter and sit as bishop as it was for him to have refused entrance at the Latrocinium to Eusebius. To which the Commissioners replied : ' Bishop Eusebius and Bishop Theodoret sit in the rank of accusers, as also you sit in the place of those under accusation ' :[1] *i.e.* Dioscorus was himself admitted as bishop, so that he could not complain. Thus Eusebius had accused Dioscorus of violating canonical order,[2] and Dioscorus's only defence was that the Imperial Commissioner took the lead, and that the Chalcedonian fathers had themselves admitted Theodoret to the rank of bishop—a plea which was not recognised as sufficient.

5. When they now came to the place where Cyril's pacificatory letter to John of Antioch had been read in the Council of Constantinople under[3] Flavian, the Illyrian

---

[1] Mansi, vi. 645.

[2] ἀκολουθία—ἀκολούθως, used absolutely, always = canonically. *Cf. supra*, p. 85, and Christianus Lupus, *Scholia in Canones et Decreta*, i. 903 (Brussels, 1673).

[3] The minutes of the Council under Flavian were read at the

bishops, always on the watch for the name of Cyril to throw it against the adversaries of Eutyches, whom they wrongly imagined to be anti-Cyrilline, exclaimed : ' So we believe, as Cyril.' Theodoret here, by way of justifying the position provisionally conceded to him, exclaimed : ' Anathema to him who says there are two Sons. For we adore one Son, our Lord Jesus Christ the Only-begotten.' This was his act of reparation for past antagonism to Cyril.[1]

The reading of Cyril's letter also gave occasion to Dioscorus, à propos of an explanation of that letter by one of he bishops, to disavow any adhesion to the supposed teaching of Eutyches on the ' confusion of natures' in our Divine Lord. His emphatic words were: ' We neither speak of confusion, nor division, nor conversion '—of one into the other. ' Anathema to anyone who speaks of confusion, or conversion, or commixture.'[2]

At length they came to Flavian's declaration of his own faith—his *ecthesis*, as it is uniformly called.[3] Hereupon the Imperial Commissioners asked the bishops of the Synod for their judgment on Flavian's exposition of the faith. The Papal legate at once rose and said that Flavian had expounded the faith '[4] rightly, for it agrees with the letter (*i.e.* the Tome) of Leo. Anatolius simply said that ' Blessed ' Flavian had ' expounded the faith '

Latrocinium, and as the 'Acts' of the Latrocinium were being read at Chalcedon, those minutes necessarily formed part of this reading.

[1] Mansi, vi. 673.

[2] *Ibid.* 676.

[3] *Ibid.* 680, 681, 683. All through this scene, St. Flavian is spoken of as having ' expounded ' (ἐξέθετο) and promulgated an ' exposition ' (ἔκθεσιν) of the faith. From which it will be seen that it is idle to confine the words ἐκθεῖναι and ἔκθεσις to the Creed.

[4] In each case the Greek is πίστιν ἐξέθετο.

of our fathers in an orthodox way. Lucentius, the Papal legate, said that it agrees with the Apostolic See and the traditions of the fathers; Maximus of Antioch, that Flavian 'expounded the faith' in orthodox wise and agreeably with Leo; Thalassius, that he had spoken in accord with Cyril, which in some sense was the most emphatic thing to say, since Flavian had been condemned at the Latrocinium as though disagreeing with Cyril. After Eusebius of Ancyra and Eustathius of Berytum had spoken to the same effect, Dioscorus put in a word. He asked that more of what Flavian had expounded should be read and it would be found that he contradicted himself, for he said that there were 'two natures after the union,' which Dioscorus implied Cyril had not taught.

And now Dioscorus's right hand man, Juvenal of Jerusalem, next to whom he had sat when at the opening of the session he took his place in the circle of judges, came prominently forward. He said that if they read Flavian's words to the end, they would find that they were in perfect accord with Cyril.[1] He thus contradicted Dioscorus point blank, and hereupon he rose from his seat and passed over to the other side. Bishop after bishop now did the same. This brought Dioscorus to his feet again, and led to an important utterance of his belief. In spite of the defection of bishop after bishop, he stood his ground, and told the assembly that 'Flavian was manifestly condemned *because he spoke of two natures after the union*, *i.e.* after the Incarnation. So that in spite of his having disavowed the doctrine of

---

[1] Mansi, vi. 681. Harnack calls this change of opinion disgraceful (*Hist. of Dogma*, iv. 218, Tr.). The disgrace was in the original deference to Dioscorus.

any confusion or conversion of the natures in our Lord, he maintained the proposition which underlay that false doctrine. He declared now that his teaching was to be found in the Fathers, and that he had carefully compiled the evidence from their writings.[1]

As they proceeded with the reading at Dioscorus's request, a declaration by one of the bishops at the Council of 448 elicited a fresh heretical declaration from Dioscorus. The bishop had spoken of Cyril's *ecthesis*, or exposition,[2] as countenancing the expression 'of two natures' in reference to the Incarnation; whereupon Dioscorus said, '"Of two natures" I accept; "two natures," I do not'—*i.e.* he did not agree that there are two natures in our Incarnate Lord. He added that he was obliged to speak without shame, for his soul was concerned. He thus deliberately adopted the expression 'of two natures' (as opposed to 'in two natures') in vogue among the Apollinarians, and in after time perpetually repeated by the Eutychians. Had he stopped with the mere assertion that Christ was 'of two natures,' he would not have enunciated a heresy, but only (as

---

[1] The expression, as has been said in a previous chapter, on which they built was that there is 'one nature of the Word incarnate'—*i.e.* one nature which was incarnate. Dioscorus and the Egyptians generally professed to ground their belief, not only on Cyril, but on a passage in Athanasius; but there is no such passage. Leontius of Byzantium says that Theodore of Mopsuestia quoted St. Athanasius, but that he (Leontius) could not find the passage in Athanasius's writings (*Lib. de Sectis*, cap. 8). St. John Damascene speaks of the phrase just quoted as, not Athanasian, but as first used by Cyril, and he explains that 'nature' (*i.e.* φύσις) was sometimes used for 'person' (*De Orthod. Fide*, lib. iii. c. 11).

[2] The bishop speaks of Cyril thus: τὸ δόγμα ἐν τῇ ἐπιστολῇ ἐξέθετο (Mansi, vi. 689). I mention this as some writers are for confining the words ἐκθεῖναι and ἔκθεσις to the Creed.

Leontius expresses it) an *imperfect* description of the Incarnation. But the Council of Chalcedon refused to canonise this phrase, however innocent it might be on the lips of some. It was in reality, as used at that time, opposed to the orthodox doctrine that Christ exists 'in two natures.' Presently Dioscorus took occasion from another passage in the minutes of the Constantinopolitan Council under Flavian (which condemned Eutyches) to say distinctly, ' I object to this, for after the union there are not two natures.'[1] And further on, when Eutyches was reported to have said at Constantinople in 448, ' I confess that our Lord was of two natures before the union; but after the union' (*i.e.* the Incarnation) ' I confess one nature,' Dioscorus was found to have said at Ephesus (in 449) 'We all agree to this'—an account of matters which the Antiochenes now repudiated at Chalcedon.[2]

And so they read on hour by hour, with intermingled exclamations from the Antiochenes on the one side, and the Egyptians on the other, the great bulk of the bishops simply sitting and watching the case, which was being conducted with every respect to normal judicial procedure, until at length they had to light the great waxen candles,[3] and the sentence passed by Dioscorus on Flavian at the Latrocinium was read out to these 600 fathers at Chalcedon in the half-darkened church at the same hour at which, two years before, that sentence had been passed. At the conclusion, which ended with the one word in Latin from the Papal legate, *Contradicitur*, the Orientals and their party exclaimed: 'Anathema to Dioscorus. At this very hour he passed sentence: at this same hour let him be condemned. Holy Lord,

---

[1] Mansi, vi. 692. [2] *Ibid.* 774. [3] κηρίων, 901.

avenge Thyself. Catholic Emperor, avenge Flavian. Long live Leo! Long live the Patriarch!'[1]

The session ended with a proposal on the part of the Imperial Commissioners that Dioscorus, Juvenal, Thalassius, Eusebius (of Ancyra), Eustathius and Basil (of Seleucia) should all be deposed, and, after some excited rather than edifying exclamations from the Orientals (Antiochenes), in favour of this wholesale deposition of the presidents, the Commissioners ordered that each bishop should prepare a profession of faith, and the Council was adjourned till the following day.

So far Dioscorus had been convicted of having taken upon himself to degrade the Papal legates from the Presidency of the Synod at Ephesus in 449; of having not read the letter of Leo to the Synod, including the Tome; of having refused to allow Eusebius of Dorylæum a hearing before acquitting Eutyches; of having sanctioned Eutyches's heretical teaching as to the Flesh of Christ having 'descended from Heaven,' and as to only one nature remaining in Him after the Incarnation; of having committed great violence at the Robber-Synod; and of having condemned Flavian for heresy, when his (Flavian's) teaching agreed with that of Leo and all the Fathers.

[1] Mansi, vi. 911. This is the first instance of the word *Patriarch* being used in a General Council. It had been used of Leo by Valentinian, but not in Synod. It was a word in use among the Jews for the supreme judge in religious matters (cf. *Codex Theodos.* Lib. II. tit. i. c. 10). It was transferred first to Leo, then to the Bishop of Alexandria and others, and eventually to metropolitans and primates in general—its use fluctuating somewhat, and its application in legal documents to the Jews gradually dying out. Justinian never applies it to Jews. *Cf.* Lupus, *Canones et Decreta,* i. 910.

§ 3. *His Contumacy. The Papal Legates deliver Sentence*

The position of Dioscorus was at this moment that of a bishop—but of a bishop who was now under a sentence of condemnation ready at any moment to descend upon him and deprive him of the rank of bishop and of a place within the Christian fold. St. Leo had declared him worthy of deposition, but had expressly committed the act of deposition, if he proved obdurate, to the Council of bishops under his legates; the Imperial Commissioners, after a minute investigation of his doings at the Latrocinium, had declared also that he was worthy of deposition; but the actual ecclesiastical sentence had not yet been pronounced. This was left to the bishops assembled, as a matter belonging strictly to the functions of the episcopate by themselves alone, without the magistrates.

'What,' it has been asked, 'is the province of the Episcopate in the monarchy of the Church? It is certain, not only that the episcopal body can never be superseded in the Church by the Pope, but also that it can never be deprived of its inherent jurisdiction in the general government of the Church, although there is no difficulty as to restrictions and limitations being placed by the Pope upon the exercise of their jurisdiction, should necessity require such a course. . . . The power of the aristocratic episcopal body was not intended by Christ to control or to reform the government and the teaching of the supreme ruler of the Church, but to give efficacy to his action on the whole body, to diffuse to every part the streams of divine life, and to draw tighter the bonds of unity which link together the whole structure.' These are the words of a writer who received the special approbation of Pius IX. for his works on the subject of Papal infallibility. What, therefore, we shall be careful to notice, if we wish to scrutinise the witness of history, is, *not* whether the Pope appears as an absolute monarch—for no one who accepts the Vatican decrees claims for him such a position as that—but whether he appears as 'head of all the Churches,' as he has been already definitely called in our Council.

When the bishops reassembled,[1] Dioscorus did not make his appearance. But Eusebius of Dorylæum, who had been 'deposed' by him, and had now to make good his case against him, demanded his presence. They searched the precincts of the church, but nowhere could he be found. They accordingly sent an embassy to him, and, this failing, wrote to him, and persisted until the canonical rule of thrice summoning a bishop under accusation had been complied with. Dioscorus first said that he was under surveillance, being in the hands of the Imperial Guard, having (we presume) been placed under arrest after the decision of the first session. But when the officer in command gave him leave to go, he refused to move. He next insisted that the Imperial Commissioners and the Senate should be present at the session. He then gave illness as his reason for not coming. Again, he insisted that not he alone but the others who were prominent in the late Synod should be placed in the dock with him, to which it was replied,

[1] This was not, according to the common opinion, the next—*i.e.* the second—but the third session. But there is considerable authority for supposing that it was. I have, however, given the account of it here, without presuming to settle the question, merely by way of presenting a consecutive narrative of the treatment of Dioscorus.

R

in effect, that he alone was accused by Eusebius. Lastly he recurred to the absence of the magistrates as his ground of refusal. This was the same as contempt of court.

Meanwhile three clerics of Alexandria and a layman were admitted to the Synod, to prefer their several complaints against their patriarch. Their petitions were each one of them addressed to 'the Œcumenical Archbishop and Patriarch of great Rome, Leo, and the holy and Œcumenical Synod,' the priest from Alexandria concluding his petition with repeating 'I, miserable Athanasius, presbyter of the most renowned city of Alexandria, have presented these petitions to the most holy and *Œcumenical Archbishop* and Patriarch Leo, and to the most holy Œcumenical Synod of most holy bishops and fathers.' The layman, Sophronias, concluded in the same way.[1] These documents contained accusations against Dioscorus, which the petitioners said they were prepared to substantiate, of intolerable tyranny and dishonest peculations in his rule at Alexandria. The layman averred that Dioscorus had quashed an appeal to the Emperor, and said that Egypt 'was his own rather than the Emperor's province.'

The Synod considered that these accusations were sufficiently serious to demand explanation. But Dioscorus absolutely refused to put in an appearance.

---

[1] Dr. Bright says that this term 'Œcumenical' was 'obviously put in to please Leo,' and he compares it to the use of the term 'angelical' used by the memorialists of the company of Bishops (*Roman See*, p. 182). But (1) the memorialists had to ingratiate themselves with the Council —not with Leo; and (2) they called the Synod 'Œcumenical' in the same breath; and (3) to call the bishops 'angelical' involved no doctrine, whereas to call Leo 'Œcumenical Patriarch' did.

Dioscorus had now definitely refused to obey the summons of the Synod, and had thus involved himself in an offence against the canons, which rendered all further accusations superfluous. Accordingly, the Papal legate, Paschasinus, asked the bishops to declare with their own mouth what he deserved. The Synod said that he incurred the penalty assigned by the canons to contumacy. Paschasinus put question after question, that everything might be done by the Synod itself in due order and with the utmost plainness of speech. He was desirous that the punishment should be the act of the entire Synod. Not a voice was raised in favour of the contumacious Archbishop. No Egyptian clamours, no Illyrian shouts, but in perfect calmness and without hesitation, the Synod decided that this, the highest offence known to canon law, should be visited with the proper sentence. Then Julian, Bishop of Hypæpæ, rose and said: 'Holy Fathers, listen. At that time Dioscorus held the authority of judgment[1] in the city of the Ephesians and meanwhile he deposed the most holy Flavian and the most God-fearing bishop Eusebius, himself passing the unrighteous judgment first, and all followed by compulsion. Now, your Holiness holds the authority of the most holy Archbishop Leo, and your Holiness and the whole holy Synod assembled by the grace of God and the command of our most God-fearing Emperors, know all the injustice perpetrated at Ephesus[2] as your Holiness also knows; and thrice has it summoned

[1] τὸ κῦρος . . . τοῦ κρίνειν.

[2] I have followed the oldest Latin versions here. Cf. Baluze's note q in Mansi, vi. 1043. The Greek, literally translated, makes Julian say that the whole Synod holds the authority of Leo. But it hardly seems likely that they would bring this in here, considering the context: though I cannot be sure that the Greek is not correct.

Dioscorus and he has refused to obey. We [therefore] entreat your Holiness, who holds, or rather who hold, the place of the most holy Archbishop Leo, to give sentence against him, and to decree against him the penalty included in the canons. For all of us, the whole of the Œcumenical Synod, is of one accord with your Holiness.'[1] Paschasinus said: 'Once more I say, "What pleases [or meets the wishes of] your Blessedness?"' And Maximus of Antioch said: 'What seems good to your Holiness, we also agree thereto.'

Accordingly the legates 'passed sentence.'[2]

§ 4. *The Sentence.*

The sentence proceeded on the following grounds.

1. 'He received Eutyches, holding the same opinions,

[1] Lit. 'becomes one in vote with'—σύμψηφος γίνεται. The context seems to give the meaning as 'will vote with,' or 'pass the same sentence as.' So Dr. Bright translates the answer of Maximus: 'We will vote with you.'

[2] ἀπεφήναντο. Cf. Liddell and Scott *s. v.*, and Evagrius, *H. E.* i. § 4, used of the sentence of the Synod deposing Nestorius. Dr. Bright (*Roman See*, p. 293) renders 'proposed a sentence.' This is nothing less than a mistranslation. The legates did not propose, but 'gave,' or 'issued'—not 'a' but 'the' sentence, and the bishops had promised to accept it. Dr. Bright's account of Julian's speech is very inadequate (p. 293, note) and misleading. He omits Julian's saying that Dioscorus had 'the authority in judging' (τὸ κῦρος . . . τοῦ κρίνειν), with which he compares the position of the Papal legates; he translates παρακαλοῦμεν 'request' (*Lat.* petimus), and he translates σύμψηφος γίνεται ' the whole Council was σύμψηφος with them,' instead of, as on p. 293, 'we will vote with you,' which is the real meaning. Then he calls the legates' sentence 'their speech,' and quotes Tillemont's misleading representation of ἀπεφήναντο as 'avis.' Then he asks 'If it was *the* Synodical sentence'—whereas it was *the* sentence adopted by the Synod beforehand—'why did it conclude with "the Synod ψηφίσεται according to the canons"?' Because the Synod had promised to accept the sentence. The future is equivalent to 'shall' in legal documents.

[3] Mansi, vi. 1045.

into communion, although he had been regularly deprived by his own bishop, Flavian. This he did ' on his own authority, before he sat in Council with the God-beloved bishops.'

2. 'The Apostolic See pardoned the latter for what was done by them against their will.' 'They have continued up to this hour obedient to the most holy Archbishop Leo and the whole of the holy Œcumenical Synod, on which account he received them as one in faith into communion with himself. But Dioscorus has continued up to the present to glory in these things which should be his shame.'

3. 'He did not consent to the Epistle of Leo to Flavian being read, although frequently entreated to read it and indeed after promising on oath that he would. Through this letter not being read, the Churches of God throughout the world have suffered loss.'

4. All these things might have been pardoned, but 'his next iniquity exceeded all these, for he dared to dictate a sentence of excommunication against the most holy and most sacred Archbishop of great Rome, Leo.'

5. Add to all this that ' when a number of memorials accusing him of irregularities were presented to the Synod, and he was thrice summoned to attend its session, he refused to come, evidently pricked in conscience; and he received those who had been canonically deprived by various Synods. Thus he bore sentence against himself.'

Such were the grounds of Dioscorus's condemnation as summarised by the Papal legates. It will be noticed that they refer to the matter of faith; they mention that Dioscorus was ' of the same opinion ' as Eutyches, that he suppressed the Tome of Leo, and that the bishops whose action at the Latrocinium was condoned were one in teaching (at least they came to be so) with Leo, whereas Dioscorus remained obdurate, and so the condition attached by Leo to his condemnation was fulfilled. He was proved to be not only heterodox, but a heretic. But as he did not present himself to the Synod to be examined by the bishops in this strictly episcopal session they condemned him for what he was proved to have done. Had he come to the Synod at this session, he would have been convicted of heresy also.[1]

And now for the sentence itself. The legates continued:

'Wherefore Leo, the most holy and blessed Archbishop of great and elder Rome, by us and the present most holy Synod, in union with the thrice-blessed and all-glorious Peter, the Apostle, who is the rock and foundation of the Catholic Church, and the foundation of the orthodox faith, has stripped him of the episcopate and deprived him of all sacerdotal rank.

'*Therefore* this most holy and great Synod will vote the penalties assigned by the canons.'[2]

The bishops are not here asked to consider the sentence or to revise it, or to make any suggestions: but the legates simply say that the bishops will as a matter of course accept the sentence now pronounced and proclaim their adhesion to it.

The act of deposition was thus proclaimed to be the act of Leo, and to be accomplished '*with* Peter the Apostle, the rock and foundation of the Church.' 'Leo

---

[1] So Leontius, *De Sectis*, act. 6.
[2] Mansi, vi. 1048: τὰ δόξαντα τοῖς κανόσιν. *Cf.* the legates' request, given above, that the bishops would declare the penalties attached by the canons to Dioscorus's offence.

... has deprived him.' But Leo could not thus act ' with Peter' and with Peter as 'the rock of the Church and the foundation of the orthodox faith' and in such an act lead the Church astray. Else Peter would not prove to be the 'rock.'

But the act of Leo was rendered extrinsically greater by the action of the Synod. The bishops are real judges, and by their adhesion bore witness to the visible unity of the Catholic Church. The Papal sentence then having been delivered, those bishops who were orthodox would as a matter of course connect themselves with the judgment of the Apostle Peter. '*Therefore* the Synod will adjudge the things decreed by the canons' were the words of the legates.

Many has been the struggle in the last three centuries to evade the force of these plain words. Appeal has been made to the words of the bishops that follow. But so far as the doctrine of Papal infallibility is concerned, the appeal is in vain. They only say exactly what would be expected in accordance with that doctrine. They publicly averred that they adjudged the case in the same way as Leo had done. They added nothing to the intrinsic value of the judgment, but they added much to its persuasive force. The judgment became fuller, but not more certain. The unity of the Church was more conspicuous and the accidental reasons for accepting its judgment were increased.

And so Anatolius of Constantinople led the way. He avowed that, 'being of one mind with the Apostolic throne, he voted with it, or adjudged in harmony with it, on the deposition of Dioscorus,' on the ground that he had incurred the penalties of the canons for having disobeyed its threefold summons. Maximus, the Patriarch of Antioch, agreed with Leo and (as he could now add) with Anatolius. Stephen, the Exarch of Ephesus, said the same. Others could now say that they agreed with these 'fathers' or with the Synod, for it was all one to say it either way. The act of Leo was taking up into itself the action of the Synod. It had indeed already spoken for the Synod, for before any episcopal signatures or affirmations the legates had said: 'Leo . . . by us and this present holy Synod . . . has stripped Dioscorus of the episcopate.'

Each bishop's declaration was a definition, each was a judgment, each was a decision, as the action of the limbs in the human body is at once different from, and yet one with, the head. Those limbs that do not move concentrically with the head have to be restored to their proper dependence, or to be cut away. So with the affirmations of the bishops in Council. They themselves selected this metaphor in writing to Leo. He was their head, they the members. The origination of the movement was his; the continuance of the action in regular form was theirs.[1]

The sentence as communicated to Dioscorus did not give the bishops' reasons in full, but merely mentioned the technical point of his disobedience to the summons of the Synod, besides 'his other offences.'[2] This was

[1] The calculations of Dr. Bright (*Roman See*, p. 183, note) as to the number of times the words 'decide' 'define' &c. are used, add nothing to the argument. It was the duty of all bishops to 'define' and 'decide,' but as members, not as head, of the Synod—revolving round their centre, and not out of their orbit. Dr. Bright on another page (p. 293) renders ἐγύμνωσεν [Leo] 'deprives.' As he is summarising, this is presumably not meant for a translation. But it misses a shade of meaning conveyed by the Greek. The act originated with Leo the head, and received its external completion at the Synod. It is 'Leo . . . . deprived.'

[2] Mansi, vi. 1093.

sufficient for the purpose. Those who expect that it
should bring in the name of Leo and who find an argument in its describing the deposition as its own act
might as well deduce something from their not mentioning the Holy Trinity as they did on one occasion, but did
not in their short summary communication to Dioscorus,
contained in a single sentence. In communicating the
deposition to the clergy of Constantinople they allude to
the many ways in which he was caught violating the
holy canons and the discipline of the Church, but in
their very brief document they lay the stress on his
refusal to obey the summons of the Council.[1]

But they wrote two official reports, one to the
Emperors, and a second, when their numbers were
thinned, to St. Leo himself. The two together contain
a vast amount of teaching as to the discipline of the
Church. The latter assigns the origination of the whole
matter to Leo; but it will be better to deal with this in
its proper place. The letter to the Emperors is of high
importance, as in this they give the grounds of their
condemnation in full.[2]

First, Dioscorus had prevented the Pope's letter to
Flavian being read at Ephesus.

Next, he had restored Eutyches 'sick with the impiety of the Manichæans' to his priesthood and position
in his monastery, 'and this after the Bishop of Rome

---

[1] Mansi, vi. 1096. Dr. Bright remarks that 'instead of accepting even constructively [*sic*] the position of being Leo's minister, the Council repeatedly describes the deposition as its own act' (*Roman See*, p. 184). The 'construction' that most people would put on their words is that they did not feel it necessary to include the whole theology of the matter in every communication. It *was* their own act, but not exclusively such. It was originated by Leo. *Cf.* p. 228.

[2] Mansi, vi. 1097.

had by that same letter decreed what was fitting, and had condemned the perfidy of Eutyches in saying, " I confess, indeed, that our Lord Jesus Christ was of (ἐκ) two natures before the union, but there is one nature after the union." '

The quotation is from the Tome of Leo, and shows that they understood the latter part of the Tome as a juridical sentence. Dioscorus had seen this sentence which the Pope passed on Eutyches, and had suppressed the Tome in which it occurred. The significance of this reason must not be overlooked.

Thirdly, his misconduct to Eusebius of Dorylæum was scandalous.

Fourthly, he had received into communion those who had been put out of communion, thereby offending against the canon which 'teaches that those who are excommunicated by one should not be received into communion by another.'

But all this (the Synod says) might have been forgiven; in fact, the Pope had expressly said that a door of repentance was to be left to the last. But Dioscorus (possibly just before the Council met) gathered together ten bishops and induced them to execute the farce of excommunicating St. Leo himself. This was the climax of his madness. And so the Synod continues its report to their Imperial Majesties by saying that—

Fifthly, 'beyond all this, he has also opened his mouth like a mad dog against the Apostolic See itself, and has endeavoured to frame letters of excommunication against the most holy and blessed Pope Leo.'

And, lastly, 'has persisted in his iniquities and been contumacious against the holy and Œcumenical Synod, refusing to answer to various accusations brought against him.'[1]

He remains, therefore (so they wrote at the same time to the Empress Pulcheria), 'a pillar of salt, and the rulers of the various Churches have regained their sees, Christ our Lord having prosperously directed their course, Who shows the truth in the wonderful Leo; for as He used the sapient Peter, so He uses also this champion of the truth,' viz. Leo.[2]

Such, then, was the faith of the Church in the East at that hour, viz. that Peter is the rock in Matt. xvi; Leo acted 'with' him; and that in the Church's government of souls, Leo takes the place of the blessed Apostle Peter. The bishops of the Eastern world had gathered round their centre, 'the Apostolic throne,' as they called the See of Rome, and having at the desire of that 'throne' used their judgment in the matter, they had endorsed its decision, and thus manifested the unity of the Church. The Papal had become a Conciliar judgment, not as though the Œcumenical Council were a thing apart, for it included the Pope; but the Papal

[1] Dr. Bright (*Roman See*, p. 184) says: 'Mr. Rivington stops just short of the momentous words, "He has been fittingly deprived of his episcopate *by the Universal Council*."' I do not know why these words are particularly 'momentous,' considering that the report is giving the reasons of the Council's action. But Dr. Bright appears to suggest that there is some 'suppression' in my account, because these words are not tacked on in this place. That, however, cannot be, for I have *begun* with stating what he imagines to be suppressed, since it is 'of their condemnation,' as I have called it, that I am professedly treating. Here I am giving the *grounds of the Synodical condemnation*. The fact itself is placed in the forefront, that it is '*their* condemnation,' of which the *grounds* are given. This was not one of the grounds. In fact Dr. Bright's remark is trivial: it gives the impression of some terrible suppression, when there is none whatever.

[2] Mansi, vi. 1101.

judgment had extended itself so as to gather up into itself the orthodox Episcopate.

Three times had an Alexandrian 'Pope' deposed a Bishop of Constantinople in this century: Chrysostom in 403, Nestorius in 431, Flavian in 449. Here at length a Bishop of Constantinople takes the first place, under Rome, in deposing an Alexandrian 'Pope.'[1]

There are some 'moments' of history which determine a long future. Centuries of national life are affected by a single incident, which, of course, has its roots in the past. The deposition of Dioscorus from the pinnacle of power to which he had climbed in 449 was one of these. The Egyptians clung to him, eventually formed a national independent community, and passed out of the unity of the Church. Separate in their religious life from that of the great Catholic stream, their country came under the domination of Islam, to be delivered from the thraldom of the most debasing tyranny in this nineteenth century of the Christian era, when a Gordon died for their deliverance, and a conqueror has taken his name from the centre of the Khalifa's rule.

But the faith remained, not with Constantinople, who concurred with Rome in the deposition of the Alexandrian Patriarch, but with Rome herself, who had now to settle the balance disturbed by the new heresy.

NOTE ON DIOSCORUS BEING PUT ON HIS TRIAL.

Dr. Bright (1) (*Roman See*, pp. 278 and 181) endeavours to make capital out of the fact that the Imperial Commissioners did not send Dioscorus out of the building altogether, but only

[1] *Cf.* Duchesne, *Les églises séparées*, p. 192.

turned him out of his seat among the bishops, as though this showed that they owned no obedience to the Pope as 'head of all the Churches.' Also (2) he understands them to reprove Lucentius, the legate, for wishing to act, or actually posing, as accuser of Dioscorus, whom he was going to judge (*ibid.*).

To prove (1), he translates the words αὐτοῦ εἰσελθόντος ἀναγκαῖόν ἐστιν ἐκείνῳ ἀντιτεθῆναι (Mansi, vi. 581) thus : ' When he comes in—*i.e.* after having first gone out—it will be necessary to state objections against him ' (*Roman See*, 277, 278). There is nothing about ' first going out.' The literal translation is : ' He having entered [*i.e.* since he has entered], it is necessary that he should have been opposed (or objected to),' *i.e.* that his sitting side by side with the rest of the Council should have been protested against. This, viz. the not sitting with the Council, was all that the Pope had enjoined, ὅπως Διόσκορος μὴ συγκαθεσθῇ τῷ συνεδρίῳ ; the going outside the four walls and coming in again was merely a detail which the legates suggested. The essence of the Papal injunction was clearly that Dioscorus was to be put on his trial, and not to be admitted as judge of anyone. So Evagrius seems to take it (*H. E.* II. iv. and xvii.). And so Quesnel expresses the legates' contention : ' Id mandatum a Leone ne ut judex sed ut reus admitteretur ' (*Diss. de Vit. Leonis*, Chalc. Act. I.). The Commissioners themselves later on say to Dioscorus, when outside the circle of bishops, ' You sit in the place of those under accusation ' (Mansi, vi. 645). So Natalis Alexander : ' Petentibus legatis, decernentibus magistratibus, Dioscorus in synodo sedere prohibitus est ut judex, jussus in medio sedere ut reus ' (*H. E.* Vol. IX. cap. III. Art. xiii. § 17). And Mansi himself thus writes : ' Item enituit dominativa S. Leonis in synodum potestas quia jusserat Dioscorum in synodum tamquam episcopum non recipi sed solum audiri, atque ejus præceptis synodus obtemperavit ' (Nat. Alex. Diss. xii. *Animadv. in potestatem dominativam quam exercuit S. Leo in concilium* &c. § 1). The Pope, I repeat, had not entered into details, but merely ordered that Dioscorus should not be judge, but on his trial the legates insisted that by way of executing this order, Dioscorus should leave his seat at once, 'go out,' else they would themselves withdraw. The Imperial Commissioners hesitated at this strong measure, and wished the legates to accuse him there and then before he left his seat. This the legates refused to do. And here we come to Dr. Bright's second misrepresentation of the scene;

For (2) the magistrates did not say, either 'sharply' or at all, to the legate Lucentius, as Dr. Bright maintains (*Roman See*, p. 278), 'If *you* claim to judge, do not be accuser too,' or, as he elsewhere translates (*ibid.* p. 182), 'If you represent a judge, you must not be accuser as well;' neither, as the same writer expresses himself elsewhere, did 'the Commissioners tell a legate that he had no business to be both judge and accuser' (*Waymarks*, p. 226, note 4). The words to which Dr. Bright in each case refers his readers are these : εἰ δικαστοῦ ἐπέχεις πρόσωπον, ὡς δικαζόμενος οὐκ ὀφείλεις δικαιολογεῖσθαι— 'If you hold the character of judge, you ought not (or you are under no obligation) to plead your case as one on trial.' How Dr. Bright gets 'accuser' out of δικαζόμενος . . . δικαιολογεῖσθαι, I do not know. Possibly he has been misled by the corrupt Latin text, which, however, he must have seen was corrected in the margin. And no one pretends that we have the Latin original even of Lucentius's speeches in this case. Neither did the Imperial Commissioners speak in Latin. Besides Dr. Bright, in each instance, gives his references to the Greek. The fact is that the words in question were obviously addressed, not to Lucentius the legate at all, but to Dioscorus. It is inconceivable that they should be addressed to Lucentius, since he had refused to be the accuser of Dioscorus; and the Commissioners, as representatives of the Emperor, were on the side of the legates, so far as sympathy went;[1] whereas these words, as

[1] *Cf.* Harnack, *Hist. of Dogma*, iv. 217 (Tr.).

addressed to Dioscorus, explain the next three lines, in which we are told that Dioscorus [left the seat he had dared to occupy and] 'sat in the middle,' the place for the accused. In other words, he was transferred at the instance of the legates, pleading the order of 'the head of all the Churches,' from the bench to the dock. So that what, according to the Greek text, the magistrates had said to Dioscorus was : 'If you hold the place (or represent the person) of a judge, you must not (= cannot) plead your cause as one on trial (δικαζόμενος).' The suppressed inference is that 'since you *have* to answer for yourself as under accusation, it follows that you cannot sit in the place of a judge.' The magistrates in fact had given in to the legate. Accordingly, Dioscorus left the seat of judge for the place of accused. It will be noticed that Dr. Bright not only mistranslates δικαζόμενος as 'accuser,' but he translates εἰ δικαστοῦ ἐπέχεις πρόσωπον, 'If *you* claim to judge.' This is doubly wrong. There is nothing in the Greek to justify the *italicised* 'you'; and ἐπέχεις is invariably followed by the dative when it signifies to 'aim at,' so that, even if it *could* here mean 'claim,' it would naturally have been followed by the dative, whereas πρόσωπον is in the accusative case.

Dr. Bright accuses me of culpable omission in the first edition of this work because certain words to the legate were not given. But these are (1) the very words which he has mistranslated, and their omission, if they are correctly translated, does not interfere with the substantial accuracy of the narrative as I have given it; and (2) the other (omitted) words are those which Dr. Bright takes to be an order for Dioscorus to leave, not merely his place as judge, but the building itself, a detail which does not alter the argument as to the deference paid to the decision of Leo. And as for omissions, it is only right to say that Dr. Bright in his somewhat detailed account of the opening scene at Chalcedon in *Waymarks*, p. 226, omits (1) the crucial words 'who is the head of all the Churches,' though this was the ground of the obedience claimed for Leo's order; also (2) the words about Dioscorus having to give account of his own judgment 'because he took upon himself the office or character (πρόσωπον) of judging which he did not possess,' words which give the key to the sentence misunderstood by Dr. Bright; and, lastly (3), he omits the important words 'which is not competent to be done' from Lucentius's explanation of the reason why Dioscorus should stand out as under trial.

On the whole, when we remember that the Emperor had not expressly and explicitly summoned Dioscorus for trial, and yet that he was now put in the dock, after some vacillation on the part of the Imperial Commissioners, in obedience simply and solely to the statement of the legates that Leo, as 'the head of all the Churches,' had ordered that it should be so, this witness of the opening incident in the Council to the prerogative of the See of Peter is as decisive as anything could be. A year before, the Archbishop of Alexandria was master of the position throughout the East; at this hour he was in the dock by order of the Bishop of Rome.

CHAPTER III

THE COUNCIL'S DEFINITION

§ 1. *The Need of a Definition*

THE Emperor Marcian in his letter to Leo concerning the Council had said that 'those things which conduce to the [maintenance of the] Catholic faith shall be laid down as *your Holiness in accordance with the canons of the Church has ruled*,'[1] in allusion to the Tome, or letter to Flavian. The Empress Pulcheria had also said to Leo, that the Council was summoned in order that the bishops '*may decide by your authority* in accordance with what the faith and the Christian religion demands.'[2] These two utterances must be borne in mind if we are to have a clear view of the situation.

But besides this, we must not forget that Leo had also written to the Emperor Marcian saying that he ought to 'order that what had been established by the ancient Council of Nicæa, should remain firm.'[3] He had also said to the Synod itself that they were to take care 'that the decisions against Nestorius in the Council of Ephesus, over which Cyril presided, should be undisturbed;'[4] and, to the Empress Pulcheria, saying that he 'had given injunctions to his legates as to the "form" [*i.e.* of sound teaching] which they were to preserve.'[5]

---

[1] διετύπωσε. *Cf.* Ball. in *Leon. Ep.* 76.   [2] *Ep.* 77.
[3] *Ep.* 90.   [4] *Ep.* 93.   [5] *Ep.* 95.

Further, the Emperors had written to the bishops of the Council saying that 'the holy Synod in the city of Nicæa . . . was to be confirmed.'[1]

Now it was not possible to 'confirm' the Nicene faith by merely reciting the Nicene Creed. St. Cyril had expressly told Nestorius that it was not sufficient for him to do that. He must also accept the authorised explanations of that Creed.[2] At the Council of Ephesus, however, the bishops had not themselves drawn up any doctrinal formulary; they had simply accepted the ruling of Celestine as to the Hypostatic union as in harmony with the Nicene faith, and thereupon excommunicated Nestorius.[3] But the Council of Chalcedon in its fifth session issued a new doctrinal formulary, based on the Tome of Leo; and in this it stood alone up to this time. Its formulary was not a Creed, but an explanation of one point in the Creed of Nicæa; and it was to be presented to those suspected of heresy, not in lieu of, but in addition to, the Nicene Creed. The work of drawing up this definition of faith now occupied the Council during three sessions, and it advanced to its issue by three stages. First, many of the bishops refused to entertain the idea of framing any such definition, but they were overruled; next, their conciliar adhesion to the Tome on which the definition was based had to be publicly proclaimed, that their unity might be clear and emphatic as to the doctrine to be defined; and lastly, they had to be guided into an accurate expression of the salient point set forth in that Tome.

And all through this matter the Imperial Commissioners acted in concert with the Papal legates. As

[1] Mansi, vi. 552.   [2] Ibid. iv. 1071.   [3] Cf. supra, p. 77.

NEED OF A DEFINITION

Hefele remarks, the practical good sense exhibited by the Commissioners, even from a theological point of view, leads us to ask whether they were not inspired in their conduct of the business by the Papal legates. Professor Harnack deplores the ascendency of Leo in the Council through his legates; he thinks that the definition of faith framed in the fifth session had been prepared by them beforehand and shown to Dioscorus at the meeting between him and the Emperor and Empress previous to the Council, and he considers that 'the disgrace attaching to this Council consists in the fact that the great majority of the bishops who held the same views as Cyril and Dioscorus finally allowed a formula to be forced upon them which was that of strangers, of the Emperor and the Pope, and which did not correspond to their belief.'[1]

Harnack's theological position, unfortunately, does not allow him to sympathise with the Christology taught then and ever since by the Catholic Church; and he draws such a sharp line of distinction between East and West as to obscure the unity of the Church, so that the Eastern Emperor and the Pope are in his view of matters 'strangers' to the Eastern bishops; yet his account is so far true that the issue of the Council of Chalcedon was (as events proved) a purely external conformity to the Tome of Leo on the part of some of the bishops; but Harnack immensely overrates the minority that thus submitted.

We have now to see how the Commissioners conducted their delicate task of fulfilling the Emperor's order that 'what was expedient for the Catholic faith should be laid down as his Holiness [Leo] in accordance with the

[1] *Hist. of Dogma*, iv. 215 (Tr.).

canons of the Church decided,' and how the legates executed the order of Leo to keep to the 'form' which he had given them in his Tome.

The matter of Dioscorus having been so far settled at the first session as that he was judged by the Imperial Commissioners worthy of deposition, though the sentence was not then pronounced but deferred until the second or third,[1] the Commissioners and Senate had closed the first session with saying that on the following day each of the bishops must forthwith 'expound his faith in writing.'[2] They at the same time bade them take note that the Emperor himself 'believes in accordance with the "exposition" of the 318 holy fathers at Nicæa and in accordance with the "exposition" of the 150 after that, and with the canonical epistles and "expositions"[3] of the holy fathers Gregory, Basil, Athanasius, Hilary, Ambrose, and the two canonical letters of Cyril confirmed and published in the first Synod of Ephesus.' And they added: 'For moreover Leo, the most reverend Archbishop of older Rome, has sent forth[4] his epistle to Flavian of holy memory against the doubts raised by Eutyches in contradiction to the faith of the Catholic Church.'

One or two points need to be noticed in this injunction of the Commissioners which is the keynote to three following sessions. In the first place, the Constantino-

[1] I have anticipated the acts of the third session in the account given of Dioscorus's deposition, in order to give the narrative a certain unity. It is, however, possible, though (it seems to me) improbable, that the sequence has been disturbed in the ordinary accounts.

[2] Mansi, vi. 936: ὅπως πιστεύει, ἐγγράφως ἐκθέσθαι σπουδασάτω, γινώσκων κ.τ.λ.

[3] ἐκθέσεις.

[4] φαίνεται ἐκπέμψας, the equivalent of ἐξέθετο which is used by the Emperor of Leo's sending forth his Tome, ibid. 937; also cf. vii. 465, for a similar use.

politan Creed is expressly mentioned in opposition to its indirect repudiation at the Latrocinium by Dioscorus and his followers. In the next place, no room for doubt is left as to the *ex animo* reception of Leo's Tome by the Emperor and his representatives, the Imperial Commissioners. Thirdly, what the Emperor and his representatives considered the subject matter for the Council's action was not, in reality, the truth of Leo's teaching, but the extent of the assent given to it by the bishops. For the Commissioners distinctly spoke of Leo's Tome already in this stage as having opposed the teaching of Eutyches 'in contradiction to the faith of the Catholic Church.'

In fact, the *Récits de Dioscore* lets us know that before the Council the Emperor and Empress had done their best to persuade Dioscorus to accept Leo's Tome, but in vain.

And now in entering upon the session in which the matter of faith was mooted it must be remembered that Dioscorus's party, though small, was strong, and that their position was this. Flavian had been condemned by virtue of a misrepresentation of the seventh canon, more properly called simply a decree, of the Œcumenical Council of Ephesus. Dioscorus had read the decree as though it forbade any 'exposition'[1] of the faith other than that made by the 318 fathers of Nicæa. Eutyches had by implication excluded even the Constantinopolitan form of the Nicene Creed, and had been defended by Dioscorus. But Flavian had 'expounded'[2] the faith so as to show that there was in the Nicene Creed enough to condemn Eutyches, and he was himself condemned by Dioscorus on the technical ground that by publishing an

[1] ἔκθεσις. [2] ἐξέθετο.

'exposition' beyond that of the Nicene fathers, he had offended against the Ephesine rule.[1] This was the standpoint of the faction among the bishops that secretly adhered to Dioscorus. This the Commissioners knew well, and they had added a reason why the bishops should make an 'exposition,' viz. 'that those who seem not to have been of one mind with the rest might be brought back to harmony by the full knowledge of the truth.' When, therefore, it was proposed, as it was in the next session, in the same terms as in the first, that the bishops should make an 'exposition,' they, or rather some of them,[2] exclaimed against such a course. They had, doubtless, other grounds for protesting; they were in secret sympathy with Dioscorus. The Commissioners, then, having spoken again of the Emperor's adhesion to 'the faith handed down by the 318, *and by the* 150, and moreover by the rest of the holy and illustrious fathers' (those mentioned at the end of the first session), and having asked the bishops 'to expound the faith clearly,'[3] the latter burst into the exclamation: 'No one makes another exposition, nor do we attempt nor dare to "expound"; for the fathers have taught, and the expositions made by them are preserved in writing: besides those we cannot say [anything].'

[1] Mansi, vi. 907.
[2] *Ibid.* 953. Rusticus in his Annotation here says expressly that it was only some of the bishops that thus exclaimed. He apparently argues from the omission of the word 'all.' And Rusticus's experience and the fact that he studied the records in Chalcedon, or Constantinople, in the following century, make him an important witness. I have treated his suggestion as one of great value. If all the bishops thus exclaimed, all one can say is that they afterwards all changed their minds and made an 'exposition,' which, of course, was not a Creed. There was no question about framing a *Creed*.
[3] ἐκθέσθαι.

NEED OF A DEFINITION

Cecropius, Bishop of Sebastopol, by way of strengthening their contention, added: 'The Eutychian matter has sprung up; on this a "form"[1] has been given by the most holy archbishop at Rome, and we go by it,[2] and have all subscribed the letter.' Upon which the bishops shouted: 'This we all say; the expositions suffice; it is not competent to us to make another exposition.' In other words, 'We all agree that we are guided by the authoritative decision of Leo on the Eutychian heresy, so that no exposition is needed in regard to that: therefore the expositions already made suffice—we are not permitted to make another.' They were, as the event shows, mistaken in their application of the Ephesine rule. It did not forbid a fresh conciliar 'exposition' such as was contemplated in this case, for such an exposition would not consist in inserting anything into the Creed itself, to be presented to converts; it would only be an explanation.[3]

The Imperial Commissioners were by no means satisfied with this. They therefore proposed that 'the patriarchs of each diocese' (using 'diocese' in the sense of a group of provinces) should gather in the middle of the church and deliberate about the faith in common, and then, if all agreed, well and good; if not, they would make their opinions known. But again the bishops

[1] τύπος, here, an authoritative mould, an ordinance, in the full sense of the term.

[2] στοιχοῦμεν αὐτῷ.

[3] Of course, it was also true that the authority of the Council of Chalcedon was equal to that of Ephesus. And what the purely Eastern Council of Constantinople could do, that the Œcumenical Council of Chalcedon could also do, viz. develop the Creed. But it decided not to do that. These same persons actually proposed, in the fifth session, to insert the word Θεοτόκος into the Creed.

shouted : 'We make no exposition : the canon rules that the expositions suffice; the canon rules that no fresh exposition should be made; let those of the fathers prevail.'

In fact, as has been already observed, no doctrinal definition had been issued by the Œcumenical Council of Ephesus. Nestorius had been condemned on the *ex cathedra* judgment of Celestine, which contained a mention of the Hypostatic union,[1] and decided that this doctrine was expressed in the term 'Mother of God,' but the Council itself was not called upon to frame any exposition of the faith in explanation of its teaching. And these bishops at Chalcedon seem to have argued that it was not competent for them to engage in such work, but that it came under the prohibition of the Ephesine Synod. They appear to have thought that if they could not 'expound' in the shape of a Creed, they could not expound at all. In this they were mistaken, and eventually they submitted to the proposal of the Imperial Commissioners, inspired as these evidently were by the Papal legates.[2]

Florentius, Bishop of Sardis, was the first to give in, if indeed, as may be doubted, he had joined in the cries of protest. By way of executing the wishes of the magistrates, he first deprecated being called on to draw up anything offhand.[3] He described himself as among those—indeed he seems to have spoken for all—'who had been taught to follow the Nicene and Ephesine Synods in accordance with the faith of the holy fathers,

---

[1] Mansi, iv. 548-552.

[2] See note on p. 292 for a criticism of Dr. Bright's remarks on this incident.

[3] σχεδιάσαι.

Cyril, and Celestine, *and with the epistle of the most holy Leo.*' He asked therefore for a time to be fixed, 'so that we may approach the truth of the matter with becoming consideration, although certainly as regards our own selves, who have subscribed the letter of Leo, we need no setting right.' In other words, to have subscribed the Tome of Leo was a sufficient guarantee of orthodoxy. His request for an interval of delay was a reasonable one, for some time was necessarily required to frame a doctrinal definition expounding the truth which was denied by Eutyches, and, as he must have known well, was not clearly (if at all) held by the faction of Dioscorus. Cecropius, accordingly, spoke again, and proposed what was a natural preliminary to the work before them. 'The faith,' he said, 'has been well expressed[1] by the 318 holy fathers, and has been confirmed by the holy fathers—Athanasius, Cyril, Celestine, Hilary, Basil, Gregory, and now again by the most holy Leo; and we beg that the [expositions] of the 318 fathers and of Leo be read.'[2]

It will be noticed that he omits any mention of the 150 fathers or of Cyril: probably because the Imperial and Papal order was that whatever was decreed was to be in accordance with the faith of Nicæa as explained by Leo. It was necessary, therefore, to have at least these two documents read publicly.

The Commissioners accordingly had the Nicene Creed read, which was followed by exclamations such as 'In this we were baptised,' 'Blessed Cyril thus taught,' 'Pope Leo thus believes,' 'Pope Leo has thus interpreted'—declarations which must be borne in mind

[1] εἴρηται is undoubtedly the right reading. *Cf.* Evagrius, *H. E.* ii. 18.
[2] Simply τὰ τῶν . . . πατέρων κ. τ. Λέοντος.

when we come to the bishops' signatures to the Tome in the succeeding session.

Next the Constantinopolitan form of the Creed was read, which had been obliquely depreciated at the Latrocinium. The exclamations as given in the record were few: nothing was said about their having been baptised into it.[1] As a matter of fact, most Churches of the East still gave the original form of the Nicene Creed to their candidates for baptism. The Roman Church presented only the Apostles' Creed. At Antioch the Constantinopolitan was not sung at every solemn Mass until the time of Peter the Fuller, but only on Easter Sunday. But it received here at Chalcedon a more public welcome than it had received before. For the record says, '*All* the most reverend bishops cried out, "This is the faith of all; we all believe thus."'

Next, at the proposal of Aetius, Archdeacon of Constantinople, two letters of Cyril were read—his second letter to Nestorius and his letter to John of Antioch, both of which as the archdeacon remarked, had received the Church's sanction. Their recitation was followed by cries of the bishops to the effect that Cyril and Leo were really at one.

Then was read the Tome of Leo, after which the bishops burst into the following cries, probably as a kind of war song, with slight intonations: 'This is the faith of the fathers, this the faith of the Apostles. We all believe thus; the orthodox thus believe. *Anathema to him who does not thus believe.* Peter has uttered these things through Leo. The Apostles taught thus. Leo has taught piously and truly. Cyril thus taught. Everlasting be the memory of Cyril. Leo and Cyril

[1] Mansi, vi. 957.

have taught alike. *Anathema to him who does not thus believe.* This is the true faith. We the orthodox thus think. This is the faith of the fathers. Why was not this read at Ephesus? This is what Dioscorus concealed.'[1]

Two things need to be noticed. First, even if the Tome of Leo had not before this been part of the rule of faith (as, nevertheless, we have seen it was) it certainly was such at this hour. The 'anathemas' settle that question. This is to be borne in mind in view of the next session. Secondly, it is only when we come to Leo's Tome that the mention of the Apostles and the name of Peter occurs in the exclamations.

But during the reading of St. Leo's Tome, the Imperial secretary was three times interrupted by the Illyrian and Palestinian bishops. It must be remembered that the latter were under the jurisdiction of Juvenal of Jerusalem, who had failed so conspicuously at the Latrocinium. Why the Illyrians made so much trouble in the Council, it is difficult to say. But the two together formed but an infinitesimal portion of the vast assembly. They were not joined in this action of theirs by the Egyptian bishops, who, as we shall see, had their own line of action. But these forty-eight bishops (out of 600) from Illyria and Palestine were dealt with in most considerate fashion. Three passages in St. Leo's Tome caused them difficulty. They could not understand how they could be reconciled with Cyril's teaching, which yet had been sanctioned by the Church. It was, as they said in the next session, a matter of phraseology which confused them;[2] they did not presume to imply that the occupant of the Holy See was not orthodox. This they distinctly asserted.[3] Two of these passages

[1] Mansi, vi. 972. [2] ἃ ἡ φράσις διιστᾶν ἠνίττετο (*ibid.* vii. 32). [3] *Ibid.* 30.

were explained by Aetius the Archdeacon, and the third by Theodoret. In each case some passages from Cyril were produced to show the conformity of teaching.

At the conclusion the Commissioners and Senate asked if any doubted, and the answer shouted out was ' No one.' But it was assumed that not all joined in the cry, and accordingly Atticus of Nicopolis asked that an interval of a few days should be allowed them and that since ' the letter of our lord [1] and most holy father and archbishop Leo ' had been read, they might be allowed to take with them for perusal the letter of Cyril to which the twelve Anathematisms were attached, so that in the time of discussion—*i.e.* as to the definition of faith to be drawn up—' they might be fully provided.' Five days were granted and they were to meet at the house of Anatolius and ' consult in common concerning the faith, so that those who doubt may be taught.' ' All the bishops ' then repudiated the idea that anyone doubted, for they had signed the Tome of Leo. Still the Commissioners, who knew well that some needed instruction, as their interruptions had shown, persisted that Anatolius should select some of those who signed (*i.e.* the enormous majority) and who were fitted to teach the others.

The Nestorians, in after times, adduced this treatment of the Illyrian and Palestinian bishops as a flaw in the Council of Chalcedon, for, they urged, the bishops were placed under Anatolius to be taught, when Anatolius was a known sympathiser with Dioscorus and tinged with Eutychian tendencies. But Anatolius had signed the Tome of Leo and publicly proclaimed his intention to

---

[1] Mansi, vi. 974. The word δεσπότης is used in the Council of Chalcedon (i) of our Divine Lord, (ii) of the Emperor, (iii) of the Pope, and of no one else.

force it on the acceptance of those under him under anathema; although it is true that he was still somewhat leavened with, *not Eutychian, but Alexandrian* sympathies. And his action in the fifth session was corrected by that of the Papal legates.

So far, it will be seen, there was no conciliar investigation or examination of the Tome of Leo, unless anyone were to dignify with such a name the interruptions of these few Illyrian and Palestinian bishops, who were immediately set right by the Archdeacon and Theodoret, or unless we consider the decision of the Commissioners and Senate to refer these few bishops to Anatolius to be 'taught' in his house, a conciliar examination. In truth, the objection that has been so confidently raised, that the Tome of Leo was sanctioned by the Synod after examination as by a superior authority, collapses for want of evidence, so soon as we take the whole of the facts into consideration. So far, it had been made from the very beginning the test of orthodoxy. The bishops, by signing it, witnessed to their own orthodoxy rather than set a seal to that of Leo. Their witness, however, did give to the Tome that external recommendation which, though not needed for the strong, was calculated to assist the weak by its impressive exhibition of the Church's unity. And as events proved, every help was needed to preserve the faith in the coming century.

CHAPTER IV

THE COUNCIL'S DEFINITION

§ 2. *The Adhesion to Leo's Tome as a necessary Preliminary*

WE have now reached the second stage in the proceedings immediately concerning the faith. That part of the minutes of the previous session was re-read in which the Commissioners and Senate had requested that each bishop should make an 'exposition,' to *teach* (that is, to exercise their office of teaching in a solemn way) what all were to hold. The object had been distinctly stated, viz. that as there were a few who appeared to differ from the great majority, ' these might be brought into harmony by a *full* knowledge of the truth '—the ' truth ' being, according to the Emperor's faith, the Nicene Creed, as amplified by the 150 fathers at Constantinople in 381, and as interpreted by the Council of Ephesus under Cyril in 431 in respect to the heresy of Nestorius, and again as interpreted by the Tome of Leo in regard to the heresy of Eutyches.[1] It is of the utmost importance to bear this expressly stated object in mind. They were not engaged in investigating any *question* as to whether the Nicene Creed was true, or whether its amplification at Constantinople, or its interpretation at Ephesus and again by Leo, was valid ; they were asked

[1] Mansi, vi. 252.

simply to *confirm* all four by a public conciliar adhesion and a fresh pronouncement of the Episcopate as to the agreement of these four expositions. There was, however, a difference between the Tome or epistle of Leo and the three former: these latter had been already conciliarly promulgated; the Tome had not. The bishops had, indeed, pronounced, and collectively pronounced, an anathema on anyone who did not believe in the teaching of Leo on the subject of the Incarnation; they had, with very few exceptions, signed that document as expounding the orthodox faith; and when they found that a small handful of bishops could not see how three passages in it could be reconciled with the teaching of Cyril—through ignorance, as it proved, of Cyril's writings—they had committed these to the care of Anatolius and some others, to be 'taught'; they had also, during the last five days, considered the best way of formulating their faith on the basis of Leo's Tome.

But now they issued forth from their more private considerations, and were to teach before the world what their faith was, that (so the Commissioners had said in effect) proclaiming their own unity they might teach the world with one voice. They themselves, or rather a minority of them, the least naturally disposed to exalt unduly the Apostolic See, afterwards described their situation thus: they spoke of 'the knowledge of the Lord' 'which the Saviour brought us from above,' 'which you yourself' (Leo) 'preserved as a golden chain reaching down to us by the precept of the Lawgiver, being constituted the interpreter of the voice of Peter to all, and yourself bringing the blessedness of his faith to all, whence we also, using you as the originator of what was good [*i.e.* the true faith], showed forth the inheritance of the truth to the children of the Church.'[1] Such is their own account of what took place. Let us compare this with the actual minutes of the Council.

The Commissioners thus addressed the reassembled Synod: 'The decisions previously arrived at having now been made plain'—*i.e.* the minutes of the previous session about the duty of the bishops having been read —'let the Synod itself teach what has been decided concerning the faith.' The Papal legates at once stepped forward and said: 'The holy and œcumenical and blessed Synod holds fast the rule of faith of the 318, expounded by them at Nicæa, and likewise the definitions; and further the Synod of the 150 gathered together at Constantinople under Theodosius the Great of blessed memory: the exposition of which Creed[2] at the Synod at Ephesus under Cyril of blessed memory, in which Nestorius was condemned, it likewise embraces. But also the letter sent by the most blessed Leo, Archbishop of all the Churches, makes clear what the true faith is: likewise also the holy Synod *holds this faith*; *this it follows*; and it allows nothing further to be added or to be taken away.'[3]

This solemn exposition of the teaching of the Synod

---

[1] *Leon. Ep.* 98.

[2] Mansi, vii. 9. Notice that the Nicene faith is said to be 'confirmed' by the Eastern Synod of 381, and that the word 'exposition' is not the equivalent of 'Creed,' since here it is used of the action of putting forth the Creed: οὗτινος συμβόλου τὴν ἔκθεσιν are the Greek words. So that Dr. Bright is mistaken in identifying ἔκθεσις with the 'Creed' simply (*Roman See*, p. 186).

[3] Thus, again, Dr. Bright is mistaken in imagining that the bishops thought that the Ephesine rule did not forbid additions to documents like the Tome (*ibid.*). Mansi says: *Fatentur nil addendum seu mutandum iis, quæ S. Leo in sua epistola docuerat* (*Anim. in Nat. Alex. H.E.* ix. 524.)

was uttered in Latin, although Paschasinus was acquainted with Greek, but it was the custom that the utterances of Papal legates, when specially solemn, should be made in Latin, and then translated into Greek. This being done, the bishops exclaimed : ' We all believe thus ; so we were baptised ; so we believed ; so we believe.' [1]

Now these bishops were not informing the world that the Nicene Creed was true ; they were bent on no such superfluous errand : they were proclaiming that the Creed *as expounded* by the 150 fathers, by the Council of Ephesus, *and by Leo*, was the faith of the Church. They were, therefore, now asked to say this (which they had already said) in presence of the holy Gospels, which had been placed in their midst—in a word, to confirm it by oath—or, as the Commissioners put the matter, ' Since we see the holy Gospels placed in front by your Reverence, let each of the bishops assembled here *teach* ' [not merely say, but say as holders of the teaching office in common with the occupant of the Holy See] ' whether the exposition of the 318 fathers assembled at Nicæa, and after that the 150 assembled in the Imperial city, agrees with the letter of the most reverend Archbishop Leo.'

What this really comes to, if we connect it with what had gone before, is this : let each publicly and solemnly say if, as is of course the case,[2] the doubts which a few had felt, or pretended to feel, have been removed, and if the harmony of which we spoke in the beginning has been restored ' by the full knowledge of the truth,' so that you hold the same faith as the Emperor holds, viz. the Nicene Creed *as interpreted by Leo*.

[1] *Cf.* Appendix on ' The Epistle to Flavian irreformable from the first,' for the significance of the bishops' signatures in this session.
[2] The εἰ is followed by the indicative.

T

Anatolius responded at once, saying that the letter of Leo agrees with the Symbol of Nicæa, confirmed by the 150, and with the transactions of the Œcumenical Council of Ephesus under Cyril, when Nestorius was condemned. 'Wherefore I assented and willingly subscribed.'

Now Leo had told Anatolius to read his Tome carefully and to compare it with the letters of Cyril, and to sign it as 'the confession of the common faith,' and having done this to make a declaration before all the clergy and the whole flock of Constantinople, and then 'to notify the fact publicly to the Apostolic See and to all the Lord's priests [*i.e.* the bishops] and Churches.' He had at the same time sent four legates whose business it was 'to declare the exact faith which we hold, the form of our faith, so that if the Bishop of Constantinople consents to the same confession of faith, with his whole heart, we may feel secure and rejoice in the peace of the Church. If, however, there is any dissent from the purity of our faith and the authority of the fathers, a Council must be held in Italy, so that it may not be open to anyone to talk about the Nicene Creed and yet be in opposition to it.'[1] And Anatolius had done this, as we learn from a letter which Pulcheria wrote to Leo in November (450).[2] And accordingly, the Pope told Anatolius that he joined him with the legates for 'the execution of his decree.'[3] Anatolius, therefore, in this fourth session of Chalcedon merely said before the Council and in presence of the holy Gospels what he had already publicly declared to the bishops of his eparchy, and in immediately succeeding the Papal legates he was acting according to Leo's arrangement.

But Paschasinus now rose again and in the name of

Leon. Ep. 69. [2] Ep. 77. [3] Ep. 85 : 'executionem nostræ dispositionis.'

the legates made the following statement: 'It is clear and it cannot be disputed that there is one faith of Leo the most blessed Pope, prelate of the Apostolic See, agreeing with the faith of the 318 holy fathers who assembled at Nicæa, and of the 150 assembled at Constantinople, as also that those things hold which were decided at Ephesus under Cyril of holy memory, when Nestorius was deposed on account of his particular error, and that there is nowhere any discordance whatever. *Therefore* also the epistle of the most blessed Pope, which has been shown to have expounded that faith on account of the error of Eutyches, agrees in sense and spirit with that faith.'[1]

Natalis Alexander thinks that Paschasinus in these words objected to the exact shape in which the Commissioners had put the matter before the bishops. They had called on them to say *whether* the Tome agreed with the Nicene Creed and the decrees of Ephesus. This may be so; but the words used by the Commissioners do not necessarily suggest any possibility of doubt. The mere fact of thus solemnly confirming may seem to have called for an emphatic declaration from the legates that what they and the rest of the bishops were now doing involved no admission as to the possibility of the Tome being other than dogmatically true. It is to be noticed that Paschasinus does not 'ground the claim of the Tome to acceptance on its agreement with the two forms of the Creed and with the Cyrilline-Ephesine dogma,' as a recent writer has stated.[2] That

[1] Mansi, vii. 10. *Cf.* for the true reading the *Constitutum* of Vigilius, in which this speech is recited word for word (Mansi ix. 473).
[2] Bright, *Roman See*, p. 190. He refers Paschasinus's words, '*ideoque*, τούτου χάριν,' to the agreement of the Tome with the Creed. But this is to violate the syntax of the passage. Paschasinus says 'καὶ

was *a* claim to acceptance, but not the one that Paschasinus emphasised on this occasion. He said that the Tome agreed with the Nicene Creed *because it contained the faith of Leo,* and because no one could doubt that the faith of Leo agreed with the Creed of Nicæa, and with the dogma of Cyril at Ephesus. He asserted, in the language of the time, the infallibility of the Holy See. Paschasinus thus gave the keynote to the meaning of the bishops in subscribing to the Tome. As Mansi says: 'If the subscriptions of the fathers of Chalcedon be consulted, which we have in the fourth "Action,"[1] we shall find that as the rest, so the legates of St. Leo received his (Leo's) letter as most accordant with the three previous Councils. But as it is certain that they did not receive it precisely on the authority of the preceding Councils, but because it contained the definition of the Apostolic See, and so had always wished the fathers of the Synod to be conformed to that Tome and had already declared in the second 'Act' that nothing could be added thereto or taken from it, so it is to be believed the others did, although they compared it to the previous definitions

τούτου χάριν the Tome agrees with the Creed'—not, the Tome agrees with the Creed *and therefore we accept it,* but the Tome contains the faith of Leo *and therefore it agrees* with the Creed. Dr. Bright also says that 'on Mr. Rivington's showing, they ought to have proclaimed the principle of papal infallibility.' I said no such thing, but on the contrary my words were, 'What was then needed was, not an act of faith in the infallibility of the Vicar of Christ, but an intelligent adhesion to his dogmatic decree,' (p. 414, 1st ed.). But as a matter of fact Paschasinus's words do seem to involve a belief in that infallibility.

[1] Dr. Bright has a characteristic passage on these subscriptions, which he says extend, with the Latin rendering, over nearly thirty-seven columns of Mansi's seventh volume' (*Roman See,* p. 189), but which he understands in quite a different sense from Mansi himself. The meaning of one is the meaning of all. The present writer had (as above) taken Mansi's view of the matter in the first edition of this book.

of Councils the more so as nearly the whole Synod had protested that it believed as was defined in the letter, before any examination.'[1] Golden words these from the great Dominican archbishop whose name occurs on every page of Dr. Bright's work on the Roman See. Mansi warns us against 'stopping short at the rind,' as they do who, because the fathers said that the letter of Leo agreed with the definitions of previous Councils, jump to the conclusion that these fathers thought it might possibly have disagreed with those definitions. Neither is such an expression as 'we found' that the Tome agreed, or 'we have proved,' equivalent to saying 'we found to our surprise,' or 'we should not have believed in it if we had not proved it.' When we consider the character and the ignorance of some of these bishops—two of them in the Latrocinium could not sign their names—and the circumstances under which they acted, it must be felt that it was of the last importance to send them forth, not merely to say, 'the Tome *must* be right because it emanated from the Holy See,' but 'we can prove it to be right, having been carefully taught, or having learned for ourselves, that it is *as a matter of fact* in perfect accord with the standards already acknowledged as such.'

In the course of the episcopal declarations, the Illyrian bishops made a statement in which they said that their difficulty had arisen from the obscurity of language, which seemed to suggest a division—*i.e.* a Nestorian division—into two Persons,[2] but that Anatolius had set them right. The Palestinian bishops said the same.

---

[1] Nat. Alex. vol. ix. Mansi, *Animadv. in potestatem dominativam quam exercuit Leo in concilium Chalcedonense*, § iii. 1. p. 525.

[2] ἃ ἡ φράσις διιστᾶν ἠνίττετο (vii. 32).

The declarations over, some of the bishops pleaded that the five bishops, Juvenal, Thalassius, Eusebius (of Ancyra), Basil, and Eustathius, who had taken a leading part at the Latrocinium, should be admitted to the Council, as they, too, had signed the Tome of Leo. The matter was referred to the Emperor, who referred it back to the Synod. The bishops were admitted amidst cries of 'Long live the Emperor; long live the Commissioners; long live the Senate. This is the peace of the Churches.'

Peace, however, was not quite restored. A scene of excitement ensued upon the Egyptian bishops reading a petition which they had presented to the Emperor, containing a confession of faith which omitted all reference to Eutyches. It was probably the confession drawn up by Dioscorus with considerable subtlety and presented to the Emperor just before the Synod, to induce his Imperial Majesty to allow him to go to the Synod, after eluding actual subscription to the Tome.[1] These Egyptians were now called upon from all sides to anathematise Eutyches and to sign the Tome of Leo.[2] They refused to do the latter on the technical ground that no Egyptian could sign any confession of faith without his patriarch. They pleaded the sixth Nicene canon in their behalf. One of the bishops of Lower Armenia seems to have suggested (in strict accordance with the canons) that a General Council could override the powers of a single patriarch, whose jurisdiction was dormant at such a time. And another bishop (of Tyre)

---

[1] *Cf.* Lupus, *Appendix ad Sym. Chalc.* Act. iv. and also the *Récits de Dioscore*, which also shows that the Egyptian bishops were under the complete tyranny of Dioscorus. They feared to go to Chalcedon to oppose Leo. Rome and Alexandria had always been such friends.

[2] Mansi, vii. 52.

remarked that these Egyptians could not take part in the ordination of a new patriarch until they were at one with the Council.[1] In the midst of all the cries and the arguments with which they were plied, they now threw themselves on the ground and, prostrate before their fellow-bishops, called themselves dying men. They would be murdered on their return.[2] They were, they said, but few, and the bishops of Egypt were numerous; they could not dare to represent the rest of Egypt. To which it was replied that they came to the Synod for that purpose. Still they lay prostrate, and continued to plead. But the bishops did not believe them. They appealed, however, to Anatolius, who, as an Alexandrian himself, knew the Egyptian canons; and eventually they were allowed to wait until a new patriarch was ordained by the Synod, as it was within the power of a General Council to appoint a successor to Dioscorus.

And now, passing over the rest of the business of this session, which concerned certain Archimandrites and dealt with the case of Photius of Tyre, we come to the third and concluding stage in the settlement of a definition. It was the fifth session.

[1] Mansi, vii. 56.
[2] Harnack remarks that their fear of Coptic fanaticism was greater than their confidence in the Imperial police of Egypt.

CHAPTER V

THE COUNCIL'S DEFINITION

§ 3. *The legates prevail*

BISHOP HEFELE has remarked concerning the fifth session of the Council of Chalcedon that it is 'one of the most important in Christian antiquity.' It is certainly one of the most interesting.

A conflict, which at one moment seemed likely to wreck the Council, arose between the Papal legates and the Imperial Commissioners on the one side, and almost the whole of the Council on the other. Harnack thinks that the 'Robber-Synod' (a term against which he protests) does not compare unfavourably with the Council of Chalcedon. The justification of such an assertion is to be found, if anywhere, in this fifth session, in which he considers that the bishops put force on their consciences and accepted a formula merely out of deference to the Emperor and the Pope. We hold no brief for the behaviour of Eastern bishops in a Council. Being, as the Councils of Ephesus and Chalcedon were, the occasion of bringing the members of the episcopate into unity with their visible head, there might, on *a priori* grounds, be any amount of pain in stretching and setting broken or injured limbs. It is, however, absurd to compare any of the sessions of the Council of Chalcedon to the action of the Latrocinium. There was no injustice done here, as there; there was no actual violence; and as regards the bishops' submission it was a matter of mere consistency with themselves to insert in their formula what they had already asserted to be of faith, viz. the terms contained in the Tome of Leo.

In the discussion at this session everything turned upon two expressions—viz. 'of two natures' and 'in two natures.' Eutyches had said at the Council of Constantinople in 448: 'I confess that our Lord was of two natures before the union, but I confess one nature after the union,' on which words St. Leo remarked in his Tome, 'It is as impious to say that the Only-begotten Son of God was of two natures before the Incarnation as it is unlawful to assert that there is only one nature in Him after the Lord was made flesh.'[1] St. Leo thus condemned the expression 'of two natures *before the Incarnation*'; but the words 'of two natures' by themselves were perfectly capable of an orthodox sense, and had been used by St. Flavian in condemning Eutyches. They were, however, also capable of an unorthodox sense, as appears from the fact that Dioscorus used them to express his own doctrine. On the other hand the expression 'in two natures' was incapable of any such unorthodox interpretation. It did not occur, however, in the definition now presented by the bishops, whereas the expression 'of two natures' did.[2] The legates accordingly insisted upon the substitution of 'in two natures,' as conveying the teaching of Leo's Tome. They thus precluded the idea of the existence of our Lord's Humanity previous to the Incarnation, or of its

---

[1] *Ep.* 28. c. vi.
[2] This proposed definition is not extant. But what we have said

unreality after the Incarnation. They, or at any rate the majority of them, did indeed give to the word 'of' an orthodox meaning, for they did not deny the coexistence 'of two natures' *after* the union at Nazareth. But with Eutyches the expression was originally meant to suggest the unreality of the human nature, and was connected with Apollinarian teaching; and Dioscorus had himself clung to the first phrase, and repudiated the second.

When, then, the bishops met on October 22 and their exposition was read containing the expression 'of two natures' and omitting '*in* two natures,' the Bishop of Germanicia demurred to the acceptance of such a definition. Anatolius now rose and vigorously defended it, and the church was filled with the approving cries of the bishops. They declared that they all accepted it, and even went so far as to say that anyone who repudiated it was a heretic. It was, if we may so speak, a crisis in the history of the Church. If we did not know what happened, we might well hold our breath in suspense. Would a definition be accepted which, although not meant in a heterodox sense, yet contained terms which might be accepted by a Eutychian? Would a formula of comprehension find its way into the Church, so that opposing parties could sign the same formulary, setting each its own meaning on it, each retaining its own opinion on the point of dispute? Could anything be more entirely subversive of the teaching character of the Church?

The bishops, it appears, were still possessed with the idea that somehow the orthodox teaching concerning the 'two natures' in Christ involved the heresy of

results beyond dispute from what the bishops said about the one expression, and from their insisting on the insertion of the other.

Nestorius—which spoke of two *persons* in our Incarnate Lord. They even cried out for the insertion of the term 'Mother of God' in the Creed itself, and they called the objecting Bishop of Germanicia a Nestorian, as he passed across the church to the side of the legates. The situation was critical to the last degree. The Papal legates now rose from their seats with the objecting Bishop of Germanicia by their side and absolutely condemned the proposed definition. They insisted on an exact adherence to the teaching of Leo's letter, and, to show they were in earnest, they announced their determination to ask for Imperial rescripts to enable them to return at once to Rome and have a Council celebrated there, if the bishops did not consent to the letter 'of the Apostolic and most blessed man' Leo. But the Imperial Commissioners, who were present at this session without the Senate, having the management of the external [1] business of the Council, anxious to save the bishops from this humiliation, proposed that six bishops should be chosen from the 'Diocese' of Antioch, three from the region of Asia (as being not one of the Patriarchates), three from Illyricum, three from Pontus, three from Thrace, and that, Anatolius and the Roman legates being present, the matter should be arranged between them.

But no—the bishops clung to their definition. They became more emphatic, not to say excited, than ever. They demanded that their formulary should be signed at once in presence of the holy Gospels. The Commis-

---

[1] Harnack misrepresents Hefele's statement about the relation of the Imperial Commissioners to the Council. It was, according to Hefele, purely external, and as such real and official, but not (which is missed by Harnack) above that of the legates in 'spirituals.' *Cf.* Harnack, *Hist. of Dogma*, iv. 214 (Tr.), and Hefele, *Conc.-Gesch.* § 188.

sioners reminded them that Dioscorus had approved of the phrase complained of (viz. 'of two natures') and had deposed Flavian for the use of 'in two natures.' Whereupon Anatolius made the unhappy remark that Dioscorus was not excommunicated because he was a heretic but [only] because he had pretended to excommunicate Leo, and after being twice summoned had refused to attend the Council. Anatolius's sympathy with his old master showed itself in this misleading statement,[1] and the Commissioners, fully alive to the gravity of the situation, seem to have felt the necessity of intervening with a question which could only receive one answer: 'Do you accept the letter of Leo?' to which the bishops replied at once in the affirmative, appealing to the fact that they had signed it. 'Then,' replied the Commissioners at once, 'let what is inserted in it be inserted in the definition.'[2] The bishops protested that there was no difference between their definition and the Tome of Leo. They wildly averred that 'the definition contains everything.' They argued, not without a certain astuteness, that Leo and Cyril were at one in their faith, that Cyril's teaching had been confirmed by two Popes, Celestine and Xystus, and their definition (such was the supposed conclusion) being in conformity with Cyril's teaching was necessarily in conformity with that of Leo.

The Commissioners decided that the matter—not of faith, but of how the bishops were to be brought to

---

[1] Leontius of Byzantium deals very conclusively with this objection in his *Apology for the Council of Chalcedon*. He says that because Dioscorus was condemned on the formal ground of disobedience to the canons, he was not therefore absolved from the charge of heresy, which was implied in all that was done. The whole Apology is worth reading. It is printed in Mansi, vii. 800–824.

[2] Mansi, vii. 104.

submit to the exact terminology of the Tome of Leo in their definition—must be referred to the Emperor.

There was accordingly a pause while the Imperial secretary was sent across to the Imperial Palace.

The crisis that had been reached was this. The whole Council, after having formally declared the irreformable character of Leo's Tome, were yet introducing an expression into their definition which was quite insufficient to guard the truth, and which, *standing alone*, would have the effect of producing a system of 'comprehension' than which nothing could be more subversive of real unity. To put forth a document which each party could read in its own sense would be to surrender the truth. The Church would stultify herself as a teacher.

The Emperor's answer came back, clear and straightforward. Three courses were open to them, either to agree upon an authoritative decision which could not be excepted against,[1] by means of a sub-committee, exactly such as had been proposed, or each one singly to declare his faith through his metropolitan, or else the case must be carried to 'the West,'[2] i.e. *to Rome*.

The state of excitement may be measured by the answers of the bishops to this Imperial command. They exclaimed: 'Either let the definition stand, or we depart.' Cecropius asked that the definition be read and those who contradicted it could go. The Illyrian bishops cried: 'Those who contradict [the definition] are Nestorians. Let those who contradict it *go to Rome*.'[3]

The Commissioners now brought matters to a head. They said plainly: 'Dioscorus said, "The [phrase]' of two

---

[1] ἀνεπιλήπτως τυπῶσαι (vii. 105).   [2] ἐν τοῖς δυτικοῖς μέρεσιν.
[3] εἰς Ῥώμην ἀπέλθωσιν.

natures' I accept; 'two natures' [*i.e.* that there exist two natures after the union] 'I do not."' 'But,' continued the Commissioners, 'the most holy archbishop Leo says that there are two natures in the Christ united without confusion, change, or division—in the one Only-begotten Son, our Saviour. *Which, therefore, do you follow*—the most holy Leo, or Dioscorus?'

The cry rose up, 'Leo.' 'We believe as Leo; those who gainsay are Eutychians. Leo expounded[1] in an orthodox way.' 'Then,' replied the Commissioners, 'add to the definition, according to the judgment of the most holy Leo, that there are two natures united in the Christ without change, or division, or confusion.'

The commission of bishops thereupon entered into the compartment of the Church in which they had previously consulted and when they came forth, their definition contained no longer the ambiguous expression 'of two natures,' but instead, the crucial words 'in two natures :' that is to say, that, after the union effected at Nazareth when the Archangel Gabriel said, 'Hail Mary, full of grace, the Lord is with thee,' there were, and ever must be, two natures, the Divine and the human, unconfused, in the One Person of our Lord. When they returned to the church, the definition was read and accepted without dissent. The firmness of the legates had saved the situation. Their decision to withdraw, for a Council to be held in the West—which meant, of course, under Leo—helped the Imperial Commissioners to see that unless exact submission was paid to the Tome of Leo in the conciliar definition, all hope of peace was gone. And the bishops themselves, having learnt that the Emperor

---

[1] Mansi, vii. 105 : ἐξέθετο. Again, clearly ἔκθεσις cannot be absolutely identified with 'Creed.'

would insist upon the case being carried to Rome, if they did not make up their minds on a common definition, submitted their judgment, withdrew their protests, and admitted the crucial terms into their doctrinal definition. It is impossible not to feel that there is some truth in Harnack's too contemptuous remarks about the behaviour of these bishops. The deference paid to Dioscorus, the ecclesiastical Pharaoh, would not subside at once. But that they had a genuine admiration for Leo, and felt the impossibility of contradicting him, where he made anything a *sine qua non*, is also evident. This Harnack recognises, but, being out of sympathy with orthodox faith, regrets. We who hold the Catholic faith may well ask where it would have been but for Leo.

In their corrected formulary [1] the bishops included the Constantinopolitan development of the original Nicene Creed, which we now call the Nicene Creed simply, just as the Sardian canons were always called Nicene. After thus combining this later with the earlier form of the Creed, they also defend the Tome of Leo from the charge of innovation brought against the Eutychians, alleging that just as the 150 fathers at Constantinople published their decisions concerning the Holy Spirit, not as if anything were lacking to the original Creed of Nicæa, but to obviate the heretical teaching of those who endeavoured to repudiate His 'lordship,'[2] and just as the Council received the synodical letters of Cyril as against those who imagined that a mere man was born of the Virgin Mary, so too they combine with these the letter of Leo—written to countervail the false interpretation of Eutyches—as in accordance with the confession of blessed Peter and as

[1] Mansi, vii. 108–118.   [2] δεσποτείαν.

being[1] a kind of common pillar against heretics. They also renewed the Ephesine rule against making any other Symbol than the Nicene, having made it quite clear, as against Eutyches, that they combined with this the Constantinopolitan additions. They did not insert the term 'Mother of God' in the Creed, nor anything else, that they might not even appear to violate their own rule. They might have done so, for their authority was equal to that of the 150 fathers in 381, but they preferred to give no handle to the Eutychians.

The real business of the Council—that which dealt with the affairs of the universal Church and not such as were purely Eastern—was now concluded. Accordingly the Emperor appeared on the scene, attended by the heads of the various departments of the Court, with military escort and the Senate and various great patricians, counts, and tribunes, and delivered an address in the Church of St. Euphemia, where the Council had held its meetings. One passage in the Imperial allocution establishes all that has been contended for in the last few chapters, viz. that the Tome of Leo was irreformable—in other words, a standard of the faith before the Council met. His Majesty said that the original idea of the Council was that 'presumptuousness should be crushed on the part of those who dared to think or defend anything different concerning the birth of Jesus Christ from what had been proclaimed by the holy Apostles and handed down in accordance therewith by

[1] ὑπάρχουσαν—implying that it was such before they received it. Dr. Bright imagines that to 'combine' Leo's letter with these others was to assert a superiority over it. One might as well say that to bind up two books is to put oneself above the writer, or that the Church placed herself above the Apostles when she combined the Apocalypse with the rest of the canon.

the 318 fathers at Nicæa, *in the same way as also* the letter sent by the most God-beloved Leo, the Archbishop of Imperial Rome, who presides over the Apostolic Throne, to Flavian of pious memory, Bishop of the new Imperial Rome, *signifies*.'[1]

Clearly, therefore, the Council was convened not to inquire whether the Tome of Leo was accordant with the Creed of Nicæa, but to bring the Eastern bishops into unity on the basis of Leo's teaching. The 'truth,' added the Emperor, 'was to be manifested by the expositions of the Council,[2] but, as he had said more than once, on the lines laid down by the prelate of the Apostolic See.

The Archdeacon of Constantinople then read the 'definition' of the Synod. And, probably, the allocution was also read which is found in Mansi's collection at the end of the Acts.[3] It is an important document, for it defends the practice of adding 'expositions' to the Nicene Creed against the charge brought against it by the Nestorians and Eutychians, that it was the introduction of a new principle.[4] After saying that the Emperor was acting worthily of his rule, in making the things of God his first care and in beginning by gathering his forces against the devil, they at once proceed with this noteworthy declaration: 'Whence God has provided us with an invulnerable champion in regard to error[5] and

[1] Mansi, vii. 132, 133.

[2] ταῖς ὑμῶν ἐκθέσεσι. Again ἔκθεσις is not Creed, but exposition.

[3] Mansi, vii. 455. From the Synod to the Emperor.

[4] καινοτομία. It is perhaps worth while pointing out that objections such as these have no bearing on the doctrine of Papal infallibility. They are only concerned with the method of its exercise. And the objection was advanced by heretics.

[5] *Lit.* 'from error' (ἐκ πλάνης) = to bring us out of error.

has furnished the prelate of the (Church) of the Romans for victory by girding him round with the doctrines of truth on every side,[1] in order that contending,[2] as the fervent Peter, he may draw every mind to God. But lest anyone, declining to agree with his faith,[3] and wishing to shield himself from being convicted of his own private deceit [error] should misrepresent his letter as a composition unknown to and unallowed by the canons, saying that it is not lawful to make any exposition[4] of faith beyond that which was made by the fathers at Nicæa &c.'—they enter into an elaborate proof that the Nicene Creed is one thing, and an exposition by way of interpretation or explanation is another, giving instances from the Fathers. 'Let them not, therefore, produce the letters of the wonderful prelate of Rome as open to the charge of novelty (*i.e.* on technical grounds, as though it contravened the Ephesine canon): but if it is not in accordance with the Scriptures let them confute it'[5]— that is to say, let them attempt the impossible: they will only prove themselves heretics. 'For he that, out of his own mind, when there is no opponent,[6] with his

[1] *Lit.* 'from all sides.'

[2] μαχόμενος, the word they use later on when defending the proper occasion for issuing an 'exposition.'

[3] τῆς πίστεως αὐτοῦ τὴν ὁμόνοιαν—*i.e.* the Tome.   [4] ἔκθεσιν.

[5] Dr. Bright (*Roman See*, p. 191) mentions that this was omitted in the first edition of *The Primitive Church and the See of Peter*,' and accuses me in consequence of 'slurring over a critical part of the case,' incredible as it may seem that he should call this 'part of the case.' Does he think that any bishops considered that the Tome *could* be shown to be repugnant to Holy Scripture? They had publicly declared the contrary. When our Lord said 'If I have spoken evil, bear witness of the evil' (St. John xviii. 23) did He mean that they *could* prove anything against Him? Is not such a mode of speech often used as a defiance, or as a strong form of denial?

[6] μαχόμενος, as they have already said that Leo was. *Cf.* line 3.

own words out of pure ambition [makes] an exposition,[1] such a man is rightly convicted of vainglory: but he that is in conflict with those who hold wrong opinions, &c.' They then ask the Emperor to recognise the Pope's zeal for the faith, 'confirming the teaching of the See of Peter as [being] a seal of the religious dogmas, by the Synod gathered together by you.' The text is obviously corrupt, but we can hardly go wrong in interpreting it to mean that they asked the Emperor to confirm (by making it part of the law of the Empire) the definition of the Synod which was the teaching of the See of Peter. That is what he actually did.[2]

The whole of this part of the Council's action is thus summed up by the Archbishop of Constantinople in his report to Leo. Nothing can exceed the importance of this declaration. It is contained in a single sentence, which leaves no possibility of mistake as to the position which the Tome of Leo held in the minds of the orthodox bishops and the Emperor. 'Since,' says the archbishop, 'after the judgment passed on Dioscorus, it was necessary (being the chief reason why the pious Emperor was eager to assemble the Synod) that the understanding of all should agree to the utterance of your orthodox faith.'[3] In other words, the Tome of Leo was from the first the standard of faith to which all were to give an intelligent adhesion. This had now been effected.

And now the scene in the church must have been

---

[1] ἔκθεσιν. Again this word cannot mean simply a Creed, as Dr. Bright translates it elsewhere, for under no circumstances could a single individual draw up a Creed out of his own mind.

[2] Comp. Mansi, vii. 465 with 173.

[3] *Leon. Ep.* 101: ἐπὶ τὸν τῆς ὀρθῆς ὑμῶν πίστεως λόγον πάντων συνελθεῖν τὴν διάνοιαν.

striking to the last degree. It is thus described in the simplest way by the archbishop. 'The written definition of our faith in accordance with your holy epistle [*i.e.* the Tome] for the confirmation of that of our fathers' (I quote his words) drawn up 'under the protecting shield of the holy martyr Euphemia' was solemnly carried in the presence of the Emperor and Empress and their suite, and the whole Synod of bishops, with the Papal legates, and placed on the altar—that, as the Synod afterwards said, it might be presented by St. Euphemia and all the angels to Almighty God. This was done with prayers and psalms of thanksgiving and every token of holy gladness.[1] It was then taken from the altar and presented to their Imperial Majesties to be laid up in the archives, and to remain—not indeed there, for it was afterwards burnt by heretics, but in the copies taken— as the faith of the Catholic Church until the day of doom.

Note to Page 264, on the Word 'Exposition' (ἔκθεσις).

It will be well to notice here Dr. Bright's exegesis in regard to the bishops' exclamations in the second session about not making another 'exposition.' He first inverts the order of the bishops' exclamations (*Roman See*, p. 185). He unfortunately makes them *in the first instance* object on the ground of the Ephesine rule against compiling another Creed, whereas this comes afterwards, and does not govern the earlier exclamations. He next says that the expositions made 'by the fathers' mean 'the Nicene and Constantinopolitan forms of the Creed to which the Commissioners had referred.' But the Commissioners had also referred to the 'expositions' of the 'rest of the holy and illustrious

[1] μετὰ προσευχῆς, χαρᾶς καὶ εὐφροσύνης (*ibid.*).

fathers' besides those of Constantinople, and therefore in speaking of 'the fathers' we must understand them to include a great deal more than those of 325 and 381. Indeed, on the same page further on Leo is included. Then, out of order, he brings in the speech of Cecropius, about the τύπος of Leo having dealt with the Eutychian matter, and the bishops' exclamation, 'We all say this,' and he refers 'this,' not to what immediately precedes, viz. Cecropius's speech about Leo, but to the bishops' previous exclamations! Then he says that the 'expositions' [*i.e.* in each case, if his argument is to hold good] 'mean the Creed' and 'do not include the Tome.' For this he gives two reasons: first, that the Ephesine rule which is referred to as an authority would *not* have excluded any addition to documents like the Tome, which did not profess to be a Creed. But (1) the objection from the Ephesine rule is introduced *after* the first series of exclamations. And (2) some of the bishops seem to have thought that that rule did exclude additions to the Nicene faith *as already expounded by Leo*. If (as they had all professed to believe) Leo's Tome contained a true interpretation of the Nicene Creed, it is obvious that they could not add to it. Just as St. Gregory said that anyone who should add anything to the Tome must be considered a heretic. The members of the Synod were really at cross purposes. Some appear to have thought that a General Council could not add a word to the Creed of Nicæa as developed by the bishops at Constantinople in 381; others, that a General Council could not even draw up an exposition and make it of faith. It was anyhow not needed, they urged, in this instance, as Leo's Tome satisfied the needs of the case. It was, in fact, the first time that a General Council had been called upon to frame an exposition and launch it upon the world. Hence the genuine doubts of some, while others simply wished to evade giving their judgment. As a matter of fact these same bishops did, some of them, propose to insert the word Θεοτόκος into the

Creed;[1] and, all of them, eventually consented to an exposition being drawn up in the shape of a definition.

Dr. Bright's second argument is that 'in the preceding discussion at Ephesus, 'exposition' had been repeatedly used as meaning 'Creed' (*Roman See*, p. 186, note 2). But it would be more true to say that the 'exposition *of the* 318 *Fathers*' means, as a matter of fact, the Creed of Nicæa, not because it was an exposition, but because it was *their* exposition (ἔκθεσις). The question is whether the 'expositions' alluded to by the bishops, in the first exclamations recorded, *can* include the Tome of Leo. It should be noticed that the word itself is used again and again of Flavian's statement of his belief : *e.g.* by the Imperial Commissioners (Mansi, vi. 680), by the Papal legate, by the Bishop of Antioch and his bishops (*ibid.* 681), and by Athanasius of Busiris, in Egypt—good samples of an œcumenical use of the word. In each of these cases either the substantive ἔκθεσις is used, or part of the verb ἐκτίθημι. And in none of them does the word (ἔκθεσις) 'exposition' mean a 'Creed.' This, therefore, was its use by the members of the Council of Chalcedon. In the same Council it is used of Cyril's letters (vi. 681) and of the letters of Gregory, Basil, Hilary, Athanasius, and Ambrose (vii. 8), which were not Creeds. And the Egyptian bishops were said to 'expound' their faith, who certainly did not draw up a Creed, but were probably at the bottom of the objections raised to issuing a conciliar 'exposition.' Then the bishops in this very session were called upon to make an 'exposition' (vi. 952), and most assuredly it was not meant that they were to frame a Creed. Indeed the Emperor described the very object of the Council as being that 'the truth might be made manifest by your *expositions*' (vii. 133 : ἡ ἀλήθεια ταῖς ὑμῶν ἐκθέσεσι φανερούσθω), and nothing can be more certain than that he did not mean the Council to draw up a Creed. But further, Leo's Tome was itself actually called an 'exposition' in the fourth session (ἐκθέσεως τοῦ μακ.

[1] Mansi, vii. 104.

Λέοντος, vii. 40), and at the fifth session the bishops cried out with one voice : ' Leo has given an orthodox exposition ' (Λέων ὀρθοδόξως ἐξέθετο, vii. 105), and the Synod decided that no one was to go beyond the Nicene faith *as interpreted by Leo*. 'This faith the Synod holds'—*i.e.*, as the previous words say, the true faith manifested by Leo. 'And the Synod allows nothing further to be added, nor anything to be diminished from it' (*lit.* 'suffers to add' &c., vii. 9), using the very expression of the Ephesine canon, or definition, in regard to the Nicene faith as expanded by the fathers of 381 *and interpreted by Cyril and Leo*. These are expositions which are interpretations, and the bishops here accepted the Tome, *before any discussion or examination*, as an exposition which they hoped might relieve them from the necessity of making one themselves. The Ephesine rule forbade the exposition of ' another Creed ' or ' Symbol,' not of an explanation or interpretation. Harnack caustically remarks that the bishops at Chalcedon deceived themselves by drawing the delusive distinction that it was not a question of an exposition (ἔκθεσις), but of an interpretation (ἑρμηνεία) (*Hist. of Dogma*, iv. 218). But the antithesis was really between σύμβολον and ἑρμηνεία. Imagine what confusion it would make to call the ' Ecthesis ' of Heraclius a ' Creed.'

The interpretation which I have given to the first exclamations of the bishops concerning the sufficiency of the Nicene Creed *because* of the existence of the Tome, and which Dr. Bright (in his *Waymarks*, p. 227) stigmatises as 'very careless,' was given in the words of Hefele. Ballerini (*Leon. Opp.* ii. 507, note 22), Mansi (*In Nat. Alex. H. E.* ix. 522), Muzzarelli (*De Auctor. Rom. Pont.* ii. 90), Lupus (*App. in Conc. Chalced.* p. 913), Jungmann (*Diss. Eccl.* vol. ii. Diss. x. § 36), and even Quesnel, adopt the same interpretation. Muzzarelli, indeed, understands the bishops' words about ' the canon ' to refer, not to the Ephesine rule at all, but to the general rule of the Church, which forbids things once defined to be discussed as though not defined.

This would destroy Dr. Bright's interpretation root and branch. And no doubt there is a difficulty about the bishops calling the Ephesine rule 'the canon,' since the term had been expressly refused to it in the first session. On the whole, however, I have preferred the interpretation of the Ballerini, Lupus, Mansi and Hefele. I think it will anyhow be admitted by anyone really acquainted with the subject that 'carelessness' is hardly the term to apply to these great and profound students.

CHAPTER VI

THE RESTORATION OF THEODORET

BEFORE leaving the Synod, the Emperor had asked the bishops to make three authoritative regulations (τύπους) concerning monks and clerics, and had finally given them leave to moot anything they pleased during the next three or four days, after which they were free to return to their respective sees.[1] Thus the business of the Council *qua* Œcumenical was concluded. Consequently, as Pope Pelagius II. notes, several Greek manuscripts contain only six 'Acts' of the Council, ending with the session at which Marcian and Pulcheria were present.[2] The remaining sessions were occupied with matters that concerned the East alone, and which were not included in the programme as described by Leo. Of the bishops, several, such as Juvenal, Thalassius, Eustathius and Eusebius of Ancyra had been pardoned their weakness in the Robber-Synod; Dioscorus had been deposed; and the Synod had expounded its faith in strict accordance with the Tome of Leo.

But several matters concerning Eastern bishoprics called for adjustment; and first, among these, the quarrel that had long subsisted between the Bishops of

---

[1] Mansi, vii. 177.

[2] *Ep. ad Istr.*, and so St. Gregory, *Lib.* 7, *Indict.* 2, *Ep.* 53. *Cf.* Baluze in Mansi, vii. 668.

Antioch and Jerusalem as to the area of their respective jurisdictions. A settlement was now effected, Antioch taking over the two provinces of Phœnicia and that of Arabia, and Jerusalem occupying the three Palestines. The Papal legates consented, and then all the bishops.[1]

And now at length the pent-up eagerness of the small knot of bishops from Egypt, Illyria and Palestine, who had raised such a clamour against Theodoret in the first session, was allowed a vent. Their annoyance at his having been allowed to sit in the Council as a bishop must have been intense; but they had been promised satisfaction in due course of time.[2] Theodoret (as has been already noticed) had been an avowed opponent of their great Cyril, until John of Antioch made his peace with Alexandria. He had then held communion with Antioch, and so, mediately, with Cyril. He had next avowed the perfect orthodoxy of Cyril's letter of pacification to John of Antioch, and had eventually spoken well of Cyril himself.[3] His supposed letter to John of Antioch on Cyril's death, a most brutal composition, calumniating the Saint in the most savage language, is undoubtedly a forgery, if for no other reason, at least from the fact that John of Antioch died before Cyril, and Theodoret must have known of his own Patriarch's death. But on the other hand, Theodoret had never admitted the orthodoxy of Cyril's letter to Nestorius, to which were appended the celebrated twelve Anathematisms, and he had persistently maintained that, although the teaching attributed to Nestorius was certainly heresy, still the deposition of

[1] Mansi, vii. 181. [2] *Ibid.* vi. 590, and *cf. supra*, p. 226.
[3] These particulars were unknown till the discovery of the *Synodicon adv. tragœdiam Irenœi* by Lupus, which was inserted by Baluze in his Supplement to the Council, and has thence passed into the later collections of documents relating to the Councils.

Nestorius was undeserved. At the time, however, of the Council of Chalcedon there is no question but that, in spite of this, he was perfectly orthodox. He had avowed his belief that Leo and Cyril were in agreement, and had signed the Tome of Leo.

Leo had passed judgment as to his orthodoxy on his appeal to the Holy See, and had quickly sent to the Papal legates to tell them that Theodoret was to be restored to his see—the restoration presumably to be actually effected by a decree of the Synod. There was no time to do more; and indeed more was not needed, for Leo had already commissioned the bishops to restore to their office by synodical decree those who had been unjustly condemned,[1] and Theodoret would now come under this head. Judging from Leo's practice, as instanced by his treatment of Anatolius, we may feel sure that had there been no Council about to sit Theodoret would have been expressly required to anathematise both Nestorius and Eutyches by letter. Unfortunately, we do not possess Leo's letter of directions to his legates. We only know that they were able to say at the Council that Theodoret had been restored by Leo, and accepted by the Emperor—subject, *as a matter of course*, to the usual conditions of such restoration when a General Council was sitting. Accordingly, on the ground of Leo's judgment, to which the civil sanction of the Emperor had been given, the Commissioners had insisted on his being allowed to take his seat in the Council as a bishop, with the right to act as an accuser but without prejudice to the proposed action of the Egyptians and their allies. This, however, was deferred until the matter of faith had been settled.

[1] *Ep.* 93, 3.

Accordingly, the faction of Dioscorus, as those bishops had shown themselves to be in the opening of the Council,[1] now cried out that the time had come for Theodoret to anathematise Nestorius.[2] That was what he had always refused to do, although ready enough to anathematise his heresy. But this was what these few bishops were determined that he should now be made to do. Nothing would satisfy them but to hear the hated name of Nestorius from his lips after all he had said against their *quondam* patriarch, St. Cyril. And Theodoret had richly deserved to be called upon to do this. But what he did was to pass to the middle and ask to read his letters to Leo and to the Emperor to show his orthodoxy. But there was no idea of reviewing the judgment of Leo. All that was required of him was that he should anathematise Nestorius by name.

And they were in fact within their rights. For indeed any orthodox bishop might be called upon to do the same if the slightest suspicions rested on him, although it must be admitted that the demand came with an ill grace from those who had originally maintained that it was enough to sign the Nicene Creed. But the Commissioners upheld these bishops' demands, and the Papal legates stood by as consenting parties. His willingness to anathematise Nestorius was really involved in his restoration by Leo. There could be no question but that Leo would himself have approved of the demand being complied

---

[1] That it was these and not the whole Synod is certain both from the first session and from the expression here later on when '*all* the bishops' (Mansi, vii. 189) are mentioned as exclaiming that 'Leo had judged with God'—*i.e.*, as 'with' always means in such a context, 'under the protecting guidance of Almighty God.' *Cf.* 'I am with you all days' (Matt. xxviii).

[2] Mansi, vii. 188.

with, as indeed he afterwards said expressly in a letter
to Theodoret himself, whom he congratulated on coming
well out of the trial. It was not in the least allowing
Leo's judgment to be reviewed on the part of the Synod,
as though that judgment were inadequate in view of the
evidence presented, for they expressly refused to review
that evidence. They would not have his letter read. It
was merely a question of satisfying this knot of bishops
as to whether Theodoret would do what one absolved by
the Holy See must be ready to do at any moment, if called
upon by a Council. It was not a question of the infallibility of the Holy See, but of the sincerity of Theodoret.
Long years afterwards the successors of these people
maintained (quite absurdly) that Theodoret was
insincere.

Besides, all the bishops (on the principles of the
Vatican decree) had a right as bishops in a General
Council to exercise their judgment on such a case when
brought before them. Had they found that Theodoret
had been deceiving Leo, about which, however, there
could hardly be any real question after his conduct in
the Council, the matter would, on those principles, have
been referred back to Rome. But, as it was, this difficulty
did not arise. Leo proved to be right; and these
Egyptian bishops were wrong. The case, then, stands
thus : Theodoret had appealed to Leo as the occupant of
the Apostolic See ' to heal the wounds of the Church ' by
reason of his position as ' Primate in all things ' ; [1] and
Leo had already told the Synod that it was to ' apply
the medicine of justice to the wounds ' of the Churches,

[1] *Lit.* ' that we may receive from you a remedy for the wounds of
the Church. For the Primacy in all things fitly belongs to you ' (*Leon.
Ep.* 52, § 1).

whose bishops had been driven from their sees, and transported, others being placed in their stead; and that no one was to lose his proper honour, 'if all, as we desire, relinquish their error.'[1] Clearly, therefore, the Synod had an office to fulfil in the case of all the bishops who had gone astray; the only difference in the case of Theodoret being that his right to his bishopric was already established by the judgment of the Apostolic See, so far as it was possible for it to judge. What that judgment decided was that the man who wrote as Theodoret did to Rome, expounding his faith as he did, merited restoration to his see. But obviously if any one could show that the writer was not sincere, the judgment would fall to the ground. Infallibility does not confer the power of reading the heart of man. So that the execution of Leo's judgment was, as a matter of course, contingent upon the sincerity of the writer, and subject to his satisfying the Synod, if required to do so, that he had placed his case fully before the Holy See. The test of this was his anathematising Nestorius —at least in the opinion of the Egyptian party. And there was no reason why the Synod should repudiate the test. It was not reopening the question of the correctness of the decision in regard to the evidence adduced.

Theodoret, then, being called upon by these bishops to anathematise Nestorius, and probably resenting the test, wished that he should be allowed to give an exposition of his faith.[2] But he was roughly interrupted in the middle of his sentence and told that he was still a Nestorian, which, of course, was wholly false. Theodoret, seeing that nothing would satisfy his interrogators but

[1] *Leon. Ep.* 93, § 3.   [2] ἔκθωμαι ὅπως πιστεύω.

the words for which they clamoured, at once said: 'Anathema to Nestorius and to him who does not say that the holy Virgin Mary is Mother of God, and to him who divides the Only-begotten Son into two sons. Moreover, I have signed the definition of faith and the Epistle of the most holy archbishop Leo; and thus I think: and now after all this, Farewell.' The Commissioners at once stopped further proceedings, and said that all doubt about Theodoret was removed, giving their reasons thus: '(1) he has anathematised Nestorius in our hearing and (2) has been received by Leo; and he has (1) willingly accepted the definition of faith given by your Reverence [*i.e.* the Synod] and (2) moreover has subscribed to the Epistle of Leo. It remains, therefore, that a decree should be issued by yourselves, so that he may receive his Church back again, *according as Leo decided.*'

And now the whole body of the bishops[1] who had witnessed this baiting of the great Bishop of Cyrrhos joined in exclaiming: 'Theodoret worthy of the see. The orthodox to his see. . . . Long live Archbishop Leo. Leo decided with God . . . let his Church be given back to Theodoret the bishop.'

Now unless the judgment of Leo as Primate of the Church was a determining factor in the restoration of Theodoret, what need to bring in his name at every turn? It was not enough, in the opinion of the Commissioners, to say that Theodoret was restored because he had anathematised Nestorius; they must needs add that he had been received by Leo. It was not enough to say that he had signed the synodical definition of faith; they must needs add that he had subscribed the

[1] Mansi, vii. 189.

letter of Leo. It was not enough to say that a decree for his restoration must be issued by the Synod; they must needs add that this restoration was in accordance with the decision of Leo. What could this mean but that the judgment of the Apostolic See had a juridical value in the case even of a Greek bishop?

And now the sentence of the Synod was delivered by the Papal legates. They did not simply 'give a vote,'[1] they delivered the sentence of the whole Synod. They said: 'The most holy and blessed *bishop of the whole Church*, Leo, [bishop] of the city of Rome, has already received the most holy and venerable Bishop Theodoret into communion, as the letter sent to our lowliness [=our humble selves] bears witness. Since, therefore, he has shown [that he holds] the Catholic faith according to his promise, and according to the aforementioned Bishop he has sent his subscription [to the Tome] in his own document and in that sent to us; since also he has anathematised both Nestorius and Eutyches not only in writing, but with his own lips in presence of the whole assembly, *the most holy and venerable Synod*, as well as our lowliness, *has decided* by this decree that his Church be given back to him.' Thus St. Leo through his legates and the Synod decreed the actual restoration of Theodoret, who had already been restored by him *de jure*, his actual restoration by the decree of the Synod following immediately upon his anathematising Nestorius, just as Anatolius had been ordered by the Holy See to anathematise Eutyches as well as to subscribe to the Tome.

[1] I do not know how Dr. Bright defends his positive assertion that 'the legates did *not* give the decision, but simply took the lead in giving a vote' (*Roman See*, p. 194). The minutes are explicit that the legates *did* give the decision (Mansi, vii. 192).

Six bishops then recorded their assent to the sentence pronounced in their name by the Papal legates, and it is interesting to notice the selection. Anatolius, the successor of St. Flavian, and the quondam friend of Dioscorus who had deposed Theodoret, led the way, mentioning the fact that the latter had anathematised Nestorius, but saying first that he had been shown to be orthodox ' for all reasons ' (including, of course, the supreme reason—viz. Leo's judgment, given by the Papal legates in the name of the Synod), ' *and* from the fact that he had anathematised Nestorius and Eutyches.' Thus Leo's judgment was, according to Anatolius, the first factor in the process of restoration. Next, his patriarch, Maximus, deposed that he had ' known long ago and from the first that Theodoret was orthodox, when he heard [*lit.* hearing] his doctrine concerning the most holy Church,' probably in allusion to Theodoret's stay in Antioch before Maximus was bishop, which gave rise to the accusations originally brought against him by Dioscorus.[1] 'And now *much more* have I welcomed his Holiness since he has now anathematised Nestorius and Eutyches and agrees with the definition put forth [2] by this holy Synod. Whence I judge that he is properly Bishop of the city of Cyrus.' He thus gave his assent to the sentence delivered by the Papal legates. It is hopeless to argue with people who think that because Maximus does not repeat the words of the legates, he has different rather than additional reasons for agreeing to the decision about Theodoret. He merely adds his own personal witness, and lays stress, as he would necessarily do, on the latest proof of his orthodoxy, to show that Leo was right, not merely on the matter of

---

[1] Cf. *supra*, p. 126. [2] ὅρον τὸν ἐκτεθέντα (Mansi, vii. 192).

x

faith, but in his judgment on the individual, and that the Synod was right in delivering over his see to the bishop on whose letter Leo had pronounced judgment. It was an intelligent adhesion to that judgment.

Juvenal was the next to adhere to the synodical decree—the bishop who had so tamely yielded to pressure from Dioscorus in the Robber-Synod, when Theodoret was calumniated and deposed. He endorsed the words of Anatolius, which referred to Leo's judgment as well as to the anathematisation of Nestorius.

He was followed by his companion dupes at the Latrocinium, Thalassius, and Eusebius of Ancyra, each of these merely expressing their assent to what Anatolius and the other fathers had decided. Lastly, came a bishop from the neighbourhood of Theodoret's see, Constantine, whose own see lay in Arabia.

The rest of the bishops having then assented by acclamation, the Commissioners declared Theodoret restored to his see by the decree of the Synod.

I have given this scene at great length because so much turns on it in the view of certain English writers. It will be well now to notice one or two points of interest in this judicial act of the Synod.

The legates in delivering the sentence of the Synod speak of the Bishop of Rome as the Bishop of 'the whole Church,' and the Synod listens and adheres to the sentence. Clearly, therefore, Leo's judgment on Theodoret had a value which none other could have. The 'whole Church' cannot be above its own bishop.

The rule of the Pope over the whole Church is not, on Vatican principles, a despotic sway. The Episcopate has a real office of judgment, though in subordination to his.

The test imposed on Theodoret at the instance of the

impetuous theologians of Egypt, Palestine and Illyria, few in number as compared with the great throng of bishops, was not one which St. Leo had forbidden, nor one of which anyone could suppose he would disapprove. A response to it was involved in the very idea of restoration.

The Synod had distinct orders from Leo to enter into the case of the bishops deposed at the Latrocinium, of whom Theodoret was one. The actual handing over of his see, therefore, naturally lay with them.

The legates and Commissioners insisted on Theodoret being allowed to exercise some of the rights of a bishop in spite of protest, and that purely on the ground that he had been restored by Leo and consequently (for this we may certainly assume) accepted by the Emperor.

The decree of the Synod was avowedly based, not merely on Theodoret's compliance with the demand to anathematise Nestorius, but also on the judgment passed by the Bishop of Rome on this Oriental bishop, of the patriarchate of Antioch.

The Synod did not review the evidence on which Leo's judgment was based. They refused to do that, for whatever reason. But in so doing they deprived controversial writers of any right to talk of the synodical decree on Theodoret as though it were a case of reviewing Leo's decision.

Our conclusion is that there is nothing in the history of Theodoret's restoration to prejudice the doctrine of Papal supremacy, if that doctrine be understood according to the Vatican decrees, and not as teaching that the See of Peter has *absolute* sway, or is bound to govern as a despot. One alone has absolute authority. The Vicar of Him who alone absolutely rules the Church is supreme in jurisdiction over the whole Church, but is under Him and must act in harmony with the laws which He has laid down, which include a real, though subordinate, authority in the Episcopate at large.

Note on the Restoration of Theodoret.

The foregoing pages will have shown how far there is any truth in the objections drawn by Dr. Bright from the history of Theodoret against the Vatican decrees (*Roman See*, p. 193-195, and *Waymarks*, p. 231).

He says that the judgment of Leo 'on Vaticanist principles, should have been amply sufficient to place him, as a matter of course, among the constituent members of the Council of Chalcedon.' So it should. And so it did with all but a tiny section who sympathised with Dioscorus. For it was ruled that he was to be a constituent member of the Council, and his name was entered as such in the Greek lists of bishops at the second session (Mansi, vi. 944), and at the end of the fourth 'Act' he exercised the supreme function of the Episcopate in declaring the faith along with the rest of the bishops. If he was made to sit in the middle, this was not because he was not a constituent member of the Council, but because, being such, he was about to act as an accuser of Dioscorus, just as Eusebius of Dorylæum, whose right to the rank of Bishop was unquestioned, took his seat also in the middle. 'He could only take his seat in the midst as a competent accuser capable also of being accused,' says Dr. Bright. But to accept him as 'a competent accuser' at all was virtually accepting him as a constituent member of the Council. For no one not in communion with the Church could be accepted as a competent accuser, according to the Eastern regulation drawn up at Constantinople in 382 and called the 7th canon of the Œcumenical Council. The Council expressly distinguished later on—(Mansi, vi. 645) between the reason for Dioscorus sitting in the middle and Theodoret doing so. In the latter case it was, as an ' accuser.' Dr. Bright reiterates the fact that Theodoret was ' liable to be accused.' In the passage to which he refers, the word 'accused' is a misreading. All that the bishops decided was that the Egyptians should be allowed to ' have it out ' with Theodoret afterwards. This did not put him in the condition of one actually accused. To say ' liable to be accused ' is very vague.

'He did not vote except on such business as was connected with his own justification, *i.e.* as was properly doctrinal' (*ibid.*). But this exception is fatal to Dr. Bright's contention. And if it were not, it would be fatal to his other contention that the Synod in the fourth ' Act ' was a court superior to the Apostolic See. Theodoret formed part of that supposed ' superior ' court. He signed with the rest.

Then as to pronouncing anathema against Nestorius. ' Then, and not till then, the Council professed itself satisfied ' (*Waymarks*, p. 231). ' The fact remains that the bishops vehemently and persistently imposed on him a test which Leo had not imposed ' (*Roman See*, p. 194). True, not (so far as we know) *explicitly*, but that is all that could be said ; and the ' test ' was not to see if Leo's judgment on the evidence submitted to him in Theodoret's letter was correct, but whether he had properly placed his case before Leo. It was not, as Dr. Bright's account implies, the bishops in general who were ' vehement ' and ' persistent.' But no one would refuse to insist on Theodoret's answering, when thus challenged.

' He was not pronounced " worthy of his see " until he submitted ' to the test imposed (*ibid.*). Yes, he was distinctly *totidem verbis* pronounced ' worthy of his see ' in the first session, by all but a tiny knot of sympathisers with Dioscorus. The concession made to these few turbulent bishops was, not that Leo's judgment should be reviewed, but that the case (λόγος) between these bishops and Theodoret should be allowed to come on afterwards, and yet Theodoret was not to rank as an *accused* person, but as a competent accuser. The distinction (as already noticed) drawn between him and Dioscorus was notable. He sat with the orthodox Eusebius of Dorylæum. The concession was made, not because the Synod itself had thought it necessary to enter upon the case, but by reason of the clamour of the aforementioned bishops.

'The legates did *not* give the decision, but simply took the lead in giving a vote' (*ibid.*). We have seen that this is not correct.

'Six bishops followed, of whom five made no allusion referring to Leo's action, while a sixth seems to include him among "archbishops"' (*ibid.*).

There was no need to make any such allusion. They were only expressing their adhesion to the decision of the Synod pronounced by the legates. The only point of importance was to say that Theodoret, having anathematised Nestorius, was to take possession of his see. Leo's judgment took effect thereupon. He *was* an archbishop. No one denies that.

But, as a matter of fact, Anatolius alluded to 'Leo's action,' and Juvenal said he agreed with Anatolius, and the next bishop, Thalassius, agreed with 'the most holy fathers,' who included Anatolius and Juvenal, and Eusebius of Ancyra did the same, and Constantine simply expressed agreement with what had been decreed. And Maximus, as Theodoret's patriarch, naturally added his personal witness. Thus there is nothing *ad rem* in this remark of Dr. Bright's. The same may be said of his quotation of the words that Theodoret 'should regain the Church of Cyrrhos, according to the judgment of the Council.' This is a mere matter of fact, but the question is whether the judgment of the Council involved a 'review' of Leo's judgment, or was simply its execution when Theodoret had shown that he had not played false with Leo.

'The legates themselves were fain to recognise its [the Council's] decision as superadded to what their master had long before pronounced' (*Waymarks*, p. 231). But in what sense 'superadded'? As necessary to its completeness, or because the Egyptians insisted that Theodoret was not what Leo thought him to be? And, again, what was Leo's judgment *so far as it can be brought within the scope of his prerogative of infallibility*? It was simply that the letter which Theodoret wrote to him contained the true faith. This was never denied, never reviewed. The letter was not even read. It is therefore futile to quote the Vatican decree and ask, 'On this showing, how can the Fourth Œcumenical Council be acquitted of disloyal encroachment on the sovereign rights of the Church's visible head?' (*Waymarks*, p. 232). We must not stretch those 'sovereign rights' to mean what the context in the Vatican decree shows they do not include and then place them in the presence of past history.

It cannot, however, be too often repeated that on 'Vatican principles' bishops have a right to exercise their judgment in such a case as that of Theodoret; and, this being the case, the actual mention of Leo on every occasion was not needed, and in view of the new accusation raised against him it was enough to allege their reasons for adhering to Leo's judgment by themselves without explicit mention of anything besides these.

CHAPTER VII

ANTIOCH'S DEPENDENCE ON ROME

Two matters were also decided at the Synod which concerned the See of Antioch, and which brought to the front the acknowledged jurisdiction of the See of Rome over the whole Church. The first concerned a compact entered into with Juvenal of Jerusalem, by which Antioch parted with three fair provinces of its patriarchate. Juvenal had long set his heart upon the extension of his jurisdiction. He had succeeded in so completely gaining the ear of the Emperor, Theodosius II., that he had been allowed to count in his rule the two provinces of Phœnicia and also that of Arabia, together with the three provinces of Palestine, which belonged to the jurisdiction of Antioch. St. Cyril had done his utmost to oppose this iniquitous proceeding, and appealed to the Pope, entreating him with 'earnest prayer' to lend no countenance to such 'illicit attempts.' But Juvenal gained his case with the secular power by means of forged documents.[1]

This quarrel over their respective jurisdictions had continued until the time of the Council, when Maximus acquiesced in a compromise, by which Antioch was to be shorn of the three provinces of Palestine, and Juvenal was to give up all claim to the two provinces of Phœnicia and that of Arabia. But Maximus consented to this

[1] *Leon. Ep.* 119.

arrangement only 'if it was approved by our venerable father, the Archbishop of greater Rome.'[1] Thereupon the legates gave their sanction to the arrangement as though Leo had consented. This, however, Leo had never done, and when his opposition to the 28th Canon on the ground that it contravened the Nicene arrangement became known, Maximus, it would seem, discerned his opportunity and endeavoured to enlist Leo's aid in the recovery of his provinces from the jurisdiction of Jerusalem. Leo expressly disclaimed the consent given by his legates, and gave general advice to Maximus, in favour of his desire to recover his lost provinces, but abstained from any direct advice as to the present moment. The fact was, that Juvenal was then in trouble in his patriarchate in his laudable and stubborn defence of the definition of Chalcedon against his refractory monks.

But the important point to notice is that the finality of the arrangement was held to depend on the consent of the Holy See.

The other matter concerning Antioch touched its former bishop, Domnus, for whom Maximus generously asked a pension. Domnus had been Bishop of Antioch at the Latrocinium (Robber-Synod). As has been already said, this unfortunate man, the nephew of John of Antioch, had left his cell contrary to the advice of his abbot, with a view to influencing his uncle in the Nestorian controversy. At Antioch he won his way to the episcopal throne and appeared as its bishop at Ephesus to take part in the miserable tragedy there enacted under Dioscorus. Having shown the white feather, and allowed himself to be cowed by Dioscorus into consenting to the

[1] Mansi, vii. 770; also *Leon. Opp.* ii. 1223.

restoration of Eutyches and the condemnation of Flavian, he was also himself deposed by Dioscorus, on the ground of long-past sympathy with Nestorius and of having once condemned Cyril. He was accordingly exiled by Theodosius. While he was still living, Anatolius ordained Maximus bishop of Antioch in his place at Constantinople in contravention of the Nicene canons. On the restoration of the bishops who had been similarly ousted from their sees, and the deposition of the intruders, Maximus, instead of being deposed, was allowed to retain his intrusive position. The only reason given by the Council of Chalcedon for this exception was that Leo had ordered that his ordination should hold good. The Archbishop of Constantinople, Anatolius, said: 'We decide that none of those things are valid which were done in that so-called Synod [the Latrocinium] except the matter of Maximus, Bishop of Antioch, since Leo the Bishop of Rome, having received him into communion, decided that he should rule the Church of Antioch; following which decision, I also have assented and the whole of the Synod present.'[1]

The learned Jansenist, Quesnel, who always avowed the greatest regard for the prerogatives of the See of Peter, but took every opportunity of undermining their historical basis, remarks on this treatment of Domnus and Maximus, that if only the Act in which their case occurs were genuine, we should have in our hands an unequivocal testimony to 'the supreme authority of the Pontiff over Synods and over Oriental bishops, the bishops of the greater sees.' But he set to work to show that the record of this session could not be considered genuine. His arguments were dealt with by Baluze,

[1] Mansi, vii. 258.

indeed we may fairly say were crushed to atoms by that learned writer.[1] Tillemont, in spite of his theological and historical sympathies, deserted Quesnel and called his arguments nothing less than imbecile. But the matter was set at rest by a manuscript which Quesnel had not seen, but which Cardinal Casanata discovered[2] and transmitted to Baluze, and which has been edited with their usual learning by the Ballerini. This same document contains the condition which Maximus attached to his compromise with Juvenal, viz. if the Bishop of Rome consented.

The prerogative admitted in this Act as belonging to Leo covers in substance everything ever claimed by the Holy See in the way of jurisdiction. St. Leo dispensed with the irregularity in the case of Maximus's ordination to Antioch and the Synod gave this reason, and only this, for their action in accepting that ordination. They also, in the same session, assigned the invalidity of the transactions of the Robber-Synod to the decision of the Bishop of Rome. Now as we know that Leo himself contemplated their entering upon the consideration of the case of individual bishops at Chalcedon, we can only conclude that Leo's decision was regarded as the supremely invalidating factor. But the case of Maximus was more crucial. In ordaining him at Constantinople, and without any regard to the bishops of his provinces, and when Domnus was still alive, they were contravening the Nicene canons in every way, and it was in this crucial case that they quoted Leo's decision as the determining element in their own action.

[1] Baluze's arguments are given in Mansi, vii. 666-674, and the most important are repeated by the Ballerini in their *Observ. in Diss. ix. Quesnelli* (*Leon. Opp.* ii. 1215, ff).

[2] *Codex Vatic.* 1322.

St. Leo probably dispensed with the irregularity of the proceeding because Maximus had shown his adhesion to the orthodox faith, whilst Domnus, after his cowardly conduct at the Latrocinium, did not ask for reinstatement, but found his way back in a spirit of penance to the cell which he ought never to have left.

NOTE.

It has been objected to the deduction as to Papal jurisdiction drawn from the case of Maximus (1) that he 'had already approved himself orthodox by circulars throughout his provinces, so that the Council in accepting him from the outset as Bishop of Antioch, had not *merely* Leo's act to rest upon' (Bright, *Roman See*, p. 195). But, setting aside the fact that this was *à propos* of Leo's Tome, which Dr. Bright does not allow to have been of faith at that time, the point is that the only ground *which Anatolius gave for the Synod's action* was Leo's decision that Maximus should hold the bishopric (Mansi, vii. 257). It is objected also (2) that 'Stephen of Ephesus spoke of the appointment as originally "canonical"' (*ibid.*). This, however, is not the case. The word 'originally' is not there. The Ballerini point out that Stephen's words would not necessarily imply more than that Domnus by his subsequent acquiescence had contributed to the possibility of validating Maximus's ordination. The original act needed to be condoned; else why moot the matter at all? Leo expressly says that the ordination was originally irregular (*Ep.* 104). And in the same sentence Stephen spoke of Leo's decision as preceding that of the Synod, which shows that, whatever he meant by 'canonical,' there was something for Leo to do in the way of validating the act, else he would not have been mentioned at all.

As regards the condition attached by Maximus to his compromise with Juvenal, viz. if the Bishop of Rome should consent, Dr. Bright (*Roman See*, p. 196) objects (1) that it 'is not in the Greek Acts (Mansi, vii. 180).' But the 'Greek Acts' in Mansi, vii. 180, are considered by Mansi himself to be defective. He has accordingly supplemented the version on p. 180 with the version in which the said salvo occurs (*cf.* p. 770). Dr. Bright ought to have noticed this. The Latin version discovered by Casanata, which contains the salvo, represents a very old *Greek* original, as Baluze, and especially the Ballerini, have shown. Mansi himself endorses this. He thinks it older than the version used by Rusticus in the sixth century. The Ballerini give reasons for believing that parts of the Acts of the Council were sent at once to Leo, such as the definition of faith, and this Act, as Leo's consent was mentioned. Probably Maximus sent it in Greek with a translation, or it may have been translated when it reached Rome. Mansi thinks this conjecture of the Ballerini probable. He also notices, after Baluze and the Ballerini, that it is obviously the translation of a Greek version, for the salvo contains the expression 'greater Rome,' which is Greek, not Roman, style. See Mansi's note in Natal. Alex. *H.E.* ix. p. 600. Dr. Bright is thus clearly at fault in talking of the salvo as a '*Roman* invention.' See *Leon. Opp.* ed. Baller. T. ii. (*De caussa Domni*, Observ.). (2) Dr. Bright also objects that 'the legates' speech, even as there given, ignores it,' *i.e.* the salvo. But as I have shown in the text, the legates' speech, so far from ignoring it, was meant to fulfil it. (3) Again, Dr. Bright adds, 'nor does Leo mention it in his letter of 453.' But he alludes to the legates' consent, and deprecates their action being taken for his consent in any matter not explicitly mentioned by him. He is writing to Maximus himself on this very matter (*Ep.* 119, § 5).

In this same session the invalidity of the acts of the Robber-Synod is assigned by the bishops simply and solely to the decision of the Bishop of Rome. On this Dr. Bright (*ibid.* p. 185, note [1]) remarks 'as if it did not result from the proceedings *re* Dioscorus.' But in this case the bishops are speaking of *all* the proceedings of the Robber-Synod. The said proceedings had only dealt with some.

CHAPTER VIII

PREVIOUS ENCROACHMENTS OF 'NEW ROME'

It had been well for the Church if the Council had now dispersed. But it was not to be. The bishops who remained engaged in a project which had long agitated the minds of a few leading spirits.

For more than eighty years Constantinople had nursed a thought which was destined to change the course of ecclesiastical history, and plunge her into a permanent schism. Photius, who consummated the schism between the East and West in the ninth century, claimed for the Bishop of Constantinople the title and position of 'Universal Bishop.' The Bishop of Rome had been such, according to his theory, until the capital of the Empire passed from Rome to Byzantium. But the position of universal bishop was based, according to Photius, on the secular grandeur of the city; so that when Constantine left Rome it was only a matter of time for Byzantium to succeed to the honours of the original capital.

The difference between this theory and that which obtained in the fifth century involved the whole question of the property attributed to the Church in the Nicene Creed under the title 'Apostolic.' Under that title, in the mind of the early Church, was included the government of the Church by the Apostles and their successors; understanding by 'the Apostles,' as the primitive

Church did, a body of men who were associated together by our Lord under a visible head. 'It has been known to all ages,' so it was said at Ephesus, 'and it is doubtful to none, that the blessed Apostle Peter, *the Prince and head of the Apostles*, the rock and foundation of the Catholic Church, received from our Saviour the keys of the Kingdom.' And the see of that Apostle, consecrated by the blood of the two Apostles, himself and St. Paul, became, in the words of St. Irenæus and St. Cyprian, the principal or ruling Church, that which, according to St. Ignatius of Antioch, writing in the second century, 'presided over the [covenant of] love,' and in which, according to St. Augustine, 'the principalship had ever been in force,' and was designated in the terminology of the whole Church, East and West, in the fifth century, 'the Apostolic See.'

The chasm between the teaching of the schismatic Bishop of Constantinople, Photius, in the ninth century, and his predecessor in the see in the fifth century at Chalcedon, is exactly expressed in the words of the latter when he said to Leo: 'The see of Constantinople has for its parent your own Apostolic See, having specially joined itself thereunto.'[1]

But although Anatolius thus expressed the true relation between Rome and Constantinople, his action at Chalcedon prepared the way for the unhappy schism into which the East eventually plunged, under the guidance of the miserable Photius, with his claim to be 'Universal Bishop.' The term 'universal bishop' is one which might be properly used to express the relation of the Apostolic See to the rest of the Church, but even so it needed a certain care lest it should be thought to mean

[1] 'Anatolius ad Leonem' (*Ep.* 101).

that other bishops were but legates or vice-bishops of the one universal bishop. In fear of this meaning being attached to the term, St. Gregory repudiated it. It was, however, freely used at the Council of Chalcedon. And there is no fear of any Catholic nowadays giving it such an unorthodox interpretation as St. Gregory detected in John's use of the term, and so there is no ground for refusing it to the occupant of the See of Rome. But on the lips of a bishop of Constantinople it necessarily implied a heresy, for it also implied the idea that the government of the Church was not Apostolic but Erastian. The earthly Emperor, according to this theory, by moving his capital, moved the centre of the Church's unity. So Photius argued. Neither he nor his predecessors were really prepared to carry out this theory to its logical issue, for, as a Sovereign Pontiff asked of his predecessors, were they prepared to call Ravenna, or Gangra, or Sirmium, the centre of the Church's government when the Emperor made these, as he did, the centre of his rule?

The attack, however, on the original constitution of the Church, which culminated, under favourable political circumstances, in the schismatic action of the East under Photius, was commenced in fact at the Council of Constantinople in 381. There the bishops assembled under Nectarius had decreed a certain precedency of honour to the 'New Rome,' as Byzantine pride delighted to call the city of Constantine. But they had not ventured so much as to send their canon to the West. It was a purely local arrangement, not sanctioned even by the rest of the East. As *a canon*, it was no sooner born than it died. It never took effect as *a canon*; but it represented ambitions which pursued their path with almost undeviating determination until the effort was now made at Chalcedon to give them a higher sanction.

But to understand this attempt at supremacy in the East, we must recall some events which had occurred since 381, and also what took place in the later sessions at Chalcedon, when the episcopal ranks had been thinned by the departure of several hundreds.

By the Nicene settlement the arrangement of ecclesiastical matters in the 'dioceses,' or clusters of provinces, of Asia, Pontus and Thrace lay entirely with the synods of each province within the diocese;[1] and none of the great Patriarchs, so to call them, claimed any power in these regions, nor did these three groups in any way blend into one. It was, however, in the nature of things that Constantinople, as she grew, should cast her eye on these autonomous 'dioceses' and desire to form to herself a new Patriarchate, so that the Imperial city, 'New Rome,' might hold the second place after 'Old Rome' in ecclesiastical affairs, not only nominally but in an effective way.

But the advance was gradual. Patriarchal superiority included two things—honorary precedence, and effective jurisdiction.[2] Under the latter head was included the ordination of metropolitans and the right to convene, to receive the reports, and to manage the business of Provincial Synods (ἀναφορά). Honorary precedence

---

[1] It is unfortunate that our modern use of the word 'diocese' denotes a smaller region than a province. In early times the opposite was the case. The 'diocese' of Asia included Lydia, Caria, Mysia, Phrygia and Hellespont—*i.e.* Lower Asia—and also Pamphylia, Lycaonia, Pisidia, Isauria, and Cilicia, *i.e.* Upper Asia.

[2] The mere title of Patriarch was conferred on the Bishop of Chalcedon by the Emperor and the Synod at the sixth session of the Council.

(πρεσβεῖα τῆς τιμῆς) had been assigned to the see of Constantinople at the Council of 381 in the third canon—precedence even over Alexandria and Antioch—primacy of honour, but not of administration. Indeed that third canon, coming as it did after the second, could not have ascribed more than a primacy of honour without contradicting the second. Constantinople, accordingly, though situated in the very jaws of Europe and Asia, lay in the 'diocese' (or group of provinces) of Thrace; and the administration of the provinces of Thrace was expressly committed by the second canon of 381 to their Synods, Heraclea being their canonical centre. The same form of administration was laid down as regards Asia, with its centre at Ephesus, and again as regards Pontus, with its centre at Cæsarea in Cappadocia, whose bishop in 451 was Thalassius. Thus any attempts at enlarging the jurisdiction of Constantinople would centre round the sees of Ephesus, Cæsarea, and Heraclea—of which the first was vacant in 451, the second was occupied by a bishop of peculiar antecedents, viz. Thalassius, and the third was not at the Council, but was represented by Lucian, a friend of Anatolius, the Archbishop of Constantinople. This singular coincidence, much in favour of any move that might be made by Constantinople towards the enlargement of her jurisdiction, will go far towards explaining what now took place at Chalcedon.

After the Council of 381, those three 'dioceses' maintained their separate administration for a while. In the law 'de Fide Catholica' in the Theodosian Code the three groups, with their mother cities of Ephesus, Heraclea and Cæsarea in Cappadocia, are mentioned as centres of communion—while Nectarius, the Archbishop of Constantinople, was a centre of orthodoxy to that city and its suburbs alone and not to Thrace, whose metropolitan is mentioned separately.

But the honorary precedence assigned to Constantinople by the third canon of 381, was being continually converted into a primacy of jurisdiction. The most important step in this direction was taken by the establishment—not of avowed design, nor by any one act, but through circumstances—of a Synod in the Imperial city. Constantinople had no Synod of her own by canon law; no Synod to which the reports of Metropolitical Synods could be sent in—one of the great signs and instruments of jurisdiction; no Synod in which the quarrels of bishops could be dealt with; nor had she any right to ordain metropolitans. This was excluded by the second canon of 381. And yet a Patriarchal Synod was composed only of those who received ordination from the Patriarch; and, conversely, those metropolitans alone were ordained by a Patriarch who were subject to his Synod and jurisdiction.

But in spite of this what has been called the 'Resident Synod' came into being. This was not, on strict canonical principles, a Synod at all : but it served the purpose, and acquired the name, of a Synod. Some sixty bishops at a time, of the first and second rank, were wont to be temporarily resident in the Imperial city in connection with the business of their diocese or province at the Court, and these, on occasion, approached the Emperor as a body, and hence the idea, and the usurpation of the name, of a Synod. Custom soon took the place of canon, and the episcopal gatherings in the imperial city assumed the functions of a regular Synod.

An instance of the way in which this Synod sometimes

worked is found in the fourth 'Act' of the Council of Chalcedon.¹ Eustathius, Bishop of Berytus, had induced the Emperor to hand over to him the ordination to certain sees which belonged to the jurisdiction of Photius of Tyre. The Resident Synod of Constantinople had issued a decision in conformity with the Imperial rescript, and had induced Photius to sign the decision, under threats of deposition. It had also prevailed upon Maximus of Antioch, in whose patriarchate the cities in question were situated, to sign a document in favour of Eustathius, Maximus being at Constantinople at the time, although not at the Synod. But the Council of Chalcedon reversed the decision of the Imperial rescript and nullified its confirmation by the Resident Synod. It decided that Photius was within his rights in accordance with the fourth Nicene canon, which was read out, and which had decreed that the authority of the metropolitan should be respected in each province. The Council at the same time questioned the application of the term Synod to the Constantinopolitan assemblies, whereupon Anatolius the archbishop, defended their existence on the ground of custom and convenience, but not on canonical grounds.² The third canon of Constantinople was not appealed to as though it made the Imperial see a centre of metropolitan authority. That canon, as Leo said, had collapsed from the first.

But there could be no question of the utility of the Resident Synod under many circumstances. St. Chrysostom was reinstated by it after his deposition by the Synod 'at the Oak,'³ and Eutyches was condemned by Flavian in a similar gathering.

The name of Chrysostom brings us to the most signal

¹ Mansi, vii. 85, ff.   ² *Ibid.* 96.   ³ Soz. *H. E.* viii. c. 19.

instance of Constantinople's intervention in the affairs of one of the three great dioceses or eparchies, over which she always tended to exercise authority. And it affords us an insight into the real difficulties of the problem which demanded a solution as the Church developed her organisation in the East. The splendour of the Imperial see and the new dignity conferred on it, however illegitimately, by the third canon of 381 in the teeth of the Nicene settlement, naturally led to the Bishops of Constantinople mixing themselves up with the appointment and ordination of metropolitans of provinces, on invitation from the provincial bishops. On the plea of restraining the ambition of other prelates, of putting a stop to pecuniary exactions and illegal traffic in bishoprics, or, again, of calming seditions and tumults on the occasion of episcopal elections, a wide door was opened for the use of her honorary precedence in the direction of semi-authoritative jurisdiction. In the Council of Chalcedon, Philip, a Presbyter of Constantinople, quoted the action of St. Chrysostom at Ephesus in favour of the ordinations to that see being assigned to Constantinople as a matter of right.[1]

But St. Chrysostom went to Ephesus by desire of the Ephesian clergy and the rest of the bishops in that region. Antoninus had been accused of selling bishoprics but died before his case came on. On his death the city of Ephesus was torn with factions over the election of a successor, which led to St. Chrysostom going there, and, with the general feeling in his favour, consecrating his deacon Heraclides to the see. Antoninus had been accused by Eusebius at the Resident Synod, and had presented himself at this Synod in Constantinople,

[1] Mansi, vii. 293.

which thus exercised consensual jurisdiction in the matter; so that on several grounds St. Chrysostom was justified in his intervention. The second canon of Constantinople, while expressly safeguarding the rights of the exarch of Ephesus among others, had disallowed bishops going to other dioceses to ordain, but only if not invited,[1] just as the fourteenth and thirty-fourth of the Apostolic Constitutions had contemplated the possibility of intervention at the instance of 'many bishops' 'and with the most pressing invitation.'[2]

It was not, therefore, the third canon of 381 that was relied on in the advancement of Constantinople's position of authority. The growth of her authority was due sometimes to an occasion of public utility, sometimes to a move on the part of an ambitious archbishop, sometimes to an act of deference, not to say subservience, to Imperial authority, which naturally endeavoured to use the archbishop of the new capital to further its ends. As, for instance, Sisinnius, when Archbishop of Constantinople, designated Proclus for the bishopric of Cyzicum, the metropolis of Hellespont, in the 'diocese' of Asia. The Cyzicenes resisted the intrusion successfully, and whereas Sisinnius pleaded an enactment of the Emperor Theodosius, the Cyzicenes set this aside on the ground that it applied only to his predecessor Atticus, being a personal privilege. It is to be noticed that on the one hand Sisinnius did not appeal to the canon of 381, and on the other hand, the contention of the Cyzicenes shows that they also did not consider that Constantinople had received anything in the way of jurisdiction by that canon.

It was not, then, the canon of 381 that prevailed to

[1] ἀκλήτους. [2] παρακλήσει μεγίστῃ.

shelter Constantinople in her growing tendency to
exercise jurisdiction over the eparchies or ' dioceses ' that
lay close over against her ; it was rather the example of
such a saintly prelate as St. Chrysostom, misapplied ; it
was the temptation to act in conformity with Imperial rescripts ; and it was a natural fruit, human nature being
what it is, of the honorary precedence spoken of in that
third canon of 381 ; but the result was not on that
account regular or canonical. At the same time, so far
as those three Eastern dioceses of Asia, Pontus and
Thrace were concerned, it was an arrangement which, if
the Nicene settlement were set aside, would commend itself to good sense. But there was only one power which
could alter the Nicene arrangement, viz. the Church
herself acting through the Apostolic See, or through an
Œcumenical Council commissioned to act in such a
matter, or confirmed in its action by the Holy See.

Constantinople tried her best with the fragments of
an Œcumenical Council, and with the Apostolic See, in
451 and the two following years, but, as we shall presently
see, in vain. She seems from the first to have had some
idea of improving her position by means of intrigue at
the Council : such at least is the natural deduction from
the caution given to the legates not to be a party to any
alteration of the Nicene arrangement in the relative
position of sees. De Marca thinks that the subject of
ordinations was purposely introduced with a view to
leading up to the question of her position. Whether this
be so or not, that question at length came to the front,
though not in the regular sessions of the Œcumenical
Council, which ended with the sixth.

It was in this wise. In the eleventh session, the
whole subject of the relation of Ephesus to Constantinople

came before the Council through the appeal of Bassian, who claimed to be the rightful occupant of the see of Ephesus, as against Stephen, who advanced a counter-claim. The history of the matter was as follows. After the deaths of Memnon and Basilius, Bassian seized the bishopric by means of violence and bribery, without the vote of the Synod. The Emperor Theodosius on appeal confirmed him in the bishopric. Bassian forthwith went to Constantinople and ingratiated himself with Proclus, the archbishop, and was received into communion by him and by the bishops of the 'Resident Synod,' at the desire of Theodosius. Eventually, however, he was ejected by Stephen, who threw him into prison, and Stephen was elected by the vote of forty Asiatic bishops. The matter had been again referred by Theodosius to the Patriarchs, including of course the Bishop of Rome, on whose decision Stephen specially relied.[1] Their decision was in favour of Stephen, but it was intended to be executed, not by force, but through proper synodical action. Stephen, however, had used force. Consequently, both Bassian and Stephen were deposed, but permitted to retain the rank of bishop with an allotted pension.

Now in dealing with this affair the rights of Constantinople were touched upon. Lucian, the political *Vicarius* of Byza and Bishop of Heraclea, a strong partisan of Constantinopolitan privileges, pleaded that since Proclus, the archbishop, had received Bassian to communion, he had settled the matter. He spoke of Proclus as possessing authority[2] in the matter, though Bassian himself only said that he had been received into com-

[1] Mansi, vii. 289.
[2] *Ibid.* 284. ὁ ἔχων τὸ κῦρος. This latter term is that regularly used

munion at Constantinople—a different matter. Both Bassian and Stephen were treated as in communion with the Church, though not as necessarily legitimate Bishops of Ephesus. The act of Proclus was one of charity, not of superior jurisdiction.[1]

But Lucian's expression about the authority of Proclus seems to have started the all-important question in the mind of Eusebius of Dorylæum, as to where the Bishop of Ephesus ought to be ordained. At once the bishops of the diocese of Asia prostrated themselves on the ground before their fellow-bishops, terrified at the thought of the Ephesine ordinations being conducted at Constantinople. They entreated the Synod that they might not be performed in the Imperial city. The city of Ephesus would be in a tumult; it would be the destruction of the city. The Imperial Commissioners then put the question to the Synod, and the answer came at once, that the ordination should take place 'in the eparchy,' *i.e.* at Ephesus itself. Diogenes of Cyzicum then took up the cudgels for Constantinople and pleaded custom.[2] We have already seen that the Cyzicenes themselves resisted the ordination of their own bishop at Constantinople, on the ground of a custom to the contrary. Here Diogenes put forward the prevalence of custom in favour of Constantinople. Another bishop objected that from St. Timothy onwards twenty-seven bishops had been ordained in Ephesus itself; to which Philip, the cleric of Constantinople, replied that the 'blessed John,' *i.e.* St. Chrysostom, when Archbishop of Constantinople had deposed fifteen bishops in Asia and ordained

for metropolitan jurisdiction. *Cf.* De Marca, *Diss. Eccles. de Constant. Patriarch. Institutione.*
    [1] Mansi, vii. 292. [2] *Ibid.*

others in their stead; and that he had ordained Memnon in the Imperial city itself. Aetius, the Archdeacon of Constantinople, produced other instances, and especially that of Basilius (the last occupant of the see of Ephesus before Bassian or Stephen), who had been ordained at Constantinople by Proclus, and in this act the Emperor Theodosius and Cyril of Alexandria had cooperated—a fact which, as De Marca acutely remarks, indicated a sense of some need of artificial support. The bishops, however, at Chalcedon exclaimed hereupon, 'Let the canons prevail,' *i.e.* against the claim, as though this action of Constantinople was not covered by the canons.

And now for the first time, so far as the historical records go, the clergy of Constantinople, showing their hand, pleaded, to all appearance, the third canon of 381. They exclaimed: 'Let the canons *of the* 150 *fathers* prevail: let not the privileges [1] of Constantinople perish. Let the ordination take place here by the archbishop, according to custom.' It will be noticed that, after all, they had to fall back upon custom; they could not rely simply on the canon. But they seem to plead custom as the legitimate interpreter of the canon. How the alleged custom could possibly be reconciled with the *second* canon of 381, which assigned ordinations to the Synod of the eparchy, one is at a loss to conjecture. In fact it is impossible to reconcile them. The Imperial Commissioners were naturally dissatisfied; they accordingly postponed the settlement of the matter.[2]

---

[1] προνόμια (Mansi, vii. 293).

[2] τῇ ἑξῆς τοῦτο τελείως τυπωθήσεται (*ibid.* 293) = 'shall be authoritatively decided to-morrow.' Dr. Bright admits that in this passage τυπόω does mean 'authoritative regulation' (*Canons of the Councils,* p. 200).

The next day it was decided that neither Bassian nor Stephen should retain the see of Ephesus but that both should be pensioned off. Paschasinus, the Papal legate, thereupon said that 'another bishop should be decided upon according to the canons.' The Commissioners, summing up the synodical decision, quoting Anatolius's witness and that of the Papal legates—the one, we may presume, because of his connection with the affair, and the other, because of their special position as legates— decreed the ejection of both Bassian and Stephen, and their maintenance by the Church of Ephesus; and then concluded with saying that 'another bishop shall be ordained according to the canons of the Church.' This was received by acclamation as a pious decree ($\tau \acute{v} \pi o s$). Thus far, then, the clergy of Constantinople had endeavoured to base a custom on such instances as that of Proclus's ordination, in contravention of the canons, both of Nicæa and of Constantinople in 381, *i.e.* of the second canon, and the third canon of that Synod had not been explicitly quoted in favour of their wishes.

As regards Alexandria and Antioch, Constantinople had not as yet claimed to act upon the third canon of Constantinople. That canon, indeed, had never received the adhesion of Alexandria, whose Bishop Timothy was absent when it was drawn up.[1] And it had been enacted when the Bishop of Antioch was in a peculiar relation to Constantinople. Flavian of Antioch, contrary to all rules of justice, had just been consecrated by Nectarius to the archbishopric of that city, and was neither in a mood nor in a position to resist the encroachment on the honours of his see which that canon involved. Domnus of Antioch had also recently entered into a compact with Proclus of

[1] *Cf.* Le Quien, *Oriens Christianus*, i. 16.

Constantinople, which enabled the latter to take the first place, but Dioscorus wrote indignantly to Domnus as one who was betraying the cause of Antioch, which he could not have done if the regulation of 381 had been recognised as a canon of the Church.[1] Seventeen years after the enactment of the canon, Theophilus of Alexandria consecrated St. Chrysostom to Constantinople,[2] and then, in his place, Arsacius in 406. And in all the subsequent troubles between Theophilus and Chrysostom the canon of 381 was never appealed to: which seems inconceivable if it was held to be a really valid decision, seeing that the relation of the sees emerged again and again. At the Synod of the Oak, Theophilus did not preside, to afford an appearance of equity. He voted last.

The canon had thus, as a canon, collapsed from the outset.[3] Dioscorus's action towards Flavian of Constantinople, although in the interests of heresy, and attended with the grossest injustice, implies, nevertheless, the absence of any consciousness that the third canon of 381 had conferred a real precedence over Alexandria.[4] Flavian did not attempt to plead such precedence; indeed, in his letter to Leo he even spoke of having always *obeyed* Dioscorus;[5] neither did the Council of Chalcedon in condemning Dioscorus suggest that the primacy of the East in any sense belonged to Constantinople.

Thus between 381 and 451 the third canon of 381 had been a dead letter so far as Alexandria and Antioch were concerned; but circumstances had led to Constan-

[1] Theodoret, *Ep.* 86.
[2] 'A certain proof of his [Theophilus's] power over that see,' *i.e.* Constantinople' (Le Quien, ii. 337).
[3] 'Ab initio caducæ,' said St. Leo; he is referring to its irregularity as contravening the Nicene canon.
[4] Le Quien, *ibid.* [5] *Cf. supra*, p. 174.

tinople exercising a good deal of occasional and temporary authority over the three great 'dioceses' of Asia Minor (so to call it), Pontus and Thrace. But in the Council of Chalcedon, Constantinople's decision had in one case been reversed, and, again, its desire to ordain to the see of Ephesus had not been granted. A third case, moreover, came before the Council which must have been equally distasteful to Constantinople, connected again with ordinations. In the thirteenth session the Bishop of Nicomedia was supported by the bishops at the Council in his metropolitical rights in the province of Bithynia as against the Bishop of Nicæa, the quarrel between them turning on their respective rights to ordain a bishop to Basilinopolis in that province. Hereupon Aetius, the Archdeacon of Constantinople, suddenly stepped forward and put in a claim for the Imperial see, saying that it had been itself accustomed to ordain to Basilinopolis or else by letters dimissory to permit others to ordain. But the Synod at once exclaimed, as in the previous instances: 'Let the canons prevail. Let the canons obtain their due.' The Imperial Commissioners accordingly pronounced in favour of Eunomius, Bishop of Nicomedia, and then went on to say that 'whatever is suitable for the throne of Constantinople concerning ordinations in the " eparchies "' (*i.e.* the three 'dioceses' of Asia Minor, Pontus and Thrace) 'shall be examined in its proper order before the Synod.' Eunomius publicly thanked the Synod for keeping to the canons, and at the same time in a somewhat cringing tone averred his affection for the Archbishop of Constantinople.[1]

Now it must be remembered that in the fourth session the Imperial Commissioners had asked the

[1] Mansi, vii. 92.

bishops in full Synod to settle two questions—first, 'whether it was lawful for Anatolius the most holy Archbishop of Constantinople to send an excommunication to the most reverend Bishop Photius and to order that certain Churches in the province should be taken from him; and [secondly] whether he ought to call the assembly of bishops in the Imperial city a Synod.' Neither of these questions was answered, so far as their essential points were concerned. It was decided that Anatolius ought not to have condemned a man in his absence. And the second question was left severely alone. Thus a slur had been cast upon Constantinople's method of action at its core, viz. its use of the 'Resident Synod' to determine such matters at all. And now the Council had withdrawn Basilinopolis, in the 'diocese' of Pontus, from the jurisdiction of Constantinople, and had ordered that the whole question of her rights as to ordinations in the provinces of those three great dioceses, or eparchies, should be regularly examined.[1]

It is a singular and unfortunate fact that the records of the next session are missing. Had they been to the credit of Constantinople, we can hardly suppose that she would have allowed them to disappear. But so it is. We have only a list of canons, twenty-seven of which are supposed by the Ballerini and others to have been enacted

[1] Dr. Bright (*Roman See*, p. 197) says that 'the Council had not refused to call the Sojourning Synod a Synod, but simply blamed it for condemning a bishop unheard.' It did more. It refrained from answering the question as to whether the 'Sojourning Synod' was a Synod. And it at once quoted the fourth Nicene canon (Mansi, vii. 93), which decreed that bishops should be ordained 'in the eparchy'—a sufficiently plain rebuff for Constantinople, which was thus declared to be wrong in two ways—first, in condemning a bishop unheard, and, secondly, in interfering in the province of another.

in an earlier session, while the twenty-eighth was not even entered as a canon of Chalcedon in the Greek collections, until much later on. But it is this twenty-eighth canon which has been the sheet-anchor of the Anglican position : with what justice, we shall now see. What we know of it is gathered from the record of the Papal legates' protest, and of the struggle that ensued, in the session which followed upon its enactment.

CHAPTER IX

THE BYZANTINE PLOT: OR, THE TWENTY-EIGHTH CANON

THE circumstances under which Constantinople made her supreme effort to gain synodical sanction for the position she was assuming over the dioceses of Asia, Pontus and Thrace were sufficiently favourable to ensure success, so far as the bishops there were concerned. The three or four days assigned by the Emperor for the bishops' stay in Chalcedon had passed, and they had left by the hundred. Hardly more than two hundred out of the original six hundred remained. And among those that lingered behind there was not one that might not be counted on for either assent or silence.

Of the two 'greater sees' Alexandria was vacant, and Antioch was occupied by a partisan of Anatolius, to whom he owed his irregular elevation, which had been pardoned by Rome only (as Leo said) 'for the sake of peace.'[1]

Constantinople, therefore, had nothing to fear from these. She only needed a lack of scrupulous fairness on her own part to enable her to press the matter to a successful issue under these favourable circumstances. But further, she could count upon at least the silence of

[1] 'Studio pacis.'

another leading prelate, viz. Juvenal of Jerusalem, who had himself just gained the object of his ambition for the last twenty years in the compromise by which he had wrested three provinces from Antioch. He at any rate was not in a position to complain of any illicit stretch of jurisdiction on the part of another. And Juvenal and Anatolius had a further bond in that both had come under the influence of Dioscorus and coquetted with Eutychianism. Then the Bishop of Heraclea, the Primate of Thrace, was absent, and he was very closely concerned in the project that Constantinople had before her of extending her actual jurisdiction as well as securing the semblance of synodical sanction for titular precedence. This primate was represented by Lucian, who was so friendly to Anatolius that he was sent by him to Rome on this very matter. Ephesus, again, of supreme importance, as one of the exarchies to be robbed of its autonomy, was vacant, Bassian and Stephen having been deposed. Thalassius of Cæsarea in Cappadocia was there, but did not subscribe, and he was Exarch of Pontus; so that no one of the three dioceses or eparchies was properly represented among the signataries; and yet it was exactly these 'dioceses' that were concerned in the matter. The Illyrians were not there, not even Thessalonica, neither was Ancyra, Corinth, Nicomedia, Cos, nor Iconium, all of them important centres. In fact, the little knot of bishops whom Constantinople gathered round herself by various means could not by any stretch of language be called a representative ecclesiastical body, for the purpose of enacting a canon concerning the jurisdiction of Constantinople. Moreover they had no leave from Rome to discuss the question now forced upon the bishops by Constantinople; it was no part of the

Council's programme. It was simply a plot against the Church's order, with hardly a name that would command the confidence of the Church except the impetuous Eusebius of Dorylæum. The legates, though pressed to attend, refused. The Imperial Commissioners were also asked to assist at the session, but they also refused, though they gave their permission for the matter to be mooted.[1] There was not a single Western bishop present. But these 'astute' Orientals, as the African bishop Facundus called them, drew up a canon which flung the Nicene settlement as to precedence to the winds, and assigned, on the one hand, the first place in the East to Constantinople, and on the other hand gave her jurisdiction over 'Asia,' Thrace and Pontus. The exarchs of these regions were to be deprived of their position as left to them by the Nicene fathers, and Constantinople was to be not only New Rome in the civil order, but in the ecclesiastical hierarchy was to stand second to Rome in point of titular precedence, and at the same time to receive an enormous extension of her jurisdiction in the East. She had hoped and tried to gain the confirmation and ordination of the provincial bishops as well as of the metropolitans, but owing to the opposition of some metropolitans she failed in this part of her project.

On the following day the Papal legates demanded an explanation of what had been done in their absence.

[1] παρεκαλέσαμεν τοὺς ἐπισκόπους τοὺς ἀπὸ Ῥώμης . . . . παρρήσαντο . . . ἀνηνέγκαμεν καὶ [sic] ἐπὶ τὴν ὑμετέραν μεγαλοπρέπειαν (Mansi, vii. 428). Dr. Bright in his criticism (*Roman See*, p. 198) on the first edition of my book on *The Primitive Church*, &c. ignores the force of the καί, which shows that the bishops asked the Commissioners to attend, but that they refused—Hefele thinks, from diplomatic considerations. They evidently thought that the bishops were skating on thin ice.

They had absented themselves on the technical ground that after the definition of faith had been drawn up, and the matter of the lapsed bishops dealt with, their commission ended. But it turned out that they had also received orders from Rome to oppose any attempt at altering the relations of bishops on the ground of the civil *status* of their sees.[1] Leo was already well aware of the ambitious projects of Constantinople.

Aetius, the archdeacon, now did his best to purge the action of the bishops of its irregularity. He said that it must be owned that the matters of faith had been decided in a fitting way, but pleaded that it was customary to take in hand other necessary matters; that they had asked the legates to be present, but without success, and that they had received the permission of the Imperial Commissioners to proceed with the business. The legates, however, maintained, and were probably justified in maintaining, that the bishops had signed in fear, and, indeed, their antecedents and the present position of those that signed, fully justify such an assertion, however little some of them may have realised it; they said also that the proposed canon contravened the Nicene settlement; that it was professedly grounded on canons which had not been enrolled among those of the Church;[2] and, lastly, that if Constantinople had been benefiting by the said canon up till now, what need of anything further?—and if she had not, why did she now apply for sanction for that which is an infringement of the canons?—reasoning which was unanswerable.

In consequence of this mention of the canons, the

---

[1] For an answer to Dr. Bright's accusation against the legates (*Roman See*, p. 198) see note at the end of this chapter.

[2] 'Non conscripti,' *i.e.* the third of Constantinople.

Commissioners requested that each side should read those on which they relied. The legates accordingly read the sixth canon of Nicæa, in which Alexandria and Antioch, and not Constantinople, came next to Rome. They also read the seventh canon, which by anticipation reproved Juvenal. Aetius is then supposed to have produced first a slightly different version of the same canon, and then (omitting the seventh of Nicæa) the third of Constantinople was read. But this is in the highest degree improbable, since his supposed reading of that version of the sixth canon makes nothing for the point at issue. The rise of Constantinople took place after the Council of Nicæa; no one pretends, or pretended, that the Nicene canons in any way assisted Constantinople in its present aims; on the contrary, they were dead against the new canon. Constantinople was then an inferior see, and left so by the Nicene fathers. It was on the third canon of Constantinople that these bishops took their stand. The Nicene canon was their difficulty.[1] Indeed, in one of the oldest versions of the Acts of Chalcedon that we possess the production of the sixth canon by Aetius does not appear.[2] There are also other indications that the text has been tampered with here; for between the supposed recitation of the sixth canon and that of the third of Constantinople occurs the statement that 'the same secretary read from the same codex the synodicon of the

---

[1] Dr. Bright thinks that 'if the legates' version of the canon was alone read, then the Greek text' (he ought to have said the Constantinopolitan version) 'was practically thrown overboard' (*Roman See*, p. 203). But why? Each was to read the canons on which each relied, not those on which the other relied. The legates did not rely on the opening words, but the latter part, which is admittedly genuine.

[2] The *Codex Julianus*, now called *Parisiensis*. Baluze first noticed this, and has been followed by the Ballerini.

second Synod,' which Mansi rightly transferred to the margin, as an impossible statement to have occurred in the original. The Council of Constantinople was not called 'the second Synod' at that time—not until in the compilations of canons the four Œcumenical Councils came to be separated from the local Councils, which took place later on. The expression, therefore, belongs to a later period than the original of the Council of Chalcedon. Accordingly, Rusticus, who had before him very early manuscripts, omits this whole sentence, although (inconsistently enough) the sixth canon appears in his manuscript. The insertion, therefore, had been made before his time, doubtless, as has been suggested above, by a Greek scribe, who, seeing a Greek version of the sixth canon in the margin, put there as a note by some previous scribe, inserted it in the text, and some later copyist inserted the remark about the second Synod. And most people will feel with Hefele that if two conflicting versions of the Nicene canon had been read, some remark must have been made on such a subject.[1]

What, however, is of greater importance is the conclusion which the Imperial Commissioners now drew from the whole discussion. The legates had quoted the sixth and seventh Nicene canons, beginning 'Rome has always held the primacy,' and had read onwards about *Alexandria*,

---

[1] Ballerini, *De Antiq. Collect. Canonum*, Part I. cap. vi. 8. Dr. Bright (*Notes on the Canons*, &c., 1892, p. 227) refers to the expression 'œcumenical,' meaning 'of the whole East,' used by the Council of 382 in reference to the Council of 381; but this would not account for the expression 'second Synod,' which only came into use when the canons were collected in the way stated in the text. *Cf.* Ballerini, *Opp. Leon.* iii. p. xxxvii; *De Antiq. Coll.* I. vi. § 8. The reference to Theodoret which Dr. Bright gives adds nothing to the authorities. It only contains the letter of the Council of 382.

Antioch and Jerusalem, this latter portion being that on which they relied. The Archdeacon of Constantinople had had the third canon of Constantinople read with a long addition (which was dishonestly joined on) placing Asia, Pontus and Thrace under the jurisdiction of the Imperial city. Several of the bishops had taken the side of Constantinople, and expressed their perfect willingness to subordinate their sees to that of the imperial city; Eusebius of Ancyra, however, while he proclaimed his willingness to do the same, protested against the pecuniary exactions with which this subordination had been accompanied. The Commissioners, however, decided that two things were plain from the Acts and depositions: first, that the primacy (πρωτεῖα—the very word used in the sixth Nicene canon, as cited by the Papal legate) belonged to Old Rome. About this there had been no question, and it is obvious that the Imperial Commissioners could decide nothing about that. But, secondly, they decided that New Rome ought to have—not a primacy (πρωτεῖα) such as Rome had, which the whole history of the Council proves to have involved jurisdiction in the minds of all the bishops—but the same honorary privileges (πρεσβεῖα) as Rome, besides her primacy and as a consequence of it, also possessed. Rome, they had said, possessed two things—honorary precedence and primacy; Constantinople ought to possess in the East that honorary precedence which Rome possessed over the whole Church.[1]

---

[1] πρὸ πάντων μὲν τὰ πρωτεῖα καὶ τὴν ἐξαίρετον τιμὴν κατὰ τοὺς κανόνας τῷ τῆς πρεσβύτιδος Ῥώμης θεοφιλεστάτῳ ἀρχιεπισκόπῳ φυλάττεσθαι. I do not see how, in view of this undisputed original, it can be maintained, as it is by so many Anglican writers, that the legates' version was a forgery. The Council clearly accepted the

Thus Constantinople laid the foundation of her desired patriarchate over the East, and supplied the premiss from which Photius was one day to draw the conclusion in claiming universal jurisdiction.

It is difficult to understand how Canon Gore could manage to see 'Rome's self-assertion' at the bottom of all this. Canon Bright also reproduces with approval the sentence in which Canon Gore makes the strange statement, that it is 'more than probable [sic] that the self-assertion of Rome excited the jealousy of the East, and thus Eastern bishops secretly felt that the cause of Constantinople was theirs.' It must have been *very*

Papal legate's quotation as expressing the truth (*cf.* Appendix I.). τὰ πρωτεῖα, primacy, and πρεσβεῖα τῆς τιμῆς, honorary precedence, are distinguished throughout. Primacy in general is assigned to Rome in the legates' version of the Nicene canon. It is assigned to Alexandria and Antioch over their respective restricted jurisdictions in the same canon, and to the other eparchies. Honorary precedence, ἀκολουθία τῆς τιμῆς, is assigned to Jerusalem. The 28th canon now in dispute said that 'the [Nicene] fathers naturally rendered precedence to the see of older Rome on account of the Imperial position of that city' (Mansi, vii. 428). They did not say 'gave,' nor 'gave the primacy.' But they said ἀποδεδώκασι = 'rendered.' It is the word used in Matt. xxii. for 'Render unto God the things that are God's.' It was presently used in the same session by Eusebius of Ancyra for rendering in the sense of paying up what was owing: πολλὴν ὁλκὴν ἀπέδωκα (Mansi, vii. 452). The πρεσβεῖα, rank, or dignity, rendered to Rome was the result of τὰ πρωτεῖα = her primacy as the See of Peter. 'The 150 fathers,' says the 28th canon, 'assigned' (ἀπένειμαν, not 'rendered') 'equal honours [*i.e.* in the East] to the see of New Rome.' It desired to confirm the 3rd canon of 381, which decreed that the Bishop of Constantinople should have honorary precedence (πρεσβεῖα τῆς τιμῆς) after the Bishop of Rome. Thus the *primacy* of Rome was never in question, but only the honorary precedence that resulted from the primacy. The latter was mentioned in the legates' version of the 6th Nicene canon, and conceded as a matter of course. Constantinople wanted to usurp honorary precedence over Alexandria and Antioch and effective jurisdiction over the 'dioceses' of Asia, Pontus and Thrace.

'secretly' felt, for there is not a solitary allusion in their speeches to such an idea, while they are from end to end of the Council brimful of acknowledgments of the service which Leo had rendered to the Church of God. So far as the records go, the bishops, whatever they 'secretly felt,' were open in their avowals that, to use their own words, 'God has given the Synod an invulnerable champion against every error in the person of the Roman bishop, who, like the ardent Peter, desires to lead everyone to God.' (Synod's letter to Marcian.[1]) Pope Nicholas I. said to Photius, of the crisis which arose in consequence of the Latrocinium, 'If the great Leo had not been divinely moved to open his mouth, the Christian religion would have perished outright.'

Canon Gore's suggestion bears, indeed, no serious relation to the facts. It may be fairly said of it, as Canon Bright has said of a contention of the Ballerini, mentioned above, that 'nothing but an intelligible bias could account for a suggestion so futile.'[2] The 'self-assertion' was all on the part of Constantinople.

The legates entered their protest on the technical ground that the Apostolic See had not been consulted as to the discussion of this question,[3] and that the proposal was a violation of the Nicene canons. They asked that the proceedings of the previous day be cancelled, or else that their opposition be recorded, 'so that we may know what we ought to report to the Apostolic man, the Pope of the Universal Church, so that he himself may pass sentence on the injury done to his see or on the overthrow

---

[1] Quoted in the 'Collectio Lacensis,' *Acta Concilii Vaticani*, vii. 449.
[2] Bright's *Notes on the Councils*, p. 148.
[3] This seems to be the meaning of the legates' words. Cf. *Leon. Ep.* 119, 5.

of the canons'—the injury done to the Holy See by debating the question without its consent, and the overthrow of the canons by displacing Alexandria in favour of Constantinople.

In spite, however, of the legates' protest the bishops voted the canon, the Commissioners calling them 'the whole Synod,' *i.e.* all except the Papal legates.

The matter could not, of course, stand there. Comparatively speaking, as we have seen, they were but a handful of bishops, most of them of sees grouped round Constantinople, and their leaders far from enjoying the esteem of the Catholic world. Their canon was the work 'rather of Greek sophists than of Fathers of the Church.'[1] They had adroitly tacked on their new claim over three large eparchies (which by the Nicene Council had been left autonomous) to the third canon of Constantinople, so that the new and old parts read like one: in which, as Canon Bright remarks, they were more 'astute than candid.'

The matter, then, could not rest there. Indeed these bishops themselves did not entertain the idea that their act was final; and accordingly they set to work to gain a favourable decision from Leo, in spite of his legates' protest. They had the Emperor on their side, and the game was worth pursuing; for even if they lost in the present, they had taken a step forward for the future.

It is certainly astonishing that writers who are so full of Rome's supposed 'self-assertion' and 'exorbitant claims' should not see the worthlessness of what these comparatively few bishops said and did, two-thirds of the bishops of the original Synod being absent, and the Presidents of the same refusing their assent. Yet it is

[1] Rohrbacher, *Hist.* iv. 539.

the case that the most universally accepted writers among Anglicans have for the last three centuries taken their stand on this canon, and seen in it an acceptance, *by the Church*, of the principle that Rome owed *all* her privileges, not to her relationship to the Apostle Peter, and through him to our Lord's institution, but to her secular position as the capital of the Roman Empire. How, it may be asked, can the Church be identified with these Eastern adventurers, men whose antecedents were in almost every case sufficiently suspicious to deprive their judgment on such a matter of half its value? Anatolius, originally secretary to Dioscorus, and wavering in the Eutychian troubles; Juvenal, one of the leaders at the Robber-Synod, and himself involved in an ambitious scheme for the stretch of his jurisdiction; Maximus, who had been irregularly ordained by Anatolius himself, his ordination only sanctioned by Leo for the sake of peace; Alexandria vacant; the Exarch of Ephesus, so deeply concerned, not there; and the rest, most of them, in no position to withstand the pressure which the legates, who knew the position of matters well, asserted had been put upon them by Constantinople—how can these be taken to represent the Church?

It may be asked how did the Emperor Marcian come to second Constantinople's ambition? Perhaps the true answer is, that he saw in the proposed arrangement certain conveniences which commended it to his mind from a political point of view.[1] And it was undoubtedly the case that the proposed arrangement had much in its favour, and might have passed muster had it not conflicted with a higher principle of action. As things then

---

[1] *Cf.* Hefele, *in loco.*

stood, Constantinople having become the actual centre of life in the East, it was certainly a natural position for a politician to adopt, that the ecclesiastical apparatus should adapt itself to the new circumstances, and that the London of the East should become the root and womb of the Church in the future. But Marcian did not see that another principle was being introduced which, if admitted, must have been subversive of the Church's spiritual and supernatural order, as, indeed, it proved to be under Peter the Czar. When Marcian found that St. Leo was opposed to the arrangement, he dropped his patronage of the scheme. But the bishops braced themselves to the work of persuading Leo that their canon was harmless and worthy of that sanction which they felt to be all important.

NOTE ON DR. BRIGHT'S ACCUSATION AGAINST THE LEGATES.

Dr. Bright accuses the Papal legates roundly of telling a falsehood at the fifteenth session. 'Their former reply, then, was a falsehood which had served its purpose' (*Roman See*, p. 198). Now the legates were asked in the fifteenth session *to take a share in* (κοινωνοὺς γίγνεσθαι) certain matters which the Church of Constantinople said that she had to transact (διαπράξασθαι), without mentioning exactly what they were. The legates, however, knew perfectly well that the business was concerned with the jurisdiction of Constantinople in the matter of ordinations in the three 'dioceses' of Asia, Pontus and Thrace, for it was of this that the Commissioners had said that the rights of the see of Constantinople must be investigated. They accordingly 'refused, saying that they had received no such orders' (Mansi, vii. 428). This was, according to Dr. Bright, their falsehood. But it was absolutely true. For they afterwards, in the sixteenth session, read to the

Synod the instruction which they *had* received, viz. 'Suffer not the constitution of the holy fathers to be violated or diminished by any rashness, preserving in every way the dignity of our person' (*i.e.* of Leo) 'in yourselves whom we have sent in our stead; and if it should happen that any, trusting in the power of their cities, shall have attempted any usurpation, repudiate this with proper constancy' (*ibid.* 443). There was, therefore, not the remotest approach to a falsehood in what they said. Their instructions gave them no leave to enter upon the discussion of matters such as the relationship between Alexandria, Antioch and Constantinople, nor the subjugation of those 'other eparchies,' mentioned in the sixth Nicene canon, whose mutual relationship had been there settled. This was a recognised principle, laid down in regard to the matter of Maximus in a subsequent letter by Leo (*Ep.* 119). Accordingly, when the affair of Constantinopolitan jurisdiction was thus brought on, they refused to have anything to do with its discussion: they had no orders *to take part in it*, as they said with the strictest accuracy. Celestine gave definite orders to his legates not to take part in discussions, but to give their judgment on the sentences of the bishops in the Council of Ephesus; and the legates here could truthfully say that they also had no orders to enter upon a discussion on such a matter. But they had orders to repudiate certain attempts at usurpation, if they should be made. They *were* made, and, accordingly, when the 28th canon was read at the next session, having been carried by a mere remnant of bishops, they repudiated it, as Leo told them to do. They protested against it, appealing to the judgment of 'the bishop who presides over the whole Church' (Mansi, vii. 453). Dr. Bright was bound before he accused men who had boldly stood up for the foundation of our Christian faith, and had been appointed for the office of presiding in place of Leo, to produce some instructions bidding the legates take a share in the transaction of business (κοινωνοὺς γίγνεσθαι τῶν πραττομένων—the present tense) which had not been allotted to the Council. An order to oppose any violation of the Nicene settlement is not an instruction to take part in a meeting improperly held for the obvious purpose of promoting such a violation. Until Dr. Bright can produce such an instruction, he stands convicted of a false accusation. His translation is grievously misleading; the legates did not say, as he makes them say, that 'they had no instructions about such a matter,' *i.e.*, as he applies it, the subject of Constantinopolitan jurisdiction. They said that 'they had no such orders,' *i.e.* as to be sharers (κοινωνοὺς) in the transactions of a particular meeting held to promote it by a comparative handful of bishops under sinister influence. It would be possible to construct a falsehood out of the legates' speech as mistranslated by Dr. Bright; but it is not possible to invent one from the words correctly translated and applied to their actual context. It is to be regretted that Dr. Bright perpetrates the same mistranslation in a book intended for young men at one of our universities. He there translates the words of the legates 'we have no instructions on the matter' (*Canons of the first four General Councils*, p. 220, 2nd ed. 1892). The words of the legates as given by the bishops are παρῃτήσαντο λέγοντες, ἐντολὰς μὴ εἰληφέναι τοιαύτας, and what they were asked was κοινωνοὺς γίγνεσθαι τῶν πραττομένων. It will be seen that their actual instructions fully justified them in refusing to attend a meeting to promote, or even discuss the affairs of Constantinople's jurisdiction in the matter of ordinations. *Cf.* Mansi, vii. 428 and 444.

It is clear that this is how their words of refusal were understood by the bishops, for in the following session the legates were asked if they had any orders 'about this,' *i.e.* about the matter decided by the bishops, and they then read their order (Mansi, vii. 442, 444). But they could not have been asked this, if they had been understood in the fifteenth session to mean what Dr. Bright understands them to have meant, *i.e.* that they had no instructions on the matter.

CHAPTER X

EASTERN RECOGNITION OF PAPAL SUPREMACY

No one will deny the incomparable importance of the letter which was now addressed to Leo by the remnant of the Synod concerning their new proposal. The twenty-eighth canon of Chalcedon has long been the sheet-anchor of the Anglican position. Relying as that position does on the first four General Councils, it is maintained that the judgment of the Council of Chalcedon, supposed to be expressed in this canon, establishes the theory that the primacy of the Bishop of Rome was considered in the East to be due, not to his relation to St. Peter, but to the Imperial position of the city of Rome. The belief in any real relationship to St. Peter postulates a divine origin for the primacy of the Bishop of Rome, for it involves the belief that our Lord included that primacy in His words to the Apostle. And if the primacy be in any sense divine, it is indispensable. No amount of misconduct on the part of its representatives can justify us in altering the lines laid down by our Divine Lord Himself. But this twenty-eighth canon proves, so it is confidently asserted, that the Bishop of Rome only held a certain primacy by reason of his being bishop of the Imperial City. He was, so it is said, only *primus inter pares*. Constantinople (it is urged) was placed by this canon in the second position on a principle which proves that Rome's primacy was one of mere presidency, of honour 'without definite powers'—in a word that the Bishop of Rome was only the 'First Patriarch.'

Now it is important to remember that the Bishop of Rome *was* the first patriarch, and this canon recognises him as such. There is no dispute about this. Leo XIII. is to-day not only Bishop of Rome, but Patriarch of the West. The fault of the so-called twenty-eighth canon, therefore, did not lie in its recognition of Rome's patriarchal position; its mistake lay in attributing even that position purely to her connection with the Imperial city, whereas the matter really stood thus:—St. Peter selected Rome, and Rome was the capital of the empire. His successors reaped the fruit of his wise choice, and utilised, as they were meant to do, the advantages of a natural centre. Ecclesiastical Rome was able to be what she was because she was the See of Peter: she was also able to do her work at first as she did because her influence radiated from the metropolis of the Empire. Her patriarchal sway was subordinate to her apostolical jurisdiction; but it was a reality. It is difficult to draw the line between the apostolical and patriarchal elements of her position, for the latter is necessarily overshadowed, and coloured, and informed by the former; but her relationship to Peter, the prince and head of the Apostles, is clear, and occupied an unmistakable place in the thoughts of the bishops at Chalcedon. It was expressed emphatically and in the most precise terms by the comparatively few bishops who passed this canon in favour of Constantinople. The terms which they use in their letter to Leo cannot all of them, without doing violence to the laws which govern men's minds, be attributed simply to flattery or general Eastern courtesy. This, which is the favourite Anglican explanation of these bishops' statements, is excluded by the circumstances which produced the letter.[1]

The bishops were, it is true, concerned to flatter St. Leo, if possible: they wanted to gain something from him. But what they wanted to gain was of that nature that the particular terms used by them were the last in the world that they would have dreamt of addressing to him at this juncture, merely with a view to flatter, even if they supposed that Leo was the man to be seduced by honeyed words in a matter of such supreme importance. Consider the circumstances under which they wrote. Leo had shown himself above all things zealous for the canons of the Church. It was this trait which the Emperor Marcian singled out for praise in his encomium of the Pontiff during this whole transaction. And the bishops at Chalcedon who passed the twenty-eighth canon were, as the African bishop Facundus described them in the next century, 'astute as serpents.' Is it to be supposed that these astute bishops would give away their case by telling St. Leo that he was in precisely that position which their canon, according to the Anglican interpretation, was concerned to deny or ignore? If they admitted that St. Leo was their 'head,' they were admitting that their position next after him was secondary in the sense of subordinate, and that their canon was valueless without his sanction. If they asserted that St. Leo was the instrument whereby the teaching of the Prince of the Apostles was made known *to them*, they were giving away the whole position which our Anglican friends consider essential to their own

[1] *Leon. Ep.* 98.

security. Terms which expressed, in plain Greek and Latin, a truth which Leo had all along maintained and acted upon, and which his legates had stated in the Council, cannot be called mere compliments; they denote the acceptance of the position.

Now the bishops did tell St. Leo that 'he was their head, and they but members.' What could be their idea in using, by way of compliment, such an expression as that? Did they suppose that Leo would not take them at their word and treat them as members and act as their head?

Then, again, they did tell St. Leo that he was their 'leader' in the Council, through his legates. They used the very word which our Lord used to His Apostles when He told them that there should be a leader (or ruler) among them, and that their leader should be as He Himself was in their midst—'Even as I am among you' not lording it over them, but teaching, guiding, governing. Did they suppose that Leo would smile at the term and take no advantage of it?

Again, they did tell St. Leo that he had been to them 'the interpreter of the voice of Peter.' It was, on the Anglican supposition, exactly the wrong occasion to say that. They were not Eastern heathens addressing heathen rajahs, or Hindu suppliants before their conquerors. They were Christian bishops—not, it is true, the best specimens; but still, all Eastern as they were, they had not lost all Christian sense of truth in spite of their Eastern cunning. On the other hand, they knew that it was the teaching of Leo that he was the successor of Peter, and as such the ruler of the Christian Church. And they were not so utterly devoid of all sense of truth, and of ordinary common sense, as to suppose that in putting such a weapon into Leo's hand as their own recognition of his position as successor of Peter, they would advance the cause of Constantinople. Whereas if the Christian world held that Leo was their head, their language was natural, for then they lost nothing by saying so.

Again they did tell St. Leo that 'the vineyard had been entrusted to him by the Saviour,' in a way which implied that he stood in a different relation to that vineyard from the rest of the bishops. And they did tell him that he was the 'father' of Constantinople, and trusted that he would 'extend his *wonted care* over that part of the vineyard.' In fact they as much as said there is no such thing as an independent national Church. Although we are the East, and under one Emperor, and you are in the West and under another, still you have responsibilities towards the East, and a paternal relation to it, and you acted as our ruler in the Council, and were the interpreter to us of the Prince of the Apostles, and we apply to you for that sanction without which our canon can never be the voice of the Catholic Church. This was what they said in effect.

Indeed, they said more than this; for they told St. Leo that their own delivery of the truth to the children of the Church was but as the flowing forth of a stream from him as its Apostolic source. 'Thou wast constituted the interpreter of the voice of blessed Peter to us all, and didst bring to all the blessing of his faith. *Whence we also* show the inheritance of truth to the children of the Church.'[1] And hence unity of teaching

---

[1] ὅθεν καὶ ἡμεῖς . . . τῆς ἀληθείας τοῖς τῆς ἐκκλησίας τέκνοις τὸν κλῆρον ἐδείξαμεν (*Leon. Ep.* 98, § 1).

is secured by what they distinctly state as the mediatorial position of their head.

Of Eutyches, who, be it remembered, was deposed by the Synod of Constantinople, the Acts of which were sent to Leo, as to a court of revision, these bishops say that 'his dignity was taken away by your Holiness'—which is the result arrived at above from a consideration of the facts (*Leon. Ep.* 98, § 2).

And of Dioscorus they say that he meditated an excommunication 'against thee, when thou wast all eager to unite the Church,' and 'he repudiated the letter of your Holiness.'

They speak also of being eager to 'confirm' the mercy of the Saviour towards him (which was what Leo had desired them to do)—not as if 'confirming' necessarily implies the action of a superior court, but in obedience to their Saviour's words (*ibid.* § 3).

They speak of the actual help derived from St. Euphemia—'God was with us and Euphemia was with us'—on whose altar we know they placed their definition, for the entire Synod believed in the Invocation of Saints.

And then they ask that Leo will 'accept and confirm' their canon.

When they mention the legates' opposition to their canon, they profess to ascribe that opposition to the idea in the legates' minds that everything ought to originate with his Holiness, 'so that even as the right settlement of the faith is set down to your account, so also should that of good discipline.' They in fact acknowledge that the matter of faith was settled by Leo, but they thought that they might initiate a matter of discipline, which they had now brought before his

Holiness for his acceptance and confirmation. 'Therefore, we entreat thee, honour the decision with your favourable judgment, that as we have introduced harmony with the head in the things that are excellent, so the head may supply to the children that which is becoming.'

They have (they say) sent the Acts to Leo for his approval and sanction.[1]

Now these are, many of them, positive statements of doctrine. Is sentence by sentence, one after the other, to be dismissed as mere compliment? Could anything but the exigencies of controversy have led Canon Bright and Canon Gore, and other Anglican writers, to set aside all these definite statements on the part of the bishops on the ground that they were mere compliments?

If they were 'compliments,' they were those of men who found themselves compelled to couch their compliments in terms which, if they wished to be independent of Rome, cut the ground from under their feet, sentence after sentence. They are not in the place in which compliments would come, nor are they of the nature of honorific expletives. They form the substance of the letter.

If insincerely used, they testify to the necessity under which these bishops found themselves, of crouching at the feet of a master in order to gain the object of their desires. If used in sincerity, they are the testimony of witnesses, naturally the most unwilling, to the position of headship which the East recognised in the occupant of the See of Peter. We cannot claim for them the authority of the Council, for these men were

---

[1] τῶν παρ' ἡμῶν πεπραγμένων βεβαίωσίν τε καὶ συγκατάθεσιν (*Leon. Ep.* 98, last line).

not the Council; but we are compelled to see in these terms the strongest possible evidence that the idea of the connection between Rome and St. Peter, and of such a consequent 'headship' of Rome over Constantinople that the latter could not arrange its own relations with other sees in the East without the acquiescence of Rome—we are compelled, I say, to acknowledge that this was so deeply rooted in the mind of the Eastern Church that it was simply useless to ignore it, and that the only thing to be done was to admit it plainly and to win the adhesion of Rome to their projected canon.

But side by side with this letter of the bishops is another, written by Anatolius himself, not less emphatic in its witness to the Constantinopolitan conviction as to the Pope's supremacy. Anatolius speaks of the bishops at Chalcedon having confirmed 'the faith of the blessed and venerable fathers' of Nicæa, 'and also your Holiness's letter agreeing with them'—showing that the attitude of the Synod towards the Tome was the same in one respect as towards the Nicene faith—viz. that their confirmation of it was an acceptance of an authoritative statement.[1] He then says that Bishop Lucentius is bringing the Acts of the Synod, since 'it was a matter of necessity that all things should be brought to the cognisance of your Holiness.'[2] But beside these things, since some matters were transacted which specially

[1] In the first edition this sentence was without the words 'in one respect.' I have added these words because Dr. Bright managed to misunderstand my meaning, as though I had stated that the attitude of the Synod towards the Nicene Symbol and the Tome of Leo was in all respects the same, which it would be absurd to suppose.

[2] ἔδει ἅπαντα ἀναγκαίως (*Leon. Ep.* 101, cap. 1). This could not be said of other absent bishops. Sending the Acts was treating Leo as a higher court.

concerned themselves,[1] and these *must also of necessity be brought to the knowledge of his Holiness*, Anatolius says that he sent these letters by the same messengers, to receive an answer concerning them. He then mentions the acts in order. First came Dioscorus's excommunication, which he feels sure will obtain his Holiness's assent. Next (*Leon. Ep.* 101, c. 3) he speaks of the reception of the Tome in exact accordance with what we have seen above. He says that it was needful that 'the understanding of all should agree with the meaning of your orthodox faith,' and that this was the end for which the Emperor convened the Council—words which are completely corroborative of the view of the matter taken in this book (pp. 270-292). Anatolius's words express the object of the session held after Dioscorus's excommunication, as that of obtaining an *intelligent adhesion* to the faith as propounded by Leo. Consequently, Anatolius says, that with prayers and tears, and with the help of Leo himself, assisting in spirit and co-operating by means of the well-beloved men whom his Holiness sent to the Council, and under the protection of St. Euphemia, he and those with him had devoted themselves to the work—in allusion to the 'instruction' given in Anatolius's house to the Illyrian bishops. And when the time had come for all to issue an harmonious definition, they had done so, in spite of some contentious opposition from the first, and for the confirmation of their definition 'in accordance with that holy epistle of yours,' they placed it on the holy altar. This latter remark explains the statement of the bishops that their definition was offered by Euphemia to her divine Spouse.

[1] διὰ τὸ ἰδικῶς ἡμῖν πέπραχθαί τινα—called 'negotia privata' in Pelagius II.'s letter to the Istrian bishops.

So that Anatolius, writing thus publicly an account of the Synod, emphasises (1) the *necessity* of agreement with the definition of faith issued by Leo, and (2) the *necessity* of reporting to the Pontiff whatever was done at the Synod; and (3) describes the confirmation of their canon by Leo as at once necessary for them and free on his part.[1]

Having thus described the relation of the Council to the Pope, in exact accordance with all that has been said in these pages, Anatolius proceeds to introduce the subject of the canon. He describes it as having for its object the confirmation of the canon of the 150 Fathers, who decreed that the Bishop of Constantinople should have honour and precedence (not $\pi\rho\omega\tau\epsilon\hat{\iota}\alpha$, primacy) next after the most holy throne of Rome, by reason of her being 'New Rome.' And he says it (*i.e.* the canon drawn up at Chalcedon) decided that the ordination of the metropolitans of the diocese of Pontus, of Asia and of Thrace should rest with Constantinople; but that the bishops under them should not be ordained, as had been the case for sixty or seventy years, by the latter, but by their own metropolitans.

He then complains of the legates' opposition to all this, and speaks of the sanction of the Emperor. He says that they paid all possible respect to the legates, but that they have now reported their decision to his Holiness, in hope of gaining his assent and confirmation, which they entreat him to give. 'For the throne of Constantinople has your Apostolic throne as its Father, having specially attached itself to you.' And so he asks for the ratification of the canon.

Later on (in 454) the archbishop tells the Pope that

[1] Cf. *Leon. Ep.* 101, ed. Ballerini, *note.*

'all the force and confirmation of what was thus done was reserved for the authority of your Blessedness.'[1]

Now after these two letters—the one from the enacting bishops at Chalcedon, and the other from the Archbishop of Constantinople himself—it is idle to talk of the 'self-assertion' of Rome as having anything to do with the twenty-eighth canon. St. Leo doubtless knew how to magnify his office. But, indeed, there was no need to do that here; it was already done for him. He was recognised publicly and unmistakably by these bishops of the Eastern part of the Church as the natural and, indeed, the necessary guardian of the canons of the whole Church, and this, too, in virtue of his relationship, through his see, to the blessed Apostle Peter. To attribute all this plain dogmatic and public exposition of the relationship of the Holy See to the rest of the Church to mere courtesy can only be the shift of those who find themselves driven hard to explain untoward facts. The facts are that the bishops who drew up the twenty-eighth canon did avow their entire dependence on Rome as the See of St. Peter, and that the Archbishop of Constantinople himself counted the proposal canonically null and void without the subsequent confirmation of the Bishop of Rome. The explanation proposed and adopted by those writers who are out of communion with Rome, and have drawn up canons independently of her, is that all this plain speech was mere pretence. Even so it would require to be noticed that the pretence took that particular shape. But, in fact, pretence will not explain such statements unless these bishops were utterly regardless of truth. But

[1] *Ep.* 132, c. 4: 'Cum et sic gestorum vis omnis et confirmatio auctoritati vestræ beatitudinis fuerit reservata.'

what, then, is the value of their canon, so much relied on by our Anglican friends?

The letters of St. Leo in regard to all this are full of Christian royalty. Majestic, uncompromising, and tender, they would by themselves be sufficient to establish his claim to the title which Christendom has accorded to him—Leo the Great.

To Anatolius he wrote,[1] reminding him of the suspicion which had originally attached to his orthodoxy, praising the faith which he now exhibited, but regretting that he had allowed himself to be influenced by the lust of honour and power. He blames him for endeavouring to use a Council, assembled for the matter of faith, for his ambitious projects, and for imagining that any number of bishops could override the Nicene settlement (cap. 2). He considers that Anatolius's blame of the Papal legates is their commendation, for they were bound to oppose any infringement of the Nicene canons (cap. 3). He says he is sure that Anatolius will please the royalties more by self-restraint than by ambition. The decision of 'some bishops,' sixty years ago, 'never transmitted to the Apostolic See,' is no support whatever. (In other words, the third canon of Constantinople is of no account.) Alexandria ought not to suffer because of Dioscorus, nor Antioch, where Peter first preached, be degraded (cap. 5). The Pontiff concludes with most earnestly and lovingly entreating Anatolius to cultivate humility and charity.

Already Leo had written to the Emperor, severely blaming Anatolius for not being content with being bishop of the royal city, but aiming at the rank of an Apostolic see, which Constantinople can never become.

[1] *Ep.* 106.

And he tells the Emperor, in answer to his Majesty's request that his Holiness would give his consent to Constantinople taking place above Alexandria and Antioch, that Nicene arrangements cannot thus be set aside, and that in their defence, by the help of Christ, it is necessary for him to be a faithful servant unto the end, 'since a dispensation has been entrusted to me' ('dispensatio mihi credita est'), 'and the guilt will be mine if the rules sanctioned by the fathers in the Synod of Nicæa, for the government of the whole Church, by the assistance of the Spirit of God, should be violated by my connivance, which God forbid.'[1]

But, as Leo's overlooking the ordination of Maximus of Antioch by Anatolius (which contravened the Nicene canon) might seem inconsistent, he adds that he has not rehandled that, out of love for the recovery of the faith and desire for peace.[2]

To Pulcheria he writes in the same strain, saying that he renders null and void ('in irritum mittimus') what the bishops agreed to contrary to the Nicene regulations, and that he does so by the authority of the blessed Apostle Peter.[3]

In the following year the Emperor wrote to St. Leo, telling him that he was unwilling to resort to extreme measures with the monks in Palestine until he could show them his (Leo's) confirmation of the Chalcedonian definition. He says that the Eutychianisers had thrown doubts on that confirmation.[4] The Emperor, in this letter, yields the point of the twenty-eighth canon, and

---

[1] *Ep.* 104.   [2] *Ibid.* § 5.   [3] *Ep.* 105.
[4] 'Whether your Blessedness has confirmed the things decreed (τυπωθέντα) in the Synod,' *i.e.* on the matter of faith and excommunication of Dioscorus. *Ep.* 110.

expresses his warm sympathy with the Pope for the stand he had made on behalf of historical veracity and the ancient ways. 'For assuredly,' wrote his Imperial Majesty, 'your Holiness did excellently well, as became the Bishop of the Apostolic See, in so guarding the canons of the Church as not to suffer any innovation on ancient custom or the order settled of old, and inviolably observed to this day.' Considering what Leo had written to Marcian, this public acknowledgment of the position of the Apostolic See as guardian of the canons, from an Eastern Emperor who had his desires as to a rise in dignity for his Imperial city, and had for a moment been led away by the Bishop of Constantinople, is at once a tribute to his real goodness and a witness, if further witness were needed, to the ingrained conviction of Christendom that the Holy See had a special dispensation committed to it, and that its charge was nothing less than the government of the universal Church. For to guard the canons of the Church, as Bishop of the Apostolic See, is to govern the universal Church.

St. Leo left Julian, Bishop of Cos, as his legate at Constantinople ('vice mea functus'), 'lest either the Nestorian or the Eutychian heresy should revive, since there is not the vigour of a Catholic in the Bishop of Constantinople.'[1] And he wrote to all the bishops who had been at Chalcedon to say that they could have had no doubt about his approval of what had been done at Chalcedon *in regard to the faith*, had Anatolius only shown the letter he had received, which he had kept back because of what concerned himself. 'In regard to the faith'—for it was for *that alone* that the Council was convoked 'by order of the Emperors, and with the

[1] *Ep.* 113.

consent of the Apostolic throne.' And he says, wherefore ' if anyone shall dare to hold the perfidy of Nestorius or Eutyches and to defend the impious dogma of Dioscorus, let him be cut off from the communion of Catholics.' At the same time they will see from his letters to Anatolius with what reverence the Apostolic See deals with the regulations of the Nicene fathers, and that, by the help of God, he (Leo) is guardian of the faith of our fathers and the canons of the Church.[1]

As it is the duty of a king to guard the laws, and himself to set an example of their observance, so Leo, as the divinely instituted governor of the Christian Church, while, for the sake of peace, he allowed Maximus, though otherwise uncanonically ordained, to remain in his episcopate, would not allow the ambition of a prelate in the Imperial city to oust Alexandria and Antioch from the position assigned to them by the Nicene fathers, on a principal fatal to the spiritual character of the Church, viz. that civil dignity could of itself, apart from the action of the See of Peter—*i.e.* without the consent of the Church—raise a see to the rank which Alexandria and Antioch then held.

[1] *Ep.* 114, c. 1.

APPENDICES

APPENDICES

APPENDIX I

DR. BRIGHT AND THE LETTER OF THE SYNOD TO LEO

THE account just given of the bishops' letter to St. Leo, asking for his confirmation of the twenty-eighth canon is almost word for word the same as in the first edition of my book on *The Primitive Church and the See of Peter*. I now subjoin Dr. Bright's criticisms on this account, with replies.

1. He protests that 'the canon must be taken in its grammatical sense and not explained away on the score of any expressions in the letter' (*Roman See*, p. 205). With that we should agree. But at the same time if we want to know what the bishops thought as to the validity of their canon in the case of its not receiving the assent of the Apostolic See —in other words, what they thought of the authority of that see—we shall find an exposition of their doctrine on this head in the letter which accompanied their canon.

2. 'Then look,' says Dr. Bright, 'at their expressions: the bishops call Leo their "head" because by his legates he was their president' (*ibid.*).

They do not say so. They say 'whom you, as head of the members, were ruling [or presiding over] in those who held your place.'[1] The words, taken in their strict literal

---

[1] ὧν σὺ μὲν, ὡς κεφαλὴ μελῶν, ἡγεμόνευες ἐν τοῖς κ. τ. λ.

sense, signify that Leo presided as being head of the members, not that he was head because he presided—in fact that he presided because of his position in the Catholic Church. The Emperor Marcian, in his letter to Leo about the Council, had said that the Emperors were assembling it with Leo's authority, σοῦ αὐθεντοῦντος (*Leon. Ep.* 63). Leo had authorised it by requesting it of Theodosius. And the Empress Pulcheria had said that the object of the Council was that its members might decide with Leo's authority (σοῦ αὐθεντοῦντος ὁρίσωσιν) the matter of the bishops who had gone wrong at the Latrocinium (*Ep.* 77). Then Leo had been called by the legates 'the head of the universal Church' at the opening of the Council. And in this letter Leo is presently called the 'head' with no reference to presidency over the Council. In this latter passage not only is the word κεφαλή used of Leo, but also κορυφή, the regular term for the Emperor, or head of the Empire (Mansi, vii. 89), and this with respect to Leo's subsequent confirmation of their canon. This could not be the act of the president merely, for that, they say, was fulfilled through the legates. 'As we have given consent to the head in good things [*i.e.* in the matter of faith, in the Council] so let the head fulfil what is becoming towards the children;'[1] the metaphor of 'father' naturally slipping in, since the Pope was the 'Holy Father,' in their language, as well as the 'head.' It is obvious that the bishops are not here speaking of presidency over the Council, but of a general headship over themselves. For the consent of which they speak was not given to the Pope as president of the Council, but to his letter or Tome, irrespective of his presidency; and the ratification asked for is compared at once with that of the Emperor in the civil order, which was given, not as president, but afterwards as Emperor.[2] Nor is this all. In the earlier passage before us, from which the word quoted by Dr. Bright is taken, the

[1] οὕτω καὶ ἡ κορυφὴ τοῖς παισὶν ἀναπληρώσοι τὸ πρέπον.
[2] βασιλεῖς . . . βεβαιώσαντες, c. iv. end.

bishops also compare the Pope with the Emperor. Their words are: 'Whom while you, as head of the members, presided over [or ruled] in the person of those who hold your place, the faithful Emperors presided over for the purpose of keeping order.'[1] Here the Pope and the Emperor are both compared and contrasted. Each has rule over the members of the Synod, but the relationship of the Emperor is external, that of the Pope is interior and intimate, being that of the head to the limbs.

3. Dr. Bright says that Leo 'had "held the position of interpreting the words" [he thus translates τῆς φωνῆς—one sees why] "of blessed Peter," inasmuch as they had accepted his Tome expressly on the ground that it truly represented the purport of Matt. xvi. 16; and by publicly affirming the true faith they had "used him as an originator of what was good"' (*ibid.*).

They say something very different. They speak of the 'faith' and 'knowledge of the Lord,' 'which the Saviour brought us from above,' 'which you yourself preserved as a golden chain reaching down to us, by the precept of the Lawgiver, being constituted interpreter[2] of the voice of blessed Peter to all' [it will be noticed that Dr. Bright unfortunately omits those words 'to all'] 'and yourself bring the blessedness of his faith to all.' The position of interpreting the voice of Peter is not here attributed to the acceptance of the Tome, but to appointment by our Lord. Then—and this is of supreme importance—they go on to say, '*Whence*' [*i.e.* since you hold the position of interpreter of the voice of Peter, and yourself bring to all (ἐφελκόμενος, present

---

[1] The word used of the Pope's presidency is ἡγεμόνευες: that used of the Emperor's is ἐξῆρχον. But they are synonymous. ἐξῆρχον is used of the presidency of Cyril and Celestine (Mansi, vii. 477), and of Osius at Nice (*ibid.* 464), and of Leo at Chalcedon (*ibid.* 85), and in this letter laity without their bishop are called ἀνηγεμονεύτων, which to those who believe in Episcopacy shows that the word implies rule.

[2] Readers of Eusebius will remember his description of St. Mark as ἑρμηνευτὴς Πέτρου in his Gospel.

middle) the blessedness of Peter's faith] *we also* by using you as originator of what was good' [*i.e.* the true faith] '*showed forth* the inheritance of the truth to the children of the Church,' *i.e.* by their common public confession of the faith, as they explain, making it known with one mind. So that Dr. Bright's interpretation needs to be exactly reversed. It was not the acceptance of the Tome that made Leo the interpreter of the voice of Peter, but Leo's action as such, that led to their common confession at the Council. Nor is this all. They proceed to liken their doings to a spiritual feast of good things 'which Christ furnished to the guests *by your letter.*' The Tome, then, was furnished them by our Lord as their spiritual food. It was not their acceptance of the Tome that made it spiritual food; that acceptance was their assimilation of the food prepared by Christ. It was not, then (to be exact), ' by publicly affirming the true faith that they had used him [Leo] as an originator,' as Dr. Bright puts it, but it was by using him ($\chi\rho\eta\sigma\acute{a}\mu\epsilon\nu o\iota$) as leader or originator ($\dot{a}\rho\chi\eta\gamma\ddot{\omega}$) that they were led publicly to affirm that faith ($\ddot{o}\theta\epsilon\nu$.. · $\dot{\epsilon}\delta\epsilon\acute{\iota}\xi a\mu\epsilon\nu$).

4. Dr. Bright further speaks of 'that curious passage which assumes that the legates only resisted the new canon that Leo might have the pleasure of approving it' (*ibid.* 206), and says: 'Mr. Rivington himself would not deny that Oriental fluency of "compliment" appears in that curious passage.'

I am sorry I cannot give Dr. Bright even this crumb of comfort. For his words are a curious misreading of a passage touching on an important point of discipline. There is doubtless Oriental ingenuity, and the truth is put in a deferential shape; but the passage (in which Dr. Bright's words do not occur) contains what they intended for a real argument. The bishops are here giving as the legates' ground for resisting the canon the contention that such a matter should be initiated by Rome,[1] so that the

---

[1] $\ddot{a}\rho\xi a\sigma\theta a\iota$.

restoration[1] of order as well as of the faith, should be set to the account of Rome, who was responsible for each. This was what the legates had actually said when they refused to attend the fifteenth session, and their instructions from Leo as to repelling any attempt to alter the relations of the sees to one another implied the same. They had 'no such instructions' from Rome,[2] *i.e.* as to take part in discussing such a question, which was not in the original programme as set forth by Leo. The bishops in this letter go on to say that they had had respect to the wishes of the Emperor, the Senate, and the whole city, and authorised 'a confirmation of its honour' (*i.e.* of the city), feeling sure that this might be considered to have emanated from his Holiness, zealous as he always was to cherish their welfare and 'knowing that every settlement made by the children redounds to their own fathers.' Here, of course, they are creeping along, insinuating, and softly persuasive. But consider what they have to concede in order to soften any possible objection from Leo. They accept the principle that such matters, if discussed in a Council, *ought* to have been part of the programme settled at Rome, but—and here comes in their 'Oriental fluency'— they pretend that the gain in this case is so obvious that they may count on Leo's acceptance of it in the spirit of a father, and may consider that practically, owing to his general goodwill (here is compliment), he may be considered to have included it in his original programme by implication. There is nothing in the letter to justify Dr. Bright's interpretation that 'the legates are said to have resisted the canon only that Leo might have the pleasure of approving it.' This is a fundamental misconception of the situation. They are said to have resisted on the ground of Rome's *right* of settling beforehand the business of the Council ($ἄρξασθαι$); the Council, however, suggest that this was a case in which Leo could not but approve. I am far from

---

[1] Or 'right settlement,' $κατόρθωμα$.
[2] Mansi, vii. 428. See note on the meaning of this above, p. 347.

denying that these Easterns were writing with diplomatic courtesy, but the Papal principles which underlie their expressions are unmistakable, and in the first part of their letter they are stating doctrine, not indulging in compliment, when they speak of the method adopted by our Divine Lord for communicating the knowledge of Himself.

5. But the next sentence in the bishops' letter is still more strangely dealt with by our critic. They say, 'We entreat you, therefore, honour also by your own decrees the decision' [*i.e.* about the exaltation of Constantinople over Alexandria and Antioch] 'as we have exhibited [*lit.* introduced] agreement with the head in those things that are good' [*i.e.*, as the same word means earlier in their letter, ' the matter of faith '] so that the head also may fulfil toward the children what is becoming.' They then speak of the Emperor having confirmed ' the judgment of your Holiness as a law,' as a counterpart to the confirmation which they hope for from the Pope. The Imperial ratification of the Papal judgment in the matter of faith was, of course, in the civil order, making it legally binding. But they ask for a similar confirmation of the matter of discipline from Leo in the ecclesiastical order, and adduce, as a proof that they have not acted in the way of favouritism or party spirit, but with the divine approval, the fact that 'we have made known to you all the force of our transactions for our own establishment [or consistency]¹ and for the confirmation and agreement with [or sanction ² of] what we have done.'

Now for Dr. Bright's translation. He says (the italics

---

¹ σύστασιν = making compact, consolidating. The ordinary Latin version of the letter has ' ad comprobationem nostræ sinceritatis,' which is a gloss rather than a translation. The older Latin translation has ' consistentiam.' I can find no authority for the gloss in the first mentioned translation.

² συγκατάθεσιν = agreement of any kind. Here, being connected with βεβαίωσιν, it probably = sanction. *Cf.* Liddell and Scott, *s.v.* The older Latin version has *dispositionem*, which is a word betokening authority.

are mine), 'They *requested* him to honour the decision by *adding* his own *vote* [ψήφοις, plural] and|so to "confirm and assent to" what had been done "by the Œcumenical Council," and, as they do not shrink from adding, "under the guidance of a Divine command"; and accordingly they "make known to him the whole purport (δύναμιν) of their proceedings"' (*Roman See*, pp. 206, 207).

Let us take this rendering point by point.

(α) παρακαλοῦμεν is transformed into 'request.' On p. 278, note ¹, Dr. Bright twice insists that this word (Lat. *obsecramur*) means urgent entreaty. Why not here, as it does so often, indeed generally?

(β) τίμησον καὶ ταῖς σαῖς ψήφοις τὴν κρίσιν is ingeniously rendered 'honour the decision by adding his own [your own] vote.' Now ψήφοις (the plural) had been already used in this very letter for the 'sentence' passed upon Eutyches by Dioscorus, and again the singular ψῆφον had been used for the sentence which Dioscorus brought upon himself by his misdeeds. Dr. Bright has himself elsewhere twice translated ψῆφον 'sentence' (*Roman See*, pp. 163, 166), and has also deduced an argument from the word ψηφίσεται as meaning 'will pass sentence.' The Latin translation is 'decretis' in Mansi, vii. 1098, and 'sententiis' in the older Latin version of the letter (*ib.* 1133). Why, then, does Dr. Bright translate καὶ . . . ταῖς σαῖς ψήφοις 'by adding your vote'?

(γ) The words 'confirm and assent to' are closely connected by our critic with those words about honouring the 'decision' with his 'vote,' whereas in the original the lines about the Imperial confirmation intervene, giving a certain complexion of authority to the word 'confirm' by the parallelism. The effect of the omission is obvious. Also the words 'by the Œcumenical Council,' are between inverted commas as though they were a quotation, whereas they do not exist in the original, and they suggest that the Council was œcumenical in its decision, without the Pope. And, translating θείῳ νεύματι as 'by a Divine command,' our critic adds : ' And accordingly they make known to him the whole purport of their proceedings.' And here Dr. Bright stops, instead of going on to the words that immediately follow, viz. ' for our own consolidation [or for our consistency] and for the confirmation and sanction of [or assent to] what we have done.' These crucial words, not exhibited by our critic in English, appear only in Greek in a note. And yet it is the application 'for the purpose of ratification and assent' or (since this would be such an anticlimax) ' ratification and sanction ' that (they say) proves that they were acting under Divine approval. I venture to submit to any impartial reader whether all this can be called adhering to the record.

(δ) Lastly, in regard to the bishops' assertion that to Leo 'had been committed by the Saviour the guardianship of the Vine,' Dr. Bright adds by way of interpretation, ' to him conspicuously and eminently, as holding a [sic] primary place, but certainly not in a sense generically unique ; for they themselves had received authority both to root up and to plant, and they treated the ' " definition " as their own ' (p. 205).

The 'certainly not' (if the words are meant to deny supreme authority) cannot be extracted from what the bishops say. Consider the context. They make the climax of Dioscorus's madness to consist in his actually extending it to ' the very person ($αὐτοῦ τοῦ$) who has been entrusted by the Saviour with the guardianship of the Vine ' : words which, occurring in such a context, do certainly convey the impression of at least a unique relationship to the Vine. This much Dr. Bright appears to admit. But seeing that the unique relationship is in the matter of guardianship to the whole Vine, the statement that others had authority to do the work of gardeners in that vineyard, cannot be held to counterbalance the impression of supreme authority conveyed by the mention of the 'guardianship of the Vine.' If we take the words by themselves, they only speak of a delegated authority ($ἐξουσίαν$) which may be either by immediate or by indirect delegation; whereas if we go outside the words of the letter, we have to remember that they had entered in the 'Acts' their sentence as delivered by Paschasinus, that Dioscorus was stripped of his episcopate by Leo, in concert with Peter the foundation of the Catholic Church, acting by the Synod as his instrument (*supra*, p. 246). In the words following the statement about the guardianship of the Vine, the bishops say of Leo, ' who didst hasten to unite the body of the Church,' thus reverting to their metaphor about the head and the members. Whether this is a position '*generically* unique ' may be questioned, but at least such a guardianship is unique and specifically preeminent, which is sufficient to satisfy the Vatican decree.

As for the bishops 'treating the "definition" as their own,' it was of course their own *quâ* Conciliar. Yet they call it (as Dr. Bright should not have omitted to notice) distinctly in this letter ' the decision of your Holiness,' and also distinctly state that they were able to make it through Leo ' being interpreter of the voice of Peter to all, and bringing to all the blessedness of Peter's faith, *whence* we showed forth, &c.'

To sum up. The steps, as we find them, in this letter, so full of doctrine as to the government of the Church, are as follows:—(1) Christ brought the knowledge of the Lord from Heaven. (2) Leo, by the ordinance of the Lawgiver extended the golden chain of teaching to the bishops, and this as being appointed [1] the interpreter, *to all*, of the voice of Peter. (3) The bishops consequently (ὅθεν) proclaimed it to the world by an harmonious confession. (4) The Emperor confirmed it in the civil order.[2] As for the relation of Alexandria and Antioch to Constantinople expressed in their twenty-eighth canon, they pretended that it might be considered to have been initiated to all intents and purposes by Leo,

[1] καθιστάμενος.
[2] The Emperors are spoken of as τὴν τῆς σῆς ὁσιότητος, ὡς νόμον, βεβαιώςαντες κρίσιν (*Ep*. 98, § 5, and Mansi, vii. 1099).

because his goodwill was sure to sanction it; but they now apply for its ratification, as a measure which pleased the Emperor and Senate and all the city, and as something that was not the offspring of likes and dislikes, since they have sent it for his confirmation and assent, or sanction, as well as for their own consolidation (εἰς σύστασιν ἡμετέραν καὶ τῶν παρ' ἡμῶν πεπραγμένων βεβαίωσίν τε καὶ συγκατάθεσιν).

That this which I have given is the true interpretation is placed beyond reasonable doubt by the words of Anatolius written in 454. He was one of the writers, probably the real author, of this letter which we have been considering, and in his letter to Leo he says that 'all the force and confirmation of what was done was reserved for the authority' of Leo.[1] This is a categorical statement by the archbishop, who was president at the session, as to a matter of fact, and must be considered decisive. Indeed, but for this, we cannot imagine the letter of the bishops being written at all. For it is not merely that expression after expression indicates their sense of Leo's authority, but the sum and substance, the very basis, of the letter, consists in an endeavour to gain the assent of a superior authority. The letter, then, cannot be regarded as a mere farce, as an attempt to gain the assent of an equal in authority by proclaiming him in every sentence their superior. Nor would Anatolius give away his case in his accompanying letter, and—which is beyond words significant—again two years later, when he wrote in the same strain. Dr. Bright's suggestion that the canon was sent to Rome because it 'mentions the See of Rome and because they expressly assign a cause for the privileges which had been "given" to it' (*Roman See*, p. 206) is futile to the last degree. This would be to suggest that it was a new thing thus to speak. And there is not a word in the letter to justify it. They actually begin their letter with another reason—nothing less than the Saviour's appointment.

[1] *Leon. Ep.* 132.

It is true that they did not act up to their words. But acts do not always say more than words in explaining what people hold to be true. Acts evince the working of love or its opposite; they may be the expression of rebellion; but faith is a distinct thing from charity in the teaching of the Catholic Church. Anyhow here are both action and language: the act of sending their canon and the words explaining why they sent it. Both show that these prelates believed that a canon had not established itself in the life of the Church until it had received the sanction of the Apostolic See, where, as the archbishop and bishops of the province of Canterbury said in 1413, 'such causes ought to be terminated.'[1] The Greek historian had said more than a thousand years before that no canon could be made for the Church without the judgment of the Bishop of Rome (Socrates, *Hist. Eccl.* ii. 8).

[1] Wilkins, *Concilia*, iii, 350.

APPENDIX II

THE EPISTLE OF LEO TO FLAVIAN (COMMONLY CALLED THE 'TOME') IRREFORMABLE FROM ITS FIRST PROMULGATION BY LEO.

THE position maintained by our Anglican friends is that it was at the 4th Session at Chalcedon that 'the Tome was solemnly accepted by the Council' (*Roman See*, p. 186), and that it was not part of the rule of the Catholic faith until then. Dr. Bright argues that as Cyril's letters were admittedly not irreformable before the Council of Ephesus set its seal upon them and thereby erected them to the position of Church standards, so with the Tome of Leo at the Council of Chalcedon. It was not (he maintains) a standard of faith until then. The special proof of this is to be found, according to Dr. Bright, in the reason given by the bishops for their subscriptions to the Tome at the fourth session of Chalcedon. It was a 'real judgment' passed at Ephesus on Cyril's letters, and it was the judgment of a superior authority; it must, therefore (he argues), have been the same in the case of Leo's Tome, because the expressions used in passing judgment are in both cases identical. In the latter case, the formal declarations made by the bishops signify, according to Dr. Bright, that they 'accept the Tome *because* they personally believe it to be conformable to

---

[1] A 'Tome,' as has already been remarked, is a doctrinal formulary. The word itself means 'a part of a book written and rolled up by itself,' a 'volume.' Liddell and Scott, *s.v.*

Church standards, just as their predecessors had dealt with Cyril's letter; *and thus by their act it acquires a place among Church standards'* (*Roman See*, p. 188, 189).

These concluding words, which I have italicised, contain the pith of the matter. Much in the preceding sentences is of the nature of an *ignoratio elenchi*. No one denies that the judgment of the bishops on the Tome was a real judgment. Neither is it denied that the bishops accepted the Tome of Leo because it was conformable to Church standards. What we do deny is that the judgment was that of superiors or equals, or that it involved the liberty of disagreeing and yet remaining within the Church or that *they thought* this liberty possible : in other words, the Tome was part of the rule of faith before its conciliar acceptance at that fourth session. We also deny that the reason given for their judgment in the fourth session was meant to comprehend the entire array of motives by which they were swayed : or that it involved the belief that the See of Peter could go wrong under such circumstances. We maintain that the bishops merely aggregated their judgment to that of the Apostolic See; and as St. Leo himself put forth his Tome as in conformity with the Nicene faith, so the fathers in Council adopted the same mode of expression, and certified to their own orthodoxy rather than guaranteed that of Leo. But they did not say so without having read the Tome and without having, indeed, carefully examined it, so that their subscription to it was not a blind act, but an intelligent adhesion to an authoritative exposition. As they said *totidem verbis*, Leo was their guide in the matter : ' Thou wast made the interpreter of the voice of blessed Peter to us all, and didst bring to all the blessing of his faith. Whence we also show the inheritance of truth to the children of the Church ' (*Leon. Ep.* 98, i.). His Tome was the *lux præfulgens*, as Vigilius called it, a kind of technical conciliar expression for a guiding light, determining the course of action : words used of the Imperial order at the Council of Ephesus

(Mansi, iv. 1261) and of the Nicene Creed in the Council of Chalcedon's definition (Mansi, vii. 110).

The point, therefore, to be proved is this, viz. that it is not correct to say, as Dr. Bright does, that 'by their act' (*i.e.* by the declarations of the bishops in the fourth session) 'it [the Tome of Leo] acquired a place among Church standards' just as Cyril's letters did at the Council of Ephesus (*Roman See*, p. 189). We say that it already held that position by reason of its emanating with such solemnity from the See of Peter.

Dr. Bright's account is not clear in this particular passage on one point, *i.e.* as to the time when the signatures were affixed to the Tome. It looks as if by 'their act' he meant 'by their subscriptions' as well as by their declarations. It must, however, be remembered that the 'subscriptions' themselves to which the bishops alluded in the fourth session were not given at that time at all, but previously— in some few (very few) cases in the house of Anatolius, in others at an earlier date. Bearing this in mind, it is capable of demonstration that before the bishops entered the Council the Tome of Leo had obtained œcumenical acceptance. The voice of the Church diffused had spoken clearly; and the Church in Council cannot contradict the voice of the Church dispersed throughout the world. The Tome was, therefore, irreformable on that account alone, were there no other reason, before the Council met. The following proofs will suffice.

1. The bishops of Gaul had received the Tome in the previous year; and three of them, writing for an exact copy, speak of this dogmatic letter as being already 'celebrated in the meetings of all the Churches, so that it is unanimously declared that the principate of the Apostolic See is deservedly placed there whence the oracles of the Apostolic spirit may still be unfolded' (*Leon. Ep.* 68). And the bishops of Gaul in a body late in the following year (451) speak of the Tome as having been already 'inscribed on the hearts of all who

care for the sacrament of redemption, having been committed to memory, as *a symbol of the faith.*' Again, they write, 'Who would think that he could sufficiently thank your Apostolate for such a gift, by which it has adorned, not only the Gauls, *but the whole world* with as it were certain most precious gems? The faithful owes it to your teaching after God that he holds with constancy what he believed; the unbelieving also owes it [or, according to another reading, 'will owe it'] thereto that he departs from his unbelief and acknowledges the truth, and, penetrated with the light of the Apostolic institution, leaves the darkness of his error and rather follows and believes what our Lord Jesus Christ teaches by your lips concerning the sacrament of His Incarnation' (*Ep.* 99). This was before the bishops in Gaul had received any report of the Council of Chalcedon. (Cp. § 4 with *Ep.* 102.) It would be difficult to express in plainer terms their conviction of the irreformable character of St. Leo's Tome, before that Council met.

2. Eusebius, the Bishop of Milan, in this same year assembled a Synod and wrote to Leo on the occasion of the return of certain bishops from the East, sent thither on the affairs of Eutyches. He then wrote to Leo in the name of the Synod. The letter is of great importance as giving the sense of the West concerning the Tome. They speak of our Lord providing for the Catholic faith 'when He placed you in the See of His Apostle, a suitable champion of His worship, ('quando vos idoneos cultus sui assertores in Apostoli sui sede Præsulem collocavit,'), who can both think what is right concerning the sacrament of the Lord's Incarnation and still more rightly guard the same.' Then, speaking of the Tome, the Synod says: 'It was clear that it shone with the full purity of the faith, with the assertions of the Prophets, with the authorities of the Evangelists, and the testimonies of Apostolic teaching, and radiated with a certain brightness of light and splendour of truth, and agreed with the ideas which the blessed Ambrose, incited by the Holy Spirit, in-

serted in his books concerning the mystery of the Lord's Incarnation.' They then say that all in the Tome agrees with the ancient faith, and that therefore they affix their signatures by way of declaring that 'all who think otherwise (*impie*) ought to be visited with befitting condemnation ; *the sentence of your authority going before*. Therefore, following the form of your letter, we show by this letter, sent through our brother-bishop Cyriacus, that we have kept the manner of the appointment prescribed,' *i.e.* have observed the appointed form prescribed by the Pope. In other words his Tome was 'a lamp to their feet' (Ps. cxviii. 105). They conclude with saying that in future ages it will be felt that this contumacious sect was permitted to arise when it did, 'that it might be for ever overthrown by your guardianship' ('ut vobis propugnatoribus in æternum prostrata succumberet,' *Ep*. 97, Baller.).[1]

It is clear, after this, that when the Council of Chalcedon met, the Tome of Leo was already of faith in the West; for these words, like those of the bishops of Gaul, were written before that Council's decision had reached the West.

3. Let us now turn to the East, and we shall see that on all sides the Tome had been accepted before that fourth session, indeed before the Council began.

(*a*). *Leo himself*, in writing to the Eastern Emperor Theodosius, treats his Tome as an irrevocable exposition of the faith. He tells him that he has sent legates to Ephesus, and speaks of the case of Eutyches as one not to be dealt with in the Council in a way that would imply any doubt about his heresy, adding that Eutyches himself had promised to correct himself in accordance with whatever Leo's sentence disapproved of in his opinions ; and that 'the letter which I have sent to our brother and fellow-bishop Flavian [*i.e.* the Tome] fully contains what the Catholic Church

[1] Muzzarelli, *De Auct. Rom. Pont.* ii. 88, noticed that Bossuet, or the author of the *Def. Cleri Gallic.* Pt. III. lib. vii. c. 17, omitted the word *præcedente*, and the last words quoted—a fatal omission.

universally believes and teaches concerning the sacrament of the Lord's Incarnation' (*Ep.* 29).

To the Council itself Leo writes saying that the Emperor wished 'the authority of the Apostolic See to be applied to his decree,' and that he 'desired to have the confession of Peter declared as it were by the most blessed Peter himself,' *i.e.* by the See of Peter. He assumes that Eutyches has erred from the faith (cap. i.). He describes the Council as assembled 'that all error may be abolished by a fuller judgment.' He does not say that its object is to investigate the truth, or decide upon the faith, but to abolish error, by more numerous judges—the idea being that they would add their witness and take the case of the individual into account. His legates are sent that in his stead 'they may decide, by a sentence in common with you, what may be pleasing to God, that, pestiferous error being condemned, the restitution of him [Eutyches] who has foolishly erred may be dealt with, if at least (*tamen*) embracing the teaching of truth he shall have fully and openly with his own voice and subscription condemned the heretical views in which his folly had been entangled, and this he actually promised in the petition sent to us, engaging to follow in all things our judgment' ('sententia,' ἀποφάσεσι). He then says that he had written to Flavian more fully about what that prelate had referred to him, 'so that, the error which appears to have arisen being destroyed, there may be one faith and one and the same confession through the whole world, to the praise and glory of God' (*Ep.* 33).

Nothing can be clearer than that Leo required the Council to regard Eutyches as a heretic unless he retracted, and that his own teaching was to be the basis of any judgment passed. That is to say, it was to be the guiding light, *lux præfulgens*, the 'lamp to their feet.'

Again, he writes to the Council of Chalcedon saying that he is present in his legates—'and I am not wanting in the proclamation of the Catholic faith, so that you who cannot be ignorant of what we believe in accordance with ancient tradition, may not doubt what our wish is.' And 'let not that be allowed a defence which it is not permitted to believe, since in accordance with the authority of the Evangelists, the voices of the Prophets, and the teaching of the Apostles, the holy and pure confession concerning the Incarnation of our Lord Jesus Christ has been most fully and clearly declared by the letter which we sent to Flavian of blessed memory' (*Ep.* 93).

Clearly the writer of these words did not contemplate the bishops sitting in judgment as superiors on this irrevocable decision as to the true faith.

(β) The Emperor Marcian took the same view of Leo's Tome. He describes the object of the Council as the furtherance of the Christian religion by the declaration of what would conduce to the Catholic faith, 'as your Holiness has defined in accordance with the ecclesiastical canons,' καθὼς ἡ σὴ ἁγιωσύνη κατὰ τοὺς ἐκκλησιαστικοὺς κανόνας διετύπωσε (Lat. *definivit*) (*Ep.* 76).

(γ) The Empress Pulcheria at the same time spoke of the Council as about to decide concerning the Catholic confession 'by your authority,' σοῦ αὐθεντοῦντος ὁρίσωσιν. She had already spoken with satisfaction of Anatolius having signed the Tome (*Ep.* 77).

(δ) Flavian himself, the (afterwards) martyred Bishop of Constantinople, had sent the Tome to the metropolitans all round to be signed (Mansi, vii. 92). And he held as a matter of principle that the whole matter could be settled by Leo himself: 'For so the heresy which has arisen, and the trouble consequent upon it, will be easily brought to an end through the Divine assistance by your holy letter' (*Leon. Ep.* 26).

All this was in accordance with what St. Peter Chrysologus, the great Bishop of Ravenna, wrote to Eutyches: 'We exhort you to listen obediently to the things written by the most blessed Pope of the city of Rome, since blessed Peter, who lives and presides in his own see, gives to those who seek, the truth of the faith' (*Leon. Ep.* 25). This was said before the Tome was known to have been written, and it stamped it with infallibility beforehand.

4. And now for the Council of Chalcedon itself. (i) In the first session, when dealing with St. Flavian's condemnation by Dioscorus, the fathers prove the orthodoxy of Flavian by the mere fact that he was in accord with the Tome of Leo—' since the exposition of the faith agrees with the letter of the most blessed and apostolic man, the Pope of Rome,' are the words of Paschasinus; 'since the faith of Flavian of holy memory agrees with the Apostolic See and the tradition of the Fathers,' are the words of Lucentius; 'Archbishop Flavian of holy memory expounded the faith rightly and in agreement with the most blessed and holy Archbishop Leo,' said Maximus of Antioch, adding 'and we all eagerly receive it,' *i. e.* that same faith. Some of the bishops then testified to the agreement of Flavian with the teaching of Cyril (Mansi, vi. 680, 681). The Tome of Leo was, then, already on a par with the teaching of Cyril, which had received Papal, conciliar, and universal sanction. It was part of the rule of faith. As Evagrius of Antioch says, it was already 'a standard of orthodox belief' (ὀρθοδοξίας ὅρον, *H. E.* ii. § 2).

(ii) Again, in the second session, the fathers had said that a ' norm.' or authoritative rule (τύπος) had been given them by the Tome of Leo ' and we follow him [or, we go by it]; we have all signed the epistle ' or Tome; and Florentius said that those who had signed the Tome needed no 'correction' of their faith; and both he and Cecropius placed together the letter of Cyril (admittedly of faith) and also the Tome, as all equally confirmatory of the faith (Mansi, vi. 954). In that same session the Nicene Creed was read, and also the Constantinopolitan, two letters of Cyril's, and the Tome of Leo, and *after each of them* the fathers said 'This is the faith of all of us,' adding in the case of Leo's Tome, ' Peter has spoken these things through Leo' (Mansi, vi. 972).

It is therefore, impossible for anyone who has regard to the history of the whole matter, to maintain with Dr. Bright and others that by the 'bishops' act' in the fourth session of Chalcedon the Tome of Leo 'acquired a place among Church standards.' We must therefore find some other meaning for the declarations of the bishops in that session to the effect that they signed the Tome because it was in accordance with the Nicene faith. Whatever their meaning, it could not have been that they were then settling the authoritative nature of that Papal utterance. Indeed when Paschasinus, the Papal legate, said that he had signed the Epistle to Flavian because it agreed with previous standards it is certain that he, at any rate, was not saying that he had examined it as something that might have disagreed with the same, or that he had ever felt himself free to repudiate its authority.

What, then, was the meaning of these declarations? Mansi expresses it thus : ' They did not approve that Epistle,' *i.e.* the Tome of Leo, ' as though without their approbation it lacked anything in the way of irrefragable authority, but to show that they themselves fully recognised in it the traditional faith of the Lord's Incarnation' (Nat. Alex. ix. 525). What sort of examination they gave to it, we do not know; there was no conciliar examination, but merely a private examination by a few for the purpose of convincing some bishops who had difficulties about two or three expressions, while even *these* distinctly and emphatically said that they did not doubt Leo's complete orthodoxy, meaning his orthodoxy as expressed in the Tome (Mansi, vii. 29). The examination, such as it was, ' served,' as Mansi comments, ' for a better understanding of the words, but not because there was room to doubt concerning what had already been defined' (Nat. Alex. ix. 526). It had been alleged that those who condemned Eutyches were unfaithful to the teaching of Cyril. No, said the bishops in effect; we have each one of us perused the great document, and we find this allegation untrue; the Tome is, as a matter of fact, in perfect accord with that teaching and in signing it we signed what we knew to be in harmony with Nicæa and Ephesus. We were guided by Leo; we followed him; he was (to quote again their own words in their letter to Leo) 'the interpreter to us of the voice of blessed Peter' (*Leon. Ep.* 98). But we signed after discerning *for ourselves* the harmony between Cyril and Leo (Mansi, vii. 44). We compared his letter with the other standards of the faith and their agréement was clear.

The question of Papal infallibility was not before them. Their declaration was in answer to the demand of the Imperial Commissioners that they should each say *whether the Creed of Nicæa was in accordance with the letter of Leo* (Mansi, vii. 9). Now, as it would be absurd to argue from this expression that Leo was placed above the Nicene Creed, so it would be a gratuitous assumption to say that in using the converse expression—namely, that the Tome of Leo was in accordance with the Creed of Nicæa—they were declaring that Leo might have gone wrong and that on that ground they examined his Tome.

Dr. Bright in maintaining his thesis refers to Mansi's seventh volume as his authority (*Roman See*, p. 189). It will be of interest, therefore, to see from the words of that great scholar and theologian, when dealing with the subject, what he would have thought of Dr. Bright's theory, which, of course, is borrowed from the *Def. Cleri Gallicani*. Mansi says that quoting the words of the bishops in the way Dr. Bright does is 'sticking to the rind,' not getting beyond the surface: 'Non est hic in verborum cortice sistendum.' 'We are not to suppose that when the Synod compared the Epistle of Leo with other Fathers and preceding Councils, it could have doubted concerning it and that it gave judgment as a superior. From what took place before the Council and until the Council was finished, it always appears that the Epistle of Leo was bound to be observed as a rule of the faith to be defined' (Mansi, in Nat. Alex. *H. E.* vol. ix. Diss. xii. *Animadversiones,* § iii. 17).

The objection drawn from the bishops saying that they signed the Tome because it was in accord with the Nicene Creed, instead of merely saying that it came from the See of Peter, has been well answered in these words: 'It has often been remarked that the general practice of the Church in enacting a decree of faith is to declare the doctrine to be in agreement with the doctrine laid down by the Fathers and the Œcumenical Councils, and therefore, when the irreformable character of a canon of faith [already] *sanctioned by a General Synod* is spoken of, this reason is alleged and not the infallibility of the assembly by which it was decreed. In proof of this, it will be enough to refer to the answer which many bishops, scattered over all parts of the Church, gave to the Emperor Leo, when consulted by him as to the irreformability of the doctrines sanctioned in the Synod of Chalcedon. They did not say [what nevertheless they unquestionably held] that the Synod was the voice of the Church, and that for this reason its decrees could not admit of reformation; they only said that the Council had not imposed any doctrine beyond that defined at Nicæa and confirmed by the following Councils' (P. Bottalla, S.J., *The Infallibility of the Pope,* 1870, p. 227; *cf.* also Mansi, vii. 539-619). Muzzarelli also, in the end of the last century, entered into this same question in his refutation of Bossuet, or the author of the *Defensio Cleri Gallicani,* and ends with saying: 'Behold the verification of the promises of Christ, who is always present *with the Pontiff when defining and with the brethren universally,* so that they may confirm with their assent what the Supreme Pontiff has previously defined; so that one can have no doubt about the assent of the brethren being given to the definition of the head; so that the same Lord gives inerrancy to the consent of the brethren in general and to the definition of the head in particular; so that that chimerical [notion of] dissidence (*discissio*) between the head and the brethren *never can* be realised in matters of faith' (*De Auctor. Rom. Pont.* II. § vi. p. 105). St. Leo has himself given us a summary of the whole matter in the following words: 'Those things which He [the Lord] had previously defined by our ministry, He confirmed by the irreformable [*irretractabili*=that cannot be rehandled with a view to being withdrawn] assent of the brethren, so as to show that that which was first formed by the first See of all, and had been received by the judgment of the whole Christian world, emanated from Himself; so that the members should agree with the head &c.' (*Ep.* 120). Here are the two steps—first, the definition by the See of Peter, *which was of God*—'the Lord had defined'—and was therefore irreformable; secondly, the reception by the whole Christian world, the members agreeing with their head, so that by a twofold emphasis the decision should be seen to be of God. And the result is, according to Leo in the same passage, that by this agreement of the members and head ' our material for rejoicing *the more increases* and the enemy *the more* smites himself, as he has the more ruthlessly risen up against the ministers of Christ' ('ut in hoc quoque capiti membra concordent in quo &c.'). The irreformable assent of the brethren *increases*, not first produces, the joy and the power of vanquishing heresy.

So that, as Fr. Bottalla says of the proceedings in the Œcumenical Council of Ephesus, 'The Fathers sitting in a General Council keep before them as a guide in their researches the doctrine defined by the Pope, and they examine the whole controversy because it is their business to confute the heretics and confirm and justify before the world the doctrine defined by the Roman Pontiff. This doctrine is clearly seen in the Acts of the Council of Ephesus' (*The Pope and the Church*, vii. 207). The only difference in the case of the Council of Chalcedon is that the Tome of Leo was not conciliarly examined, nearly 580 of the bishops having deliberately refused to do so (Mansi, vi. 974); whatever examination these had made of it having been completed, in many cases at some previous time, and in some cases in the previous year. When Pope Vigilius speaks of the Tome 'requiring these comparisons' he is referring to the comparison made in the house of Anatolius—required, not for its acceptance by the orthodox, but for the sake of teaching the few bishops who could not understand the Latin wording in some places—and to the declarations in the fourth session that all the bishops in their perusal of the same had certified to its conformity with the doctrine of the previous Councils. He is arguing that the sanction given by the Council of Ephesus to the teaching of Cyril must be held to be of the highest character, because in making this comparison that teaching was put side by side with the Council of Nicæa. Dr. Bright (*Roman See*, p. 189, and *Waymarks*, p. 229) has assumed without any warrant that Vigilius is speaking of an examination with the liberty of revision, instead of merely for the sake of elucidating its harmony with previous standards, which falls within the province of a bishop as understood by the Vatican Council. He seems to emphasise the word *exigit* instead of *his* and to give it his own interpretation. We may conclude in the words of Muzzarelli: 'Constat adeo irreformabilem [*i.e.* the Tome] ante retractationem fuisse, ut eam concilium reformare non posset nisi per apertam contradictionem cum ecclesia tum dispersa tum congregata' (*De Auct. Rom. Pont.* ii. 94). Leo's Tome was no more then and there for the first time 'erected into a Church standard' than the doctrine of the Procession of the Holy Ghost, already accepted (not to mention previous decisions) at the Second Council of Lyons, could be said to have only attained the position of a matter of faith when, for the purpose of convincing the Greeks, it was examined at the Council of Florence (*ibid.* p. 103); or the doctrine of transubstantiation when it was examined at the Council of Trent—a doctrine of which our Archbishop Lanfranc had already said, ' Hanc fidem tenuit a priscis temporibus et nunc tenet ecclesia, quæ per totum diffusa orbem Catholica nominatur' (*Lib. de Corp. et Sang. Christi*, c. xviii.), and for denying which the Province of Canterbury in 1413 had excommunicated Sir John Oldcastle (Wilkins, *Concilia*, iii. 353 *seq.*).

In each case there was a 'true personal judgment,' to use Dr. Bright's words (*Waymarks*, p. 229); but it was not the judgment of superiors, nor with the idea of possible revision, but only for the purpose of exhibiting the Church's unity. In each case there was 'confirmation,' but in the sense in which the previous standards were 'confirmed,' just as age is said to confirm the authority of truth. In each case there was 'comparison' for the sake of intelligent adhesion, and in each case the adhesion might be said to be due to such comparison, though not necessarily to that alone. When some bishops speak of having 'found' that the Tome agreed with the faith of Nicæa, it was not the finding of a superior court, nor a discovery after doubt; it was faith finding its confirmation in the order of reason— *fides quærens intellectum*. If Dr. Bright had given a more exhaustive, or more fairly illustrative, list of the bishops' declarations in the fourth session, the reader would become aware that they are clearly not speaking of themselves as giving the judgment of superiors: as when one says that he 'consents' *to the Nicene Creed*, the expression used often of their adhesion to Leo's Tome (Mansi, vii. 37); or when another says that he 'perceives' (=finds) that 'there is no difference between the expositions of Nicæa and those of the 150 fathers [at Constantinople] and knows that the *letters of Cyril* [already standards] and of Leo *agree with these*'; or when another says that he 'finds' that those things which were set forth (τὰ ἐκτεθέντα) in the first Ephesine Synod by Cyril [which were now admittedly standards of faith], and further also the letter of Leo, are in harmony with the faith of Nicæa (p. 28); or when a fourth says that 'the letter of our father and pope, Leo, and the first "Acts" of our blessed father, Cyril, at Ephesus against Nestorius, agreed with the 318 fathers of Nicæa, *as also did the* 150 *in Constantinople*, and we believe these'—using the same term of his acceptance of the Nicene-Constantinopolitan Creed as of his acceptance of the Tome of Leo (*ibid.* p. 37); or when again Theodorus says that the letter of Leo *and* the letters of Cyril agree with the Nicene exposition (*ibid.* p. 14); or when another says, 'We have learnt and received that we should believe the exposition of the 318 holy fathers at Nicæa and the 150 at Constantinople and the letter of the most blessed Archbishop Leo agreeing with the faith of the holy fathers and the interpretation of Cyril' (*ibid.* p. 41), clearly witnessing to his own orthodoxy on the whole faith; or when another says, 'I so believe, as the 318 fathers have expounded, and the 150, as also blessed Cyril, believed, and I receive the Epistle of the most blessed Pope Leo, agreeing with these' (*ibid.* p. 45); and further when they insist on the few bishops that remained not merely subscribing to the Nicene Creed but to the Tome of Leo, under pain of *ipso facto* excommunication (*ibid.* p. 54)—if, I say, Dr. Bright had given a fuller account of the session, it would have become apparent that the subscription of the bishops to the Tome was obligatory, the touchstone of their orthodoxy, and that they were not settling the question of its authority, but proclaiming their own orthodoxy by giving expression to their belief that it was already matter of faith, as they had assumed, and said that they assumed, at the opening of the Council in dealing with the case of Dioscorus. A more representative list would have made it evident that these bishops were doing what *they afterwards said they had done*, in the memorable words of their letter to Leo : ' Thou wast made to all the interpreter of the voice of blessed Peter, bringing to all the blessedness of his faith, *whence also* we, using you as the originator (ἀρχηγῷ, Lat. *inchoatore*) of good to our profit, showed forth to the children of the Church the inheritance of the truth, not each singly setting forth the teaching [of our faith] in secret, but with a common spirit, with one symphony and harmony, declaring the confession of faith' (*Ep.* 98). Whether any positive evidence results from all this, or not, in favour of Papal infallibility, one thing is certain, viz. that there is nothing in the acceptance of the Tome by the bishops which *conflicts with* a conviction that the See of Peter was the divinely constituted interpreter of the faith of Peter. The Council's own idea of its action was clearly that it was a common expression of a common faith, of which Leo was, at any rate in this case, the originator, the interpreter, and, as they afterwards say, the head. The Tome was, as Vigilius called it, the *lux præfulgens*,' the 'lamp to their feet.' And so the faith was rivetted on the minds of the faithful by a double bolt: the infallible utterance of the Apostolic See and the harmonious declarations of the bishops in Council. One of these would have sufficed for the ordinary faithful; the two together formed a bulwark of extraordinary force.

APPENDIX III

ON THE PAPAL LEGATE'S VERSION OF THE SIXTH NICENE CANON READ AT CHALCEDON.

It is certain that before the Council of Chalcedon a Codex of Canons was in use among the Easterns which contained a list distinguishing the canons by numbers carried on consecutively from Council to Council, not beginning afresh at each. We also know that in the fourth session of Chalcedon (dealing with the case of Carosus and Dorotheus) the fourth and fifth canons of the Council of Antioch were quoted by Aetius, the Archdeacon of Constantinople, as Canons 83 and 84.[1] Now if we add together the 20 canons of Nicæa, the 25 of Ancyra, the 14 of Neocæsarea, the 20 of Gangra, and the first three of Antioch, we get the number 82, which exactly brings us to the numbers (viz. 83 and 84) assigned to the two canons of Antioch read from the Codex produced by Aetius on that occasion. This Codex used to be identified with that which Dionysius Exiguus translated into Latin; but the Ballerini have shown that this cannot be maintained, as also (and this is important) that the oldest Greek Codex did not contain the canons of Laodicea, Constantinople, *or Antioch*.[2] Aetius, therefore, was not quoting from the oldest collection in existence.

The question therefore arises, From what Codex did Aetius, whose copy contained the Canons of Antioch, pro-

[1] Mansi, vii. 84. [2] Ballerini, *De Antiquis Collect. Can.* Pars I. c. 2.

duce the various Canons read at Chalcedon? And did the compilation used by him later on, in the sixteenth session at Chalcedon, exclude the exordium, or heading, of the sixth canon of Nicæa as read by Paschasinus, the Papal legate, about the primacy of the Church of Rome? And, if it did, which of the two was held by the Council to be the more accurate?

Before answering these questions, it must be remembered that it may fairly be questioned whether the sixth Nicene canon was read in any shape by the Imperial secretary at Chalcedon. As we have seen, it is highly improbable that it was, while, on the other hand, it is certain, so far as the record goes, that no objection was raised to the heading read by Paschasinus,[1] but that, on the contrary, the Imperial Commissioners appear to have taken from it part of the conclusion adopted by the bishops then present.[2]

But supposing that Aetius did give the Imperial secretary a Codex to read containing the sixth Nicene Canon, and that this canon was without the heading or exordium in question, what is the comparative value of Paschasinus's version? Seeing that no objection can be raised against it from the history of the Council, but that, on the contrary, a presumption is raised in its favour, what evidence is there in support of its being an accurate representation of the oldest Greek text? The Codex used in the earlier session by Aetius did not, as we have seen, contain the oldest collection of canons, since it included the canons of Antioch. Did, then, this Latin version from which Paschasinus read represent an older collection than that?

Now we must at once put aside Dr. Bright's gratuitous assumption that the version of the Nicene canon supposed to have been produced by Aetius contains the original Greek text. That writer assumes too much when he calls Aetius's version of that canon ' *its* Greek text ' (*Roman See*, p. 203). If this were the case, the question would be settled.

[1] Mansi, vii. 444.   [2] *Ibid.* 452.

It is only '*a* Greek text.' Dr. Bright elsewhere calls Aetius's version 'the Greek original' (*Canons of the . . . Councils*, p. 24, 1892), 'the authentic Greek text' (*ibid.* p. 226), and again 'the genuine Greek text' (*Waymarks*, p. 233), and in another place he calls it six times in one page 'the Greek text,' in a way that implies that it was that of the original autograph. But, as Hefele says, 'the original was not read.' They were each of them only copies, in Greek or Latin, which we must not begin by assuming to be identical with the original autograph.

Now Paschasinus's reading of this Nicene canon is supported by two other versions—the *Prisca* and the *Antiquissima*—which appear to represent earlier Greek Codices than that which is represented by the text produced by Aetius in the fourth session of Chalcedon when two of the Antiochene canons were read. This fact raises a presumption against the comparative superiority of Aetius's version on the score of antiquity. We cannot, however, in fairness assume that, if the Nicene canon was actually read by Aetius at the sixteenth session of Chalcedon, it was read from the same Codex as that used by him in the fourth session. If we might make this assumption, the case would be greatly in favour of Paschasinus's version being from an older Codex than that used by Aetius. But a careful attention to the titles and numbers (and the numeration of canons is, as every student of the subject is well aware, of vast importance) might justify a protest against raising this hypothesis, without further proof, into more than a conjecture. Still, as a conjecture, it must be allowed its weight against any dogmatic assumption to the contrary.

We are, then, quite in the dark as to what the Codex was from which Aetius produced (if he did produce) his copy of the sixth Nicene canon, and what is the value of the text of that canon thus produced. It agrees, however, with the Greek Codex translated in the Latin version called the *Isidorian*, both in the words quoted and in the numeration, and in the omission of the exordium. It is possibly only a transcript of the text in that same Codex.

But this Isidorian version, great as is its value, is not a conclusive authority when it is a question of something found in another Codex and not in itself. Martin Bracarensis notices two things about the Isidorian collection, viz. its frequent obscurity and the variations in which it indulges.[1] On the other hand, Paschasinus's reading of the sixth canon is supported by the *Prisca* version, which is the translation of a very old Greek Codex. That particular portion of the *Prisca* which contains the Nicene canons was translated *towards the end of the fourth century*, though the rest of the collection was not finished until after the Council of Chalcedon. The Codex, therefore, which it renders, goes, in its earlier or Nicene portion, still further back, for a Codex exists before its translation. Dr. Bright is therefore certainly mistaken when he stigmatises Paschasinus's reading as the 'fifth-century clause' (*Roman See*, p. 483).

But Paschasinus's reading is further supported by an important discovery by the Ballerini brothers in the shape of a very ancient Latin collection of the canons, including the Nicene, anterior to the *Prisca* translation mentioned above. The Greek Codex which it represents appears to have had an order of its own both in the numeration and grouping of the Nicene and Sardican canons. The rest of the collection is the same as in the *Prisca* version. Thus two ancient translations of Greek Codices older than themselves support Paschasinus's version, while the collection which agrees with Aetius's version has been proved untrustworthy in the matter of omissions.

Again, this *Isidorian* version itself (which agrees in point of omission with that of Aetius), in several of its Codices which were received in the Gallic Churches, exhibits the reading of

---

[1] St. Martin (of Bracara, in Spain) had been much in the East, and collated such Greek texts as existed in the sixth century. He had seen a Greek original of the canons of the Council of Ancyra.

Paschasinus. This is probably a recension due to the fact that the authority of the *Prisca* was considered sufficient to justify the insertion. Dr. Bright endeavours to discount from this by the fact that the regions in which that reading was received were 'dependencies' of Italy. But a collation of the numerous collections received within these 'dependencies' shows that their adhesion to Rome in this matter was not so slavish as Dr. Bright imagines. A good deal of independence discovers itself.

When, however, we speak of collections of the canons being 'received,' we must be on our guard against supposing that they were recognised by public authority. Not even in Italy was any one collection at that time officially sanctioned by Rome. Dr. Bright has fallen into an error in speaking of the version of Dionysius Exiguus as having been 'sanctioned by the Roman Church' (*Roman See*, p. 482), from which he argues that the reading of Paschasinus at the Council of Chalcedon was 'officially withdrawn in the early part of the sixth century.' This is incorrect. Cassiodorus, in the middle of the sixth century speaks indeed of the Dionysian collection as 'hodie usu celeberrimo,' 'in most frequent use,' in the Roman Church; but, as the Ballerini point out, it is of use, not of definite public sanction, that he speaks.[1]

We have, then, if we admit (which is here only admitted for argument's sake) that the sixth Nicene canon was read in Greek by the secretary at Chalcedon, a Greek text of the canon brought from Constantinople, and a Latin text brought (possibly from Sicily) by the Papal legate. The former, on the supposition just mentioned, lacks an exordium, or heading, which the latter contains—an exordium, however, which has no bearing on the point at issue in that session. The difference between the two versions may be explained by supposing either that Aetius's Greek version was defective, or that Paschasinus's reading was in excess of the

[1] Ball. *De Ant. Coll. Can.* Pars III. c. 1, § 2. *Cf.* also Bouix, *Tract. de Princ. Juris Can.* Pars III. 5, § 1.

original Greek text. Both of these explanations can claim some standing ground in the midst of the numerous representations of the original Greek copies, none of which we possess. But they cannot both be true. Which, then, is the more probable? The first supposition seems to be attended with the fewest difficulties. The omitted clause, or heading, whichever it may have been, viz. 'The Roman Church always held the Primacy,' contained a truth denied by none, and implicitly contained in the rest of the canon. Indeed, I presume that even Dr. Bright would not reject such terms as containing no truth, though he would have his own explanation to give of the term 'primacy' ($\pi\rho\omega\tau\epsilon\hat{\iota}a$).

But our choice does not really lie between these two explanations. A third explanation is that the sixth canon was not read at all by the Constantinopolitan party, as being their real difficulty.[1] It was Leo's contention throughout the controversy with Anatolius that the sixth Nicene canon gave an order which was being overturned by the bishops at Chalcedon who proceeded on the ground of the third canon of Constantinople.[2] And if we were to suppose that the clause in question had been added without authority, in order to push a doctrine such as that of Papal supremacy, it is in the highest degree improbable that those Eastern bishops would sit like 'dumb dogs' and express no surprise or indignation at the alteration of a Nicene canon, if Paschasinus's reading contained anything contrary to their teaching. Silence would be impossible under such circumstances, and out of keeping with their bearing throughout the Council. Their native element was clamour. Still less would the Imperial Commissioners have inserted in a statement as to what they all believed, the crucial word of this heading or exordium, and conceded it to Rome.

In truth, the mention of primacy would most naturally be welcomed by an advocate of the Constantinopolitan projects. For the bishop of the Imperial city wished to have a

[1] Cf. *supra*, p. 340.   [2] *Leon. Ep.* 35.

primacy in the East on the ground that Old Rome had a peculiar primacy, as Patriarch in the West, which she had formed as being the central city of the Empire, over and above her relation to the universal Church. Paschasinus's reading, therefore, did not in any way help his case. It was the rest of the canon which supplied the ground of Rome's objection to the displacement of Alexandria and Antioch in favour of Constantinople.

And as regards forgery, for which we have now seen there was no sufficient motive, or 'the false use of documents,' of which the Bishop of Lincoln, following Dr. Bright, accuses Paschasinus,[1] it must in all fairness be conceded that anything coming from Constantinople was more likely to be in that direction than what came from Rome. For while Rome had been distinguished for her courageous maintenance of the respect due to Nicene decrees, and indeed had given her public sanction to them alone and to the Sardican as one with them, the see of Constantinople had richly deserved a character for loose dealing with orthodox documents. The Arians, who had their way plentifully in that city from time to time, were specially addicted to the occupation of forging and mutilating canons. Other heretics had also tampered in Constantinople with the Acts of a Council more recent still, viz. those of Ephesus, in the interests of Pelagianism, and the Greek originals at Constantinople of the Council of Chalcedon were destined to be destroyed outright in the interests of Monothelism and Erastianism. It would be well, therefore, to drop the explanation of forgery, as though any difference between Rome and the East about documents necessarily implied forgery on the part of the former and accuracy on the part of the latter. St. Gregory tells Narses that it was exactly the other way. He gave the Easterns credit for cleverness in this matter, but claimed for the Romans less astuteness with greater integrity. 'Our Roman books are much more

[1] *The Primitive Saints*, &c., by Rev. F. W. Puller, *Preface*, p. xxi.

truthful than the Greek ones, because, as we are blessed with fewer brains than you, we are not such good hands at imposture.' Such was the verdict of one who had first-hand experience in this matter, having investigated it in Constantinople itself—one, too, of unquestioned integrity and ability and who has earned the name of 'Great.'

But, indeed, in the very act of reading the canons or canon at this sixteenth session of Chalcedon, Aetius was acting dishonestly in producing and making the secretary Constantine read a tremendous addition as though it were part of the canons of Constantinople.[1] The man who would do this would omit with equal readiness. Dr. Bright calls this procedure 'more astute than candid.' What eloquence we should have had from him if a Roman legate had done the same!

The conclusion is, that the accusation which Dr. Bright has launched (though indeed he has been preceded by certain German Protestants) against the Roman legate, and which has been recently so readily caught up by Anglican writers of less learning, has no premisses to support it, except the eagerness with which some people catch at anything that seems to score a point against the Church of Rome.

N.B.—Dr. Bright altogether misses the point of my contention as to the improbability of Aetius having had the sixth Nicene canon read, when he asks, 'If it was *ad rem* for a legate to quote his version of a Nicene canon, why was it irrelevant for a Constantinopolitan to read its [sic] Greek text?' (*Roman See*, p. 203). It was *ad rem* for the legate to read the sixth canon, because it placed Alexandria and Antioch, and not Constantinople, next to Rome; it was not *ad rem* for a Constantinopolitan to touch that sixth canon with the tip of his fingers, because the only justification of the Constantinopolitan contention lay in the third canon of 381, which dictated a fundamental alteration of the Nicene settlement as to the relative position of the sees.

[1] *Mansi*, vii. 445.

INDEX

AETIUS, Archdeacon, 339, 394 ff
Alexandria, its position, 5
Anatolius, Archbishop of Constantinople, 204 ff; discussion of the *Tome*, 268, 274
Antioch. See *John, Domnus, Maximus*

BARSUMAS, monk, 152
Bishops. See *Council*
Bossuet, 20, 52, 55, 98, 382

CANDIDIAN, Count, 60, 63, 92
Canons, violated by Nestorius, 51; third of Constantinople (A.D. 381), 323 ff, 330, 340; null from beginning, 332, 342; twenty-eighth of Chalcedon, 338, 343, 345, 360. See *Nicene*, and Preface, xii
Capreolus, Bishop of Carthage, 49
Celestine I., St., Pope, character, 6, *ex cathedrâ* definition, 7, 19; sentence on Nestorius, 12; president of Council, 35; letter read, 48; obedience to, 50; instructions to legates (*Commonitorium*, 66; last letter, 115
Chrysaphius, Imperial Chamberlain, 125, 135
Chrysologus, St., 132, 384
hrysostom, St., action at Ephesus, 325

Constantinople, people of, Leo's children, 187; desire for a Patriarchate, 321 ff; position at Chalcedon, 336
— Council of, in 381, detested by Dioscorus, 125; slighted at the Latrocinium, 151, 156, 160; when inserted in list of Œcum. Councils, 341. See *Synod*
— Council of, A.D. 448, 158
— Creed of, 232, 261, 266, 287
Council, function of Œcumenical, 39, 301; Leo's idea of, 145, 383, 389; the Emperor's idea of, 288; Bottalla on, 389, 391
Cyprus, quarrel with Antioch, 110
Cyril, St., of Alexandria, on the Incarnation, 4; his position in A.D. 430, 5; asks Celestine to define, 10; his Synod, 29; president at Ephesus, 34; on the Apostolic See, 84; Eutyches's use of his name, 222. See *Union*

DALMATIUS, monk, 93
Diocese, meaning of, 34, 323
Dioscorus, Archbishop of Alexandria, 124, 135, 151; object in the *Latrocinium*, 154; treatment of Flavian, 164; made to sit in the middle, 224, 252; his trial, 229 ff; his heresy, 238; sentence on, 244
Domnus, Bishop of Antioch, 124 126, 165, 313

EGYPT, effect of Eutychianism, 252
— Bishops of, 225, 226 *note*, 278, 298, 301
Ephesus, people of, against Nestorius, 30 ; Bishop of, at Florence, 105 ; ordination of its bishops, 329
— Council of, question at issue, 3 ; a device of Nestorius, 24 ; absence of John of Antioch, 31 ; condemnation of Pelagianism, 49 ; no definition issued, 264
Episcopate, its function in a Council, 39 ; relation to the Pope, 48, 240. See Preface
Eulogius, St., on Council of Ephesus, 109
Euphemia, St., 223, 292
Eusebius, of Dorylæum, accuses Eutyches, 128 ; not admitted to the *Latrocinium*, 156, 158 ; appeals to Rome, 164, 165 ; his letter of appeal, 176, 232 ; his position at Chalcedon, 308
Eutyches, character, 123 ; accused, 128 ; appeals, 130 : defence at *Latrocinium*, 154 ff ; claims agreement with Cyril, 222 ; his confession of faith, 232

FIRMUS, Bishop of Cæsarea in Cappadocia, 69
Flavian, Archbishop of Constantinople, 125, 128, 133 ; correspondence with Leo, 136 ; reporting to Leo, 149 ; accused by Eutyches, 155, 159 ; appeals to Rome, 164 ; his letter of appeal, 173 ff ; his *ecthesis*, 235

GALLA PLACIDIA, Empress, 188, 193

HARNACK, 259, 283
Hilarus, legate, 181
Hypostatic. See *Union*

IRENÆUS, Count, 60, 126

JOHN, Bishop of Antioch ; letter from Cyril, 17 ; urges Nestorius to obey, 20 ; his delay near Ephesus, 31 ; schismatic action, 60 ff ; summoned to the Council, 96 ; excommunicated, 98
Juvenal, Bishop of Jerusalem. 44, 46, 48, 96, 152, 236, 239, 337

LATROCINIUM (or Robber-Synod), literature on, 150 ; irregular features, 152 ; Dioscorus's object thereat, 154 ; Council of 381 slighted, 151 ; ill-treatment of Flavian, 164
Legates, Papal, sent to Ephesus, 65 ff ; deference to, 79 ; Philip's speech, 81, 85, 338 ; Dr. Bright's accusation, 347, 371. See *Paschasinus, Philip*
Leo, Eutyches's appeal to, 130 ; correspondence with Flavian, 134 ; asked to settle matters without a Council, 137 ; zeal for the faith, 140 ; his *Tome*, 142 ff ; claim to absolve Eutyches, 146 ; relation to St. Peter, 122, 147 ; Petrine prerogatives relied on, 167 ff, 186, 190, 194, 195, 209, 211 ; invalidates the *Latrocinium*, 182 ; deprecates a Council, 202 ; decides Theodoret's case, 218 ; directions about Eastern bishops, 221 ; his *Tome* read, 266 ff : the *Tome* to be followed, 286 ; its promulgation defended by the Council, 287 ; his judgment on Theodoret not reviewed, 299 ; dispenses in Maximus's case, 313, 315 ; care for the canons, 352 ; head of the Church, 368, 369

MANSI, Archbishop, on the Council of Ephesus, 88 ; on the sufficiency of the *Tome*, 295 ; on Maximus of Antioch, 317 ; on the bishops' declarations as to

INDEX 405

the *Tome*, 386; on the Council of Chalcedon's attitude towards the *Tome*, 387
Marcian, Emperor, 199, 288, 346, 362
Maximus, Bishop of Antioch, 165; compact with Juvenal, 312; dispensed by Leo, 315, 317
Memnon, Bishop of Ephesus, 30, 61, 63

NESTORIUS, his pride, 6; condemned by Pope Celestine, 8; his idea of a Council, 24; his reception at Ephesus, 30; condemned by the Council, 50; banished to Antioch, thence to the Thebaid, 114, 115
Nicene, Canons, Sardican called thus, 185
— Sixth Canon, version read at Chalcedon, 340, 394
— Creed, its enlargement in A.D. 381, 105; signing Nicene Creed not sufficient, 106; additions to, slighted by Dioscorus, 154; and by Eutyches, 156; Leo's guardianship, 184 (and see Preface); confirmed at Chalcedon, 222

ŒCUMENICAL, applied to Leo, 242. See *Council*

PASCHASINUS, legate, 223, 225, 243, 275, 395. See *Legate*
Patriarch, meaning of, 239; position of, 321; Western Patriarchate, 351

Pelagians, 25; condemnation renewed, 49
Philip, legate, 67, 71, 81 (speech on See of Peter)
Placidia. See *Galla*
Pulcheria, St., Empress, 133, 146, 186, 199 (character), 201, 208

ROBBER-SYNOD. See *Latrocinium*

SARDICAN, Canons. See *Nicene*
Socrates (historian), 86
Synod, 'Resident' or 'Home,' at Constantinople, 155, 323, 334
— Roman, 171 ff, 174, 178

THALASSIUS, Bishop of Cæsarea in Cappadocia, 153, 322, 337
Theodoret, Bishop of Cyrus (or Cyrrhos), 179, 212 ff (letter to Leo), 215 (letter to Renatus); at Chalcedon, 225, 228, 232, 298 ff (restoration)
Theodosius II., influenced by Nestorius, 27; dislike of Cyril, 29; misled by Candidian, 92; visited by Dalmatius, monk, 93; intercedes for Eutyches, 134; refuses second Council, 182, 187, 195
Theotokos (Θεοτόκος), meaning, 4; repudiated by Nestorius, 9; not inserted in Creed, 108, 109, 283

UNION, Hypostatic, the question at Ephesus in A.D. 431, 3, 4, 5; Pope Celestine's definition, 7, 107
Universal, Bishop, 116, 319

April 1899.

A Selection of Works
IN
THEOLOGICAL LITERATURE
PUBLISHED BY
Messrs. LONGMANS, GREEN, & CO.

London : 39 Paternoster Row, E.C.
New York : 91 and 93 Fifth Avenue.
Bombay : 32 Hornby Road.

Abbey and Overton.—THE ENGLISH CHURCH IN THE EIGHTEENTH CENTURY. By Charles J. Abbey, M.A., Rector of Checkendon, Reading, and John H. Overton, D.D., Canon of Lincoln. *Crown 8vo. 7s. 6d.*

Adams.—SACRED ALLEGORIES. The Shadow of the Cross—The Distant Hills—The Old Man's Home—The King's Messengers. By the Rev. William Adams, M.A. *Crown 8vo. 3s. 6d.*
  The four Allegories may be had separately, with Illustrations. 16mo. *1s. each.*

Aids to the Inner Life.
  Edited by the Venble. W. H. Hutchings, M.A., Archdeacon of Cleveland, Canon of York, Rector of Kirby Misperton, and Rural Dean of Malton. *Five Vols.* 32mo, *cloth limp, 6d. each; or cloth extra, 1s. each.*
  OF THE IMITATION OF CHRIST. By Thomas à Kempis.
  THE CHRISTIAN YEAR
  THE DEVOUT LIFE. By St. Francis de Sales.
  THE HIDDEN LIFE OF THE SOUL.
  THE SPIRITUAL COMBAT. By Laurence Scupoli.

Alexander.—THE CHRISTIANITY OF ST. PAUL. By the Rev. S. A. Alexander, M.A., Reader of the Temple Church.

Barnett.—THE SERVICE OF GOD : Sermons, Essays, and Addresses. By Samuel A. Barnett, Warden of Toynbee Hall, Whitechapel; Canon of Bristol Cathedral; Select Preacher before Oxford University. *Crown 8vo. 6s.*

Bathe.—Works by the Rev. Anthony Bathe, M.A.
  A LENT WITH JESUS. A Plain Guide for Churchmen. Containing Readings for Lent and Easter Week, and on the Holy Eucharist. 32mo, *1s.; or in paper cover, 6d.*
  AN ADVENT WITH JESUS. 32mo, *1s.; or in paper cover, 6d.*
  WHAT I SHOULD BELIEVE. A Simple Manual of Self-Instruction for Church People. *Small 8vo, limp, 1s.; cloth gilt, 2s.*

Bathe and Buckham.—THE CHRISTIAN'S ROAD BOOK. 2 Parts. By the Rev. Anthony Bathe and Rev. F. H. Buckham.
  Part I. DEVOTIONS. *Sewed, 6d.; limp cloth, 1s.; cloth extra, 1s. 6d.*
  Part II. READINGS. *Sewed, 1s.; limp cloth, 2s.; cloth extra, 3s.; or complete in one volume, sewed, 1s. 6d.; limp cloth, 2s. 6d.; cloth extra, 3s. 6d.*

Benson.—Works by the Rev. R. M. BENSON, M.A., Student of Christ Church, Oxford.

THE FINAL PASSOVER: A Series of Meditations upon the Passion of our Lord Jesus Christ. *Small 8vo.*

Vol. I.—THE REJECTION. 5s.
Vol. II.—THE UPPER CHAMBER.
Part I. 5s.
Part II. 5s.

Vol. III.—THE DIVINE EXODUS. Parts I. and II. 5s. each.
Vol. IV.—THE LIFE BEYOND THE GRAVE. 5s.

THE MAGNIFICAT; a Series of Meditations upon the Song of the Blessed Virgin Mary. *Small 8vo.* 2s.

SPIRITUAL READINGS FOR EVERY DAY. 3 vols. *Small 8vo.* 3s. 6d. each.

I. ADVENT.   II. CHRISTMAS.   III. EPIPHANY.

BENEDICTUS DOMINUS: A Course of Meditations for Every Day of the Year. Vol. I.—ADVENT TO TRINITY. Vol. II.—TRINITY, SAINTS' DAYS, etc. *Small 8vo.* 3s. 6d. each; or in One Volume, 7s.

BIBLE TEACHINGS: The Discourse at Capernaum.—St. John vi. *Small 8vo.* 3s. 6d.

THE WISDOM OF THE SON OF DAVID: An Exposition of the First Nine Chapters of the Book of Proverbs. *Small 8vo.* 3s. 6d.

THE MANUAL OF INTERCESSORY PRAYER. *Royal 32mo.*; cloth boards, 1s. 3d.; cloth limp, 9d.

THE EVANGELIST LIBRARY CATECHISM. Part I. *Small 8vo.* 3s.

PAROCHIAL MISSIONS. *Small 8vo.* 2s. 6d.

Bickersteth.—YESTERDAY, TO-DAY, AND FOR EVER: a Poem in Twelve Books. By EDWARD HENRY BICKERSTETH, D.D., Lord Bishop of Exeter. *One Shilling Edition*, 18mo. *With red borders*, 16mo, 2s. 6d.

The Crown 8vo Edition (5s.) may still be had.

Blunt.—Works by the Rev. JOHN HENRY BLUNT, D.D.

THE ANNOTATED BOOK OF COMMON PRAYER: Being an Historical, Ritual, and Theological Commentary on the Devotional System of the Church of England. 4to. 21s.

THE COMPENDIOUS EDITION OF THE ANNOTATED BOOK OF COMMON PRAYER: Forming a concise Commentary on the Devotional System of the Church of England. *Crown 8vo.* 10s. 6d.

DICTIONARY OF DOCTRINAL AND HISTORICAL THEOLOGY. By various Writers. *Imperial 8vo.* 21s.

DICTIONARY OF SECTS, HERESIES, ECCLESIASTICAL PARTIES AND SCHOOLS OF RELIGIOUS THOUGHT. By various Writers. *Imperial 8vo.* 21s.

THE REFORMATION OF THE CHURCH OF ENGLAND: its History, Principles, and Results. 1574-1662. *Two Vols.* 8vo. 34s.

IN THEOLOGICAL LITERATURE. 3

Blunt.—Works by the Rev. JOHN HENRY BLUNT, D.D.—*contd.*
THE BOOK OF CHURCH LAW. Being an Exposition of the Legal Rights and Duties of the Parochial Clergy and the Laity of the Church of England. Revised by the Right Hon. Sir WALTER G. F. PHILLIMORE, Bart., D.C.L., and G. EDWARDES JONES, Barrister-at-Law. *Crown 8vo.* 9s.
A COMPANION TO THE BIBLE: Being a Plain Commentary on Scripture History, to the end of the Apostolic Age. *Two Vols. small 8vo. Sold separately.* OLD TEST. 3s. 6d. NEW TEST. 3s. 6d.
HOUSEHOLD THEOLOGY: a Handbook of Religious Information respecting the Holy Bible, the Prayer Book, the Church, etc., etc. *Paper cover,* 16mo. 1s. *Also the Larger Edition,* 3s. 6d.

Body.—Works by the Rev. GEORGE BODY, D.D., Canon of Durham.
THE LIFE OF LOVE. A Course of Lent Lectures. 16mo. 2s. 6d.
THE SCHOOL OF CALVARY; or, Laws of Christian Life revealed from the Cross. 16mo. 2s. 6d.
THE LIFE OF JUSTIFICATION. 16mo. 2s. 6d.
THE LIFE OF TEMPTATION. 16mo. 2s. 6d.
THE PRESENT STATE OF THE FAITHFUL DEPARTED. *Small 8vo. sewed,* 6d. 32mo. *cloth,* 1s.

Boultbee.—A COMMENTARY ON THE THIRTY-NINE ARTICLES OF THE CHURCH OF ENGLAND. By the Rev. T. P. BOULTBEE, formerly Principal of the London College of Divinity, St. John's Hall, Highbury. *Crown 8vo.* 6s.

Bright.—Works by WILLIAM BRIGHT, D.D., Regius Professor of Ecclesiastical History in the University of Oxford, and Canon of Christ Church, Oxford.
SOME ASPECTS OF PRIMITIVE CHURCH LIFE. *Crown 8vo.* 6s.
THE ROMAN SEE IN THE EARLY CHURCH: And other Studies in Church History. *Crown 8vo.* 7s. 6d.
WAYMARKS IN CHURCH HISTORY. *Crown 8vo.* 7s. 6d.
LESSONS FROM THE LIVES OF THREE GREAT FATHERS. St. Athanasius, St. Chrysostom, and St. Augustine. *Crown 8vo.* 6s.
THE INCARNATION AS A MOTIVE POWER. *Crown 8vo.* 6s.

Bright and Medd.—LIBER PRECUM PUBLICARUM ECCLESIÆ ANGLICANÆ. A GULIELMO BRIGHT, S.T.P., et PETRO GOLDSMITH MEDD, A.M., Latine redditus. *Small 8vo.* 7s. 6d.

Browne.—WEARIED WITH THE BURDEN: A Book of Daily Readings for Lent. By ARTHUR HEBER BROWNE, M.A., LL.D., late Rector of St. John's, Newfoundland. *Crown 8vo.* 4s. 6d.

Browne.—AN EXPOSITION OF THE THIRTY-NINE ARTICLES, Historical and Doctrinal. By E. H. BROWNE, D.D., sometime Bishop of Winchester. 8vo. 16s.

Campion and Beamont.—THE PRAYER BOOK INTERLEAVED. With Historical Illustrations and Explanatory Notes arranged parallel to the Text. By W. M. CAMPION, D.D., and W. J. BEAMONT, M.A. *Small 8vo.* 7s. 6d.

Carter.—Works by, and edited by the Rev. T. T. CARTER, M.A., Hon. Canon of Christ Church, Oxford.

THE SPIRIT OF WATCHFULNESS AND OTHER SERMONS. *Crown 8vo.* 5s.

THE TREASURY OF DEVOTION : a Manual of Prayer for General and Daily Use. Compiled by a Priest.
    18*mo.* 2s. 6d. *; cloth limp,* 2s. Bound with the Book of Common Prayer, 3s. 6d. Red-Line Edition. *Cloth extra, gilt top.* 18*mo,* 2s. 6d. *net.* Large-Type Edition. *Crown 8vo.* 3s. 6d.

THE WAY OF LIFE : A Book of Prayers and Instruction for the Young at School, with a Preparation for Confirmation. Compiled by a Priest, 18*mo.* 1s. 6d.

THE PATH OF HOLINESS : a First Book of Prayers, with the Service of the Holy Communion, for the Young. Compiled by a Priest. With Illustrations. 16*mo.* 1s. 6d. *; cloth limp,* 1s.

THE GUIDE TO HEAVEN : a Book of Prayers for every Want. (For the Working Classes.) Compiled by a Priest. 18*mo.* 1s. 6d. *; cloth limp,* 1s. *Large-Type Edition. Crown 8vo.* 1s. 6d. *; cloth limp,* 1s.

THE STAR OF CHILDHOOD : a First Book of Prayers and Instruction for Children. Compiled by a Priest. With Illustrations. 16*mo.* 2s. 6d.

SIMPLE LESSONS ; or, Words Easy to be Understood. A Manual of Teaching. I. On the Creed. II. The Ten Commandments. III. The Sacrament. 18*mo.* 3s.

A BOOK OF PRIVATE PRAYER FOR MORNING, MID-DAY, AND OTHER TIMES. 18*mo. limp cloth,* 1s. *; cloth, red edges,* 1s. 3d.

NICHOLAS FERRAR : his Household and his Friends. With Portrait engraved after a Picture by CORNELIUS JANSSEN at Magdalene College, Cambridge. *Crown 8vo.* 6s.

MANUAL OF DEVOTION FOR SISTERS OF MERCY. 8 parts in 2 vols. 32*mo.* 10s. Or separately :—Part I. 1s. 6d. Part II. 1s. Part III. 1s. Part IV. 2s. Part V. 1s. Part VI. 1s. Part VII. Part VIII. 1s. 6d.

HARRIET MONSELL : A Memoir of the First Mother Superior of the Clewer Community. With Portrait. *Crown 8vo.* 2s. 6d.

PARISH TEACHINGS. First and Second Series. *Crown 8vo.* 4s. 6d. *each sold separately.*

SPIRITUAL INSTRUCTIONS. *Crown 8vo.*

THE HOLY EUCHARIST. 3s. 6d.	OUR LORD'S EARLY LIFE. 3s. 6d.
THE DIVINE DISPENSATIONS. 3s. 6d.	OUR LORD'S ENTRANCE ON HIS
THE LIFE OF GRACE. 3s. 6d.	MINISTRY. 3s. 6d.

    THE RELIGIOUS LIFE. 3s. 6d.

THE DOCTRINE OF THE PRIESTHOOD IN THE CHURCH OF ENGLAND. *Crown 8vo.* 4s.

THE DOCTRINE OF CONFESSION IN THE CHURCH OF ENGLAND. *Crown 8vo.* 5s.

THE DOCTRINE OF THE HOLY EUCHARIST, drawn from the Holy Scriptures and the Records of the Church of England. *Fcp. 8vo.* 9d.

VOWS AND THE RELIGIOUS STATE. *Crown 8vo.* 2s.

Coles.—LENTEN MEDITATIONS. By the Rev. V. S. S. COLES, M.A., Principal of the Pusey House, Oxford. 18mo. 2s. 6d.

Congreve.—CHRISTIAN LIFE A RESPONSE. With other Retreat Addresses and Sermons. By GEORGE CONGREVE, Mission Priest of the Society of St. John the Evangelist, Cowley St. John, Oxford. *Crown 8vo.* 5s.

Conybeare and Howson.—THE LIFE AND EPISTLES OF ST. PAUL. By the Rev. W. J. CONYBEARE, M.A., and the Very Rev. J. S. HOWSON, D.D. With numerous Maps and Illustrations. LIBRARY EDITION. *Two Vols. 8vo.* 21s. STUDENTS' EDITION. *One Vol. Crown 8vo.* 6s. POPULAR EDITION. *One Vol. Crown 8vo.* 3s. 6d.

Creighton.—A HISTORY OF THE PAPACY FROM THE GREAT SCHISM TO THE SACK OF ROME (1378-1527). By Right Hon. and Right Rev. MANDELL CREIGHTON, D.D., Lord Bishop of London. *Six volumes. Crown 8vo.* 6s. each.

DAY-HOURS OF THE CHURCH OF ENGLAND, THE. Newly Revised according to the Prayer Book and the Authorised Translation of the Bible. *Crown 8vo. sewed,* 3s.; *cloth,* 3s. 6d.
SUPPLEMENT TO THE DAY-HOURS OF THE CHURCH OF ENGLAND, being the Service for certain Holy Days. *Crown 8vo. sewed,* 3s.; *cloth,* 3s. 6d.

Devotional Series, 16mo, Red Borders. *Each* 2s. 6d.

BICKERSTETH'S YESTERDAY, TO-DAY, AND FOR EVER.
CHILCOT'S TREATISE ON EVIL THOUGHTS.
THE CHRISTIAN YEAR.
HERBERT'S POEMS AND PROVERBS.
KEMPIS' (À) OF THE IMITATION OF CHRIST.
LEAR'S (H. L. SIDNEY) FOR DAYS AND YEARS.
FRANCIS DE SALES' (ST.) THE DEVOUT LIFE.
WILSON'S THE LORD'S SUPPER. *Large type.*
*TAYLOR'S (JEREMY) HOLY LIVING.
*——— ——— HOLY DYING.

* *These two in one Volume.* 5s.

Devotional Series, 18mo, without Red Borders. *Each* 1s.

BICKERSTETH'S YESTERDAY, TO-DAY, AND FOR EVER.
THE CHRISTIAN YEAR.
KEMPIS' (À) OF THE IMITATION OF CHRIST.
HERBERT'S POEMS AND PROVERBS.
WILSON'S THE LORD'S SUPPER. *Large type.*
FRANCIS DE SALES' (ST.) THE DEVOUT LIFE.
*TAYLOR'S (JEREMY) HOLY LIVING.
*——— ——— HOLY DYING.

* *These two in one Volume.* 2s. 6d.

Edersheim.—Works by ALFRED EDERSHEIM, M.A., D.D., Ph.D.
THE LIFE AND TIMES OF JESUS THE MESSIAH. *Two Vols. 8vo.* 24s.
JESUS THE MESSIAH: being an Abridged Edition of 'The Life and Times of Jesus the Messiah.' *Crown 8vo.* 7s. 6d.
HISTORY OF THE JEWISH NATION AFTER THE DESTRUCTION OF JERUSALEM UNDER TITUS. *8vo.* 18s.

Ellicott.—Works by C. J. ELLICOTT, D.D., Bishop of Gloucester.
A CRITICAL AND GRAMMATICAL COMMENTARY ON ST. PAUL'S EPISTLES. Greek Text, with a Critical and Grammatical Commentary, and a Revised English Translation. 8vo.

GALATIANS. 8s. 6d.
EPHESIANS. 8s. 6d.

PHILIPPIANS, COLOSSIANS, AND PHILEMON. 10s. 6d.
THESSALONIANS. 7s. 6d.

PASTORAL EPISTLES. 10s. 6d.

HISTORICAL LECTURES ON THE LIFE OF OUR LORD JESUS CHRIST. 8vo. 12s.

ENGLISH (THE) CATHOLIC'S VADE MECUM: a Short Manual of General Devotion. Compiled by a PRIEST. 32mo. limp, 1s.; cloth, 2s.

PRIEST'S Edition. 32mo. 1s. 6d.

Epochs of Church History.—Edited by Right Hon. and Right Rev. MANDELL CREIGHTON, D.D., Lord Bishop of London. Small 8vo. 2s. 6d. each.

THE ENGLISH CHURCH IN OTHER LANDS. By the Rev. H. W. TUCKER, M.A.

THE HISTORY OF THE REFORMATION IN ENGLAND. By the Rev. GEO. G. PERRY, M.A.

THE CHURCH OF THE EARLY FATHERS. By the Rev. ALFRED PLUMMER, D.D.

THE EVANGELICAL REVIVAL IN THE EIGHTEENTH CENTURY. By the Rev. J. H. OVERTON, D.D.

THE UNIVERSITY OF OXFORD. By the Hon. G. C. BRODRICK, D.C.L.

THE UNIVERSITY OF CAMBRIDGE. By J. BASS MULLINGER, M.A.

THE ENGLISH CHURCH IN THE MIDDLE AGES. By the Rev. W. HUNT, M.A.

THE CHURCH AND THE EASTERN EMPIRE. By the Rev. H. F. TOZER, M.A.

THE CHURCH AND THE ROMAN EMPIRE. By the Rev. A. CARR, M.A.

THE CHURCH AND THE PURITANS, 1570-1660. By HENRY OFFLEY WAKEMAN M.A.

HILDEBRAND AND HIS TIMES. By the Rev. W. R. W. STEPHENS, M.A.

THE POPES AND THE HOHENSTAUFEN. By UGO BALZANI.

THE COUNTER REFORMATION. By ADOLPHUS WILLIAM WARD, Litt. D.

WYCLIFFE AND MOVEMENTS FOR REFORM. By REGINALD L. POOLE, M.A.

THE ARIAN CONTROVERSY. By the Rev. H. M. GWATKIN, M.A.

EUCHARISTIC MANUAL (THE). Consisting of Instructions and Devotions for the Holy Sacrament of the Altar. From various sources. 32mo. cloth gilt, red edges. 1s. Cheap Edition, limp cloth. 9d.

Farrar.—Works by FREDERICK W. FARRAR, D.D., Dean of Canterbury.

THE BIBLE: Its Meaning and Supremacy. 8vo. 15s.

TEXTS EXPLAINED; or, Helps to Understand the New Testament. Crown 8vo. [In the press.

ALLEGORIES. With 25 Illustrations by AMELIA BAUERLE. Crown 8vo. 6s.

CONTENTS.—The Life Story of Aner—The Choice—The Fortunes of a Royal House—The Basilisk and the Leopard.

Fosbery.—Works edited by the Rev. THOMAS VINCENT FOSBERY, M.A., sometime Vicar of St. Giles's, Reading.
  VOICES OF COMFORT. *Cheap Edition. Small 8vo.* 3s. 6d.
    The Larger Edition (7s. 6d.) may still be had.
  HYMNS AND POEMS FOR THE SICK AND SUFFERING. In connection with the Service for the Visitation of the Sick. Selected from Various Authors. *Small 8vo.* 3s. 6d.

Geikie.—Works by J. CUNNINGHAM GEIKIE, D.D., LL.D., late Vicar of St. Martin-at-Palace, Norwich.
  HOURS WITH THE BIBLE: the Scriptures in the Light of Modern Discovery and Knowledge. *New Edition, largely rewritten.* Complete in Twelve Volumes. *Crown 8vo.* 3s. 6d. each.

OLD TESTAMENT.
In Six Volumes. Sold separately. 3s. 6d. each.

CREATION TO THE PATRIARCHS. *With a Map and Illustrations.*

MOSES TO JUDGES. *With a Map and Illustrations.*

SAMSON TO SOLOMON. *With a Map and Illustrations.*

REHOBOAM TO HEZEKIAH. *With Illustrations.*

MANASSEH TO ZEDEKIAH. With the Contemporary Prophets. *With a Map and Illustrations.*

EXILE TO MALACHI. With the Contemporary Prophets. *With Illustrations.*

NEW TESTAMENT.
In Six Volumes. Sold separately. 3s. 6d. each.

THE GOSPELS. *With a Map and Illustrations.*

LIFE AND WORDS OF CHRIST. *With Map.* 2 vols.

LIFE AND EPISTLES OF ST. PAUL. *With Maps and Illustrations.* 2 vols.

ST. PETER TO REVELATION. *With 29 Illustrations.*

  LIFE AND WORDS OF CHRIST.
    Cabinet Edition. With Map. 2 vols. *Post 8vo.* 7s.
    Cheap Edition, without the Notes. 1 vol. 8vo. 5s.
  A SHORT LIFE OF CHRIST. *With Illustrations. Crown 8vo.* 3s. 6d.; gilt edges, 4s. 6d.
  OLD TESTAMENT CHARACTERS. *With Illustrations. Crown 8vo.* 3s. 6d.
  LANDMARKS OF OLD TESTAMENT HISTORY. *Crown 8vo.* 3s. 6d.
  THE ENGLISH REFORMATION. *Crown 8vo.* 3s. 6d.
  ENTERING ON LIFE. A Book for Young Men. *Crown 8vo.* 2s. 6d.
  THE PRECIOUS PROMISES. *Crown 8vo.* 2s.

GOLD DUST: a Collection of Golden Counsels for the Sanctification of Daily Life. Translated and abridged from the French by E.L.E.E. Edited by CHARLOTTE M. YONGE. Parts I. II. III. Small Pocket Volumes. *Cloth, gilt, each* 1s. Parts I. and II. in One Volume. 1s. 6d. Parts I., II., and III. in One Volume. 2s.

*_** The two first parts in One Volume, *large type*, 18mo. *cloth, gilt,* 2s. 6d. Parts I. II. and III. are also supplied, bound in white cloth, with red edges, in box, price 3s.

Gore.—Works by the Rev. CHARLES GORE, M.A., D.D., Canon of Westminster.
  THE MINISTRY OF THE CHRISTIAN CHURCH. 8vo. 10s. 6d.
  ROMAN CATHOLIC CLAIMS. *Crown* 8vo. 3s. 6d.

GREAT TRUTHS OF THE CHRISTIAN RELIGION. Edited by the Rev. W. U. RICHARDS. *Small* 8vo. 2s.

Hall.—Works by the Right Rev. A. C. A. HALL, D.D., Bishop of Vermont.
  THE VIRGIN MOTHER: Retreat Addresses on the Life of the Blessed Virgin Mary as told in the Gospels. With an appended Essay on the Virgin Birth of our Lord. *Crown* 8vo. 4s. 6d.
  CHRIST'S TEMPTATION AND OURS. *Crown* 8vo. 3s. 6d.

Hall.—THE KENOTIC THEORY. Considered with Particular Reference to its Anglican Forms and Arguments. By the Rev. FRANCIS J. HALL, D.D., Instructor of Dogmatic Theology in the Western Theological Seminary, Chicago, Illinois. *Crown* 8vo. 5s.

HALLOWING OF SORROW, THE. By E. R. With a Preface by H. S. HOLLAND, M.A., Canon and Precentor of St. Paul's. *Small* 8vo. 2s.

Harrison.—Works by the Rev. ALEXANDER J. HARRISON, B.D., Lecturer of the Christian Evidence Society.
  PROBLEMS OF CHRISTIANITY AND SCEPTICISM. *Crown* 8vo. 7s. 6d.
  THE CHURCH IN RELATION TO SCEPTICS: a Conversational Guide to Evidential Work. *Crown* 8vo. 3s. 6d.
  THE REPOSE OF FAITH, IN VIEW OF PRESENT DAY DIFFICULTIES. *Crown* 8vo. 7s. 6d.

Hatch.—THE ORGANIZATION OF THE EARLY CHRISTIAN CHURCHES. Being the Bampton Lectures for 1880. By EDWIN HATCH, M.A., D.D., late Reader in Ecclesiastical History in the University of Oxford. 8vo. 5s.

Heygate.—THE MANUAL: a Book of Devotion. Adapted for General Use. By the Rev. W. E. HEYGATE, M.A., Rector of Brighstone. 18mo. *cloth limp*, 1s.; *boards*, 1s. 3d. *Cheap Edition*, 6d. *Small* 8vo. *Large Type*, 1s. 6d.

Holland.—Works by the Rev. HENRY SCOTT HOLLAND, M.A., Canon and Precentor of St. Paul's.
  GOD'S CITY AND THE COMING OF THE KINGDOM. *Cr. 8vo.* 3s. 6d.
  PLEAS AND CLAIMS FOR CHRIST. *Crown 8vo.* 3s. 6d.
  CREED AND CHARACTER: Sermons. *Crown 8vo.* 3s. 6d.
  ON BEHALF OF BELIEF. Sermons. *Crown 8vo.* 3s. 6d.
  CHRIST OR ECCLESIASTES. Sermons. *Crown 8vo.* 2s. 6d.
  LOGIC AND LIFE, with other Sermons. *Crown 8vo.* 3s. 6d.

Hollings.—Works by the Rev. G. S. HOLLINGS, Mission Priest of the Society of St. John the Evangelist, Cowley, Oxford.
  THE HEAVENLY STAIR; or, A Ladder of the Love of God for Sinners. *Crown 8vo.* 3s. 6d.
  PORTA REGALIS; or, Considerations on Prayer. *Crown 8vo. limp cloth,* 1s. 6d. net; *cloth boards,* 2s. net.
  MEDITATIONS ON THE DIVINE LIFE, THE BLESSED SACRAMENT, AND THE TRANSFIGURATION. *Crown 8vo.* 3s. 6d.
  CONSIDERATIONS ON THE SPIRITUAL LIFE. Suggested by Passages in the Collects for the Sundays in Lent. *Crown 8vo.* 2s. 6d.
  CONSIDERATIONS ON THE WISDOM OF GOD. *Crown 8vo.* 4s.
  PARADOXES OF THE LOVE OF GOD, especially as they are seen in the way of the Evangelical Counsels. *Crown 8vo.* 4s.
  ONE BORN OF THE SPIRIT; or, the Unification of our Life in God. *Crown 8vo.* 3s. 6d.

Hutchings.—Works by the Ven. W. H. HUTCHINGS, M.A. Archdeacon of Cleveland, Canon of York, Rector of Kirby Misperton, and Rural Dean of Malton.
  SERMON SKETCHES from some of the Sunday Lessons throughout the Church's Year. *Vols. I and II. Crown 8vo.* 5s. *each.*
  THE LIFE OF PRAYER: a Course of Lectures delivered in All Saints Church, Margaret Street, during Lent. *Crown 8vo.* 4s. 6d.
  THE PERSON AND WORK OF THE HOLY GHOST: a Doctrinal and Devotional Treatise. *Crown 8vo.* 4s. 6d.
  SOME ASPECTS OF THE CROSS. *Crown 8vo.* 4s. 6d.
  THE MYSTERY OF THE TEMPTATION. Lent Lectures delivered a St. Mary Magdalene, Paddington. *Crown 8vo.* 4s. 6d.

Hutton.—THE CHURCH OF THE SIXTH CENTURY. Six Chapters in Ecclesiastical History. By WILLIAM HOLDEN HUTTON, B.D., Birkbeck Lecturer in Ecclesiastical History, Trinity College, Cambridge. *With* 11 *Illustrations. Crown 8vo. 6s.*

Hutton.—THE SOUL HERE AND HEREAFTER. By the Rev. R. E. HUTTON, Chaplain of St. Margaret's, East Grinstead. *Crown 8vo. 6s.*

INHERITANCE OF THE SAINTS; or, Thoughts on the Communion of Saints and the Life of the World to come. Collected chiefly from English Writers by L. P. With a Preface by the Rev. HENRY SCOTT HOLLAND, M.A. *Seventh Edition. Crown 8vo. 7s. 6d.*

Jameson.—Works by Mrs. JAMESON.

SACRED AND LEGENDARY ART, containing Legends of the Angels and Archangels, the Evangelists, the Apostles. With 19 Etchings and 187 Woodcuts. 2 *vols.* 8*vo.* 20*s. net.*

LEGENDS OF THE MONASTIC ORDERS, as represented in the Fine Arts. With 11 Etchings and 88 Woodcuts. 8*vo.* 10*s. net.*

LEGENDS OF THE MADONNA, OR BLESSED VIRGIN MARY. With 27 Etchings and 165 Woodcuts. 8*vo.* 10*s. net.*

THE HISTORY OF OUR LORD, as exemplified in Works of Art. Commenced by the late Mrs. JAMESON; continued and completed by LADY EASTLAKE. With 31 Etchings and 281 Woodcuts. 2 *Vols.* 8*vo.* 20*s. net.*

Jennings.—ECCLESIA ANGLICANA. A History of the Church of Christ in England from the Earliest to the Present Times. By the Rev. ARTHUR CHARLES JENNINGS, M.A. *Crown 8vo. 7s. 6d.*

Jukes.—Works by ANDREW JUKES.

THE NEW MAN AND THE ETERNAL LIFE. Notes on the Reiterated Amens of the Son of God. *Crown 8vo. 6s.*

THE NAMES OF GOD IN HOLY SCRIPTURE: a Revelation of His Nature and Relationships. *Crown 8vo. 4s. 6d.*

THE TYPES OF GENESIS. *Crown 8vo. 7s. 6d.*

THE SECOND DEATH AND THE RESTITUTION OF ALL THINGS. *Crown 8vo. 3s. 6d.*

THE ORDER AND CONNEXION OF THE CHURCH'S TEACHING, as set forth in the arrangement of the Epistles and Gospels throughout the Year. *Crown 8vo. 2s. 6d.*

THE CHRISTIAN HOME. *Crown 8vo. 3s. 6d.*

Knox Little.—Works by W. J. KNOX LITTLE, M.A., Canon Residentiary of Worcester, and Vicar of Hoar Cross.

THE PERFECT LIFE: Sermons. *Crown 8vo. 7s. 6d.*

CHARACTERISTICS AND MOTIVES OF THE CHRISTIAN LIFE. Ten Sermons preached in Manchester Cathedral, in Lent and Advent. *Crown 8vo. 2s. 6d.*

SERMONS PREACHED FOR THE MOST PART IN MANCHESTER. *Crown 8vo. 3s. 6d.*

THE MYSTERY OF THE PASSION OF OUR MOST HOLY REDEEMER. *Crown 8vo. 2s. 6d.*

THE LIGHT OF LIFE. Sermons preached on Various Occasions. *Crown 8vo. 3s. 6d.*

SUNLIGHT AND SHADOW IN THE CHRISTIAN LIFE. Sermons preached for the most part in America. *Crown 8vo. 3s. 6d.*

Lear.—Works by, and Edited by, H. L. SIDNEY LEAR.

FOR DAYS AND YEARS. A book containing a Text, Short Reading, and Hymn for Every Day in the Church's Year. 16mo. 2s. 6d. *Also a Cheap Edition*, 32mo. 1s.; *or cloth gilt*, 1s. 6d.; *or with red borders*, 2s. 6d.

FIVE MINUTES. Daily Readings of Poetry. 16mo. 3s. 6d. *Also a Cheap Edition*, 32mo. 1s.; *or cloth gilt*, 1s. 6d.

WEARINESS. A Book for the Languid and Lonely. *Large Type. Small 8vo. 5s.*

JOY: A FRAGMENT. With a slight sketch of the Author's life. *Small 8vo. 2s. 6d.*

CHRISTIAN BIOGRAPHIES. *Nine Vols. Crown 8vo. 3s. 6d. each.*

MADAME LOUISE DE FRANCE, Daughter of Louis XV., known also as the Mother Térèse de St. Augustin.

A DOMINICAN ARTIST: a Sketch of the Life of the Rev. Père Besson, of the Order of St. Dominic.

HENRI PERREYVE. By PÈRE GRATRY.

ST. FRANCIS DE SALES, Bishop and Prince of Geneva.

THE REVIVAL OF PRIESTLY LIFE IN THE SEVENTEENTH CENTURY IN FRANCE.

A CHRISTIAN PAINTER OF THE NINETEENTH CENTURY.

BOSSUET AND HIS CONTEMPORARIES.

FÉNELON, ARCHBISHOP OF CAMBRAI.

HENRI DOMINIQUE LACORDAIRE.

[continued.

Lear.—Works by, and Edited by, H. L. SIDNEY LEAR—*continued.*

DEVOTIONAL WORKS. Edited by H. L. SIDNEY LEAR. *New and Uniform Editions. Nine Vols.* 16mo. 2s. 6d. *each.*

FÉNELON'S SPIRITUAL LETTERS TO MEN.

FÉNELON'S SPIRITUAL LETTERS TO WOMEN.

A SELECTION FROM THE SPIRITUAL LETTERS OF ST. FRANCIS DE SALES. Also *Cheap Edition*, 32mo, 6d. *cloth limp;* 1s. *cloth boards.*

THE SPIRIT OF ST. FRANCIS DE SALES.

THE HIDDEN LIFE OF THE SOUL.

THE LIGHT OF THE CONSCIENCE. Also *Cheap Edition*, 32mo, 6d. *cloth limp;* and 1s. *cloth boards.*

SELF-RENUNCIATION. From the French.

ST. FRANCIS DE SALES' OF THE LOVE OF GOD.

SELECTIONS FROM PASCAL'S 'THOUGHTS.'

Lepine.—THE MINISTERS OF JESUS CHRIST: a Biblical Study. By J. FOSTER LEPINE, Curate of St. Paul's, Maidstone. *Crown* 8vo. 5s.

Liddon.—Works by HENRY PARRY LIDDON, D.D., D.C.L., LL.D.

SERMONS ON SOME WORDS OF ST. PAUL. *Crown* 8vo. 5s.

SERMONS PREACHED ON SPECIAL OCCASIONS, 1860-1889. *Crown* 8vo. 5s.

EXPLANATORY ANALYSIS OF ST. PAUL'S FIRST EPISTLE TO TIMOTHY. 8vo. 7s. 6d.

CLERICAL LIFE AND WORK: Sermons. *Crown* 8vo. 5s.

ESSAYS AND ADDRESSES: Lectures on Buddhism—Lectures on the Life of St. Paul—Papers on Dante. *Crown* 8vo. 5s.

EXPLANATORY ANALYSIS OF ST. PAUL'S FIRST EPISTLE TO TIMOTHY. 8vo. 7s. 6d.

EXPLANATORY ANALYSIS OF PAUL'S EPISTLE TO THE ROMANS. 8vo. 14s.

SERMONS ON OLD TESTAMENT SUBJECTS. *Crown* 8vo. 5s.

SERMONS ON SOME WORDS OF CHRIST. *Crown* 8vo. 5s.

THE DIVINITY OF OUR LORD AND SAVIOUR JESUS CHRIST. Being the Bampton Lectures for 1866. *Crown* 8vo. 5s.

ADVENT IN ST. PAUL'S. *Two Vols. Crown* 8vo. 3s. 6d. *each. Cheap Edition in one Volume. Crown* 8vo. 5s.

CHRISTMASTIDE IN ST. PAUL'S. *Crown* 8vo. 5s.

PASSIONTIDE SERMONS. *Crown* 8vo. 5s.

EASTER IN ST. PAUL'S. Sermons bearing chiefly on the Resurrection of our Lord. *Two Vols. Crown* 8vo. 3s. 6d. *each. Cheap Edition in one Volume. Crown* 8vo. 5s.

SERMONS PREACHED BEFORE THE UNIVERSITY OF OXFORD. *Two Vols. Crown* 8vo. 3s. 6d. *each. Cheap Edition in one Volume. Crown* 8vo. 5s.

[*continued.*

Liddon.—Works by HENRY PARRY LIDDON, D.D., D.C.L., LL.D.—*continued.*
THE MAGNIFICAT. Sermons in St. Paul's. *Crown 8vo.* 2s. 6d.
SOME ELEMENTS OF RELIGION. Lent Lectures. *Small 8vo.* 2s. 6d. [*The Crown 8vo. Edition* (5s.) *may still be had.*]
SELECTIONS FROM THE WRITINGS OF. *Crown 8vo.* 3s. 6d.
MAXIMS AND GLEANINGS. *Crown 16mo.* 1s.

Linklater.—TRUE LIMITS OF RITUAL IN THE CHURCH. Edited by Rev. ROBERT LINKLATER, D.D., Vicar of Stroud Green. *Crown 8vo.* 5s.
CONTENTS.—Preface—Introductory Essay, by the Rev. ROBERT LINKLATER, D.D.—The Ornaments Rubric, by J. T. MICKLETHWAITE, V.P.S.A.—The Catholic Principle of Conformity in Divine Worship, by the Rev. C. F. G. TURNER—A Plea for Reasonableness, by the Rev. JOHN WYLDE—Intelligible Ritual, by the Rev. HENRY ARNOTT—The English Liturgy, by the Rev. T. A. LACEY—Eucharistic Ritual, by the Rev. W. F. COBB, D.D.—Suggestions for a Basis of Agreement in Matters Liturgical and Ceremonial, by the Rev. H. E. HALL.

Luckock.—Works by HERBERT MORTIMER LUCKOCK, D.D., Dean of Lichfield.
THE HISTORY OF MARRIAGE, JEWISH AND CHRISTIAN, IN RELATION TO DIVORCE AND CERTAIN FORBIDDEN DEGREES. *Second Edition. Crown 8vo.* 6s.
AFTER DEATH. An Examination of the Testimony of Primitive Times respecting the State of the Faithful Dead, and their Relationship to the Living. *Crown 8vo.* 3s. 6d.
THE INTERMEDIATE STATE BETWEEN DEATH AND JUDGMENT. Being a Sequel to *After Death. Crown 8vo.* 3s. 6d.
FOOTPRINTS OF THE SON OF MAN, as traced by St. Mark. Being Eighty Portions for Private Study, Family Reading, and Instruction in Church. *Crown 8vo.* 3s. 6d.
FOOTPRINTS OF THE APOSTLES, as traced by St. Luke in the Acts. Being Sixty Portions for Private Study, and Instruction in Church. A Sequel to 'Footprints of the Son of Man, as traced by St. Mark.' *Two Vols. Crown 8vo.* 12s.
THE DIVINE LITURGY. Being the Order for Holy Communion, Historically, Doctrinally, and Devotionally set forth, in Fifty Portions. *Crown 8vo.* 3s. 6d.
STUDIES IN THE HISTORY OF THE BOOK OF COMMON PRAYER. The Anglican Reform—The Puritan Innovations—The Elizabethan Reaction—The Caroline Settlement. With Appendices. *Crown 8vo.* 3s. 6d.
THE BISHOPS IN THE TOWER. A Record of Stirring Events affecting the Church and Nonconformists from the Restoration to the Revolution. *Crown 8vo.* 3s. 6d.

A SELECTION OF WORKS

MacColl.—Works by the Rev. MALCOLM MACCOLL, D.D., Canon Residentiary of Ripon.
THE REFORMATION SETTLEMENT: Examined in the Light of History and Law. With an Introductory Letter to the Right Hon. W. V. Harcourt, M.P. *Crown 8vo.*
CHRISTIANITY IN RELATION TO SCIENCE AND MORALS. *Crown 8vo. 6s.*
LIFE HERE AND HEREAFTER : Sermons. *Crown 8vo. 7s. 6d.*

Mason.—Works by A. J. MASON, D.D., Lady Margaret Professor of Divinity in the University of Cambridge and Canon of Canterbury.
THE CONDITIONS OF OUR LORD'S LIFE UPON EARTH. Being the Bishop Paddock Lectures, 1896. To which is prefixed part of a First Professorial Lecture at Cambridge. *Crown 8vo. 5s.*
THE PRINCIPLES OF ECCLESIASTICAL UNITY. Four Lectures delivered in St. Asaph Cathedral. *Crown 8vo. 3s. 6d.*
THE FAITH OF THE GOSPEL. A Manual of Christian Doctrine. *Crown 8vo. 7s. 6d. Cheap Edition. Crown 8vo. 3s. 6d.*
THE RELATION OF CONFIRMATION TO BAPTISM. As taught in Holy Scripture and the Fathers. *Crown 8vo. 7s. 6d.*

Maturin.—Works by the Rev. B. W. MATURIN.
SOME PRINCIPLES AND PRACTICES OF THE SPIRITUAL LIFE. *Crown 8vo. 4s. 6d.*
PRACTICAL STUDIES ON THE PARABLES OF OUR LORD. *Crown 8vo. 5s.*

Medd.—THE PRIEST TO THE ALTAR; or, Aids to the Devout Celebration of Holy Communion, chiefly after the Ancient English Use of Sarum. By PETER GOLDSMITH MEDD, M.A., Canon of St. Alban's. Fourth Edition, revised and enlarged. *Royal 8vo. 15s.*

Meyrick.—THE DOCTRINE OF THE CHURCH OF ENGLAND ON THE HOLY COMMUNION RESTATED AS A GUIDE AT THE PRESENT TIME. By the Rev. F. MEYRICK, M.A. *Crown 8vo. 4s. 6d.*

Mortimer.—Works by the Rev. A. G. MORTIMER, D.D., Rector of St. Mark's, Philadelphia.

JESUS AND THE RESURRECTION: Thirty Addresses for Good Friday and Easter. *Crown 8vo. 5s.*

CATHOLIC FAITH AND PRACTICE: A Manual of Theology. Two Parts. *Crown 8vo.* Sold separately. Part I. *7s. 6d.* Part II. *9s.*

HELPS TO MEDITATION: Sketches for Every Day in the Year.
Vol. I. ADVENT to TRINITY. *8vo. 7s. 6d.*
Vol. II. TRINITY to ADVENT. *8vo. 7s. 6d.*

STORIES FROM GENESIS: Sermons for Children. *Crown 8vo. 4s.*

THE LAWS OF HAPPINESS; or, The Beatitudes as teaching our Duty to God, Self, and our Neighbour. *18mo. 2s.*

THE LAWS OF PENITENCE: Addresses on the Words of our Lord from the Cross. *16mo. 1s. 6d.*

SERMONS IN MINIATURE FOR EXTEMPORE PREACHERS: Sketches for Every Sunday and Holy Day of the Christian Year. *Cr. 8vo. 6s.*

NOTES ON THE SEVEN PENITENTIAL PSALMS, chiefly from Patristic Sources. *Fcp. 8vo. 3s. 6d.*

THE SEVEN LAST WORDS OF OUR MOST HOLY REDEEMER: with Meditations on some Scenes in His Passion. *Crown 8vo. 5s.*

LEARN OF JESUS CHRIST TO DIE: Addresses on the Words of our Lord from the Cross, taken as Teaching the way of Preparation for Death. *16mo. 2s.*

Mozley.—Works by J. B. MOZLEY, D.D., late Canon of Christ Church, and Regius Professor of Divinity at Oxford.

ESSAYS, HISTORICAL AND THEOLOGICAL. *Two Vols. 8vo. 24s.*

EIGHT LECTURES ON MIRACLES. Being the Bampton Lectures for 1865. *Crown 8vo. 3s. 6d.*

RULING IDEAS IN EARLY AGES AND THEIR RELATION TO OLD TESTAMENT FAITH. *8vo. 6s.*

SERMONS PREACHED BEFORE THE UNIVERSITY OF OXFORD, and on Various Occasions. *Crown 8vo. 3s. 6d.*

SERMONS, PAROCHIAL AND OCCASIONAL. *Crown 8vo. 3s. 6d.*

A REVIEW OF THE BAPTISMAL CONTROVERSY. *Crown 8vo. 3s. 6d.*

Newbolt.—Works by the Rev. W. C. E. NEWBOLT, M.A., Canon and Chancellor of St. Paul's Cathedral.

RELIGION. *Crown 8vo. 5s.* (*The Oxford Library of Practical Theology.*)

PRIESTLY IDEALS; being a Course of Practical Lectures delivered in St. Paul's Cathedral to 'Our Society' and other Clergy, in Lent, 1898. *Crown 8vo. 3s. 6d.*

THE GOSPEL OF EXPERIENCE; or, the Witness of Human Life to the truth of Revelation. Being the Boyle Lectures for 1895. *Crown 8vo. 5s.*

COUNSELS OF FAITH AND PRACTICE: being Sermons preached on various occasions. *New and Enlarged Edition. Crown 8vo. 5s.*

SPECULUM SACERDOTUM; or, the Divine Model of the Priestly Life. *Crown 8vo. 7s. 6d.*

THE FRUIT OF THE SPIRIT. Being Ten Addresses bearing on the Spiritual Life. *Crown 8vo. 2s. 6d.*

THE MAN OF GOD. *Small 8vo. 1s. 6d.*

THE PRAYER BOOK: Its Voice and Teaching. *Crown 8vo. 2s. 6d.*

Newman.—Works by JOHN HENRY NEWMAN, B.D., sometime Vicar of St. Mary's, Oxford.

LETTERS AND CORRESPONDENCE OF JOHN HENRY NEWMAN DURING HIS LIFE IN THE ENGLISH CHURCH. With a brief Autobiography. Edited, at Cardinal Newman's request, by ANNE MOZLEY. *2 vols. Crown 8vo. 7s.*

PAROCHIAL AND PLAIN SERMONS. *Eight Vols. Cabinet Edition. Crown 8vo. 5s. each. Cheaper Edition. 3s. 6d. each.*

SELECTION, ADAPTED TO THE SEASONS OF THE ECCLESIASTICAL YEAR, from the 'Parochial and Plain Sermons,' *Cabinet Edition. Crown 8vo. 5s. Cheaper Edition. 3s. 6d.*

FIFTEEN SERMONS PREACHED BEFORE THE UNIVERSITY OF OXFORD *Cabinet Edition. Crown 8vo. 5s. Cheaper Edition. 3s. 6d.*

SERMONS BEARING UPON SUBJECTS OF THE DAY. *Cabinet Edition. Crown 8vo. 5s. Cheaper Edition. Crown 8vo. 3s. 6d.*

LECTURES ON THE DOCTRINE OF JUSTIFICATION. *Cabinet Edition. Crown 8vo. 5s. Cheaper Edition. 3s. 6d.*

⁂ A Complete List of Cardinal Newman's Works can be had on Application.

Osborne.—Works by EDWARD OSBORNE, Mission Priest of the Society of St. John the Evangelist, Cowley, Oxford.
 THE CHILDREN'S SAVIOUR. Instructions to Children on the Life of Our Lord and Saviour Jesus Christ. *Illustrated.* 16mo. 2s. 6d.
 THE SAVIOUR KING. Instructions to Children on Old Testament Types and Illustrations of the Life of Christ. *Illustrated.* 16mo. 2s. 6d.
 THE CHILDREN'S FAITH. Instructions to Children on the Apostles' Creed. *Illustrated.* 16mo. 2s. 6d.

Ottley.—ASPECTS OF THE OLD TESTAMENT: being the Bampton Lectures for 1897. By ROBERT LAWRENCE OTTLEY, M.A., Vicar of Winterbourne Bassett, Wilts; sometime Principal of the Pusey House. 8vo. *New and Cheaper Edition.* 7s. 6d.

The Oxford Library of Practical Theology.

PRODUCED UNDER THE EDITORSHIP OF

The Rev. W. C. E. NEWBOLT, M.A., Canon and Chancellor of St. Paul's, and the Rev. F. E. BRIGHTMAN, M.A., Librarian of the Pusey House, Oxford.

The Price of each Volume will be Five Shillings.

The following is a list of Volumes as at present arranged:—

1. RELIGION. By the Rev. W. C. E. NEWBOLT, M.A., Canon and Chancellor of St. Paul's. *Crown 8vo.* 5s.
2. BAPTISM. By the Rev. DARWELL STONE, M.A., Principal of the Missionary College, Dorchester. *Crown 8vo.* 5s. [*In the press.*
3. CONFIRMATION. By the Right Rev. A. C. A. HALL, D.D., Bishop of Vermont.
4. HOLY MATRIMONY. By the Rev. W. J. KNOX LITTLE, M.A., Canon of Worcester.
5. THE HOLY COMMUNION. By the Rev. F. W. PULLER, M.A., Mission Priest of St. John Evangelist, Cowley.
6. THE PRAYER BOOK. By the Rev. LEIGHTON PULLAN, M.A., Fellow of St. John's College, Oxford.
7. RELIGIOUS CEREMONIAL. By the Rev. F. E. BRIGHTMAN, M.A., Librarian of the Pusey House, Oxford.
8. PRAYER. By the Rev. A. J. WORLLEDGE, M.A., Canon of Truro.
9. VISITATION OF THE SICK. By the Rev. E. F. RUSSELL, M.A., St. Alban's, Holborn.

CONFESSION and ABSOLUTION.	DEVOTIONAL BOOKS and READING.
FASTING and ALMSGIVING.	ORDINATION.
RETREATS, MISSIONS, ETC.	FOREIGN MISSIONS.
CHURCH WORK.	THE BIBLE.

IN THEOLOGICAL LITERATURE. 17

OUTLINES OF CHURCH TEACHING : a Series of Instructions for the Sundays and chief Holy Days of the Christian Year. For the Use of Teachers. By C. C. G. With Preface by the Very Rev. FRANCIS PAGET, D.D., Dean of Christ Church, Oxford. *Crown 8vo.* 3*s.* 6*d.*

Oxenham.—THE VALIDITY OF PAPAL CLAIMS : Lectures delivered in Rome. By F. NUTCOMBE OXENHAM, D.D., English Chaplain at Rome. With a Letter by His Grace the ARCHBISHOP OF YORK. *Crown 8vo.* 2*s.* 6*d.*

Paget.—Works by FRANCIS PAGET, D.D., Dean of Christ Church.
STUDIES IN THE CHRISTIAN CHARACTER: Sermons. With an Introductory Essay. *Crown 8vo.* 6*s.* 6*d.*
THE SPIRIT OF DISCIPLINE : Sermons. *Crown 8vo.* 6*s.* 6*d.*
FACULTIES AND DIFFICULTIES FOR BELIEF AND DISBELIEF. *Crown 8vo.* 6*s.* 6*d.*
THE HALLOWING OF WORK. Addresses given at Eton, January 16-18, 1888. *Small 8vo.* 2*s.*

Percival.—SOME HELPS FOR SCHOOL LIFE. Sermons preached at Clifton College, 1862-1879. By J. PERCIVAL, D.D., LL.D., Lord Bishop of Hereford. New Edition, with New Preface. *Crown 8vo.* 3*s.* 6*d.*

Percival.—THE INVOCATION OF SAINTS. Treated Theologically and Historically. By HENRY R. PERCIVAL, M.A., D.D., Author of 'A Digest of Theology,' 'The Doctrine of the Episcopal Church,' etc. *Crown 8vo.* 5*s.*

POCKET MANUAL OF PRAYERS FOR THE HOURS, ETC. With the Collects from the Prayer Book. *Royal 32mo.* 1*s.*

Powell.—THE PRINCIPLE OF THE INCARNATION. With especial Reference to the Relation between our Lord's Divine Omniscience and His Human Consciousness. By the Rev. H. C. POWELL, M.A. of Oriel College, Oxford ; Rector of Wylye and Prebendary of Salisbury Cathedral. 8*vo.* 16*s.*

PRACTICAL REFLECTIONS. By a CLERGYMAN. With Prefaces by H. P. LIDDON, D.D., D.C.L., and the LORD BISHOP OF LINCOLN. *Crown 8vo.*

THE BOOK OF GENESIS. 4*s.* 6*d.*	THE MINOR PROPHETS. 4*s.* 6*d.*
THE PSALMS. 5*s.*	THE HOLY GOSPELS. 4*s.* 6*d.*
ISAIAH. 4*s.* 6*d.*	ACTS TO REVELATION. 6*s.*

PRIEST'S PRAYER BOOK (THE). Containing Private Prayers and Intercessions ; Occasional, School, and Parochial Offices ; Offices for the Visitation of the Sick, with Notes, Readings, Collects, Hymns, Litanies, etc. With a brief Pontifical. By the late Rev. R. F. LITTLEDALE, LL.D., D.C.L., and Rev. J. EDWARD VAUX, M.A., F.S.A. *New Edition, Revised.* 20*th Thousand. Post 8vo.* 6*s.* 6*d.*

Pullan.—LECTURES ON RELIGION. By the Rev. LEIGHTON PULLAN, M.A., Fellow of St. John's College, Lecturer in Theology at Oriel and Queen's Colleges, Oxford. *Crown 8vo. 6s.*

Pusey.—SPIRITUAL LETTERS OF EDWARD BOUVERIE PUSEY, D.D. Edited and prepared for publication by the Rev. J. O. JOHNSTON, M.A., Principal of the Theological College, Cuddesdon; and the Rev. W. C. E. NEWBOLT, M.A., Canon and Chancellor of St. Paul's. *8vo. 12s. 6d.*

Randolph.—Works by B. W. RANDOLPH, M.A., Principal of the Theological College and Hon. Canon of Ely.

MEDITATIONS ON THE OLD TESTAMENT for Every Day in the Year. *Crown 8vo. 6s.*

THE THRESHOLD OF THE SANCTUARY: being Short Chapters on the Inner Preparation for the Priesthood. *Crown 8vo. 3s. 6d.*

THE LAW OF SINAI: being Devotional Addresses on the Ten Commandments delivered to Ordinands. *Crown 8vo. 3s. 6d.*

Rede.—Works by WYLLYS REDE, D.D., Rector of the Church of the Incarnation, and Canon of the Cathedral, Atalanta, Georgia.

STRIVING FOR THE MASTERY: Daily Lessons for Lent. *Cr. 8vo. 5s.*

THE COMMUNION OF SAINTS: a Lost Link in the Chain of the Church's Creed. With a Preface by LORD HALIFAX. *Crown 8vo. 3s. 6d.*

Reynolds.—THE SUPERNATURAL IN NATURE: A Verification by Free Use of Science. By JOSEPH WILLIAM REYNOLDS, M.A., Late President of Sion College, and Prebendary of St. Paul's Cathedral. *New and Cheaper Edition, Revised. Crown 8vo. 3s. 6d.*

Sanday.—Works by W. SANDAY, D.D., Margaret Professor of Divinity and Canon of Christ Church, Oxford.

THE CONCEPTION OF PRIESTHOOD IN THE EARLY CHURCH AND IN THE CHURCH OF ENGLAND: Four Sermons. *Crown 8vo. 3s. 6d.*

INSPIRATION: Eight Lectures on the Early History and Origin o the Doctrine of Biblical Inspiration. Being the Bampton Lectures for 1893. *New and Cheaper Edition, with New Preface. 8vo. 7s. 6d.*

Scudamore.—STEPS TO THE ALTAR: a Manual of Devotion for the Blessed Eucharist. By the Rev. W. E. SCUDAMORE, M.A. *Royal 32mo. 1s.*

On toned paper, with red rubrics, 2s: The same, with Collects, Epistles, and Gospels, 2s. 6d; Demy 18mo. cloth, 1s; Demy 18mo. cloth, large type, 1s. 3d; Imperial 32mo. limp cloth, 6d.

Simpson.—THE CHURCH AND THE BIBLE. By the Rev. W. J. SPARROW SIMPSON, M.A. Vicar of St. Mark's, Regent's Park. *Crown 8vo.* 3s. 6d.

MEMOIR OF THE REV. W. SPARROW SIMPSON, D.D., Sub-Dean of St. Paul's Cathedral. Compiled and Edited by W. J. SPARROW SIMPSON. With Portrait and other Illustrations. *Crown 8vo.* 4s. 6d.

Strange.—INSTRUCTIONS ON THE REVELATION OF ST. JOHN THE DIVINE: Being an attempt to make this book more intelligible to the ordinary reader and so to encourage the study of it. By Rev. CRESSWELL STRANGE, M.A., Vicar of Edgbaston, and Honorary Canon of Worcester. *Crown 8vo.* 6s.

Strong.—CHRISTIAN ETHICS : being the Bampton Lectures for 1895. By THOMAS B. STRONG, B.D., Student of Christ Church, Oxford, and Examining Chaplain to the Lord Bishop of Durham. *New and Cheaper Edition.* 8vo. 7s. 6d.

Tee.—THE SANCTUARY OF SUFFERING. By ELEANOR TEE, Author of 'This Everyday Life,' etc. With a Preface by the Rev. J. P. F. DAVIDSON, M.A., Vicar of St. Matthias', Earl's Court; President of the 'Guild of All Souls.' *Crown 8vo.* 7s. 6d.

Whishaw.—THE CHILDREN'S YEAR-BOOK OF PRAYER AND PRAISE. By C. M. WHISHAW, Compiler of 'Being and Doing.' *Crown 8vo.* 3s. 6d.

Williams.—Works by the Rev. ISAAC WILLIAMS, B.D.
A DEVOTIONAL COMMENTARY ON THE GOSPEL NARRATIVE. *Eight Vols. Crown 8vo.* 5s. *each.*

THOUGHTS ON THE STUDY OF THE HOLY GOSPELS.	OUR LORD'S MINISTRY (Third Year).
A HARMONY OF THE FOUR GOSPELS.	THE HOLY WEEK.
OUR LORD'S NATIVITY.	OUR LORD'S PASSION.
OUR LORD'S MINISTRY (Second Year).	OUR LORD'S RESURRECTION.

FEMALE CHARACTERS OF HOLY SCRIPTURE. A Series of Sermons. *Crown 8vo.* 5s.
THE CHARACTERS OF THE OLD TESTAMENT. *Crown 8vo.* 5s.
THE APOCALYPSE. With Notes and Reflections. *Crown 8vo.* 5s.
SERMONS ON THE EPISTLES AND GOSPELS FOR THE SUNDAYS AND HOLY DAYS. *Two Vols. Crown 8vo.* 5s. *each.*
PLAIN SERMONS ON CATECHISM. *Two Vols. Cr. 8vo.* 5s. *each.*

Wilson.—THOUGHTS ON CONFIRMATION. By Rev. R. J. WILSON, D.D., late Warden of Keble College. 16mo. 1s. 6d.

Wirgman.—Works by A. THEODORE WIRGMAN, B.D., D.C.L., Vice-Provost of St. Mary's Collegiate Church, Port Elizabeth, South Africa.
THE DOCTRINE OF CONFIRMATION. *Crown 8vo.* 7s. 6d.
THE CONSTITUTIONAL AUTHORITY OF BISHOPS IN THE CATHOLIC CHURCH. Illustrated by the History and Canon Law of the Undivided Church from the Apostolic Age to the Council of Chalcedon, A.D. 451. *Crown 8vo.* 6s.

A SELECTION OF THEOLOGICAL WORKS.

Wood.—THE STORY OF A SAINTLY BISHOP'S LIFE—
LANCELOT ANDREWES, Bishop of Winchester, 1555-1626. By
Lady Mary Wood. *Crown 8vo. 1s. 6d.*

Wordsworth.—Works by CHRISTOPHER WORDSWORTH, D.D.,
sometime Bishop of Lincoln.

    THE HOLY BIBLE (the Old Testament). With Notes, Introductions, and Index. *Imperial 8vo.*
        Vol. I. THE PENTATEUCH. 25s. Vol. II. JOSHUA TO SAMUEL. 15s. Vol. III. KINGS to ESTHER. 15s. Vol. IV. JOB TO SONG OF SOLOMON. 25s. Vol. V. ISAIAH TO EZEKIEL. 25s. Vol. VI. DANIEL, MINOR PROPHETS, and Index. 15s.
        Also supplied in 12 Parts. Sold separately.
    THE NEW TESTAMENT, in the Original Greek. With Notes, Introductions, and Indices. *Imperial 8vo.*
        Vol. I. GOSPELS AND ACTS OF THE APOSTLES. 23s. Vol. II. EPISTLES, APOCALYPSE, and Indices. 37s.
        Also supplied in 4 Parts. Sold separately.
    A CHURCH HISTORY TO A.D. 451. *Four Vols. Crown 8vo.*
        Vol. I. TO THE COUNCIL OF NICÆA, A.D. 325. 8s. 6d. Vol. II. FROM THE COUNCIL OF NICÆA TO THAT OF CONSTANTINOPLE 6s. Vol. III. CONTINUATION. 6s. Vol. IV. CONCLUSION, TO THE COUNCIL OF CHALCEDON, A.D. 451. 6s.
    THEOPHILUS ANGLICANUS: a Manual of Instruction on the Church and the Anglican Branch of it. *12mo.* 2s. 6d.
    ELEMENTS OF INSTRUCTION ON THE CHURCH. *16mo.* 1s. *cloth.* 6d. *sewed.*
    THE HOLY YEAR: Original Hymns. *16mo.* 2s. 6d. *and* 1s. *Limp,* 6d.
        ,, ,, With Music. Edited by W. H. MONK. *Square 8vo.* 4s. 6d.
    ON THE INTERMEDIATE STATE OF THE SOUL AFTER DEATH. *32mo.* 1s.

Wordsworth.—Works by JOHN WORDSWORTH, D.D., Lord
Bishop of Salisbury.

    THE EPISCOPATE OF CHARLES WORDSWORTH, D.D., D.C.L., Bishop of St. Andrews. With Two Portraits. *8vo.* 15s.

    THE HOLY COMMUNION: Four Visitation Addresses. 1891. *Crown 8vo.* 3s. 6d.

    THE ONE RELIGION: Truth, Holiness, and Peace desired by the Nations, and revealed by Jesus Christ. Eight Lectures delivered before the University of Oxford in 1881. *Second Edition. Crown 8vo.* 7s. 6d.

    UNIVERSITY SERMONS ON GOSPEL SUBJECTS. *Sm. 8vo.* 2s. 6d.
    PRAYERS FOR USE IN COLLEGE. *16mo.* 1s.

5000/4/99.

Printed by T. and A. CONSTABLE, Printers to Her Majesty
at the Edinburgh University Press.

www.ingramcontent.com/pod-product-compliance
Lightning Source LLC
Chambersburg PA
CBHW022135300426
44115CB00006B/196